Study Guide for Use with

MACROECONOMICS

Ninth Canadian Edition

McCONNELL • BRUE • BARBIERO

PREPARED BY

TORBEN ANDERSEN
Red Deer College

WILLIAM B. WALSTAD
University of Nebraska, Lincoln

ROBERT C. BINGHAM

McGraw-Hill Ryerson

Toronto Montréal Boston Burr Ridge, IL Dubuque, IA Madison, WI New York San Francisco
St. Louis Bangkok Bogotá Caracas Kuala Lumpur Lisbon London Madrid
Mexico City Milan New Delhi Santiago Seoul Singapore Sydney Taipei

McGraw-Hill
Ryerson Limited

A Subsidiary of The McGraw-Hill Companies

Study Guide for use with
Macroeconomics
Ninth Canadian Edition

ISBN: 0-07-088671-7

1 2 3 4 5 6 7 8 9 0 JFM 0 9 8 7 6 5 4 3 2

Printed and bound in Canada.

Senior Sponsoring Editor: Lynn Fisher
Economics Editor: Ron Doleman
Marketing Manager: Kelly Smyth
Developmental Editor: Maria Chu
Production Coordinator: Jennifer Wilkie
Printer: J.F. Moore

CONTENTS

Preface

Welcome to the study of economics. This *Study Guide* is intended to directly complement the textbook, *Macroeconomics*, 9th Canadian edition, by McConnell, Brue and Barbiero. The design of the *Study Guide* is based on the conviction that active study is superior to passive study. To benefit from an aerobics class, you must not only watch the instructor's demonstrations — you must do the exercises yourself. To learn carpentry you cannot merely read a book — you must practise using the tools. Learning economics is a lot like aerobics or carpentry: you must do exercises, and you must handle the tools.

The *Study Guide* lets you practise using the tools of economics, and gives you feedback along the way. It provides a range of questions that require verbal, numerical, and graphical answers. These are the three main modes of analysis in economics, and skill in all three areas will likely be expected of you on your economics exams.

I hope that you will make good use of this *Study Guide* and that, as a result, you have more success and more fun in your economics course. Please e-mail me at torben.andersen@rdc.ab.ca   with any comments you would like to offer. I would appreciate hearing from you.

■ WHAT THE STUDY GUIDE IS

For each chapter in the text there is a chapter in the *Study Guide*. Each *Study Guide* chapter has twelve sections. The first five sections identify and explain the basic content of each chapter.

1. An introduction relates the chapter to other chapters, and gives an overview of the chapter.

2. A list of learning objectives notes the key things you will learn in the chapter.

3. A chapter outline summarizes the whole chapter, piece by piece.

4. A list of terms and concepts shows what terminology is introduced in the chapter.

5. Selected hints and tips alert you to common pitfalls and points you cannot afford to overlook.

The final sections provide questions and answers:

6. Fill-in questions.

7. Problems and projects.

8. True-false questions.

9. Multiple-choice questions.

10. Discussion questions.

11. Answers to all fill-in questions, true-false questions, multiple-choice questions, and most of the problems.

12. Answers to key questions from the textbook can be found at the back of the *Study Guide*.

■ A BIT OF ADVICE

Try to work several times each week with both the text and the *Study Guide*. Economics is absorbed most effectively in small, frequent doses.

You might find it useful to preview the *Study Guide* introduction, chapter outline, and checklist before tackling a new chapter in the textbook. However, most of your time with the *Study Guide* should come after reading the chapter in the textbook, and probably after your instructor has dealt with the material in class.

Make a serious attempt to answer a question before looking at its solution. Evaluate your results to assess your areas of strength and weakness. If you don't have time to do all of the questions, choose ones that seem more important given your instructor's emphasis.

When reviewing for exams, you will not have time to re-read all of the textbook chapters. Use the overviews and chapter outlines in the *Study Guide* for quick review and to focus on key areas that you might need to review in more detail in the textbook.

■ ACKNOWLEDGEMENTS

I thank Cyril Grant, William Walstad, and the late Robert Bingham, whose work on earlier editions of the *Study Guide* made my work much easier. Thanks to Tom Barbiero for preparing a fine text for Canadian students. Once again, I've enjoyed wonderful support from the McGraw-Hill Ryerson team: especially Ron Doleman, Lynn Fisher, Erin Moore, and Maria Chu.

Finally, I am grateful to my students at Red Deer College who continue to teach me a great deal about what is important in introductory economics.

Torben Andersen

CHAPTER 1

The Nature and Method of Economics

Chapter 1 introduces you to economics — the social science concerned with the efficient use of scarce resources to achieve maximum satisfaction of wants. You are given a sense of the kinds of topics economists study, how economists analyze these topics, and why economics is useful and important. You also learn about eight widely accepted economic goals that are important to our society.

At the heart of economics is the idea of scarcity: the fact that our limited resources are insufficient to produce all the goods and services we want. Accordingly, we must make choices about how to allocate our resources, and in these choices we face tradeoffs. When we choose to allocate resources to producing one thing we sacrifice the production of something else. This sacrifice is known as an opportunity cost.

Economic explanations of human behaviour are based on the assumption of "rational self-interest" and on "marginal analysis." People make rational decisions to maximize satisfaction of their personal goals. These goals differ between individuals and are not limited to material goals or to selfish goals. When people make decisions they weigh the marginal benefits and marginal costs of different courses of action. It is rational to do more of an activity if the marginal benefit exceeds the marginal cost.

The discipline of economics uses the scientific method. Based on observations of facts and data, we formulate hypotheses that are possible explanations of the causes and effects of economic phenomena. While these explanations may be somewhat abstract and simplified representations, they must be based on facts in the real world. Therefore, we test the predictions of our hypotheses to see whether they are supported by the data. Those explanations that produce predictions that are highly consistent with the data become accepted theories; those that have passed the test over and over are referred to as laws or principles. Policy economics entails the application of theories and data to formulate policies to solve economic problems or achieve certain economic goals.

In Canada we have eight economic goals for our society: economic growth, full employment, economic efficiency, price-level stability, economic freedom, equitable distribution of income, economic security, and a balance in foreign trade. Policy questions often centre on how these goals should be interpreted, and on the relative importance of different goals when there are tradeoffs between goals. Such questions move us from economic theory and positive economics, which investigates *what is*, to normative economics, which incorporates subjective or value-laden views of *what ought to be*.

Economics is divided into two broad categories: microeconomics and macroeconomics. Microeconomics studies the behaviour of individual or specific economic units. Macroeconomics studies economy-wide aggregates. Though they focus on different sorts of questions, both microeconomics and macroeconomics use the scientific method and are based on the scarcity principle.

Clear thinking about economic questions requires that we avoid many common pitfalls. Errors in thinking can occur from bias, loaded terminology, imprecise definitions, fallacies of composition, and causation fallacies. Awareness of these pitfalls will help you think more objectively about economic issues.

■ CHAPTER LEARNING OBJECTIVES

In this chapter you will learn:

☐ The Ten Key Concepts to retain a lifetime.

☐ The definition of economics.
☐ About the economic way of thinking.
☐ How economists construct theories.
☐ The distinction between microeconomics and macroeconomics.
☐ The pitfalls to objective thinking.

■ CHAPTER OUTLINE

1. Economics is the social science concerned with the efficient use of scarce resources to achieve maximum satisfaction of human wants.

2. The economic perspective on human behaviour is described in three interrelated ideas:
   (a) Scarcity of resources forces people to make choices and incur opportunity costs.
   (b) People make rational decisions based on their own self-interest.
   (c) People make choices by comparing marginal costs and marginal benefits.

3. Economists develop economic principles (also called theories, laws or models) to help us to understand the economy and formulate policies that will solve economic problems.
   (a) The object of economic theorizing is to systematically arrange and analyze facts so that we may discover regularities or trends. Without bringing such order to facts we could not discover the relationships between facts.
   (b) Economic theories are generalizations which are expressed as tendencies or trends. These tendencies need not hold true in every single case in order for theories to be useful.
   (c) Economic theories are abstractions from reality because they are simplifications designed to omit irrelevant facts.
   (d) An explanation that has not yet been tested is often called an hypothesis; one that has been tested and supported by the data is often called a theory; one that has been tested many times, and is regularly supported by the data, is often called an economic law or principle.
   (e) As an analytical tool, economists use the assumption of *ceteris paribus*, or "other things equal," in order to focus on only the variables of main interest.

4. Economic policy involves the application of economic principles to reach specific goals. The three steps in policy design are stating the goals, determining the policy options for achieving the chosen goals, and implementing and evaluating the effects of the selected policy.

5. At least eight major economic goals are widely accepted in Canada: economic growth, full employment, economic efficiency, price-level stability, economic freedom, equitable distribution of income, economic security, and balance of trade. Economic goals may be complementary or conflicting. When goals conflict, the tradeoffs must be assessed and value judgments made about how to balance them.

6. Economists derive principles of economic behaviour at the macroeconomic and the microeconomic level. Macroeconomics deals with the economy as a whole by examining aggregate measures (such as employment at the national level). Microeconomics looks at specific economic units (such as the real estate market in a particular city).

7. Economists deal with both positive economics and normative economics. Positive economics concerns the study of facts to determine *what is*, whereas normative economics involves value judgments to determine *what ought to be*. Sound economic policy decisions involve both because solutions cannot be implemented before the current situation is understood and value judgments are made about the desired situation.

8. Common pitfalls to avoid in order to think clearly and logically using the economic perspective include:
   (a) bias or preconceptions not warranted by facts
   (b) loaded terminology that appeals to emotions
   (c) careless use of terms that have precise technical definitions
   (d) the fallacy of composition, or the assumption that what is true for one is necessarily true for the group
   (e) the *post hoc* fallacy, or the mistaken belief that if event A precedes event B, A is the cause of B
   (f) confusion of correlation with causation

■ TERMS AND CONCEPTS

economics	tradeoffs
economic perspective	macroeconomics
marginal analysis	aggregate

scientific method
principles
generalizations
"other-things-equal"
  assumption
policy economics

microeconomics
positive economics
normative economics
fallacy of composition
"after this, therefore
  because of this" fallacy

■ HINTS AND TIPS

1. You may have difficulty accepting the claim that economics is a science, especially because its theories are inexact. Economics is a science by virtue of its methodology. That economic generalizations are inexact does not disqualify economics from being a science, nor does it negate the value of these generalizations. Think of generalizations from cancer research, or from meteorology. Scientists have proven a link between smoking and lung cancer, even though their knowledge is not exact enough to identify which specific smokers will get cancer. Meteorologists' weather forecasts are not always correct, but we often follow these forecasts because they are generally better than the forecasts we could generate ourselves without the benefit of the inexact science of meteorology.

2. A way to remember the pitfalls to objective thinking in economics is to associate each with a specific example. Choose examples that are funny, or that have personal application. For example: "The day I ate ice cream at the lake it was really hot, so next time it gets too cool I will eat some ice cream." Which fallacy is this an illustration of?

■ FILL-IN QUESTIONS

1. Economics is concerned with the _____ use of _____ resources to attain the _____ satisfaction of human wants.

2. Deriving principles or theories is called _____ economics, whereas applying economic principles to solve problems is called _____ economics.

3. Studying the economy in aggregate is called (microeconomics, macroeconomics) _____, whereas studying a specific business or market is called _____.

4. The three steps involved in the formulation of economic policy are:

(a) _____
(b) _____
(c) _____

5. Eight economic goals that are widely accepted in Canada include:

(a) _____
(b) _____
(c) _____
(d) _____
(e) _____
(f) _____
(g) _____
(h) _____

6. Two different types of statements can be made about economic topics. A (positive, normative) _____ statement explains *what is* by offering a scientific proposition about economic behaviour that is based on theory and facts. A _____ statement includes a value judgment that suggests *what ought to be*. Many of the reported disagreements among economists usually involve _____ statements.

7. The economic perspective has three interrelated features: (1) It recognizes that scarcity requires _____; (2) that people make decisions in a _____ manner based on their _____; and (3) that weighing the costs and benefits of a decision is based on _____ analysis.

■ PROBLEMS AND PROJECTS

1. Use the idea of opportunity cost to provide some possible explanations for these observations:
(a) Ashley's parents offered her a free trip to California but she declined because the trip was the week before her midterms.
(b) Dennis decided to use a realtor to sell his house, even though he could have avoided the realtor's fee by selling it himself.
(c) The St. Amand family buys a dishwasher from Sears because they didn't know that the same model was available at a lower price at a discount warehouse store.

2. Below are five statements, each containing an example of a common pitfall in thinking about economics. Indicate, in the space following each statement, the type of pitfall involved.

(a) The Second World War resulted in forty-five years of economic expansion in Canada. _____

(b) "An unemployed worker can find a job if he or she looks diligently and conscientiously for employment; therefore, all unemployed workers can find employment if they search diligently and conscientiously." _____

(c) "Just tell me when rain will be needed and I will schedule my vacation for that week." _____

(d) "The players, not the team owners, deserve to benefit from the recent explosion in revenues experienced by the National Basketball Association; after all, it is the players that fans pay to see." _____

(e) "The North American Free Trade Agreement is making Canadian workers pawns of the powerful corporations who can move their sweat shops to Mexico." _____

3. Indicate in the space beside each statement whether it is positive (P) or normative (N).

(a) Tuition fee increases are causing university enrolments to decrease. _____

(b) Agricultural subsidies in Europe are killing small towns in Saskatchewan. _____

(c) Higher income tax rates reduce the number of people willing to be employed. _____

(d) The Employment Insurance program is too generous because it gives people the incentive to quit their jobs. _____

(e) Free trade can improve the standard of living of a country. _____

(f) The federal government should do more to eliminate regional disparity in Canada. _____

4. Match the following terms on the left-hand list with the descriptions on the right-hand list.

(a) hypothesis   (i) explanation supported by data

(b) law   (ii) proposed explanation

(c) theory   (iii) explanation supported by data many times

■ **TRUE-FALSE**

Circle T if the statement is true, F if it is false.

1. Economics deals with the activities by which people earn their living and try to improve their standard of living.   **T F**

2. The "other things equal" or *ceteris paribus* assumption is made in order to simplify the reasoning process.   **T F**

3. Abstraction in economic theory is useful because it eliminates unnecessary complexity and irrelevant facts.   **T F**

4. A common reason that individuals disagree on what economic policy should be chosen is that they disagree on the goal or desired result.   **T F**

5. Making value judgments as to preferred goals of an economy is known as positive economic analysis. **T F**

6. The statement: "Increased patent protection for the Canadian pharmaceutical industry will result in increased research and development activity in Canada" is a positive statement.   **T F**

7. Rational self-interest is the same thing as being selfish.   **T F**

8. If two variables are correlated with one another, changes in one must be causing changes in the other.   **T F**

9. Microeconomic analysis is concerned with the behaviour of individual households and business firms.   **T F**

10. Scarcity is caused by the fact that people make choices.   **T F**

11. In economics the word "marginal" means additional, or extra.   **T F**

■ **MULTIPLE-CHOICE**

Circle the letter that corresponds to the best answer.

1. Which statement is the best one to complete a short definition of economics? "Economics is the study of:

(a) how businesses maximize profits."

(b) the triumph of the capitalistic system over communism."

(c) monetary transactions."

(d) the efficient use of scarce resources."

2. The statement that "there is no free lunch" refers to what economic concept?

(a) correlation does not imply causality
(b) everything has an opportunity cost
(c) nothing is free because government taxes everything
(d) individuals have different tastes and preferences

3. One economic principle states that, *ceteris paribus*, the lower the price of a commodity the greater will be the quantity of the commodity consumers will wish to purchase. On the basis of this principle alone, it can be concluded that:

(a) if the price of mink coats falls, consumers will purchase more mink coats
(b) if the price of mink coats falls, there must have been a decrease in the demand for clothes made of fur
(c) if the price of mink coats falls and there are no important changes in the other factors affecting their demand, consumers will purchase more mink coats
(d) if more mink coats are purchased this month than last month, it is because the price of mink coats has fallen

4. An economic model is *not*:

(a) an ideal type of economy or economic policy that we should strive to achieve
(b) a tool economists employ to enable them to predict
(c) an abstract representation of the economy or some part of the economy
(d) an explanation of how the economy or a part of the economy functions in its essential details

5. Which of the following is *not* among the dangers encountered when constructing or applying an economic model?

(a) it may contain irrelevant facts and be more complex than necessary
(b) it may come to be accepted as "what ought to be" rather than as "what is"
(c) it may be overly simplified and so be a very poor approximation of the reality it explains
(d) it may result in a conclusion that is unacceptable to people

6. A theory in economics:

(a) is useless if simplifying assumptions are used
(b) is of little use if it is abstract

(c) is useful if the predictions of the theory usually correspond to actual economic occurrences
(d) is useless if its predictions are not always correct

7. Which of the following would not be contained in an economic theory?

(a) predictions that follow from that theory
(b) definitions that clearly set out the variables included in the model
(c) statements of the relationships among the variables in the model
(d) normative statements about the most preferred outcomes

8. During World War II, Canada used price controls to prevent inflation; some people called this "a fascist and arbitrary restriction of economic freedom" and others called it "a necessary and democratic means of preventing ruinous inflation." Both labels are examples of:

(a) economic bias
(b) the fallacy of composition
(c) misuse of common-sense definitions
(d) loaded terminology

9. If one individual decides to consume less beef, there will be little or no effect on beef prices. To argue, therefore, that if all individuals consume less beef there will be little or no effect on beef prices is an example of:

(a) the *post hoc, ergo propter hoc* fallacy
(b) the fallacy of composition
(c) an oversimplified generalization
(d) using loaded terminology

10. The Great Depression that began in 1929 was preceded by a stock market crash. To conclude that the Depression was therefore caused by the crash in the stock market is an example of:

(a) the *post hoc, ergo propter hoc* fallacy
(b) the fallacy of composition
(c) the *ceteris paribus* assumption
(d) using loaded terminology

11. Which of the following is not a widely accepted economic goal?

(a) price-level stability
(b) zero taxation
(c) economic efficiency
(d) economic freedom

12. Which of the following would be studied in microeconomics?

(a) the output of the entire economy
(b) the national unemployment rate
(c) the effect of money supply changes on the Consumer Price Index
(d) the price and output of apples

13. If economic growth tends to produce a more equitable distribution of income among people in a nation, then the goals of growth and equitable income distribution seem to be:

(a) deductive
(b) conflicting
(c) complementary
(d) mutually exclusive

14. To say that two economic goals are conflicting means that:

(a) there is a tradeoff in the achievement of the goals
(b) some people do not agree with these goals
(c) the achievement of one goal results in achievement of the other goal
(d) it is impossible to quantify both goals

15. Which of the following is a macroeconomic topic?

(a) the effect of cigarette tax reductions on cigarette consumption
(b) the effect of government set stumpage fees on the amount of lumber being exported to the United States
(c) the effect of the cod fishery closure on the unemployment rate in Halifax
(d) the effect of the falling Canadian dollar on Canada's exports and imports

■ **DISCUSSION QUESTIONS**

1. What are some issues that you face in your personal or work life for which a knowledge of economics could provide you with useful skills?

2. What is a "laboratory experiment under controlled conditions?" Why are such experiments not normally possible in economics? What does economics have instead of a laboratory?

3. What is the relationship between facts and theory?

4. Why are economic principles and models necessarily generalizations and abstractions?

5. Sketch a map showing me how to get from your home to the nearest grocery store. In what ways is your map realistic, and in what ways is it unrealistic (abstract)? Would your map necessarily be more helpful to me in finding the store if it was more realistic? Would it be worth making it more realistic? How do these issues concerning your map relate to issues concerning economic theories?

6. Explain each of the following:
(a) fallacy of composition
(b) loaded terminology
(c) the *post hoc, ergo propter hoc* fallacy

7. Explain briefly the difference between:
(a) macroeconomics and microeconomics
(b) correlation and causation

■ **ANSWERS**

FILL-IN QUESTIONS
1. efficient, scarce, maximum
2. theoretical, policy
3. macroeconomics, microeconomics
4. (a) stating goals; (b) analyzing policy options; (c) evaluating policy effectiveness
5. full employment; economic growth; price-level stability; balance of trade; equitable distribution of income; economic efficiency; economic security; economic freedom
6. positive, normative, normative
7. choices; rational; self-interest; marginal

PROBLEMS AND PROJECTS
1. Each of these decisions was presumably made because the opportunity cost was too high: (a) by going to Disneyland, Ashley would lose study time and her exam results would suffer; (b) selling his own house would have cost Dennis some time, and perhaps some money if he couldn't get as high a price as a professional realtor; (c) shopping at every store to find the absolute lowest price is not usually worth the cost for time and travel.
2. (a) *post hoc ergo propter hoc* fallacy; (b) the fallacy of composition; (c) confusing correlation and causation; (d) bias; (e) loaded terminology
3. P; (b) P; (c) P; (d) N; (e) P; (f) N
4. (a)-(ii); (b)-(iii); (c)-(i)

TRUE-FALSE
1. T
2. T
3. T
4. T
5. F   Value judgments imply normative economics
6. T   The statement is positive, whether true or false
7. F   Generosity may be in one's self-interest
8. F   Don't confuse correlation with causation

9. T
10. F The other way around
11. T

MULTIPLE-CHOICE

1. (d) This is the most comprehensive one
2. (b) Everything has a cost in some form
3. (c) *Ceteris paribus* means "other things remaining constant"
4. (a) An economic model explains how the world is, not how we want it to be
5. (d) Perhaps the conclusion will be unacceptable to some people, but this should not affect the theory
6. (c) Good theories always involve assumptions and abstractions, and may not predict correctly in *every* case.
7. (d) Theories are limited to positive aspects
8. (d) Loaded terminology appeals to emotions
9. (b) What is true for one need not be true for all
10. (a) Because B happened *after* A does not prove that B *caused* A
11. (b) Zero taxation is the only one not on the list of eight goals
12. (d) Only this topic deals with a single market
13. (c) Complementary because they can be achieved together, without tradeoff
14. (a) To move towards one goal entails moving away from the other
15. (d) All of the others deal with specific markets

APPENDIX TO CHAPTER 1
Graphs and Their Meaning

The old saying that "a picture is worth a thousand words" is true in economics because economists use graphs to "picture" relationships between economic variables. A graph can display a lot of information in a manner that is precise yet quick to comprehend. Because we rely so much on these "pictures," you need to be skilled in constructing and interpreting graphs. Even if you are already familiar with the fundamentals of graphing, perhaps from previous classes in math and sciences, you should review this appendix. If none of this material seems familiar, relax: all of the basics that you need are explained in this appendix.

The appendix shows how to construct a graph from a table of data on two variables (using the example of income and consumption). Each variable is represented on one of the two axes, so each axis should be labelled with the variable name, its units of measurement, and marked off with a consistent measurement scale. Once the data points are plotted and a line drawn to connect the plotted points, one can determine whether there is a direct or inverse relationship between the variables.

Economists usually, but not always, measure the independent variable on the horizontal axis and the dependent variable on the vertical axis of a graph. The curve plotted to illustrate the relationship between the two variables is drawn based on the *ceteris paribus* condition. If any other variable that influences the dependent variable happens to change, then we must plot a whole new curve through a different set of points. This is called a shift in the curve.

A relationship that is linear (a straight line on the graph) can be defined by two simple elements: the slope and the vertical intercept of the line. The slope is the ratio of the vertical change (rise) to the horizontal change (run). The slope often has economic meaning, because slopes measure effects of mar-

ginal changes. As discussed in Chapter 1, marginal analysis is key in economics.

For a nonlinear curve the slope is not constant; it varies as one moves along the curve. The slope at a particular point can be estimated by determining the slope of a straight line drawn tangent to the curve at that point. The vertical intercept of a line is the value on the vertical axis when the value of the horizontal axis variable is zero. A linear relationship is easily expressed in equation form once the slope and the vertical intercept are found from a graph or table of data.

■ APPENDIX LEARNING OBJECTIVES

When you have studied this appendix, you should be able to:
☐ Understand why economists use graphs.
☐ Construct a graph of two variables using numerical data from a table.
☐ Construct a table with two variables from an algebraic function or from data on a graph.
☐ Determine whether a graph shows a direct or an inverse relationship between two variables.
☐ Identify dependent and independent variables in economic examples and graphs.
☐ Determine the slope of a straight line.
☐ Determine the vertical intercept of a line.
☐ Write and interpret a linear equation using the slope and the vertical intercept.
☐ Estimate the slope of a nonlinear curve at a point using a line tangent to the curve at that point.

■ APPENDIX OUTLINE

1. A graph is a visual representation of the relationship between variables and is helpful in describing economic theories and models.

2. To construct a simple graph, plot numerical data about two variables from a table. Sometimes the tabular data must be found first by using an equation relating the two variables.

(a)   Each graph has a horizontal and a vertical axis that is labelled for each variable and then scaled for the range of the data points that will be measured on the axis. Along a given axis a certain increment of distance represents a consistent increment in the variable.

(b)   Data points are plotted on the graph by drawing perpendiculars from the scaled points on the two axes to the place on the graph where the perpendiculars intersect.

(c)   A line or curve can then be drawn to connect the points plotted on the graph. If the line is straight the relationship is "linear."

3. The slope of the line on a graph indicates the relationship between the two variables.

(a)   A line that is upsloping to the right indicates a positive or direct relationship between the two variables: an increase (a decrease) in one is associated with an increase (a decrease) in the other.

(b)   A line that is downsloping to the right indicates a negative or inverse relationship between the two variables because the variables are changing in opposite directions: an increase (a decrease) in one is associated with a decrease (an increase) in the other.

4. Economists are concerned with determining cause and effect in economic events.

(a)   An independent variable is the variable that changes first, and causes another variable to change.

(b)   A dependent variable is one that changes as a result of a change in another variable.

(c)   Economists do not always follow the convention used in mathematics whereby an independent variable is placed on the horizontal axis and a dependent variable on the vertical axis.

5. A two-variable graph is a simplified representation of an economic relationship. In such a graph there is an implicit assumption that all other factors are being held constant. This "other things equal" or *ceteris paribus* assumption is a simplification that helps us focus on the two variables of interest. If another variable that influences the dependent variable does change, then the curve on the graph will shift to a new position.

6. A slope and vertical intercept can be calculated for a linear relationship (straight line graph). These values also define the equation of the line.

(a)   The slope of a straight line is the ratio of the vertical change to the horizontal change between two points.

(b)   The slope measures the marginal effect on one variable of a small change in the other.

(c)   A positive (negative) slope indicates a direct (inverse) relationship between the two variables.

(d)   The vertical intercept is the value where the line intersects the vertical axis of the graph.

(e)   A linear equation is written as $y = a + bx$. If the values for the intercept a and the slope b are known, then given any value of variable x, the value of variable y can be determined.

7. A straight line has a constant slope, but a nonlinear curve has a continually changing slope. To estimate the slope of a nonlinear curve at a point, calculate the slope of a line tangent to the curve at that point.

■   **APPENDIX TERMS AND CONCEPTS**

horizontal axis	independent variable
vertical axis	dependent variable
direct relationship	slope of a straight line
inverse relationship	vertical intercept

■   **HINTS AND TIPS**

1.   Some students are comfortable with economic graphs right away, but others initially have an aversion to graphs. If you are in the first group, you are fortunate because economics will come more easily to you. If you are in the second group, do not run because you cannot hide! It is incredibly important that you quickly develop basic skills with graphing. If you find this appendix very difficult you should seek extra help with these tools.

2.   The text includes a number of graphs of real world data showing relationships between two variables. These graphs often take the form of a "scatter diagram" with a "best-fitting line." That is, the data points may be somewhat scattered, rather than lying exactly on a curve. In many of these graphs no precise relationship is evident in the data, but there is a discernible tendency or pattern in the data, indicating that the variables are related. A "best-fitting line" through the data points indicates this pattern. If you take a statistics course you will learn the proper techniques for determining such best-fitting lines, and for judging when you can be confident that the points in a scatter diagram do indicate some relationship. To understand this textbook you need only have a rough idea of a "best-fitting line."

3. All graphs in this appendix have actual numerical values marked on the axes. Later in the text you will see graphs without any numbers on the axes. In such cases the specific numbers are not necessary for the explanation, but you should recognize that there are numbers implicit on the axes. If at first you have difficulty comprehending such abstract graphs, you could pencil in arbitrary values on the axes until you get used to such graphs.

■ **FILL-IN QUESTIONS**

1. The relationship between two economic variables can be visualized with a two-dimensional graph.
   (a) The (dependent, independent) _____ variable is said to change because of a change in the _____ variable.
   (b) The vertical and horizontal (scales, ranges) _____ on the graph are calibrated to reflect the _____ of values in a table of data points on which the graph is based.

2. The graph of a straight line that slopes downward to the right indicates that there is (a direct, an inverse) _____ relationship between the two variables. A graph of a straight line that slopes upward to the right tells us that the relationship is (direct, inverse) _____. When the value of one variable increases and the value of the other variable increases, then the relationship is _____; when the value of one increases, and the other decreases, the relationship is _____.

3. The slope of a straight line between two points is defined as the ratio of the (vertical, horizontal) _____ change over the _____ change. The point at which the line meets the vertical axis is called the _____.

4. We can express the graph of a straight line with a linear equation that can be written as $y = a + bx$.
   (a) a is the (slope, intercept) _____ and b is the _____.
   (b) If a was 2, b was 4, and x was 5, then y would be _____.

5. The slope of a (straight line, nonlinear curve) _____ is constant throughout; the slope of a _____ varies from point to point. The slope of a nonlinear curve at a point can be estimated by calculating the slope of a straight line that is _____ to the point on the curve.

■ **PROBLEMS AND PROJECTS**

1. The data below represent the relationship between the mortgage interest rate and the number of new houses built.

Mortgage Rate (% per year)	Housing Starts (thousands per year)
12	70,000
10	90,000
8	110,000
6	130,000
4	150,000

   (a) Which variable is dependent? _____ Which is independent? _____
   (b) On the axes of the graph below, set up the scales to best suit these data. Label each axis of the graph (including the units of measurement).
   (c) Plot the five data points given in the table.

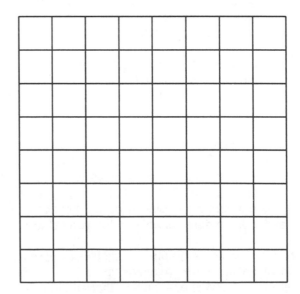

   (d) The curve is (up-, down-) _____ sloping, meaning that the relationship between the mortgage interest rate and housing starts is (direct, inverse) _____.

2. (a) Based on the relationship found in question 1, if the mortgage rate increases by 1%, *ceteris paribus*, then housing starts will (decrease, increase) _____ by _____ thousands per year.

(b) If household incomes rise, new homes would become more affordable, so there would be more new housing starts at the same interest rate as before. On the graph, this would cause a (leftward, rightward) _____ shift of the curve in question 1.

(c) If lumber prices increase, new homes would become less affordable, so there would be fewer new housing starts at the same interest rate as before. On the graph, this would cause a (leftward, rightward) _____ shift of the initial curve.

3. The Hammerheads, a very mediocre club band, have just released a CD. They will immediately sell 10 copies to their parents and friends. Thereafter, they can sell 4 copies for each performance they give in a club.

(a) Based on this information, complete the table below.

Performances	CD Sales
0	_____
5	_____
10	_____
15	_____
20	_____

CD Sales

Performances

(b) Which variable is dependent? _____ Which is independent? _____
(c) Plot the data on the graph below.
(d) The vertical intercept value is _____.
(e) The slope value is _____.
(f) Write the equation for this relationship:

_____.

4. This question is based on the graph below.
(a) The function has a negative slope between the X values of _____ and _____. Over this range the relationship between X and Y is (direct, inverse) _____.
(b) Find the slope of the curve at the following points:
A: _____, B: _____, C: _____

5. An economist is hired to determine the relationship between real estate value and proximity to the waterfront in a Manitoba lakeshore resort community. The table below gives recent selling prices for undeveloped building lots.

(a) On the graph provided, create a "scatter diagram" with lot prices on the vertical axis and distance to shore on the horizontal axis.
(b) The scatter diagram suggests that lot prices are (directly, inversely, not) _____ related to their proximity to the waterfront.
(c) With a ruler, draw in what appears to be the "best-fitting" line through these data points.
(d) The value of the vertical intercept is _____. This value indicates price for a lot that is _____.

(e)   The value of the slope is _____. This value indicates that price (falls, rises) _____ by $_____ for each metre from the waterfront.

(f)   The expression for the equation of this line is: _____.

Lot	Distance to Shore (m)	Price ($)
A	200	9,000
B	0	18,000
C	50	16,000
D	100	15,000
E	50	17,000
F	150	10,000
G	200	7,000
H	125	12,000

Price (thousand $)

Distance to shore (m)

■   **TRUE-FALSE**

Circle T if the statement is true; F if it is false.

1. Graphs provide a visual representation of the relationship between two variables.   **T F**

2. If the straight line on a two-variable graph is upward sloping to the right, then there is a positive relationship between the two variables.   **T F**

3. A variable that changes as a consequence of a change in another variable is considered to be a dependent variable.   **T F**

4. *Ceteris paribus* means that the value of all other variables is set equal to zero.   **T F**

5. In the ratio for the calculation of the slope of a straight line, the horizontal change is divided by the vertical change.   **T F**

6. If the slope of the linear relationship between consumption (on the vertical axis) and income (on the horizontal axis) is 0.90, then it tells us that for every $1 increase in income there will be a $0.90 increase in consumption.   **T F**

7. The slope of a straight line is 0.   **T F**

8. If a linear equation is $y = 10 + 5x$, the vertical intercept is 10.   **T F**

9. A function with a constant slope becomes steeper as the independent variable increases. **T F**

10. If the slope of a straight line on a two-variable (x, y) graph is 2 and the vertical intercept is 6, then if the value for x is 10, the value for y is 22.   **T F**

11. A slope of 4 for a straight line in a two-variable graph indicates the two variables are inversely related.   **T F**

12. If there is an inverse relation between price and quantity demanded, the graph of this function will be downward-sloping.   **T F**

13. In the relationship between snowfall and demand for snowblowers, snowfall is the dependent variable.   **T F**

14. If the line tangent to a nonlinear curve is up-sloping, this indicates that the slope of the curve is positive at that point.   **T F**

15. If two points described by the (x, y) combinations of (13, 10) and (8, 20) lie on a straight line, then the slope is 2.   **T F**

16. On a graph relating the number of visitors to Canada's national parks to the price of admission to the parks, an increase in levels of rainfall would likely shift the curve to the left.   **T F**

■ **MULTIPLE-CHOICE**

Circle the letter that corresponds to the best answer.

1. If an increase in variable *A* is associated with a decrease in variable *B*, then we can conclude that *A* and *B* are:
  (a) nonlinear
  (b) directly related
  (c) inversely related
  (d) positively related

2. Economists:
  (a) always put the independent variable on the vertical axis
  (b) always put the independent variable on the horizontal axis
  (c) sometimes put the dependent variable on the horizontal axis
  (d) use only linear functions

3. If the curve in a two-variable graph shifts, what does this indicate?
  (a) the two variables are positively related
  (b) the two variables are negatively related
  (c) the relationship between the two variables must be nonlinear
  (d) some third variable must have changed

4. If *y* is plotted on the vertical axis and *x* is on the horizontal axis, which of the following is a false statement regarding the equation $y = 100 + 0.4 x$?
  (a) the vertical intercept is 100
  (b) the slope is 0.4
  (c) when *x* is 20, *y* is 108
  (d) the graph is nonlinear

5. If a straight line drawn tangent to a nonlinear curve has a slope of zero, then at the point of tangency the curve is:
  (a) vertical
  (b) horizontal
  (c) upsloping
  (d) downsloping

6. Consider a graph relating gasoline consumption (on the vertical axis) to population (on the horizontal axis). All of the following will affect gasoline consumption, but which one will **not** shift the curve?
  (a) increased consumer incomes
  (b) increased availability of public transit
  (c) increased population

  (d) more efficient gasoline engines

Answer questions 7 through 10 on the basis of the following diagram.

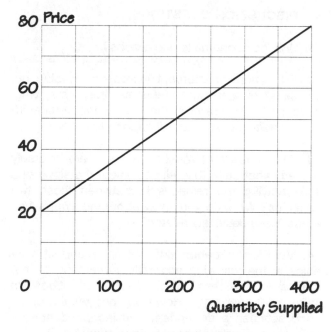

7. The graph indicates that price and quantity supplied are:
  (a) positively related
  (b) negatively related
  (c) indirectly related
  (d) nonlinear

8. The slope of the line is:
  (a) 0.15
  (b) 0.20
  (c) 1.50
  (d) 6.67

9. The vertical intercept is:
  (a) 0
  (b) 10
  (c) 20
  (d) 80

10. The linear equation for the function is:
  (a) $p = 20 + 0.15q$
  (b) $q = 20 + 6.67p$
  (c) $p = 20 + 6.67q$
  (d) $q = 20 + 0.15p$

11. Which of the following statements is true?
  (a) a vertical line has a slope of zero
  (b) a horizontal line has a slope of infinity

(c) a nonlinear curve has different slopes at different points

(d) an upsloping line has a negative slope

■ **DISCUSSION QUESTIONS**

1. Why do economists use graphs?

2. If the vertical intercept increases in value but the slope of a straight line stays the same, what happens to the graph of the line? If the vertical intercept decreases, what will happen to the line?

3. If you know that variables X and Y are inversely related, what does this tell you about the slope of a line showing the relationship between these two variables? What do you know about the slope when X and Y are positively related?

4. Identify the dependent and independent variables in the following economic statement: "A decrease in business taxes gave a big boost to investment spending." How does one tell the difference between a dependent and independent variable when examining economic relationships?

5. Why is an assumption made that all other variables are held constant when we construct a two-variable graph of the price and quantity of a product?

6. If you were to plot a two-variable graph of the price of gasoline versus per capita use of gasoline, using the data for various nations, what sort of graph would you expect, and what sort of relationship would this represent? The data points would probably be somewhat scattered, rather than consistently located along a precise line or curve. Give some reasons why the data points might be somewhat scattered.

■ **ANSWERS**

FILL-IN QUESTIONS

1. (a) dependent, independent; (b) scales, ranges

2. an inverse; direct; direct, inverse

3. vertical, horizontal; vertical intercept

4. (a) intercept, slope; (b) 22

5. straight line; nonlinear curve; tangent

PROBLEMS AND PROJECTS

1. (a) housing starts; mortgage interest rates; (d) down; inverse; (b) and (c):

2. (a) decrease, 10; (b) rightward; (c) leftward

3. (a) 10, 30, 50, 70, 90; (b) CD sales; performances; (d) 10; (e) 4; (f) CD Sales = 10 + 4 Performances; (c) see graph

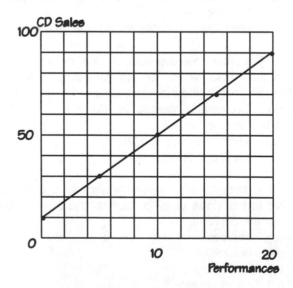

4. (a) 8; 17; inverse; (b) 3.0; 0; -2.1.

5. (a) see graph; (b) inversely; (c) see graph; (d) about $19,000; on the waterfront; (e) vertical change/horizontal difference is approximately = (8,000-19,000)/(200-0) = -11,000/200 = about -55; falls; about $55. (f) Price = 19,000 - 55 Distance.

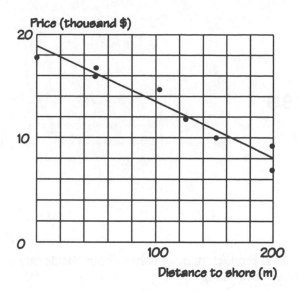

Price (thousand $)

Distance to shore (m)

7. (a) The curve is upsloping
8. (a) (80-20)/(400-0) = 0.15
9. (c)
10. (a) See the answers to questions 8 and 9
11. (c)

TRUE-FALSE

1. T
2. T
3. T
4. F   It means "other things equal"
5. F   Vertical change divided by horizontal change
6. T
7. F   A slope of zero indicates a horizontal line
8. T   Yes, the vertical intercept is the simple constant term in the equation
9. F   A constant slope means constant steepness
10. F   The equation is $y = 6 + 2x$; at $x = 10$, $y = 26$
11. F   The slope would be negative for an inverse relationship
12. T
13. F   The amount of snowfall does not depend on how many snowblowers are purchased
14. T   An upsloping curve
15. F   (20-10)/(8-13) = -2
16. T   Rainfall would likely be one of the variables held constant on the original graph, so if rainfall changes the curve will shift

MULTIPLE-CHOICE

1. (c) Variables changing in opposite directions are inversely or negatively related
2. (c) There is no consistent convention
3. (d) The original curve assumed "other things equal"
4. (d) Because the slope is a fixed number, the graph is a straight line
5. (b)
6. (c) Population change is reflected in a movement along the original curve

CHAPTER 2

The Economic Problem: Scarcity, Wants, and Choices

The field of economics is based on two fundamental facts: our wants are unlimited or insatiable, and the resources available for satisfying these wants are limited, or scarce. Consequently, we face the economic problem, or the need to make choices about how to allocate our scarce resources. The main categories of these resources are land, capital, labour, and entrepreneurial ability. Given scarcity, all resources must be fully employed and used efficiently in order to satisfy wants to the fullest possible extent. Efficiency has two elements: productive efficiency is achieved if resources are used in the least cost manner, and allocative efficiency is achieved if resources are used to produce those goods society wants most.

The production possibilities table and the production possibilities curve are useful for illustrating many concepts in this chapter: scarcity, choice, the law of increasing opportunity cost, allocative and productive efficiency, unemployment, and economic growth. The production possibilities model is both very basic and very important.

Every society uses some sort of economic system to address the problem of scarcity. No two economies use exactly the same system, but there are two general types: the market system and the command system. In a market system most resources are owned privately and economic activity is coordinated spontaneously, with little government interference. In a command system government owns most of the property resources and economic activity is centrally planned. Canada's economy is mainly a market system, but with some elements of a command system.

The circular flow model illustrates how businesses and households interact in a market system. These economic agents interact in resource markets (where households sell and businesses buy), and in product markets (where households buy and businesses sell).

■ CHAPTER LEARNING OBJECTIVES

In this chapter you will learn:
☐ The foundation of economics.
☐ The nature of economic efficiency.
☐ How to achieve economic growth.
☐ The two general types of economic systems society can choose to coordinate production and consumption decisions.
☐ What the circular flow model is.

■ CHAPTER OUTLINE

1. The study of economics rests on two facts:
(a) Society's wants are essentially unlimited and insatiable.
(b) The resources for producing goods and services to satisfy these wants are limited or scarce.

2. The four categories of resources are land, capital, labour, and entrepreneurial ability. The payments received by those who provide resources are, respectively: rental income, interest income, wages, and profits.

3. Economics is the social science concerned with the problem of using scarce resources to attain the maximum fulfillment of society's unlimited wants. To achieve this goal society must use its resources efficiently, achieving both full employment and full production.
(a) Full employment occurs when all available resources are being used.

(b) Full production occurs when the resources are being used as efficiently as possible. Two kinds of efficiency must be achieved:

(i) productive efficiency — where any particular mix of goods and services is produced in the least costly way.

(ii) allocative efficiency — where the resources are used to produce that particular mix of goods and services most wanted by society.

4. The production possibilities table, or a production possibilities curve, indicates the alternative combinations of goods and services an economy can produce when it has achieved full employment and productive efficiency.

5. Four assumptions are made when constructing a production possibilities table or curve:

(a) full employment and productive efficiency

(b) fixed resources

(c) fixed technology

(d) two goods are being produced

6. Any point on the production possibilities curve is attainable, but society must choose one point (one particular combination of goods). If the chosen combination provides the greatest satisfaction, the economy is said to be allocatively efficient.

7. Points outside the curve are unattainable, so the production possibilities curve illustrates the condition of scarcity.

8. Given full employment and full production, society can produce more of one good only by producing less of the other good. This foregone output is termed the opportunity cost and arises because resources must be shifted from producing one good to producing the other.

9. The marginal opportunity cost of producing additional units of a product usually increases as more of that product is produced. This generalization is the law of increasing opportunity costs.

(a) Opportunity costs are increasing because resources are not perfectly adaptable from one production use to another.

(b) Increasing opportunity costs cause the production possibilities curve to be concave (bowed out from the origin).

10. The amount of resources allocated to the production of a good is optimal where the marginal benefit received from the last unit produced equals its marginal cost. This marginal cost is the opportunity cost in terms of other goods that could have been produced with the same resources.

(a) The optimal production level corresponds to the point of allocative efficiency.

(b) Marginal benefit falls as more is produced.

(c) Marginal cost rises as more is produced.

11. Dropping the assumptions underlying the production possibilities model gives some additional results.

(a) An economy experiencing unemployment and productive inefficiency is operating at a point inside its production possibilities curve, and is therefore failing to meet its productive potential.

(b) Economic growth occurs through improvements in technology or expansions in resource supplies, causing the production possibilities curve to expand, or shift outward.

(c) Resource allocation decisions made today help to determine production possibilities in the future; the more capital or future goods that we produce today, the more the production possibilities curve will expand in the future.

(d) If a nation specializes and trades with other nations, then the nation is not limited to points inside the production possibilities curve.

12. Many current and historical events and problems can be analyzed with the production possibilities model. These include: recessions, discrimination, land-use controversies, priorities for government spending, and technological change.

13. Different societies use different economic systems for addressing the fundamental economic problem of scarcity. Systems differ mainly in the ownership of resources, and in the method used to coordinate and direct economic activity.

(a) At one extreme is the market system, or capitalism, which relies upon private ownership of resources, the profit motive, and coordination through the use of prices and markets. The type of capitalism used in Canada also relies on government having a significant role in the economy.

(b) At the other extreme, the command economy uses public ownership of resources and decisions are made by central planning. In recent years a number of command economies have incorporated elements of the market system.

14. The circular flow model illustrates the interaction between businesses and households in resource markets and product markets. In exchange for resources that households supply to firms, firms pay incomes that households in turn use to demand goods and services produced by firms.

■ TERMS AND CONCEPTS

economic problem	production
utility	possibilities table
resources	production
land	possibilities curve
capital	opportunity cost
investment	law of increasing
labour	opportunity cost
entrepreneurial ability	economic growth
factors of production	economic system
full employment	capitalism
full production	market system
productive efficiency	command system
allocative efficiency	resource market
consumer goods	product market
capital goods	circular flow model

■ HINTS AND TIPS

1. The production possibilities curve is the first instance where graphing skills are needed. If you have serious difficulty mastering the graphical analysis you may have a general weakness in graphing that you should address immediately. Graphs are used constantly in the chapters that follow. Spend extra time on the graphical questions in this study guide, the relevant sections of the chapter, and with Appendix 1A of this study guide. Your instructor may also have additional resources or advice for you.

2. A movement from one point on the production possibilities curve to another point on the same curve indicates a change in what combination of products society *chooses*. In contrast, a shift of the whole production possibilities curve indicates a change in the *set of choices* available to society.

3. Many students initially confuse the coordinates of a point on the production possibilities curve with the intercepts of the curve. The intercepts indicate the *maximum*, or *potential*, production for each good (if all resources are dedicated to producing that

good), whereas the coordinates of the production point show *actual* production for each good.

■ FILL-IN QUESTIONS

1. The two fundamental facts that provide the foundation of economics are:
  (a) Society's wants are _____ .
  (b) Society's resources are _____ .

2. Consumer goods satisfy human wants (directly, indirectly) _____ and capital goods satisfy these wants _____ .

3. Economic efficiency requires that there be both full _____ of resources and full _____ .

4. Below is a production possibilities curve for tractors and suits of clothing.

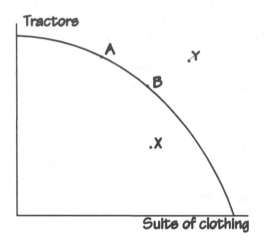

(a) If the economy moves from point *A* to point *B*, it will produce (more, fewer) _____ tractors and (more, fewer) _____ suits.
(b) If the economy is producing at point *X*, some of the resources of the economy are either _____ or _____ .
(c) If the economy is to produce at point *Y*, it must either expand its supply of _____ or improve its _____ .

5. The quantity of other goods and services an economy must go without in order to produce more low-cost housing is the _____ of producing the additional low-cost housing.

6. If Canada attempts to expand her apple industry, the opportunity cost per apple produced will tend to increase because resources are not completely

_____ to different uses. This is an example of the generalization known as the law of _____.

7. For each situation below, indicate whether there is overallocation, underallocation, or optimal allocation of resources to the production of the good in question.

(a) marginal benefit is greater than marginal cost at the current output level _____

(b) marginal benefit equals marginal cost at the current output level _____

(c) marginal benefit is less than marginal cost at the current output level _____

8. If some available resources are unemployed, productive efficiency (is, is not) _____ met, and the economy is (inside, outside, on) _____ its production possibilities curve.

9. Productive efficiency means that the _____ production techniques are used in the production of wanted goods and services.

10. Production is allocatively efficient when, given the distribution of resources, the economy produces that combination of goods _____ by society.

11. All points on the production possibilities curve are _____ efficient but some points are not _____ efficient.

12. Full production implies that both _____ efficiency and _____ efficiency are achieved.

13. Improvements in oil drilling technology would shift Canada's production possibilities curve to the (right, left) _____. Depletion of forest resources would shift our production possibilities curve to the _____.

14. In pure capitalism property resources are (publicly, privately) _____ owned; in a command economy resources are _____ owned.

■ **PROBLEMS AND PROJECTS**

1. Match the resources on the left with the corresponding resource payments on the right.

labour   rental income
capital   profits
land   wages
entrepreneurial ability   interest income

2. Below is a list of resources. Indicate in the space to the right of each whether the resource is land (Ld), capital (K), labour (L), or entrepreneurial ability (EA).

(a) fishing grounds in the North Atlantic _____

(b) a farmer's inventory of wheat _____

(c) Maple Leaf Gardens in Toronto _____

(d) the work performed by the late Henry Ford _____

(e) Cavendish beach in Prince Edward Island _____

(f) Stelco's steel plant in Hamilton, Ontario ___

(g) the tasks accomplished in making the Apple Computer a commercial success _____

(h) the work done by a welder on an assembly line _____

3. An economy produces two products, timber (T) and fish (F), according to the production possibilities table below. The usual assumptions apply.

(a) Plot the data from the production possibilities table on the graph provided. Place T on the vertical axis and F on the horizontal axis.

(b) Can the economy produce 4 of F and 22 of T? _____ If not, why? _____ What is the maximum amount of T that can be produced in combination with 4 of F? _____

Combination	Timber	Fish
a	0	6
b	7	5
c	13	4
d	18	3
e	22	2
f	25	1
g	27	0

(c) If the economy is producing 2F and 15T, what problem is being experienced? _____

(d) Assuming that the economy is productively efficient, what is the opportunity cost of producing 1F instead of none? _____ What is the opportunity cost of the second unit of F? _____ And the third F? _____

(e) As more units of F are produced, what is the trend in the number of units of T that must be given up to get the extra F? _____. Due to this trend, the shape of the production possibilities curve is _____ to the origin.

4. For each case below you are given an initial production possibilities curve between timber and fish. Sketch a new curve to show the result of the events given.

(a) The nation's supplies of labour and capital expand.

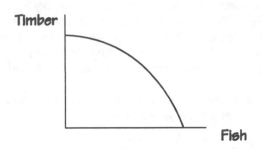

(b) New tree-planting techniques improve the success of reforestation operations.

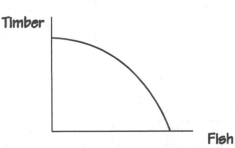

(c) An ecological disaster wipes out a large part of the fish stocks.

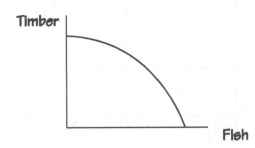

5. An economy is achieving full production, producing a combination of automobiles and food. Now a technological advance occurs which enables this economy to produce automobiles with fewer resources than previously. How is it possible for the society to consume more automobiles *and* more food as a result? Illustrate below using the production possibilities diagram.

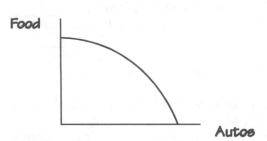

6. Below is a list of economic goods. Indicate in the space beside each whether the good is a consumer good (C), a capital good (K), or that it depends (D) upon who is using it and for what purpose.

(a) a dairy cow _____
(b) a tractor _____
(c) a shopping mall parking lot _____
(d) a telephone pole _____
(e) a telephone _____
(f) your refrigerator _____
(g) a refrigerator in a restaurant _____

7. A department store is installing video cameras to reduce shoplifting. The marginal costs and marginal benefits of additional cameras are:

Camera	MB ($/month)	MC ($/month)
1	300	100
2	250	125
3	160	150
4	50	175

(a) If the store must choose one of the numbers shown in the table, the optimal number of cameras is _____.

(b) How much better off is the store with the optimal number than with one camera fewer? $___

(c) How much better off is the store with the optimal number than with one camera more? $___

■ **TRUE-FALSE**

Circle T if the statement is true, F if it is false.

1. If you must stand in line for six hours to get into a free concert by the Tragically Hip, there is no opportunity cost to you for seeing the concert. **T F**

2. Money is a resource and is classified as "capital." **T F**

3. A Canada Savings Bond is classified as a capital good. **T F**

4. Profit is the reward paid to those who provide the economy with capital. **T F**

5. If the main opportunity cost of going to college is the foregone earnings, college enrolment should increase during periods of high unemployment, other factors remaining constant. **T F**

6. The opportunity cost of producing wheat tends to increase as more wheat is produced because land less suited to its production must be reallocated from other uses. **T F**

7. A production possibilities curve that is concave to the origin reflects the law of increasing opportunity costs. **T F**

8. The problem of scarcity is likely to be solved someday by technological progress. **T F**

9. An economy that is employing the least cost productive methods has achieved allocative efficiency. **T F**

10. Given full employment and full production, it is impossible for an economy that can produce only two goods to increase production of both. **T F**

11. Economic growth can be represented by a shift of the production possibilities curve to the right. **T F**

12. The more capital goods an economy produces today, the greater will be its ability to produce all goods in the future, *ceteris paribus*. **T F**

13. Most nations use economic systems somewhere between the extremes of pure capitalism and command economy. **T F**

14. In a command economy most resources are privately owned and are allocated by the market system. **T F**

15. In the circular flow model, households act on the demand side of resource and product markets. **T F**

■ **MULTIPLE-CHOICE**

Circle the letter that corresponds to the best answer.

1. In her role as an "innovator" an entrepreneur:
   (a) makes policy decisions in a business firm
   (b) combines factors of production to produce a good or service
   (c) invents a new production process
   (d) takes risks in the market place

2. An economy is efficient when it has achieved:
   (a) full employment
   (b) full production
   (c) either full employment or full production
   (d) both full employment and full production

3. When a production possibilities curve is drawn, four assumptions are made. Which is **not** one of those assumptions?
   (a) only two goods are produced
   (b) wants are unlimited
   (c) the economy has both full employment and full production
   (d) the quantities of all resources available to the economy are fixed

Answer the next four questions on the basis of the following diagram.

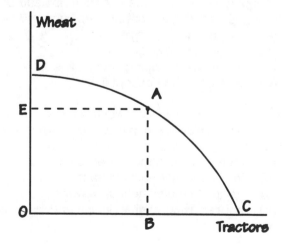

4. At point *A* on the production possibilities curve:
   (a) less wheat than tractors is being produced
   (b) fewer tractors than wheat are being produced
   (c) the economy is employing all its resources
   (d) the economy is not employing all its resources

5. The opportunity cost of producing 0*B* of tractors is:
   (a) 0*D* of wheat
   (b) 0*E* of wheat
   (c) *ED* of wheat
   (d) 0*C* of tractors

6. If there occurred a technological improvement in the production of tractors but not wheat:
   (a) point *D* would remain fixed and point *C* shift to the left
   (b) point *C* would remain fixed and point *D* shift upward
   (c) point *D* would remain fixed and point *C* shift to the right
   (d) point *C* would remain fixed and point *D* shift inward

7. From one point to another along the same production possibilities curve:
   (a) resources remain fixed but are reallocated between the production of the two goods
   (b) resources are increased and are reallocated between the two goods
   (c) resources are increased and production of both goods increased
   (d) idle resources are put to work to increase the production of one good

8. If opportunity costs are constant, instead of increasing, the production possibilities curve will be:
   (a) concave to the origin
   (b) convex to the origin
   (c) a downward sloping straight line
   (d) parallel to the horizontal axis

9. Which of the following would cause a nation's production possibilities curve to shift inward toward the origin?
   (a) more people in the labour force
   (b) increased international trade
   (c) rising unemployment of workers
   (d) not replacing capital equipment as it wears out

10. Which of the following will slow down the rate at which Canada's production possibilities curve shifts rightward?
    (a) increasing rate of technological change
    (b) increased immigration
    (c) depletion of Canada's oil and gas deposits
    (d) freer trade between Canada's provinces

11. The opportunity cost of providing a governmentally financed stadium for a city's baseball team is:
    (a) the interest on the money borrowed to finance the stadium
    (b) the future tax increase the public will be forced to bear to pay for the stadium
    (c) the other goods and services that must be sacrificed so that resources can be used for stadium construction
    (d) there is no opportunity cost since Ottawa will finance the stadium under a regional development program

12. Private ownership of property resources, use of the market system to direct and coordinate economic activity, and the presence of the profit motive are characteristic of:
    (a) pure capitalism
    (b) the command economy
    (c) market socialism
    (d) communism

13. Central planning is associated with which economic system?
    (a) pure capitalism
    (b) laissez-faire capitalism
    (c) market economy
    (d) command economy

14. Productive efficiency is attained when:
    (a) resources are all employed
    (b) output is produced at least possible cost
    (c) there is no government involvement in the economy
    (d) the production possibilities curve is concave

15. The term "laissez-faire" refers to:
    (a) the absence of government intervention in markets
    (b) the absence of monopoly
    (c) the absence of competition in markets
    (d) efficient use of employed resources

■ DISCUSSION QUESTIONS

1. Explain what is meant by the "economic problem." Why are resources scarce?

2. When is a society economically efficient? What is meant by "full production," and how does it differ from "full employment"?

3. What four assumptions are made in drawing a production possibilities curve? How do technological progress and an increased supply of resources in the economy affect the curve?

4. Why cannot an economist determine which combination in the production possibilities table is "best"? What determines the optimum product-mix?

5. What is opportunity cost? What is the law of increasing opportunity costs? Why do opportunity costs increase?

6. Would the economic problem disappear if the affluent countries, including Canada, offered to pay more for the products of the Third World countries? Explain.

7. During the Cold War, Russia seemed to be quite competitive with the United States in terms of military strength even though Russia's overall production capabilities were much lower than America's. Use the production possibility curve model to resolve this paradox.

8. If resources in an economy are fully employed, what would be the effect on living standards if the government decided to increase the output of goods for the future? Explain using the production possibilities curve.

9. Explain why you agree or disagree with the statement: "The opportunity cost of allocating large numbers of people to clean up Ontario's lakes during a recession is different from the opportunity cost during a period of full employment."

10. Explain the difference between productive and allocative efficiency.

11. What are the roles of households and of businesses in the resource market and the product market?

■ ANSWERS

FILL-IN QUESTIONS

1. (a) unlimited; (b) scarce (or limited)

2. directly; indirectly

3. employment, production

4. (a) fewer, more; (b) unemployed, underemployed; (c) resources, technology

5. opportunity cost

6. adaptable; increasing opportunity costs

7. (a) underallocation; (b) optimal allocation; (c) over-allocation

8. is not; inside

9. least costly

10. most wanted

11. productively, allocatively

12. productive, allocative

13. right; left

14. privately, publicly

PROBLEMS AND PROJECTS

1. labour: wages; capital: interest income; land: rental income; entrepreneurial ability: profits

2. (a) Ld; (b) K; (c) K; (d) EA; (e) Ld; (f) K; (g) EA; (h) L

3. (b) No; this combination lies outside the production possibilities curve; 13 T; (c) productive inefficiency (unemployment or underemployment); (d) $2T = 27T - 25T$, 3T, 4T; (e) increasing, concave

4. (a) Both T and F intercepts shift out; (b) T intercept shifts out, F intercept is unchanged; (c) F intercept shifts in, T intercept is unchanged

5. More automobiles can now be produced with a given amount of resources, so the automobiles intercept shifts out. By moving some resources from autos to food, the

society can produce more food and more automobiles. Show this on your diagram by shifting the production possibilities curve, then showing a movement to a new point that is northeast of the original point.

6.   (a) K, (b) K, (c) K, (d) K, (e) D, (f) C, (g) K

7.   (a) 3 cameras, because for each of the first three, the MB > MC; (b) $10/month is the net benefit for the 3rd camera ($160-150); (c) $125/month is the net loss for the 4th camera ($50-175)

TRUE-FALSE

1.   F   Your time has value
2.   F   Money is not an economic resource
3.   F   CSB's are financial assets, not real capital
4.   F   Profit goes to entrepreneurs; capitalists earn interest income
5.   T   High unemployment means more people would not lose wages by choosing to go to college
6.   T
7.   T
8.   F   Even as we become able to produce more our wants will continue to expand
9.   F   Allocative efficiency is not achieved unless the most wanted combination of goods is being produced
10. T
11. T
12. T
13. T
14. F   The statement describes capitalism or market system
15. F   Households are suppliers, not demanders, in resource markets

MULTIPLE-CHOICE

1.   (c) The others are roles of entrepreneurs, but not the innovator role
2.   (d) Both forms are necessary conditions
3.   (b) Demands for goods are not relevent to production possibilities
4.   (c) Because point A is on the curve
5.   (c) Wheat production falls from point D to point E
6.   (c) Maximum tractor output increases; maximum wheat does not change
7.   (a) Increased resources would imply a shift; if resources were previously idle the economy was not on the curve
8.   (c) Such a line would have a constant slope, or trade-off ratio between the two goods
9.   (d) The capital stock would shrink, meaning a reduction in the supply of resources
10. (c) Reduction in our supply of resources
11. (c) Ultimately the opportunity cost must be measured in other goods given up
12. (a) All are critical to a capitalist or market economy

13. (d) Including socialism and communism
14. (b) Using resources in the most productive way, and minimizing cost of production go hand in hand
15. (a) "Let it be" is government's attitude toward the economy in a "laissez faire" system

CHAPTER 3

Individual Markets: Demand and Supply

This chapter presents the most important tool of economic analysis: the demand and supply model. We use this model to analyze how various events affect the price and quantities of goods and services traded in highly competitive markets where there are many buyers and sellers trading a standardized product.

The law of demand asserts an inverse relationship between price and quantity demanded, *ceteris paribus*. The law of supply states a positive relationship between price and quantity supplied, *ceteris paribus*. The demand and supply relationships can be expressed in several ways: as algebraic equations, schedules in tables, or graphs. Given the demand and the supply in a market, there is only one price at which the quantity demanded by consumers exactly equals the quantity supplied by sellers. This is the equilibrium or market-clearing price. The equilibrium quantity is the quantity demanded and supplied at the equilibrium price.

Starting from an equilibrium, a change in any demand or supply determinant will shift the demand or supply curve, and throw the market out of equilibrium — creating either a shortage or a surplus. To eliminate the shortage (or surplus) the price must rise (or fall) to restore the balance between how much consumers are willing and able to buy and producers are willing and able to sell.

The first step in analyzing how an event affects the market equilibrium is to determine which curve is directly affected by the event: supply or demand. The second step is to decide whether that curve increases or decreases. From there it is a simple matter to decide the direction of change for the equilibrium price and quantity.

To master the supply and demand model one must clearly understand the definitions of demand and supply, and the key distinctions between "de-mand" and "quantity demanded" and between "supply" and "quantity supplied." Practice with the graphical model of demand and supply will greatly help clarify these concepts.

■ CHAPTER LEARNING OBJECTIVES

In this chapter you will learn:
□   What markets are.
□   What demand is and what factors affect it.
□   What supply is and what factors affect it.
□   How demand and supply together determine market equilibrium.

■ CHAPTER OUTLINE

1. A market is any institution or mechanism that brings together the buyers and sellers of a particular good or service. In this chapter we assume that markets are highly competitive.

2. Demand is the relationship between the price of a product and the amount of the product that the consumer is willing and able to purchase in a specific time period. The relationship can be expressed in a table, graph, or equation.

3. The law of demand states that, other things being equal, as price falls, the quantity demanded rises. That is, there is an inverse relationship between price and quantity demanded.

4. Along with plenty of strong evidence for the law of demand, there are also three analytical reasons:
   (a) If consumers experience *diminishing marginal utility* then they will be willing to buy additional units of a good only if price is reduced.

(b) When price falls there is an *income effect*: the consumer's overall buying power increases so the consumer buys more of the good.

(c) When price falls there is a *substitution effect*: the consumer is motivated to buy more of the good that is now relatively less expensive instead of other goods for which it is a substitute.

5. The demand curve is a graphic representation of the law of demand.

(a) The graph has price on the vertical axis, and quantity demanded on the horizontal axis.

(b) A change in price leads to a movement along the demand curve. This is called a change in quantity demanded.

6. The market demand is derived by "adding up" the individual consumer demands at each possible price. The law of demand applies to both individual and market demand curves.

7. The price determines the quantity demanded of a good, but factors other than price determine the location of the whole demand curve. These factors are known as the demand determinants:

(a) tastes (or preferences) of buyers;

(b) number of buyers in the market;

(c) incomes of consumers;

(d) prices of related goods (substitutes and complements);

(e) expectations.

8. A change in a demand determinant will shift demand to the left (a decrease) or the right (an increase), creating an entirely new demand curve. This is called a change in demand.

(a) If tastes shift in favour of a good, its demand will increase.

(b) If the number of buyers of a good increases, its demand will increase.

(c) If consumer incomes increase, demand will increase if the good is normal, and demand will decrease if the good is inferior.

(d) If an increase in the price of one good causes the demand for another good to decrease, the two goods are complements; if the price increase causes demand for the other good to increase, the two goods are substitutes.

(e) If consumers expect prices or incomes to rise in the future they may increase their demand now.

9. A change in demand and a change in the quantity demanded are not the same thing. This is obvious on the graph where a change in the price of the good causes a change in the quantity demanded, or movement along the curve, whereas a change in demand shifts the entire curve to a new location.

10. Supply is the relationship between the price of a product and the amount of the product that suppliers will offer to sell in a specific time period. The law of supply states that, other things being equal, as price rises, the quantity supplied rises. That is, there is a positive relationship between price and quantity supplied. The quantity supplied rises with price because the supplier can profitably produce more output at a higher price.

11. The supply curve is a graphic representation of supply and the law of supply.

(a) The graph has price on the vertical axis, and quantity supplied on the horizontal axis.

(b) A change in price leads to a movement along the supply curve. This is called a change in quantity supplied.

12. The determinants of supply are:

(a) resource prices;

(b) technology;

(c) taxes and subsidies;

(d) prices of other goods;

(e) price expectations;

(f) number of sellers in the market.

13. A change in any of the determinants will shift supply to the left (a decrease) or the right (an increase), creating an entirely new supply curve. This is called a change in supply.

(a) If prices of production resources fall, supply will increase.

(b) A technological change will improve the efficiency of production and increase the supply.

(c) A new tax will raise the producer's costs and reduce the supply; a new subsidy will increase the supply.

(d) Producers may reallocate their resources if the price of a related good changes. Depending on the case, supply could increase or decrease.

(e) It is also difficult to generalize about how a change in expectations about the future price will change today's supply.

(f) An increase in the number of sellers will increase the supply.

14. A change in supply and a change in the quantity supplied are not the same thing. The difference is most obvious on a graph. A change in the price of the good causes a change in the quantity supplied, which on the graph is a movement to a different point on the same supply curve, whereas a change in supply involves a shift to a whole new supply curve.

15. The market-clearing or equilibrium price of a good is that price at which quantity demanded and quantity supplied are equal; the equilibrium quantity is equal to the quantity demanded and supplied at the equilibrium price.

(a) If price is above the equilibrium, quantity demanded is less than quantity supplied, so there is a surplus. This will cause price to fall.

(b) If price is below the equilibrium, quantity demanded is greater than quantity supplied, so there is a shortage. This will cause price to rise.

(c) The only sustainable price is the equilibrium price.

(d) The rationing function of price is to create consistency between the decisions of sellers and of buyers, so as to eliminate any shortages or surpluses from a market.

16. Any change in a determinant of demand or supply will cause the curve to shift, and result in a new equilibrium price and quantity.

(a) Most changes shift only one of the two curves.

(b) When demand changes, and supply is unchanged, equilibrium price and quantity change in the same direction as the change in demand.

(c) When supply changes, and demand is unchanged, quantity moves in the same direction as the supply change, but equilibrium price moves in the opposite direction.

(d) In complex cases where both supply and demand change, both curves will shift; either the direction of price change or quantity change will be predictable, the other will be indeterminate.

17. It is always important to keep in mind that specific demand and supply curves show relationships between prices and quantities demanded or supplied, holding all other determinants equal.

■ **TERMS AND CONCEPTS**

market	**change in quantity**
demand	**demanded**

demand schedule	**supply**
law of demand	**supply schedule**
diminishing marginal	**law of supply**
utility	**supply curve**
income effect	**determinants of**
substitution effect	**supply**
demand curve	**change in supply**
determinants of	**change in quantity**
demand	**supplied**
normal goods	**surplus**
inferior goods	**shortage**
substitute good	**equilibrium price**
complementary good	**equilibrium quantity**
change in demand	**rationing function of**
	price

■ **HINTS AND TIPS**

1. This chapter is the most important one in the book. Be sure to spend extra time on it, and to return to it to review the fundamentals if you run into difficulties in later chapters.

2. You have not mastered the chapter until you can clearly distinguish between a change in demand and a change in quantity demanded; the same for supply vs. quantity supplied. You should be able to articulate the difference verbally, and graphically.

3. Perhaps more than any other chapter, this chapter requires active practice. Pick up your pencil and draw graphs. Begin by plotting demand and supply schedules onto graphs. Study carefully the examples in the text and study guide to learn the appropriate labels for such graphs. Once you are confident of working with graphs with concrete numbers, go to the next step of drawing abstract graphs where numbers are implied on the axes, but not explicitly given.

4. If algebraic work with demand and supply is relevant in the economics course you are studying, please look at the Appendix to Chapter 3.

■ **FILL-IN QUESTIONS**

1. A market is the institution or mechanism that brings together the _____ and the _____ of a particular good or service.

2. The demand schedule reflects a (positive, negative) _____ relationship between price and quantity demanded. The supply schedule reflects a _____ relationship between price and quantity supplied.

3. Factors that shift the demand curve when they change are called demand _____.

4. The Latin phrase meaning "all other things being equal" is _____.

5. When demand or supply is graphed, price is placed on the _____ axis and quantity on the _____ axis.

6. The graph of the demand schedule is called the demand _____ and according to the law of demand is _____ sloping.

7. A change in price causes a change in (demand, quantity demanded) _____, and results in a (movement along, shift in) _____ the demand curve. A change in consumer incomes causes a change in (demand, quantity demanded) _____, and results in a (movement along, shift in) _____ the demand curve.

8. Marianne tends to buy more books when the price of books falls because:
   (a)   her purchasing power is increased, so she can afford to buy more books and other goods; this is called the _____ effect.
   (b)   books become less expensive relative to magazines, so Marianne tends to buy more books and fewer magazines; and this is called the _____ effect.

9. Don likes to have spare drill bits for various projects around the house. He is willing to pay less for each successive drill bit because he is successively less likely to actually need each extra one he buys. This is an example of the principle known as diminishing _____.

10. A change in price causes a change in (supply, quantity supplied) _____, and results in a (movement along, shift in) _____ the supply curve. A change in resource costs causes a change in (supply, quantity supplied) _____, and results in a (movement along, shift in) _____ the supply curve.

11. An increase in supply is shown by a shift of the entire supply curve to the (left, right) _____. A

decrease in supply is shown by a shift of the entire supply curve to the _____.

12. If quantity demanded exceeds quantity supplied, price is (above, below) _____ the equilibrium price. This creates a (shortage, surplus) _____ that will cause the price to (rise, fall) _____.

■   **PROBLEMS AND PROJECTS**

1. (a) Plot the demand and supply schedules below on the graph provided. Indicate on the graph the equilibrium price and quantity by drawing lines from the intersection of the demand and supply curves to the price and quantity axes, and labelling the values P* and Q*.

Price per Unit	Quantity Demanded	Quantity Supplied	Shortage (-) or Surplus (+)
$13	18	54	_____
12	21	48	_____
11	24	42	_____
10	27	36	_____
9	30	30	_____
8	33	24	_____
7	36	18	_____
6	39	12	_____

(b)   At equilibrium, P* = _____, and Q* = _____.
(c)   Fill in the last column of the table showing the amount of shortage or surplus that would exist at each price shown.

2. (a) Three individuals' demand schedules for bread are shown below. Assuming these are the only buyers, fill in the market demand schedule for bread.

Price (per loaf)	Quantity Demanded (loaves per month)			
	Doug	Leslie	Chong	Total
$1.20	10	6	8	_____
1.10	12	8	10	_____
1.00	15	11	12	_____
0.90	19	15	14	_____
0.80	24	18	16	_____

(b) If the market supply of bread is fixed at 48 loaves per month, what will be the equilibrium price, and how many loaves will each consumer buy at this price?

Price = $_____ per loaf

Doug: _____ loaves; Leslie: _____ loaves; Chong: _____ loaves

3. Below are some events that affect the market for wine. In each space, indicate whether the event shifts demand (D) or supply (S), and whether it is an increase (+) or decrease (-) in the curve.

(a) Increase in the price of grapes _____
(b) Increase in population of consumers _____
(c) Increase in the price of cheese _____
(d) Improvement in production technology _____
(e) New subsidies for wine production _____
(f) Increase in the price of beer _____
(g) Consumers expect a new tax on wine _____

4. Suppose that the demand and supply model is applicable to the Canadian beef market. For each of the following events, sketch a demand and supply graph showing the effect on the equilibrium price and quantity of beef in Canada.

(a) A popular singer remarks that red meat in the diet may be a contributing factor in heart and circulatory diseases.

(b) The East Coast cod fishery is closed due to depleted fish stocks.

(c) Hoof and mouth disease in Europe leads to destruction of much of the supply of beef imported from Europe.

(d) The price of livestock feed grains falls sharply due to a record harvest.

(e) Agriculture Canada discovers a new growth hormone that will increase the weight of beef cattle by 20% with the same feed intake.

(f) Numerous hamburger restaurants go out of business as a result of sharp increases in the minimum wage rate.

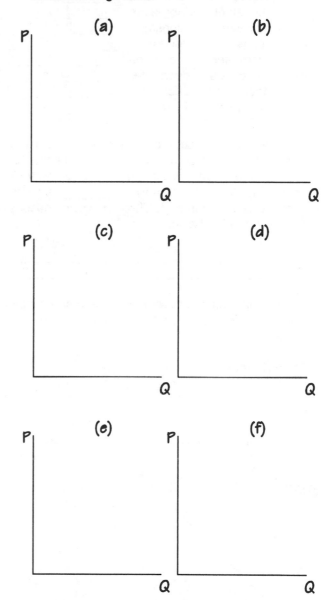

5. The table on the next page shows a number of different cases of a change in demand and/or supply. In the columns for price change and quantity change, fill in the direction in which the equilibrium will change: increase (+), decrease (-), or indeterminate (?).

Case	Demand	Supply	Price change	Quantity change
a	increases	constant	____	____
b	constant	increases	____	____
c	decreases	constant	____	____
d	constant	decreases	____	____
e	increases	increases	____	____
f	increases	decreases	____	____
g	decreases	decreases	____	____
h	decreases	increases	____	____

6. In the 1990s, most golf courses in Canada raised their green fees (the price of playing golf), but also had more golfers coming to play at their courses. This case (is, is not) _____ a violation of the law of demand. Three possible reasons for the observed behaviour are:

(a) _____

(b) _____

(c) _____

7. The graph below shows the demand and supply for daily parking spots in the downtown core of a Canadian city.

Price ($/spot)

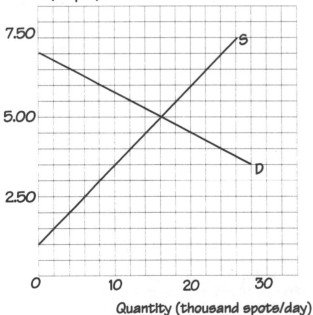

Quantity (thousand spots/day)

(a)   The current equilibrium price is _____ per spot, and _____ spots are rented each day.

(b)   Suppose that city council levies a new tax on parking lot operators in order to raise revenue to pay for a rapid transit system. The tax is set at $1.50 per spot rented. If the consumer pays

$6.00, the supplier keeps $6.00-$1.50=$4.50. If the consumer pays $5.00, the supplier keeps

_____.

(c)   Show the new supply curve reflecting the tax. (The supply curve will shift upward by the amount of the tax because suppliers require this much extra in order to be willing to maintain the same supply as before.)

(d)   The new equilibrium price is _____ per spot, and _____ spots are rented each day. Accordingly, the price consumers pay for one spot has (fallen, risen) _____ by $_____ , and the price that suppliers keep has _____ by $_____. Therefore, the consumers' burden of the tax is _____ percent, and the suppliers' burden is _____ percent.

8. The table below shows the demand and supply schedules for firewood in two small towns, Eastwick and Westwood. At first each town is a separate competitive market because there is no passage across the river separating the towns.

	Eastwick		Westwood		Total	
Price	Qd	Qs	Qd	Qs	Qd	Qs
$225	80	100	45	105	____	____
200	90	90	55	95	____	____
175	100	80	65	85	____	____
150	110	70	75	75	____	____
125	120	60	85	65	____	____

(a)   In Eastwick the equilibrium price is _____ per cord, and the equilibrium quantity is _____ cords per year.

(b)   In Westwood the equilibrium price is _____ per cord, and the equilibrium quantity is _____ cords per year.

Now a bridge is built across the river, turning Eastwick and Westwood into one combined market.

(c)   Fill in the market demand and supply schedules in the blank columns.

(d)   The new equilibrium price is _____ per cord. This represents an increase in (Westwood, Eastwick) _____ and a decrease in

_____.

(e)   In Westwood quantity demanded is now _____ cords per year, and quantity supplied is now _____ cords per year. In Eastwick quantity demanded is now _____ cords per year, and quantity supplied is now _____ cords per year. Therefore, the town of _____ must import

_____ cords per year from the town of _____.

9. How would a lengthy strike by transit drivers in a major city affect the market for gasoline in that market? Work this out by considering the relationships between buses and cars, and between cars and gasoline.

■ **TRUE-FALSE**

Circle T if the statement is true, F if it is false.

1. The classified ads section of a student newspaper could be considered a market.　　　**T F**

2. The law of demand states that as price increases, the demand for the product decreases, *ceteris paribus*.　　　**T F**

3. In graphing supply and demand schedules, supply is put on the horizontal axis and demand on the vertical axis.　　　**T F**

4. A fall in the price of snowboards will cause the demand for skis to decrease.　　　**T F**

5. If two goods are complements, an increase in the price of one will cause the demand for the other to decrease.　　　**T F**

6. An increase in income increases the demand for normal goods.　　　**T F**

7. If Wimpy experiences diminishing marginal utility, then the additional satisfaction he gets from eating his sixth hamburger of the day is less than the satisfaction from the fifth hamburger.　　**T F**

8. Since the amount purchased must equal the amount sold, demand and supply must always equal each other.　　　**T F**

Questions 9-11 are based on the accompanying graph.

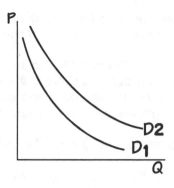

9. If the demand curve moves from D_1 to D_2 demand has increased.　　　**T F**

10. The shift of the demand curve from D_1 to D_2 could be caused by a decrease in the price of complements.　　　**T F**

11. The shift of the demand curve from D_1 to D_2 could be caused by a decrease in supply.　　**T F**

12. A decrease in quantity supplied can be caused by an increase in production costs.　　　**T F**

13. If the supply curve for green lipstick shifts to the right, the supply of green lipstick has decreased.　　　**T F**

14. When quantity supplied exceeds quantity demanded, the market price will tend to fall.　　**T F**

15. The equilibrium price is also referred to as the market-clearing price.　　　**T F**

16. The rationing function of prices is the elimination of shortages and surpluses.　　　**T F**

17. There is an inverse relationship between a change in supply and the resulting change in equilibrium price.　　　**T F**

■ **MULTIPLE-CHOICE**

Circle the letter that corresponds to the best answer.

1. An increase in the quantity demanded of oranges can be caused by:
　(a) a shift to the left of the supply curve of oranges
　(b) a shift to the right of the supply curve of oranges

(c)   a decline in the demand for orange juice

(d)   a rise in the demand for orange juice

2. A decrease in the quantity demanded:

(a)   shifts the demand curve to the left

(b)   shifts the demand curve to the right

(c)   is a movement down along the demand curve

(d)   is a movement up along the demand curve

3. If skiing at Banff and skiing at Whistler are substitutes, an increase in the price of skiing at Banff will:

(a)   decrease the demand for skiing at Whistler

(b)   increase the demand for skiing at Whistler

(c)   decrease the quantity demanded of skiing at Whistler

(d)   increase the quantity demanded of skiing at Whistler

4. Which pair of goods would most consumers regard as complementary goods?

(a)   coffee and tea

(b)   hockey sticks and skates

(c)   hamburger meat and bus rides

(d)   books and televisions

5. Which of the following is **not** among the determinants of demand?

(a)   consumer incomes

(b)   consumer expectations of future prices

(c)   prices of substitute goods

(d)   cost of resources

6. If an increase in income causes the demand for a particular good to decrease, then that good is:

(a)   normal

(b)   inferior

(c)   substitute

(d)   complement

7. According to the law of supply:

(a)   equilibrium quantity will increase when equilibrium price increases

(b)   equilibrium quantity will decrease when equilibrium price increases

(c)   the supply curve has a negative slope

(d)   if other things remain the same, the quantity supplied increases whenever price increases

8. A supply curve indicates:

(a)   the profit-maximizing quantities sellers place on the market at alternative prices

(b)   the minimum quantities sellers place on the market at alternative prices

(c)   the maximum quantities sellers will place on the market at different prices for inputs

(d)   the quantities sellers place on the market in order to meet consumer demand at that price

9. The supply curve of the firm slopes upward in the short run because:

(a)   the increased production requires the use of inferior inputs

(b)   hiring more inputs for the extra production requires the payment of higher input prices

(c)   the increased technology to produce more output is expensive

(d)   productive efficiency declines because certain productive resources cannot be expanded quickly

10. A movement along a supply curve for a good would be caused by:

(a)   an improvement in the technology of production

(b)   an increase in the price of the good

(c)   an increase in the number of suppliers of the good

(d)   a change in expectations

11. Which of the following would increase the supply of books?

(a)   an increase in the demand for books

(b)   an increase in the price of books

(c)   an increase in the cost of paper

(d)   a decrease in the wages paid to printers

12. A market is in equilibrium when:

(a)   inventories of the good are not rising

(b)   suppliers can sell all of the good they decide to produce at the prevailing price

(c)   quantity demanded equals quantity supplied

(d)   demanders can purchase all of the good they want at the prevailing price

13. When the price of toothpaste falls, what will happen?

(a)   quantity demanded decreases

(b)   demand increases

(c)   supply decreases

(d)   quantity supplied decreases

Questions 14 to 17 are based on the following diagram.

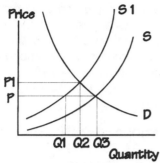

14. Given the original demand and supply curves are D and S:

(a) the equilibrium price and quantity were P and Q_1

(b) the equilibrium price and quantity were P and P_1

(c) the equilibrium price and quantity were P_1 and Q_1

(d) the equilibrium price and quantity were P and Q_3

15. The shift of the supply curve from S to S_1 is termed:

(a) an increase in supply

(b) an increase in quantity supplied

(c) a decrease in supply

(d) a decrease in quantity supplied

16. The shift in the supply curve from S to S_1 could be caused by:

(a) an increase in the price of the good

(b) a technological improvement in the production of the good

(c) a decrease in demand

(d) an increase in the cost of the resources used in the production of the good

17. If the price were prevented from adjusting when the supply shifted from S to S_1 the result would be:

(a) a surplus of Q_3 - Q_1

(b) a shortage of Q_2 - Q_1

(c) a shortage of Q_3 - Q_1

(d) a surplus of Q_3 - Q_2

18. Which of the following events would likely cause a furniture manufacturer to increase his supply of oak tables:

(a) an increase in the price of oak tables

(b) an increase in the cost of oak lumber

(c) a decrease in the demand for pine tables

(d) an increase in wages paid to staff

19. An increase in supply and an increase in demand will:

(a) increase price and increase the quantity exchanged

(b) decrease price and increase the quantity exchanged

(c) affect price in an indeterminate way and decrease the quantity exchanged

(d) affect price in an indeterminate way and increase the quantity exchanged

20. If scalping NHL playoff game tickets is profitable, this is a sign that the initial price at which the tickets were issued was:

(a) below the equilibrium price

(b) equal to the equilibrium price

(c) above the equilibrium price

(d) unreasonably high

21. A shortage of paper would cause the price of paper to go up. This would in turn alleviate the shortage by:

(a) giving buyers incentives to use less paper

(b) giving producers incentives to find ways to supply more paper

(c) increasing the amount of paper being recycled

(d) all of the above

22. In 2001 fewer tents are sold, and the price of tents is higher, as compared to 2000. Which one of the following might have caused the change?

(a) demand for tents was greater in 2001

(b) demand for tents was less in 2001

(c) supply of tents was greater in 2001

(d) supply of tents was less in 2001

23. Which of the following could raise the price of movie rentals in Saskatoon?

(a) a drop in the number of movie rental stores

(b) an increase in the price of VCRs

(c) a decrease in the population of Saskatoon

(d) a decrease in the price of admission to movie theatres

24. If new reserves of natural gas were discovered and brought into production, and population were to grow at the same time:

(a) the price of natural gas would rise

(b) the price of natural gas would fall

(c) the price of natural gas would not change

(d) the price of natural gas might rise or fall

■ DISCUSSION QUESTIONS

1. What is a market? For what kinds of goods does a laundromat bulletin board, or classified pages in a student newspaper, often serve as a market?

2. Carefully state the law of demand and explain the three reasons presented in this chapter to justify downward sloping demand curves.

3. The last time OPEC succeeded in sharply increasing the price of oil, drivers reacted by significantly reducing their gasoline consumption. Explain this in terms of the income effect and substitution effect.

4. Explain the difference between an increase in demand and an increase in quantity demanded. What factors cause a change in demand?

5. Define supply and explain why supply curves are upward sloping.

6. Explain the differences between a change in supply and a change in quantity supplied. What are the factors that cause a change in supply?

7. Neither demand nor supply remains constant for long. Economic circumstances are always changing so the actual prices we see are often not equilibrium prices. Why then do economists spend so much time trying to determine the equilibrium price and quantity if these magnitudes change so frequently?

8. How are normal, inferior, substitute, complementary, and independent goods defined? During a recession (when consumer incomes are falling), who would fare better, firms that sell normal goods, or firms that sell inferior goods?

9. Analyze the following quotation and explain the fallacies contained in it. "An increase in demand will cause price to rise; with a rise in price, supply will increase and the increase in supply will push price down. Therefore, an increase in demand may or may not result in a price increase."

10. To reduce emissions of greenhouse gases, Canada wants to reduce the burning of fossil fuels. Explain why a new tax on automobiles or a subsidy for bicycles would help the pursuit of this goal.

11. From the supply and demand perspective, what would you say has happened in the market for cell phones in the last decade? Are the falling prices and increased numbers of cell phones in use consistent with our economic theory?

■ ANSWERS

FILL-IN QUESTIONS

1. buyers, sellers (either order)

2. negative, positive

3. determinants

4. *ceteris paribus*

5. vertical, horizontal

6. curve, downward (negative)

7. quantity demanded, movement along; demand, shift in

8. (a) income; (b) substitution

9. marginal utility

10. quantity supplied, movement along; supply, shift in

11. right, left

12. below; shortage, rise

PROBLEMS AND PROJECTS

1. (b) $9, 30; (c) from top to bottom: +36, +27, +18, +9, 0, -9, -18, -27.

2. (a) 24, 30, 38, 48, 58; (b) $0.90 (where Qd = Qs). Doug: 19; Leslie: 15; Chong: 14.

3. (a) S-; (b) D+; (c) D- (complements); (d) S+; (e) S+; (f) D+ (substitutes); (g) D+ (buy more now before price rises).

4. (a) D shifts left: P -, Q -; (b) Fish and beef are complements for consumers, so as fish prices rise, then in the beef market D shifts right: P +, Q +; (c) S shifts left: P +, Q -; (d) Resource prices fall, so S shifts right: P -, Q +; (e) Improved production technology causes S to shift right; P -, Q +; (f) Less buyers of beef, so D shifts left: P -, Q -.

5. (a) +, +; (b) -,+; (c) -,-; (d) +,-; (e) ?,+; (f) +,?; (g) ?,-; (h) -,?

6. is not; (a) population growth, (b) increased incomes, (c) increased preferences for golf, or increased prices for substitute recreation activities, etc.

7. (a) $5.00, 16,000; (b) $3.50; (c) the new S curve is parallel to the original and $1.50 above it; (d) about 5.50, 12,000, risen, 0.50, fallen, 1.00; 33, 67.

8. (a) $200, 90; (b) $150, 75; (c) Qd = 125, 145, 165, 185, 205; Qs = 205, 185, 165, 145, 125; (d) $175, West-wood, Eastwick; (e) 65, 85; 100, 80; Eastwick, 20, West-wood.

9. Cars and buses are substitutes, so when buses are not available more people will drive cars. Cars and gasoline are complements, so more gasoline will be used. The demand for gasoline shifts to right. Equilibrium price and quantity both increase.

TRUE-FALSE

1. T
2. F   The change is in quantity demanded, not demand
3. F   Quantities of supply and demand are both on the horizontal axis and price is on the vertical
4. T   Assuming skis and snowboards are substitutes
5. T
6. T
7. T
8. F   They are necessarily equal only at the equilibrium price
9. T
10. T
11. F
12. F   The decrease is in supply, not quantity supplied
13. F   The supply has increased
14. T
15. T
16. T
17. T   As supply increases, price decreases

MULTIPLE-CHOICE

1. (b) There is a movement along the demand curve when the supply shifts, changing the equilibrium price
2. (d) This is caused by a rise in price
3. (b) Some skiers choose Whistler instead of Banff
4. (b) Complementary goods are used together
5. (d) Cost of resources affects supply, not demand
6. (b) For example, generic macaroni and cheese
7. (d) This law states a positive relationship between quantity supplied and price
8. (a) Sellers try to maximize profits
9. (d) For example, a restaurant cannot quickly expand its kitchen facilities

10. (b) All of the others shift the supply curve
11. (d) Lower wages means lower production costs and an increase in supply
12. (c) The other choices are only partially correct
13. (d) A movement down along the supply curve
14. (d) Where S and D intersect
15. (c) Less is supplied at every possible price
16. (d) S to S1 is a decrease in supply
17. (c) At the moment after supply shifts, Qd is still at Q3, but Qs is now at Q1
18. (c) The supply of oak tables could shift right if producers move their resources away from making pine tables and more into making oak tables
19. (d) Depending on which shifts more, demand or supply, price could rise or fall
20. (a) Scalpers depend on there being a shortage at the price at which tickets are first issued
21. (d) These are all aspects of the rationing function of prices
22. (d) Of the possibilities given, only the supply decrease affects both price and quantity as specified
23. (a) Fewer stores would mean a decrease in supply
24. (d) Both supply and demand shift to the right, so the price change depends on the relative extent of the two shifts

APPENDIX TO CHAPTER 3

The Mathematics of Market Equilibrium

This appendix shows how the demand and supply model can be represented mathematically. The demand curve and the supply curve can be expressed in equation form as functions of price. Only at the equilibrium price do both functions generate the same value for quantity. Therefore, given the equations for demand and supply, we can set the two equal to solve for equilibrium price and quantity.

This appendix deals with only straight-line demand and supply curves, so their equations can be represented as simple linear equations. Demand is given by $P = a - bQd$, and supply is given by $P = c + dQs$. Each parameter in the equations has an economic meaning. If the price reaches a or higher, the amount demanded will be zero. If the price reaches c or lower, the amount supplied will be zero. The value b indicates the amount by which price would have to rise to reduce quantity demanded by one unit. The value d indicates the amount by which price would have to increase to increase quantity supplied by one unit.

Normally the values for a, b, c, and d are known. With these parameters known, P and Qd are unknown in the demand equation, and P and Qs are unknown in the supply equation. There appear to be three unknowns (P, Qd, and Qs), but at the equilibrium price, Qd and Qs are equal. Therefore the only unknowns are equilibrium price and quantity, which can be represented as Q^* and P^*.

■ APPENDIX LEARNING OBJECTIVES

When you have studied this appendix, you should be able to:
□ Understand how demand and supply curves can be represented in equations.
□ Solve supply and demand equations to find equilibrium price and quantity.

■ APPENDIX OUTLINE

1. A market equilibrium can be expressed as a price and quantity pair (Q^*, P^*) and occurs where quantity demanded equals quantity supplied $(Qd = Qs)$.

2. The market equilibrium results from the negotiating process that brings together the sellers' behaviour and the buyers' behaviour.

3. The buyers' behaviour is represented in the equation: $P = a - bQd$. Buyers will buy only at prices below a, and b reflects how quantity demanded and price are related.

4. The sellers' behaviour is represented in the equation: $P = c + dQs$. Sellers will sell only at prices above c, and d reflects how quantity supplied and price are related.

5. The equilibrium values are solved from the parameter values as follows:
$$P^* = (ad + bc)/(a + d)$$
$$Q^* = (a-c)/(b + d)$$

■ HINTS AND TIPS

1. Solving for the equilibrium price at which the demand and supply equations are equal is no different from locating the intersection on a demand and supply graph to find the equilibrium price. There is only one value for price at which the two equations, or the two curves, have the same value for quantity.

2. If price is not at the equilibrium value there will be a shortage or a surplus, which can also be de-

termined from the equations by substituting the given price into both equations and then comparing the resulting values for quantity demanded and quantity supplied.

■ FILL-IN QUESTIONS

1. The maximum price that buyers are willing to pay for a product is given by the (slope, intercept) _____ term in the (demand, supply) _____ equation.

2. The extent to which the producers are willing to supply more when price increases is reflected in the (slope, intercept) _____ term in the (demand, supply) _____ equation.

3. If demand is given by $P = a - bQd$, an increase in the value of parameter a indicates that the demand curve shifts to the (left, right) _____, and equilibrium price will (decrease, increase) _____.

4. If supply is given by $P = c + dQs$, a decrease in the value of parameter c indicates that the supply curve shifts to the (left, right) _____, and equilibrium price will (decrease, increase) _____.

■ PROBLEMS AND PROJECTS

1. The demand and supply in the market for jeans are given by the following equations:
$P = 100 - 0.1\ Qd$ $P = 50 + 0.4\ Qs$
(a)   Rewrite the demand equation as a function of Qd: _____
(b)   Rewrite the supply equation as a function of Qs: _____
(c)   Using these new equations, fill in the table.
(d)   Solve for the equilibrium price: _____

Price ($/pair)	Qd (pairs/yr)	Qs (pairs/yr)
100	_____	_____
90	_____	_____
80	_____	_____
70	_____	_____
60	_____	_____
50	_____	_____

2. Suppose that the market for lemons can be characterized by the following equations:

$P = 4 - 0.01\ Qd$
$P = 1 + 0.02\ Qs$
(a)   Solve for the equilibrium quantity: _____
(b)   Solve for the equilibrium price: _____
(c)   If price was fixed by government policy at $P = 2$, would there be a shortage or a surplus, and what would the amount be?
(d)   If price was fixed by government policy at $P = 3.5$, would there be a shortage or a surplus, and in what amount?

3. The data below represents the market for computer printers.

Price ($/printer)	Qd (printers/yr)	Qs (printers/yr)
100	4000	0
200	3000	0
300	2000	1000
400	1000	2000
500	0	3000

(a)   Based on the demand schedule, what is the demand equation? _____
(b)   Based on the supply schedule, what is the supply equation? _____
(c)   Use the supply and demand equations to solve for equilibrium: $P^* =$ _____, $Q^* =$ _____

■ TRUE-FALSE

Circle T if the statement is true, F if it is false.

1. If the demand curve is given by $P = 12 - 2\ Qd$, then quantity demanded will be 3 if price is 6.   **T F**

2. If the supply curve is given by $P = 5 + 4\ Qs$, then price will be 7 if quantity supplied is 2.   **T F**

3. A change in either of the parameters in the demand equation will change the market equilibrium price.   **T F**

4. A change in either of the parameters in the supply equation will change the market equilibrium price.   **T F**

5. A change in either of the parameters in the demand equation will change the parameters in the supply equation.   **T F**

■ MULTIPLE-CHOICE

Circle the letter that corresponds to the best answer.

Answer questions 1 through 6 on the basis of the following demand and supply equations:

$P = 100 - 2\ Qd$

$P = 40 + 4\ Qs$

1. The equilibrium price, P^*, will be:
   - (a) 50
   - (b) 60
   - (c) 70
   - (d) 80

2. The equilibrium quantity, Q^*, will be:
   - (a) 10
   - (b) 20
   - (c) 30
   - (d) 40

3. The lowest price at which producers are willing to begin selling output is:
   - (a) 10
   - (b) 20
   - (c) 30
   - (d) 40

4. Quantity demanded would become zero if the price rises above what level?
   - (a) 70
   - (b) 80
   - (c) 90
   - (d) 100

5. If price were 60, what would the situation be in this market?
   - (a) a surplus of 15
   - (b) a shortage of 15
   - (c) a surplus of 20
   - (d) a shortage of 20

6. The demand equation given could also be re-written as:
   - (a) $Qd = 100 - 2\ P$
   - (b) $P = 50 - Qd$
   - (c) $Qd = 100 - 0.5\ Qd$
   - (d) $Qd = 50 - 0.5\ P$

■ DISCUSSION QUESTIONS

1. What aspect of a demand equation shows that the equation is consistent with the law of demand? What aspect of the supply equation ensures that there is a positive relation between price and quantity supplied?

2. Sketch a hypothetical straight-line demand curve. How would the position of this curve change if there were an increase in the parameter *a*? What if there were an increase in *b*?

3. Sketch a hypothetical straight-line supply curve. How would the position of this curve change if there were an increase in the parameter *c*? What if there were an increase in *d*?

■ ANSWERS

FILL-IN QUESTIONS

1. intercept, demand

2. slope, supply

3. right, increase

4. right, decrease

PROBLEMS AND PROJECTS

1. (a) $Qd = 1000 - 10\ P$; (b) $Qs = 125 + 2.5\ P$: (c) from top to bottom: Qd: 0, 100, 200, 300, 400, 500; Qs: 375, 350, 325, 300, 275, 250: (d) by setting the two equations equal, or by reading the table, we see that $P^* = 70$, where $Qd = Qs = 300$.

2. (a) 100; (b) 3; (c) $Qd = 200$, $Qs = 50$, so a shortage of 150; (d) surplus of 75

3. (a) $P = 500 - 0.1\ Qd$; (b) $P = 200 + 0.1\ Qs$; (c) $P^* = 350$, $Q^* = 1500$

TRUE-FALSE

1. T Substitute in 6 for P and solve for Qd
2. F Substitute in 2 for Qs and $P = 13$
3. T If *a* or *b* changes the demand curve will shift
4. T If *c* or *d* changes the supply curve will shift
5. F The parameters for one curve have no effect on the parameters for the other curve

MULTIPLE-CHOICE

1. (d) Set $Qd = Qs$ and solve for $P*$
2. (a) Substitute $P* = 80$ into either the Qd or the Qs equation
3. (d) Set $Qs = 0$
4. (d) Set $Qd = 0$
5. (b) Find that $Qd = 20$ and $Qs = 5$ at this P
6. (d)

CHAPTER 4

An Overview of the Market System and the Canadian Economy

Chapter 3 explained how prices and quantities are determined in individual markets. This chapter widens the focus to consider the nature of the market system as a whole, with emphasis on describing the Canadian economy in particular.

The market system or capitalism has six defining characteristics: the institution of private property; freedom of choice for consumers and freedom of enterprise for suppliers; the pursuit of self-interest; competition among economic units; coordination through markets and prices; and an active, but limited, role for government. Households make choices about supplying the resources that they own, and about spending the incomes from these resources on those goods and services that will best satisfy their wants. Firms employ resources to produce goods that seem to them likely to yield the greatest profit. The profits depend on producing goods that consumers are willing to pay for, and on producing these goods using the most efficient techniques. These demand and supply decisions determine market prices; these in turn provide incentives and signals to consumers and producers, thereby providing a coordinating mechanism for allocating society's resources.

Consumers and producers have the freedom to follow their self-interest as they exchange their property. Where these interactions occur in competitive markets with large numbers of independent buyers and sellers, and where there is easy entry and exit, no individual will have significant power or control in the market. The discipline of competition ensures that self-interested choices made by individual consumers or producers are also in the interests of society — as though individuals are guided by an "invisible hand" to serve the public interest. Accordingly, the role of government is quite limited.

Modern industrial economies have three other characteristics that increase dramatically the amount of goods and services that can be produced: (1) extensive use of advanced technology and capital goods; (2) specialization in production; and (3) use of money. Specialization stimulates the creation of new technology and capital goods, and creates the need for a monetary system that can facilitate exchanges and eliminate the reliance on barter.

The challenge for any market economy can be summarized in four fundamental questions: (1) what goods and services will be produced; (2) how will the goods and services be produced; (3) who will get the goods and services; and (4) how will the system accommodate change?

The market system features three key virtues: efficiency, incentives, and freedom. However, in some cases the market fails to produce an efficient allocation of resources. When spillover effects occur, some of the costs or benefits of production or consumption of a good affect someone other than the immediate producer or consumer. Since these "spillover" costs or benefits are ignored by those choosing the levels of production or consumption, the levels will end up being too high or too low. Goods that everyone can benefit from collectively, and which non-payers cannot be excluded from enjoying, are called public goods. Users' incentives to "free-ride" rather than pay may make it impossible for private firms to supply such goods. Such inefficiencies can be corrected by government intervention.

40

The chapter closes with a thumbnail sketch of the structure of the Canadian economy and its evolution. In recent decades the tertiary (service) sector has grown as a share of Canada's employment and output while the primary sector (e.g., agriculture, forestry, mining) and secondary (manufacturing) sector have declined. High levels of foreign ownership are prevalent in many sectors.

■ **CHAPTER LEARNING OBJECTIVES**

In this chapter you will learn:
☐ The basic institutions required for a market economy.
☐ The Four Fundamental Questions any economy faces.
☐ How the "invisible hand" helps to close the gap between private and public interests.
☐ The role of government in the market economy.
☐ About the structure of the Canadian economy.

■ **CHAPTER OUTLINE**

1. The market system, or capitalism, is an economic system with six defining characteristics: private property, freedom of enterprise and choice, self-interest, competition, self-regulating markets, and an active, but limited role for government.

(a) Resources are the private property of households and firms who are free to obtain, control, employ, and dispose of their property as they see fit.

(b) Freedom of enterprise means that firms are free to make business decisions about what to produce, where to sell, etc. Freedom of choice means that consumers can spend their incomes on whatever goods they want, and resource owners can supply their land, labour, etc. as they see fit.

(c) Self-interest is the motivating force behind decisions: consumers try to maximize their satisfaction, and entrepreneurs try to maximize their profits.

(d) Because each market has many independent buyers and sellers, each of whom are free to enter or exit the market, competition is pervasive and no individual buyer or seller has much economic power.

(e) In the market system signals and incentives are conveyed through prices. Because buyers and sellers respond spontaneously to price changes, resource allocation is coordinated in a decentralized and spontaneous fashion, as if by an "invisible hand."

(f) Markets create a sufficiently self-regulating, self-adjusting, and efficient allocation of resources that the government plays a limited, though active, role in the economy.

2. All modern industrial economies have three other main characteristics:

(a) There is extensive use of new technologies and the use of roundabout production whereby complex capital goods (e.g., tools, machinery, and computers) are produced in order to raise the efficiency of producing final goods for consumers.

(b) Specialization prevails at all levels. Division of labour among workers means that each person produces only a very narrow range of goods, and relies on the existence of markets and prices to be able to trade for goods that others have specialized in producing. The same is true of regions and nations. Specialization creates efficiencies by making use of ability differences, by allowing learning by doing, and by saving time.

(c) In order to overcome the inconvenience and transactions costs of bartering, some system of money emerges in every modern society. It is impossible to sustain a highly specialized economy without some form of money to facilitate exchanges. Anything that is generally accepted by sellers in exchange for goods and services is considered money.

3. The competitive market system functions with two primary groups of decision makers: households (consumers) and firms (businesses). Households are the ultimate suppliers of resources, and firms are the suppliers of goods purchased by consumers with the incomes from their resources. The market system communicates the decisions of millions of individual households and firms, and coordinates these decisions in a coherent allocation of resources.

4. Faced with unlimited wants and scarce resources, every economy must find answers for the Four Fundamental Questions: what goods and services will be produced; how will the goods and services be produced; who will get the goods and services; how will the system accommodate change.

5. The market system, or price mechanism, is a communication and coordination system that provides answers to the Four Fundamental Questions.

(a) Consumer demands for products and firms' desires for profits determine the types and amounts of goods to be produced, and at what price. Goods that can be produced at a profit will be produced, and those whose production would lead to loss will not be produced.

(b) The desires of businesses to maximize profits motivate them to use production methods that economize on resources, especially those resources that are relatively expensive.

(c) Goods are distributed to consumers on the basis of their willingness and ability to pay the existing market prices for these goods. Consumers' incomes are determined by the quantities and prices of the labour, property, and other resources they supply in resource markets. The market system does not guarantee an equitable distribution of income and consumer goods.

(d) Changes in consumer tastes, technology, and resource supplies are signalled by price changes that give households and firms incentives to adjust their choices; thus the economy spontaneously accommodates changes.

6. Competition in the economy compels firms and households acting in their own self-interest to promote (as though led by an "invisible hand") the interests of society as a whole, though this is not their intention. Adam Smith first noted this concept in his 1776 book, *The Wealth of Nations*.

7. The market system has several merits. The two economic virtues of the system are the efficient allocation of resources and the incentives for using resources productively. The personal freedom allowed in a market economy is its major noneconomic virtue.

8. Market failure occurs when the competitive market system results in the "wrong" production level for some goods, or fails to produce any of certain goods. Spillover effects and public goods are two main kinds of market failure. Both can be corrected by government action.

9. Government can be added to the circular flow model. Government buys goods and services from the product market, employs labour, capital, etc. from resource markets, and finances its expenditures from net tax revenues collected from businesses and households.

10. Any economy can be divided into three major sectors: primary, secondary, and tertiary. The tertiary (service) sector has become a much bigger part of the Canadian economy. Employment in agriculture and manufacturing have been shrinking, particularly due to tremendous amounts of technological change that have decreased the amount of labour needed in these sectors.

11. Canada's economy has high levels of foreign ownership and control: particularly by American companies and investors.

■ **TERMS AND CONCEPTS**

private property	**consumer sovereignty**
freedom of enterprise	**dollar votes**
freedom of choice	**derived demand**
self-interest	**guiding function of**
competition	**prices**
roundabout	**creative destruction**
production	**"invisible hand"**
specialization	**spillover costs**
division of labour	**spillover benefits**
medium of exchange	**exclusion principle**
barter	**public goods**
money	**free-rider problem**
Four Fundamental	**quasipublic goods**
Questions	

■ **HINTS AND TIPS**

1. The crux of the market system is the dual role played by prices: to provide both signals and incentives. An increase in the price of a product signals that for some reason scarcity of this product has increased. The price increase gives consumers the incentive to reduce their consumption (as they ration their limited incomes) and gives producers the incentive to produce more (in order to maximize profits).

2. Think about what an amazing thing it is that a market system works at all! How can millions of independent decisions by consumers and producers possibly add up to a coherent allocation of resources that virtually guarantees that your neighbourhood store will have milk and bread every time you come to buy them? The system coordinates resource allocation in a spontaneous and decentralized manner. Nobody is in control of the whole economy; nobody has the responsibility to coordinate the allocation of resources. Yet, as if guided by an "invisible hand," the economy is coordinated.

■ **FILL-IN QUESTIONS**

1. The ownership of resources by private individuals and organizations is the institution of _____.

2. In a market system private businesses have freedom of _____ and consumers have freedom of _____.

3. In a market system, an increase in the scarcity of a product is signaled by a(n) (increase, decrease) _____ in the _____ of the product. This change gives consumers and producers the incentive to revise their choices in furthering their own _____.

4. List the six characteristics of the market system.
   (a) _____
   (b) _____ .
   (c) _____
   (d) _____
   (e) _____
   (f) _____

5. If Robinson Crusoe spends time building a canoe to help him to catch more fish, he is engaging in _____ production.

6. Economic units seeking to further their own self-interest and operating within the capitalistic system will simultaneously, as though directed by an _____, promote the _____ interest.

7. List the Four Fundamental Questions to which every society must respond.
   (a) _____
   (b) _____
   (c) _____
   (d) _____

8. Three ways in which division of labour enhances a society's output are:
   (a) _____
   (b) _____
   (c) _____

9. In an economy where specialization of labour is extensive, individuals are extremely (independent, interdependent) _____, and in order to benefit from the specialization these individuals must _____ with each other.

10. An economy based on specialization and trade cannot operate efficiently without a system of _____.

11. International specialization and exchange requires a system of exchanging _____.

12. Exchange by barter requires a _____ of wants.

13. Government frequently reallocates resources when it finds instances of _____ failure. The two major cases of such failure of the competitive market involve _____ effects and _____ goods.

14. Spillovers occur when benefits or costs associated with the production or consumption of a good are incurred by a _____ party. Spillovers are also called _____.

15. Governments can resolve the problem of spillover costs through the use of _____ or _____.

16. If spillover benefits accompany the production of a good, then resources will be _____ to the production of that good by the market economy.

17. Governments can resolve the problem of spillover benefits through _____ paid to the _____ or the _____ of the good.

18. Public goods are not subject to the _____ principle. Once a public good is produced, the benefits from the good cannot be confined to the purchaser. This results in a _____ effect.

19. A _____ good is a good that could be made exclusive, but is commonly provided by government because it has substantial spillover benefits.

20. In the expanded circular flow model, the net tax flow is obtained by subtracting all government _____ to business firms and _____ to households from the taxes paid by firms and households.

■ PROBLEMS AND PROJECTS

1. Consider a college with fewer parking spots than students who want to drive to school. At present the college offers free parking on a first-come-first-served basis. They are considering charging for parking, setting the fee high enough that there would always be a few spots open.

(a) Why would the system of charging for parking change the allocation of parking spots?

(b) Why would some students be in favour of the change while others would not?

(c) What socially beneficial incentives would be created by the proposed parking fee?

2. Suppose that a firm can produce 100 units of product X by combining labour, land, capital, and entrepreneurial ability in three different ways as shown in the table below. It can hire labour at $2 per unit, land at $3 per unit, capital at $5 per unit, and entrepreneurial ability at $10 per unit.

Resource	Method A	B	C
Labour	8	13	10
Land	4	3	3
Capital	4	2	4
Entrepreneurial ability	1	1	1

(a) Which is the least cost method of producing 100 units of X? _____

(b) If the wage for labour rises from $2 to $3 per unit, which is the least cost method to produce 100 units of X? _____

(c) If the firm produces 100 X, the increase in the wage rate gives the firm the incentive to (increase, decrease) its use of labour from _____ units to _____ units.

3. In 2001 electric power prices increased sharply in Alberta.

(a) What did the price increase signal?

(b) What incentives for consumers and producers of electric power were created by the price increase?

(c) If households and businesses responded to these incentives, how would this be socially beneficial?

(d) What is the primary motivation for consumers and producers to make choices that are socially beneficial?

4. The circular flow diagram below includes business firms, households, and government (the public sector). Product and resource markets are also shown.

(a) Identify the sector that corresponds to each box:

a. _____
b. _____
c. _____
d. _____
e. _____

(b) Supply a label or an explanation for each of the twelve flows in the model:

1: _____
2: _____
3: _____
4: _____
5. _____
6: _____
7: _____
8: _____
9: _____
10: _____
11: _____
12: _____

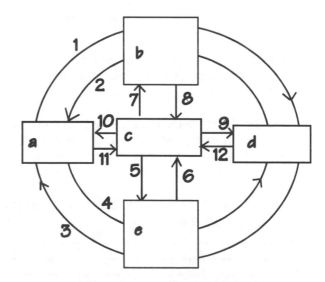

(c) If government wished to increase the production of public goods and decrease the production of private goods in the economy, which flows could it increase? _____, _____, _____.

5. The grade that you earn in your economics course this term will be the product of your work, and you probably consider this grade your private property.

(a) How would your incentives to study change if you did not have the right to communicate your grade to potential employers or other colleges or universities?

(b) How would your incentives change if you had to share your "output" on exams with your classmates (i.e., everybody is awarded the class average grade)?

(c) Are there any reasons for restricting your property rights in your grade? For example, should you be able to sell or give your grade to another student?

6. Match each example on the right with the type of situation on the left:

(a) spillover cost   (1) a radio broadcast
(b) spillover benefit   (2) a noisy house party
(c) public good   (3) vaccinations

■ TRUE-FALSE

Circle T if the statement is true, F if it is false.

1. Self-interest means the same as selfishness. **T F**

2. In the real world there are usually legal limits placed on the rights of private property. **T F**

3. In a competitive market every seller has significant influence over the market price. **T F**

4. In the market system most prices are set by a government agency. **T F**

5. If property rights did not exist for intellectual property, individuals would have less incentive to create music, books, and computer programs. **T F**

6. In the market system prices serve as signals for the allocation of resources. **T F**

7. Because the market system is efficient in resource use, it follows that every person is better off under this form of economic organization than any alternative. **T F**

8. The distribution of output in the market economy depends upon the distribution of resources. **T F**

9. In a market system competition serves to regulate self-interest for the benefit of society. **T F**

10. The employment of capital to produce goods and services implies that there will be roundabout production. **T F**

11. Specialization allows for a more efficient use of resources. **T F**

12. Money is a device for facilitating the exchange of goods and services. **T F**

13. "Coincidence of wants" means that two persons desire to acquire the same good or service. **T F**

14. The market system ensures that all households will receive an equitable share of the economy's output of goods and services. **T F**

15. The "invisible hand" refers to government intervention in the market. **T F**

16. Pollution is a cause of market failure because the price of the polluting product does not reflect all the resource costs used in its production. **T F**

17. A spillover or externality is a cost or benefit that is imposed upon an individual or group external to the market transaction. **T F**

18. A specific tax imposed on producer that create pollution will lower the marginal cost of production and increase supply. **T F**

19. A public good is any good or service that is provided free by the government. **T F**

20. For public goods the free-rider problem occurs when people can receive benefits without contributing to the cost of providing the good. **T F**

■ MULTIPLE-CHOICE

Choose the letter that corresponds to the best answer.

1. Which of the following is not one of the six characteristics of the market system?
(a) competition
(b) freedom of enterprise and choice
(c) self-interest
(d) central economic planning

2. The "invisible hand" is used to explain how in the market system:

(a) property rights are defined
(b) taxes and subsidies are determined
(c) the self-interest of individuals is harnessed for the benefit of society
(d) spillover effects occur

3. In the market system a decrease in the demand for a good should result in all but:
(a) an increase in the price of the resources producing the good
(b) a decrease in the profitability of producing the good
(c) a movement of resources out of the production of the good
(d) a decrease in the price of the good

4. Roundabout production refers to:
(a) the use of resources by government
(b) the use of resources to produce consumer goods directly
(c) the use of resources to produce services
(d) the use of resources to produce capital goods that in turn are used to produce other goods

5. Which of the following is **not** an example of a capital good?
(a) money
(b) a warehouse
(c) a forklift
(d) a computer

6. Which of the following is **not** a condition for a market to be highly competitive:
(a) the presence of a large number of buyers
(b) the freedom to enter or leave a particular market
(c) the presence of a large number of sellers
(d) a fair price determined by a public agency

7. Which of the following is a reason that specialization in production increases efficiency?
(a) trade is rendered unnecessary
(b) barter transactions are rendered unnecessary
(c) individuals usually possess very similar resources and talents
(d) experience or "learning-by-doing" results in increased output

8. Barter:
(a) is the main method of trading in a market economy
(b) is the action of haggling over the price of a good
(c) is the exchange of a good for money
(d) is the exchange of a good for a good

9. Which of the following is **not** a necessary consequence of specialization?
(a) people will barter
(b) people will engage in trade
(c) people will be dependent upon each other
(d) people will produce more of one thing than they would produce in the absence of specialization

10. Which of the following is **not** a virtue of the market system?
(a) allocative efficiency
(b) productive efficiency
(c) equitable distribution of income
(d) ability to adapt to changes in tastes, technologies, and resource supplies

11. The term "division of labour" means the same as:
(a) specialization
(b) barter
(c) economies of scale
(d) coincidence of wants

12. All modern economies have the following characteristics except for:
(a) specialization
(b) limited government interference
(c) use of money
(d) roundabout means of production

13. The economist who first wrote about the "invisible hand" was:
(a) John Maynard Keynes
(b) Karl Marx
(c) David Ricardo
(d) Adam Smith

14. If external benefits accompany the production of a good:
(a) too much of the good will be produced by a competitive market
(b) too little of the good will be produced in a competitive market
(c) a tax on the production of the good will result in the optimum production of the good
(d) the good is exported to foreign countries

15. In the case where producing a good creates spillover costs, government could promote the optimal output by:
- **(a)** banning production of the good
- **(b)** taxing the producers of the good
- **(c)** subsidizing consumers of the good
- **(d)** subsidizing producers of the good

16. Which of the following is a good example of a good or service providing spillover benefits?
- **(a)** a video game
- **(b)** landscaping
- **(c)** a sofa
- **(d)** an oil change for a car

17. Suppose that in order to relieve traffic congestion, user charges are imposed on drivers using urban expressways. This would be a response to what economic problem?
- **(a)** spillover benefits
- **(b)** spillover costs
- **(c)** the free-rider problem
- **(d)** inequitable income distribution

18. Public goods differ from private goods in that public goods are:
- **(a)** divisible
- **(b)** subject to the exclusion principle
- **(c)** not subject to the free-rider problem
- **(d)** *not* divisible and *not* subject to the exclusion principle

19. Quasi-public goods are goods and services:
- **(a)** to which the exclusion principle could be applied
- **(b)** that have large spillover benefits
- **(c)** that private producers would overproduce
- **(d)** that have large spillover benefits, and to which the exclusion principle could be applied

20. If the market system tends to overallocate resources to the production of good X:
- **(a)** good X could be a public good
- **(b)** good X could involve spillover benefits
- **(c)** good X could involve spillover costs
- **(d)** good X could be prone to the free-rider problem

21. Government expenditures, taxes, and transfer payments in the circular flow affect:
- **(a)** the distribution of income
- **(b)** the allocation of resources
- **(c)** the level of economic activity
- **(d)** all of the above

22. What is an important reason for the decrease in the percentage of Canadian workers employed in agriculture?
- **(a)** Canada's demand for food has decreased because we get food from other countries
- **(b)** fewer Canadians want to be in farming
- **(c)** technological improvements have reduced the need for labour in agriculture
- **(d)** all of the above

■ DISCUSSION QUESTIONS

1. List the Four Fundamental Questions that all economies must answer. Which of these questions does the market system answer, and how so?

2. What property rights does the owner of a motor vehicle have? What restrictions or limits are there on those rights, and why do these restrictions exist? Do these restrictions increase or decrease the value of owning a vehicle?

3. How does the pursuit of self-interest by all economic units in the market system model ultimately benefit society? Give an example of a choice you make that is in your self-interest, but not selfish.

4. At one time the world price of oil was expected to hit $100 a barrel by the 1990s. If so, the Canadian economy would presumably have allocated more resources to oil production. How would market forces have produced such a result? How would market forces have changed the gasoline consumption habits of Canadian households?

5. What are the advantages of "indirect" or "roundabout" production?

6. In order for a market to be competitive, why must there be many buyers and many sellers? What might be some consequences if there are few buyers or few sellers?

7. How does an economy benefit from specialization and division of labour?

8. What are the disadvantages of barter, and how does money overcome these disadvantages?

9. What is "market failure" and what are the two major kinds of such failures?

10. If the person living down the hall from you plays her music very loudly, is there a spillover cost or spillover benefit? If a homeowner builds an extra high fence between his house and his neighbours', is there a spillover cost or spillover benefit?

11. Based on ideas from this chapter, what is the case for government supporting needle exchange programs for intravenous drug users?

12. Discuss how the concepts of spillover effects and public goods might apply to the Internet?

13. How are private goods different from public goods? Why does there tend to be underallocation of resources to public goods in the absence of government intervention?

14. What basic method does government employ in Canada to reallocate resources away from the production of private goods and toward the production of public goods?

■ **ANSWERS**

FILL-IN QUESTIONS

1. private property

2. enterprise, choice

3. increase, price; self-interest

4. private property; freedom of enterprise and choice; self-interest; markets and prices; competition; limited, but active government

5. roundabout

6. "invisible hand," social (or public)

7. what goods and services will be produced?; how will the goods and services be produced?; who will get the goods and service?; how will the system accommodate change?

8. making use of differences in ability, fostering learning by doing, saving time

9. interdependent, trade

10. money

11. currencies

12. coincidence

13. market; spillover, public

14. third; externalities

15. specific taxes, regulations

16. underallocated

17. subsidies, consumers, producers

18. exclusion; free-rider

19. quasipublic

20. subsidies, transfer payments

PROBLEMS AND PROJECTS

1. (a) Some students currently willing and able to arrive early or to spend time hunting for a spot may be unwilling to pay for a spot, whereas others may be willing and able to pay; (b) differences in availability of money and time; (c) students who place a low value on parking would have incentive to walk, bus, carpool; firms seeking profit would have more incentive to provide near campus parking for a fee.

2. (a) B at $55; (b) A at $66; (c) decrease, 13, 8.

3. (a) increased scarcity of electricity; (b) to consume less, for instance by economizing on energy use or switching to alternate sources; and to produce more; (c) there would be electric power available, and the available amount would be allocated to highest valued uses, thus minimizing the effects of increased scarcity.

4. (a) If you could not use a good grade to help you get jobs, scholarships, etc. you may have less incentive to study; (b) If you get a better mark on an exam, your share of that improved mark would be very small, so you would have less incentive to study; (c) Restricted property rights in grades are probably justified because if students could sell their grades to other people then good grades would no longer indicate what they are supposed to, and would therefore no longer be meaningful or valuable.

5. (a) a: business firms, b: resource markets, c: government, d: households, e: product markets; (b) 1: businesses pay costs for resources that become money income for households, 2: households provide resources to businesses, 3: household expenditures become receipts for businesses, 4: businesses provide goods and services to households, 5: government spends money in product market, 6: government receives goods and services from product market, 7: government spends money in resource market, 8: government receives resources from resource market, 9: government provides goods and services to households, 10: government provides goods and services to businesses, 11: businesses pay net taxes to government, 12: households pay net taxes to government; (c) (1) 9, 10, 11.

6. (a) 2: neighbours suffer cost; (b) 3: one person being vaccinated reduces the risk of disease for other people, too; (c) 1: everybody can listen to a radio broadcast.

TRUE-FALSE

1. F You might consider it in your self-interest to help other people, or donate to charities
2. F For example, there are limits on how you can operate your vehicle, or on what you can build on your land
3. F No seller has significant influence
4. F Most prices are set mainly by market forces
5. T The prospect of earning royalties is an incentive to produce
6. T
7. F Some individuals fare poorly under a market system, particularly those who have few resources
8. T Those with more resources can earn higher incomes and have more spending power
9. T Adam Smith had this insight
10. T For example, when machine is built and used in a factory
11. T
12. T
13. F Person A must want to acquire what person B is offering to trade, and B must want to acquire what A has to offer
14. F The market offers no guarantees of equitability
15. F The "invisible hand" refers to market forces
16. T
17. T
18. F Such a tax would raise the marginal cost of production and decrease supply
19. F Many goods provided by government free of charge are not public goods
20. T Because the exclusion principle does not apply

MULTIPLE-CHOICE

1. (d) There is no central planning in the market system
2. (c) Socially beneficial results stem from self-interested behaviour, without any central control
3. (a) Less demand for the good means less demand and lower price for resources used in producing the good

4. (d)
5. (a) All of the others are human-made resources designed to help produce other things
6. (d) There is no assumption that government or any public agency would be involved
7. (d) We become more experienced, and therefore more efficient, at doing those tasks in which we specialize
8. (d) Price haggling is "bargaining"
9. (a) When we specialize we must trade, but it need not be by the inefficient barter system
10. (c) The market system often produces extreme discrepancies in incomes that do not seem equitable
11. (a)
12. (b) Many modern economies have a great deal of government interference
13. (d) In his book *The Wealth of Nations*
14. (b) Too little is produced because the producer will not take into account some of the benefits of the good
15. (b) Banning the product would reduce output to zero; this would often be below the optimal amount
16. (b) Landscaping provides benefits not only for the owner of the garden, but also for neighbours and passersby
17. (b) Each driver adds to the highway congestion, thereby slowing down other drivers and imposing time costs on them
18. (d) They cannot be divided into small units and sold to individuals, and individuals who do not pay cannot be excluded from using them
19. (d) Both aspects of this description are necessary
20. (c) All of the others are prone to underproduction
21. (d) Check the circular flow diagram
22. (c) Many Canadians who would prefer to farm have moved to other sectors because technological change has reduced the demand for labour in agriculture

CHAPTER 5

Canada in the Global Economy

As members of the global economy, Canadian consumers depend on many goods produced in other nations, and many Canadian workers and businesses depend on selling goods in foreign markets. In addition to these flows of goods and services, resources, information, technology, and financial capital flow back and forth across international borders. Why does international trade occur, and how does trade benefit us? These are fundamental questions of this chapter.

Canada's imports and exports have mushroomed in recent years. Today our exports and imports each total nearly 40% of our economic activity. We trade many different products, and many of our major exports are also our major imports (e.g., automotive products, machinery and equipment, and industrial goods and materials). The United States is our most important trading partner, and we trade mainly with industrialized countries. World trade has increased because of improved technologies for transportation and communications, and because of reductions in tariffs and other trade barriers. The number of important players in world trade has increased, especially among the newly industrializing Asian nations, including China.

The circular flow model is easily amended to add the "rest of the world" sector to the product market. Export flows are paid for by foreign expenditures, and import flows are paid for by expenditures from the domestic economy. From this diagram it is easy to understand how instability in foreign economies can introduce instability into the Canadian economy, and vice versa.

The principle of comparative advantage shows the reason that nations trade. In the simplest scenario, there are two nations, each producing two goods at constant opportunity cost ratios. If the opportunity costs differ between the two nations, each should specialize in producing that good for which their domestic opportunity cost is below the other nation's. If both nations follow this rule, both goods will be produced and traded, and both nations can end up with more output than they could produce if they remained self-sufficient. Perhaps surprisingly, all nations can reap these benefits from trade, even nations that are absolutely less productive than their trading partners.

In reality, nations usually do not barter goods with one another, as represented in the simplified scenario of the comparative advantage model. Instead, international trade is conducted through monetary transactions between households and firms in different countries acting as buyers and sellers. Such transactions require a foreign exchange market where currencies may be traded. The exchange rate, or equilibrium price of one currency in terms of another, is determined by the supply and the demand for the currency. The basic principles of supply and demand that you studied in Chapter 3 apply to foreign exchange markets also. Shifts in the supply or demand for a currency will change its price. If the currency's price rises (falls) in terms of another currency it has appreciated (depreciated) relative to the other currency.

In spite of important benefits from specialization and international trade, many nations try to limit trade. The major barriers to world trade are: (1) protective tariffs, (2) import quotas, (3) non-tariff barriers, and (4) export subsidies. So why do governments seek to reduce imports and/or increase exports? One reason may be the mistaken yet common belief that exports are beneficial because they create jobs, whereas imports are harmful because they destroy jobs at home. Another explanation is found by examining who gains and who loses from policies that limit trade. Domestic firms facing tough competition from imports often lobby governments to impose tariffs or quotas. Governments sometimes give in to such demands because the consumers who are hurt by higher prices resulting from the tariff bear costs that are relatively obscure and dispersed. Therefore, government may enjoy more political success by imposing tariffs and quotas than by supporting free trade.

Protectionist measures taken by one nation may lead other nations that lose exports to retaliate with protectionist measures of their own. In order to prevent such conflicts and to reduce existing trade barriers, various multilateral trade agreements and free trade zones have evolved. The most important agreements are the General Agreement on Tariffs and Trade (GATT), and its successor, the World Trade Organization (WTO). Important free trade zones include the European Union (EU) and the North American Free Trade Agreement (NAFTA). These agreements enable member nations to enjoy freer trade with other member nations, but critics are concerned that free trade policies may undermine national sovereignty, for instance by enabling corporations to circumvent national labour and environmental laws. Most critics and proponents do agree that freer trade increases competition and brings pressure to restructure the economy to better compete on the basis of comparative advantage.

■ **CHAPTER LEARNING OBJECTIVES**

In this chapter you will learn:
□ That trade is crucial to Canada's economic well-being.
□ The importance of specialization and comparative advantage in international trade.
□ How the value of a currency is established on foreign exchange markets.
□ The economic cost of trade barriers.
□ Multilateral trade agreements and free trade zones.

■ **CHAPTER OUTLINE**

1. The volume of international trade is now so large, and national economies so interdependent, that the world can be thought of as a "global economy."

2. Compared to most other nations, Canada relies relatively heavily on trade.
   (a)   The market in Canada is too limited to allow for efficient production of the full range of goods and services, so we import many goods, and export others to pay for the imports.
   (b)   Exports and imports are nearly 40% of our national output.
   (c)   The bulk of Canada's trade is with other industrialized nations, including over 80% with the United States.
   (d)   In 1997, Canada's three major exports, in order, were automotive products, machinery and equipment, and industrial goods and materials. Our three major imports, in order, were the same.

3. Several factors have facilitated rapid growth of world trade since World War II:
   (a)   improvements in transportation technology,
   (b)   improvements in communications technology,
   (c)   general decline in tariffs

4. In sheer volume of trade, the world's major players are the United States, Japan, and Western Europe. Despite recent problems, a number of Asian nations are becoming more important in world trade: Hong Kong, Singapore, South Korea, Taiwan, and China. Eastern European countries are also building trading relationships.

5. The circular flow model reflects the international trade dimension once we add the "rest of the world" box. This box is connected to the Canadian product market through flows of imports and exports, and the Canadian and foreign expenditures on these goods.

6. Specialization and trade among economic units (individuals, firms, provinces, regions, or nations) are based on the principle of comparative advantage. Specialization and trade increase productivity and output. Adam Smith wrote about this in 1776, and the idea was fully explained by David Ricardo in the early 1800s.

7. The basic principle of comparative advantage is shown with an example of two individuals able to do two jobs, or with an example of two nations producing two goods.
   (a)   A chartered accountant (CA) needing her house painted can paint it herself, or can hire a house painter. The CA will try to minimize her opportunity cost. By comparative advantage, even if the CA can do the job in less time than the painter can, if the CA incurs a lower opportunity cost by hiring the painter, the CA will specialize in

accounting. Likewise, the painter will specialize in painting, and hire a CA to prepare his tax return, if this minimizes his opportunity costs.

(b)   Mexico and Canada both can produce corn and soybeans. Assuming each nation has a constant opportunity cost ratio, then each nation has the lower opportunity cost — and therefore comparative advantage — in producing one of the two goods. By specializing in producing one good, each nation can trade for the other nation's good. The terms of trade, or ratio at which one good is traded for another, lies between the cost ratios for the two nations.

(c)   When two nations specialize and trade according to their comparative advantage, both nations can consume more of both goods than their domestic production possibilities curves would permit. This reduces the scarcity problem.

8. National currencies are traded in highly competitive foreign exchange markets. Such markets establish the exchange rates — the rates at which various national currencies are traded for one another. Exchange rates link all domestic prices with all foreign prices.

9. Supply and demand for a currency determine its exchange rate. Shifts in the supply and demand cause exchange rate appreciation or depreciation.

(a)   Increased demand or decreased supply for a currency will cause it to appreciate, or rise in price as measured in other currencies.

(b)   Decreased demand or increased supply for a currency will cause it to depreciate, or fall in price as measured in other currencies.

10. Governments implement protectionist policies, that is, policies to restrict trade between nations:

(a)   Such policies include protective tariffs, import quotas, non-tariff barriers, and export subsidies.

(b)   Trade restrictions may be imposed because of misunderstanding the gains from trade, or because governments have strong political incentives to protect domestic businesses from international competition.

(c)   Regardless of the government's motives, restrictive trade policies usually impose costs that outweigh the benefits. Consumers pay higher prices, exporters have less access to foreign markets, and the nation makes less efficient use of its resources.

11. To fight protectionism and promote trade, Canada and many other nations have signed arrangements to reduce tariffs, and to create free trade zones.

12. Begun in 1947, the General Agreement on Tariffs and Trade (GATT) has been the most comprehensive forum for reducing tariffs on a multilateral basis. The GATT now has 128 member nations, and has been the vehicle for eight rounds of negotiations to reduce trade barriers. Through the Uruguay Round, major changes are being phased in between 1995 and 2005: reductions in thousands of tariffs and quotas, inclusion of services, reductions in farm subsidies, and protection of intellectual property.

13. The Uruguay Round agreement also established the World Trade Organization (WTO) as a body to oversee trade agreements among member nations and rule on disputes among them.

14. The European Union (EU) is a regional free-trade zone, or trade bloc that has:

(a)   abolished tariffs between EU countries, enabled free movement of labour and capital within the EU, and developed some common economic policies.

(b)   increased trade and efficiency of production for nations in the bloc, but has also created frictions with nonmember nations.

(c)   established a common currency – the euro.

15. In 1989 Canada and the United States signed the Free Trade Agreement (FTA). In 1993 the bloc formed by the FTA was extended to include Mexico under the North American Free Trade Agreement (NAFTA). Fears that Canadian jobs would be lost to Mexico where wages are low and the workplace is less regulated seem to have been too pessimistic. Employment in Canada has grown significantly since the passage of NAFTA.

16. Globalization of trade intensifies competition for Canadian producers. Many succeed by keeping costs low, using new technology, etc. to retain market shares in Canada and to capture new markets abroad. Other firms are unable to compete and have gone out of business. Many of the unsuccessful firms previously enjoyed long periods of protection from imports (via tariffs or quotas). Note also that the increased competition tends to benefit consumers by leading to lower prices.

■ TERMS AND CONCEPTS

multinational corporations

comparative advantage

terms of trade

foreign exchange market

exchange rate

depreciation (of the dollar)

appreciation (of the dollar)

protective tariff

import quota

non-tariff barrier

export subsidies

General Agreement on Trade and Tariffs (GATT)

World Trade Organization (WTO)

European Union (EU)

trade bloc

euro

North American Free Trade Agreement (NAFTA)

■ HINTS AND TIPS

1. Finding which producer of a good has the comparative advantage depends on being able to compare opportunity costs across producers. If the data on production possibilities reflect constant costs, opportunity costs can be found easily by dividing a producer's maximum outputs of each of the two goods. For example, suppose Norway's maximum outputs are 100 fish or 20 tables. What is the cost of 1 table? Divide the number of tables into the number of fish: 100 fish/20 tables = 5 fish per table. What is the cost of 1 fish? Divide the number of fish into the number of tables: 20 tables/100 fish = 1/5 table per fish.

2. Foreign exchange rates are confusing because they can be expressed in two ways. Is Canada's exchange rate the amount of foreign currency that one Canadian dollar can buy, or the amount in Canadian dollars needed to buy one unit of foreign currency? Surprisingly, either form is correct, as long as you specify which one you are using. For example, our exchange rate with Mexico could be 5 pesos for $1, or $0.20 for 1 peso. These are reciprocal expressions of exactly the same rate! Always be clear on which form of the exchange rate you are using.

■ FILL-IN QUESTIONS

1. A nation is more likely to rely on international trade the more (diversified, limited) _____ its resource base is and the (larger, smaller) _____ its domestic market is.

2. In recent decades Canada's trade has (increased, decreased) _____ in absolute terms, and _____ as a percentage of our national income. Canada trades mainly with (developing, developed) _____ nations. Our major trading partner is _____.

3. Factors that have facilitated growth in trade since World War II include improvements in _____ and _____ technology, and a general decline in _____.

4. In the circular flow model, imports and exports are added as flows to the _____ market. Canadian expenditures pay for (exports, imports) _____, and foreign expenditures pay for _____.

5. If Nigeria can produce 10 kg of coffee at a cost of 1 barrel of oil, and Kenya can produce 25 kg of coffee at a cost of 1 barrel of oil, then _____ has the lower cost for producing oil, and _____ has the lower cost of producing coffee. The comparative advantage for oil lies with _____ and for coffee lies with _____.

6. The amount of one product that a nation must export in order to import one unit of another product is the _____.

7. When the dollar price of foreign currency increases, the dollar has (appreciated, depreciated) _____, while foreign currency has _____.

8. In the market for Japanese yen, an increase in the (demand for, supply of) _____ yen will decrease the dollar price of yen, while an increase in the _____ yen will increase the dollar price of yen. If the dollar price of yen increases, then Japanese goods imported into Canada will be (more, less) _____ expensive to Canadians, while Canadian goods exported to Japan will be _____ expensive for Japanese.

9. The major government policies that restrict trade include protective _____, import _____, _____ barriers, and _____ subsidies.

10. Governments may mistakenly intervene in trade with other nations because they mistakenly think of

(exports, imports) _____ as helpful, and _____ as harmful for their own economy.

11. Tariffs and quotas (benefit, cost) _____ domestic firms and their employees in the protected industries but _____ domestic consumers of their products in the form of (lower, higher) _____ prices than would exist if there were free trade.

12. The three cardinal principles established in the GATT are:
   (a) _____, _____ treatment for all member nations;
   (b) reduction of _____ by multilateral negotiations; and
   (c) the elimination of import _____.

13. The trade bloc first formed as the Common Market in 1958 is now known as the _____. The specific aims of the Common Market were to abolish tariffs and quotas among (member, non-member) _____ nations, to establish common tariffs on goods imported from _____ nations, to permit free movement of capital and _____ within the Common Market nations, and to adopt other common policies.

14. The FTA joined Canada in a trade bloc with _____ in the year _____. Under the name NAFTA, the FTA was extended in the year _____, when _____ joined the bloc.

■ **PROBLEMS AND PROJECTS**

1. Julius and Murray are tailors. Their production possibilities tables for trousers and jackets are given below. Initially they work independently, with Julius choosing production alternative D, and Murray choosing E from his alternatives.

JULIUS: Production Possibilities Table

Product	Production Alternative					
	A	B	C	D	E	F
Trousers	75	60	45	30	15	0
Jackets	0	10	20	30	40	50

MURRAY: Production Possibilities Table

Product	Production Alternative						
	A	B	C	D	E	F	G
Trousers	60	50	40	30	20	10	0
Jackets	0	5	10	15	20	25	30

(a) For Julius 1 pair of trousers costs _____ jackets, and 1 jacket costs _____ pairs of trousers.
(b) For Murray 1 pair of trousers costs _____ jackets, and 1 jacket costs _____ pairs of trousers.
(c) The comparative advantage in making trousers lies with _____ because his opportunity cost is (lower, higher) _____. The comparative advantage in making jackets lies with _____ because his opportunity cost is (lower, higher) _____.
(d) If Julius and Murray form a partnership, Julius should specialize in making _____, and Murray should specialize in _____.
(e) Working independently Julius and Murray would produce a total of 50 pairs of trousers and 50 jackets. If each specializes fully, their combined output will be _____ pairs of trousers, and _____ jackets. Thus, the gain from specialization is _____ pairs of trousers and _____ jackets.

2. Venezuela and Costa Rica have the production possibilities tables shown below.
(a) Find the opportunity costs:
Venezuela: 1 apple costs _____
           1 banana costs _____
Costa Rica: 1 apple costs _____
           1 banana costs _____
(b) Determine which country has the comparative advantage in each good:
Apples: _____   Bananas: _____

VENEZUELA: Production Possibilities Table

Product	Production Alternative					
	A	B	C	D	E	F
Apples	40	32	24	16	8	0
Bananas	0	4	8	12	16	20

COSTA RICA: Production Possibilities Table

Product	Production Alternative					
	A	B	C	D	E	F
Apples	75	60	45	30	15	0
Bananas	0	5	10	15	20	25

(c) From the information given we cannot determine specifically what the terms of trade will be. However, the terms of trade must be greater than _____ apples per banana, and less than _____ apples per banana.
(d) Suppose that each nation would choose production alternative C if specialization and trade were impossible. The combined production

in the two countries would be _____ apples and _____ bananas.

(e) If each nation specializes completely according to comparative advantage, their combined production will be _____ apples and _____ bananas.

(f) Their combined gains from specialization will be _____ apples and _____ bananas.

(g) Suppose that the nations specialize and then agree to trade 25 apples for 10 bananas. This trade will leave Venezuela consuming _____ apples and _____ bananas. Costa Rica will consume _____ apples and _____ bananas.

(h) Compared to production alternative C, this leaves Venezuela with a gain of _____ apples and _____ bananas. Compared to production alternative C, this leaves Costa Rica with a gain of _____ apples and _____ bananas.

3. The table below shows four different currencies and how much of each can be purchased with 1 Canadian dollar.

(a) In the blanks indicate whether the Canadian dollar appreciated (A) or depreciated (D) against these currencies from Year 1 to Year 2.

Currency per Canadian $				
Country	Currency	Year 1	Year 2	A or D
France	Franc	4.7	4.6	_____
Germany	Mark	1.40	1.44	_____
China	Renminbi	5.2	5.3	_____
Japan	Yen	80	82	_____

(b) Compute the amount of Canadian currency one would have to exchange to get 100 units of each of the four foreign currencies. Use Year 1 exchange rates.

100 Francs = $ _____
100 Marks = $ _____
100 Renminbi = $ _____
100 Yen = $ _____

■ **TRUE-FALSE**

Circle T if the statement is true, F if it is false.

1. Canada is completely dependent on other nations for many products that we do not produce domestically. **T F**

2. No nation in the world has a higher percentage of GDP represented by exports and imports than Canada does. **T F**

3. The first economists to explain the principle of comparative advantage were Adam Smith and David Ricardo. **T F**

4. The principle of comparative advantage applies just as well to individuals or regions as it does to nations. **T F**

5. If two nations produce only coal and lumber, one of the nations could have the comparative advantage over the other in both coal and lumber. **T F**

6. If two nations have identical cost conditions for producing two goods, neither nation will have a comparative advantage. **T F**

7. A nation that has resources that are more productive in every good than another nation's resources will be unable to gain by trading with the less productive nation. **T F**

8. Specialization and trade according to comparative advantage will enable a nation to have combinations of goods that lie outside the nation's production possibility curve. **T F**

9. In the foreign exchange market graph, if the British pound price of Japanese yen is plotted on the vertical axis, on the horizontal axis must be the quantity of British pounds. **T F**

10. An increase in incomes of Canadian households would tend to increase the supply of Canadian dollars in the exchange market. **T F**

11. If the supply of Canadian dollars in the foreign exchange market increases, the Canadian dollar will appreciate relative to foreign currencies, *ceteris paribus*. **T F**

12. If the U.S. dollar price of the Canadian dollar is $0.70, then the Canadian dollar price of the U.S. dollar must be $1.30. **T F**

13. An appreciation of the Canadian dollar will make our imports less expensive to Canadian consumers, and our exports more expensive to foreign consumers. **T F**

14. Export subsidies are government payments to domestic producers to encourage them to export more.   T F

15. The formation of a trade bloc encourages efficiency in production because access to larger markets enables producers to benefit from large-scale production.   T F

16. The NAFTA has benefited some Canadian firms and has harmed others.   T F

17. The NAFTA includes Canada, the United States, Mexico, and some Central American nations.   T F

18. The EU's plans call for the euro to be the only currency to be accepted for payment by July 1, 2002.   T F

■ **MULTIPLE-CHOICE**

Circle the letter that corresponds to the best answer.

1. Imports and exports amounted to roughly what fraction of Canada's GDP?
  (a) 10%
  (b) 15%
  (c) 25%
  (d) 40%

2. Based on the data in the text, which sector represents the largest percentage of Canadian exports?
  (a) agricultural products
  (b) automotive products
  (c) energy products
  (d) forest products

3. Based on recent data in the text, which sector represents the largest percentage of Canadian imports?
  (a) agricultural products
  (b) automotive products
  (c) consumer products
  (d) machinery and equipment

Questions 4 through 7 are based on the data in the table that shows maximum production levels for the regions of Heath and Cliff, both of which have constant costs of production, and are able to trade with one another.

Heath		Cliff	
Wool	Peat	Wool	Peat
100	20	120	40

4. In Heath, the domestic opportunity cost of:
  (a) 1 wool is 5 peat
  (b) 1 wool is 1/5 peat
  (c) 1 wool is 1.2 wool
  (d) 1 peat is 1/5 wool

5. In Cliff, the domestic opportunity cost of:
  (a) 1 peat is 3 wool
  (b) 1 peat is 2 peat
  (c) 1 wool is 3 peat
  (d) 1 peat is 1/3 wool

6. Which of the following statements is **not** true?
  (a) Heath has the comparative advantage in wool
  (b) Cliff should specialize in peat
  (c) Heath and Cliff could both gain from trading with one another
  (d) Heath has the comparative advantage in both wool and peat

7. The terms of trade will be:
  (a) more than 3 wool for 1 peat
  (b) fewer than 5 wool for 1 peat
  (c) between 3 and 5 wool for 1 peat
  (d) not between 3 and 5 wool for 1 peat

8. If Canada can produce 1 bottle of syrup at a cost of 2 cigars, and Cuba can produce 1 bottle of syrup at a cost of 6 cigars, what would be a mutually beneficial term of trade:
  (a) 2 cigars per 1 syrup
  (b) 3 cigars per 1 syrup
  (c) 6 cigars per 1 syrup
  (d) 8 cigars per 1 syrup

9. The foreign exchange market is a market for:
  (a) imports and exports
  (b) shares in multinational corporations
  (c) bonds sold by foreign government
  (d) currencies

10. If the equilibrium exchange rate changes so that the dollar price of Japanese yen increases:
  (a) the dollar has appreciated
  (b) the yen has depreciated

(c) Canadians can now buy more Japanese goods

(d) Japanese can now buy more Canadian goods

11. If the United States begins to demand more Mexican goods:

(a) the demand for the peso will increase, causing the peso to appreciate

(b) the demand for the peso will increase, causing the peso to depreciate

(c) the supply of U.S. dollars will decrease, causing the dollar to appreciate

(d) the supply of U.S. dollars will decrease, causing the dollar to depreciate

12. Which of the following is designed to restrict trade?

(a) export subsidies

(b) NAFTA

(c) GATT

(d) import quotas

13. If Canada imposes more stringent product packaging standards on imported food than on domestically produced food, this could be an example of:

(a) an import tariff

(b) a non-tariff barrier

(c) an import quota

(d) an export subsidy

14. Why do governments often restrict international trade?

(a) to expand their nation's production possibilities

(b) to protect domestic industries from foreign competition

(c) to encourage efficiency in production

(d) to benefit consumers

15. One important outcome of the Uruguay Round of the GATT was:

(a) elimination of services from the agreement

(b) greater restrictions on patents and copyrights

(c) increasing tariffs on manufactured products

(d) reductions in agricultural subsidies

16. The European Common Market:

(a) helped to abolish tariffs and import quotas among its members

(b) aimed for the eventual free movement of capital and labour within the member nations

(c) imposed common tariffs on products imported from countries outside the Common Market

(d) did all of the above

17. One potential problem with the European Union is that:

(a) a free flow of labour and capital within the EU is likely to create mass unemployment

(b) economies of large-scale production will result in higher consumer prices

(c) trade with nonmember nations may diminish

(d) all of the above

18. A trade bloc is the same thing as a:

(a) non-tariff barrier

(b) import quota

(c) free-trade zone

(d) trade restriction

19. For Canada, one advantage of NAFTA is:

(a) higher prices for consumer goods

(b) access for Canadian producers to larger markets

(c) the opportunity to reduce our reliance on imports

(d) more low-wage job opportunities for Canadians

20. Which Canadian firms are best able to compete effectively under a system of freer world trade?

(a) firms that were previously protected by tariffs and quotas

(b) firms in industries where Canada has a comparative advantage

(c) firms that had monopoly power in the Canadian market

(d) very few Canadian firms will be able to compete

■ **DISCUSSION QUESTIONS**

1. What are Canada's principal exports and imports? Why does Canada trade so much with the United States? Why is international trade more important to the Canadian economy than to the U.S. economy?

2. What are some factors contributing to the growth in international trade since World War II?

3. Sketch how the international trade component can be built into the circular flow model.

4. Explain how comparative costs determine which producer has the comparative advantage. What determines the terms of trade? What is the gain that results from specialization and trade according to comparative advantage?

5. Suppose that Dr. Ocula is an outstanding eye surgeon with good enough hand-eye coordination that he keyboards faster than anyone else in town. Use the principle of comparative advantage to explain why he hires someone else to do the word-processing in his office, even though he could do it faster himself.

6. How might an appreciation of the value of the Canadian dollar relative to the American dollar depress the Canadian economy? Which Canadians would be harmed, and which would benefit?

7. What are the major types of trade barriers, and how do they work to restrict international trade?

8. Hypothetically, suppose that Canada has a 20% import tariff on shoelaces. Also suppose that there are only about twenty manufacturers of shoelaces in Canada. If the tariff raises shoelace prices in Canada by about 25 cents a pair, how much would this tariff cost you each year? Estimate the annual benefit of the tariff to each Canadian manufacturer. Do you know whether in fact there is a shoelace tariff? Do you think that Canadian shoelace manufacturers know? How do you explain the difference in the knowledge, and how does this help explain why the government might have implemented this tariff?

9. What does Canada gain from participating in GATT? Which kinds of Canadian industries would be most likely to support the GATT initiatives? And which would be most likely to oppose them?

10. Is it possible that Canada, the United States, and Mexico can all gain from the NAFTA? If so, how?

11. How will the adoption of the euro as a common currency in the EU help member countries? Can you see any problems that the adoption of the euro might create?

12. "Canadian firms cannot compete in the global economy because wages are too high in Canada." Discuss this claim.

■ **ANSWERS**

FILL-IN QUESTIONS

1. limited, smaller

2. increased, increased; developed; United States

3. transportation, communications, tariffs (trade barriers),

4. product; imports, exports

5. Nigeria, Kenya; Nigeria, Kenya

6. terms of trade

7. depreciated, appreciated

8. supply of, demand for; more, less

9. tariffs, quotas, non-tariff, export

10. exports, imports

11. benefit, cost, higher

12. equal or non-discriminatory; tariffs; quotas

13. European Union; member, nonmember, labour

14. United States, 1989; 1993, Mexico

PROBLEMS AND PROJECTS

1. (a) 2/3, 1 1/2; (b) 1/2, 2; (c) Murray, lower, Julius, lower; (d) jackets, trousers; (e) 60, 50; 10, 0

2. (a) 1/2 banana, 2 apples, 1/3 banana, 3 apples; (b) Costa Rica, Venezuela; (c) 2, 3; (d) 69, 18; (e) 75, 20; (f) 6, 2; (g) 25, 10, 50, 10; (h) 1, 2, 5, 0

3. (a) D, A, A, A; (b) 21.28, 71.43, 1.25

TRUE-FALSE

1. T   for many goods we import all we consume
2. F   the Netherlands has a higher percentage
3. T
4. T   opportunity cost ratios can differ between individuals or regions
5. F   if there is comparative advantage, each nation will have the advantage in one of the two goods

6. T   so there is no gain to specialization and trade
7. F   no nation has a lower opportunity cost ratio for all goods
8. T   because imported goods can be acquired for an opportunity cost lower than the domestic production cost
9. F   quantity of yen should be on the horizontal
10. T   Canadians increase their imports
11. F   the Canadian dollar will depreciate
12. F   the reciprocal of .70 is 1.43
13. T
14. T
15. T   costs per unit are lower when more units can be sold
16. T   some gained market share and profits while others lost
17. F   only Canada, the U.S., and Mexico
18. T

MULTIPLE-CHOICE

1. (d)
2. (b)
3. (b)
4. (b) 100W = 20P, therefore 1W = 0.2P
5. (a) 120W = 40P, therefore 3W = 1P
6. (d) Heath's opportunity cost is lower than Cliff's for peat, but not for wool
7. (c) only this range is between the opportunity cost ratios in both regions
8. (b) any of the other choices benefit only one of the two nations
9. (d)
10. (d) a given number of yen can now buy more dollars, and therefore more goods in Canada
11. (a) higher demand for pesos means a higher price (appreciation) for the peso
12. (d) the others are meant to promote trade
13. (b) by raising costs for importers to get goods into Canada
14. (b) production, efficiency, and benefits to consumers all suffer
15. (d)
16. (d)
17. (c) unemployment and prices are likely to fall
18. (c) the EU is an example
19. (b) larger markets enable producers to lower their per unit production costs
20. (b) this is the central lesson of the principle of comparative advantage

CHAPTER 6

Measuring Domestic Output, National Income, and the Price Level

Macroeconomics deals with the working of the overall economy. Therefore, we need measures of such variables as the overall levels of output, income, and prices. This chapter discusses why such measures are important, defines the key measures, and discusses what the measures can and cannot tell us about the overall economy.

The measurement of the economy's overall production is called national income accounting. The key measure is gross domestic output (GDP), which measures the total market value of all final goods and services produced in the country in a year. The emphasis on final goods is to avoid the problem of multiple counting. GDP can be determined through either the "income approach" or the "expenditure approach." In total, incomes and expenditures must be equal because the value of the nation's output equals the total expenditures on this output, and these expenditures become the incomes of those in the nation who have produced this output.

By the expenditures approach, GDP has four components: personal consumption (C), gross investment (I_g), government purchases (G), and net exports (X_n). This same total GDP (after a few adjustments) is also distributed as incomes to households as: wages, rent, interest, and profit. The chapter also explains the relationship of GDP to other national income accounting measures: gross national product (GNP), personal income (PI), and disposable income (DI). The circular flow model (first presented in Chapter 2) illustrates the relationship between income flows and expenditure flows.

GDP is the market value of the nation's output, so it is measured in dollar terms. GDP measured in this way is known as "nominal GDP" and can fluctuate from year to year either because of changes in

the amount of output, or because of changes in the value of a dollar (inflation or deflation). To enable us to distinguish between price changes and real production changes, economists have developed a constant dollar measure, known as "real GDP," which is found by deflating nominal GDP by the GDP price index.

Another important overall measure of prices is the consumer price index (CPI). This index reflects variations in the prices of hundreds of consumer goods. The inflation rate, as reported in the media, is based on the annual percentage change in the CPI. Several aspects of the CPI's construction imply that the CPI will tend to overstate the inflation rate.

The final section of the chapter points out some shortcomings of the real GDP measure. It is seriously flawed as an indicator of the society's well-being, and even as a measure of our total output.

■ CHAPTER LEARNING OBJECTIVES

In this chapter you will learn:

☐ What gross domestic product (GDP) is and what it measures.

☐ The expenditure approach to measuring gross domestic product (GDP).

☐ The income approach to measuring gross domestic product (GDP).

☐ The distinction between nominal GDP and real GDP.

☐ What the Consumer Price Index (CPI) is and how it is constructed.

☐ The shortcomings of GDP as a measure of a country's well-being.

■ CHAPTER OUTLINE

1. National income accounting consists of concepts that enable economists to: (a) assess the health of the economy by measuring and comparing output at regular intervals, (b) track the long-run course of the economy growth or decline in output, and (c) formulate policies to maintain and improve the economy's health.

2. The gross domestic product (GDP) is the total market value of all final goods and services produced in a country during a given year.
   (a) GDP is a monetary measure.
   (b) To avoid multiple counting, GDP includes only final goods and services (goods and services that are not for resale or further processing). The same result can be found by including the value added by all producers in the economy.
   (c) GDP excludes nonproductive transactions such as purely financial transactions and second-hand sales.

3. Measurement of GDP can be accomplished by either the expenditure or the income approach, but the same result is obtained by the two methods.

4. In the expenditure approach, GDP is computed by adding the four components of spending for final goods and services:
   (a) Personal consumption expenditures (C) are the expenditures of households for durable and nondurable goods and for services.
   (b) Gross investment (I_g) is the sum of all final spending by business firms for machinery, equipment, and tools; all construction spending (including residential construction); and changes in inventories.
   (1) A change in inventories is included in investment because it is part of the year's output (even though it was not sold during the year).
   (2) Investment does not include expenditures for stocks or bonds or for second-hand capital goods.
   (3) Net investment equals gross investment less the depreciation allowance for capital that has been used up during the year.
   (c) Government expenditures (G) include all consumption and investment expenditures made by all levels of government, including all purchases of final goods and resource services from households, but excluding transfer payments.

(d) Net exports (X_n) equal the expenditures made by foreigners for goods and services produced in the economy less the expenditures made by the consumers, government, and businesses of the economy for goods and services produced in foreign nations.
(e) The sum or aggregate of the four major expenditure components gives gross domestic product. In symbols, $C + I_g + G + X_n = GDP$.

5. To compute GDP by the income method, we add the eight uses for the income derived from the production and sale of final goods and services:
   (a) wages, salaries, and supplementary labour income;
   (b) corporation profits before taxes;
   (c) interest and miscellaneous investment income;
   (d) farmers' income;
   (e) net income of nonfarm unincorporated business, including rent;
   (f) inventory valuation adjustment;
   (g) indirect taxes less subsidies;
   (h) capital consumption allowances (depreciation).

6. Several other national income measures are also useful.
   (a) Gross national product (GNP) measures the total of all final goods and services produced during a year by resources supplied by Canadians (whether in Canada or abroad).
   (b) Personal income (PI) is the total income received by households, earned or unearned.
   (c) Disposable income (DI) is PI less personal taxes and other transfers to government.
   (d) Figure 6-3 is a more realistic and complex circular flow diagram that shows the flows of expenditures and incomes among households, businesses, governments, and the rest of the world.

7. Because GDP is a monetary measure, it is meaningful to compare a nation's GDP level in different years only if the value of money itself does not change.
   (a) The value of money changes whenever there is inflation or deflation.
   (b) GDP calculated at current prices, and unadjusted for price level changes, is called *nominal* GDP. GDP calculated to adjust for price level changes, or measured in constant dollars, is called *real* GDP.
8. One way to adjust nominal GDP to correct for price changes is to use a price index.

(a)   The price level is stated as an index number that measures the ratio of the combined price of a market basket of goods in a given year to the combined price of a market basket of goods in a base year, with that ratio multiplied by 100.

(b)   To adjust nominal GDP figures for inflation, divide the year's nominal GDP by that year's price index (expressed in hundredths). The result is the real GDP.

(c)   When the price index in a year is below (above) its base year level of 100, the nominal GDP figure for that year is inflated (deflated) by this adjustment.

(d)   An alternative method of finding real GDP is to calculate the value of the current year's output using base year prices. The GDP price index can then be found by dividing nominal GDP by real GDP.

9. Another important price index is the consumer price index (CPI).

(a)   The CPI measures the prices of a fixed market basket of 600 goods and services purchased by typical urban consumers in 64 centres across Canada.

(b)   The CPI for a given year is found as the price of the market basket in the given year divided by the price of the same basket in the base year, all multiplied by 100.

(c)   The rate of inflation or deflation is computed as the annual percentage change in the CPI.

(d)   The GDP price index measures the prices of *all* goods and services produced in the economy, and uses the current composition of output to determine the relative importance (or weight) of each item in the basket.

10. Inflation rates calculated from the CPI overstate the rate of inflation by up to about 0.5% per year because the CPI does not account for:

(a)   consumers shifting their spending to buy less of goods that are becoming *relatively* more expensive, and more of goods that are becoming *relatively* less expensive;

(b)   new products;

(c)   quality improvements;

(d)   consumers shopping to take advantage of discounts or special sale prices at particular stores.

11. GDP is reasonably accurate and very useful for measuring the country's production, but it is a flawed measure of output and of society's overall well-being.

(a)   GDP does not capture the value of non-market transactions (e.g. home production).

(b)   GDP does not capture changes in how much leisure time we enjoy.

(c)   GDP does not capture improvements in product quality.

(d)   GDP does not capture activity in the underground economy (whether illegal activities or legal activities that are unreported for tax purposes).

(e)   GDP does not record the environmental costs that invariably accompany the production of final goods and services.

(f)   GDP does not measure changes in the composition and the distribution of society's output.

(g)   GDP does not account for population change. (However, the per capita GDP measure overcomes this criticism.)

(h)   GDP does not reflect many non-economic aspects of well-being such as levels of crime, civility, peace, and human rights.

■ TERMS AND CONCEPTS

capital consumption allowance	**multiple counting**
consumer price index (CPI)	**national income accounting**
disposable income	**net domestic income (NDI)**
expenditures approach	**net exports**
final goods	**net investment**
government purchases	**nominal GDP**
gross domestic product (GDP)	**per capita output**
gross investment	**personal consumption expenditures**
income approach	**personal income**
indirect taxes	**price index**
intermediate goods	**real GDP**
	value added

■ HINTS AND TIPS

1.   This is a fairly difficult chapter, mainly because of the number of new concepts introduced. Some memorization is inevitably required in this chapter, but the more you understand this chapter, the less you will have to rely on memorization.

2.   Accounting, in the sense used in this chapter, is really a process of adding-up. It is up to you to learn which elements to add up to arrive at each of the several income measures in this chapter.

3. Of all income measures, GDP is the most important. You must know exactly what it means, and what component parts are included in GDP. Figure 6-1 shows the components from both the expenditure approach and the income approach. Understanding of GDP is also enhanced by considering what is omitted from GDP.

4. A concept that will be crucial also in later chapters is the distinction between real GDP and nominal GDP. Make sure that you clearly understand the distinction, and that you know how to convert from one to the other.

■ **FILL-IN QUESTIONS**

1. GDP is the abbreviation for _Gross domestic product_, and measures the total market _value_ of all final goods and services (produced, sold) _produced_ in an economy in a year. The goods and services are valued at their _market_ prices.

2. GNP is the abbreviation for Gross _____ Product. Suppose that in 2001 Danish resources produce 500 billion kroner worth of final goods and services in Denmark, and 40 billion worth of final goods and services in other countries. Meanwhile, 30 billion worth of final goods and services are produced in Denmark by foreign owned resources. Denmark's GDP is _____ billion kroner, and Denmark's GNP is _____ billion kroner.

3. In measuring GDP, only final goods and services are included; if intermediate goods and services were included, the accountant would be committing the error of _____.

4. Value added is the difference between the market value of a firm's _____ and its _____ from other firms. The total value added to a product at all stages of production equals the _____ of the final product; and the total value added to all final products produced in the economy during a year is the _____.

5. GDP can be computed by adding up all spending on final goods and services produced this year. This method is the _____ approach. GDP can also be computed by adding all incomes derived from the production of this year's output. This method is the _____ approach.

6. In the expenditures approach, expenditures on final goods and services are divided into four categories or expenditure streams:
   (a) _____
   (b) _____
   (c) _____
   (d) _____

7. In symbols, the GDP by the expenditures approach = _____ + _____ + _____ + _____

8. Gross investment includes all final purchases of _____ goods (such as machinery, equipment, and tools) by businesses, all _____ of new buildings and houses, and changes in _____.

9. If gross investment is less than depreciation, net investment is (positive, zero, negative) _____ and the economy's stock of capital is (constant, declining, increasing) _____.

10. Government transfer payments are not counted as part of government purchase of goods and services because transfer payments do not represent a payment for goods _____.

11. An economy's net exports equal its _____ less its _____.

12. The net incomes of _____ businesses represent a mixture of labour income and investment income that is impossible to segregate.

13. Corporation profits are divided into three parts:
   (a) _____
   (b) _____
   (c) _____

14. Disposable income equals _____ income minus personal _____ and other personal _____ to government.

15. The price index used to adjust the nominal GDP for changes in the price level is called the _____. To obtain real or _____ dollar GDP, _____ the year's nominal GDP by that year's price index expressed in hundredths.

16. For several reasons the real GDP is not a good measure of social well-being in an economy.
   (a) It excludes _____ transactions that result in the production of goods and services,

and the amount of _____ time enjoyed by the citizens of the economy.

(b) It fails to record improvements in the _____ of the products, changes in the composition and distribution of the economy's total _____, the _____ costs that are an undesirable side-effect of producing the GDP, and the goods and services produced in the _____ economy.

17. If the population of an economy grows by 2.0% over a period of time when real GDP grows by 4.5%, real GDP per capita (rise, falls) _____ by approximately _____%, resulting in a (rising, falling, constant) _____ standard of living for the residents of this country.

■ **PROBLEMS AND PROJECTS**

1. Below are the 2001 data for some nation. Assume that there is no statistical discrepancy.

	Billion $
Exports	169
Corporate profits before taxes	46
Capital consumption allowances (depreciation)	76
Government current purchases of goods and services	133
Accrued net income of farm operators from farm production	4
Indirect taxes (less subsidies)	75
Wages, salaries, supplementary labour income	371
Gross investment	139
Personal saving	49
Corporate income taxes	17
Government transfer payments	149
Interest and miscellaneous investment income	59
Net income from nonfarm unincorporated businesses, including rent	36
Personal consumption expenditures	398
Imports	170
Inventory valuation adjustment	2
Undistributed corporate profits	7
Personal taxes	136

Compute each of the following:
(a) Dividends $_____
(b) Net Exports $ ◁1 ____
(c) Net Investment $_____

(d) Gross Domestic Product by the expenditures approach $_____
(e) Gross Domestic Product by the income approach $_____

2. Suppose the toy industry consists of three firms: a wood producer, a manufacturer, and a retailer. The tables below show their financial data.

Wood Producer			
Purchases of material inputs	$0	Sales to toy manufacturer	$84
Wages	65		
Profits	19		

Toy Manufacturer			
Purchases from wood producer	$84	Sales to toy retailer	$110
Wages	16		
Profits	10		

Toy Retailer			
Purchases from toy manufacturer	$110	Sales to consumers	$150
Wages	30		
Profits	10		

(a) Based on the firms' data, complete this table:

Firm	Gross Value of Production	Purchases from other Firms	Value Added
Wood producer	$ 84	$ 0	$ 84
Toy manufacturer	110	84	26
Toy retailer	150	110	40
TOTALS	344	194	150

(b) Compute the total incomes, or factor payments:
Wages $ 111
Profits $ 39
Total Incomes $ 150

(c) Explain why the totals in (a) and (b) should be the same.

3. In 1998 a steel company purchased $100 million worth of new machinery, $25 million worth of used machinery, and spent $113 million building new corporate headquarters. The company had $520 million worth of inventory of steel products at the beginning of the year and $482 million worth of

X–M
169 –170

inventory at year end. Depreciation was $30 million in 1998.

(a) Determine this company's contribution to the nation's gross investment for 1998.

(b) Determine the company's contribution to net investment for 1998.

4. The next table contains data on Canada's nominal GDP, constant dollar GDP, and the GDP price index for a number of years. Complete the missing entries.

Year	Nominal GDP (Billion $)	Real GDP (Billion $)	GDP Price Index
1984	$444.7	$_____	95.2
1985	477.9	489.6	_____
1986	_____	505.7	100.0
1987	551.6	526.8	_____
1988	605.9	_____	109.5
1989	_____	565.6	114.9

5. In the table below are nominal GDP figures for three years and the price index value for each of the three years. (The GDP figures are in billions.)

(a) Which of the three years appears to be the base year? __1939__ .

(b) Between:

(1) 1929 and 1933 the economy experienced (inflation, deflation) _____ .

(2) 1933 and 1939 the economy experienced (inflation, deflation) _____ .

Year	Nominal GDP	Price Index	Real GDP
1929	$104	121	$_____
1933	56	91	_____
1939	91	100	_____

(c) Use the price index values to compute real GDP in each year (rounding your answer to the nearest billion).

(d) The nominal GDP figure:

(1) for 1929 was (deflated, inflated, neither) _____ .

(2) for 1933 was _____ .

(3) for 1939 was _____ .

(e) The price level:

(1) fell by _____% from 1929 to 1933;

(2) rose by _____% from 1933 to 1939.

6. Use the information below to calculate for 2000 and 2001 the nominal GDP, the real GDP, and the GDP price index. 1986 is the base year.

Good	Output in 2000	Output in 2001	Price in 1986	Price in 2000	Price in 2001
Books	20	22	$8	$10	$12
Cards	1000	900	$1	$1	$1
Dolls	8	10	$15	$20	$21
Grain	100	80	$2	$2	$3

(a) 2000 nominal GDP $ 1560

(b) 2001 nominal GDP $ 1614

(c) 2000 real GDP $ 1480

(d) 2001 real GDP $ 1386

(e) 2000 GDP price index 105.41

(f) 2001 GDP price index 116.45

(g) The economy experienced (deflation, inflation) _____ of 9.4 % from 2000 to 2001.

(h) The economy produced (less, more) _____ goods in 2001 than in 2000.

7. The objective of measuring gross domestic product is to reflect the value of all final goods and services produced in Canada during a year. Given this, and what you have learned in this chapter about how GDP accounting works, classify each of the following as: (A) Included in calculated GDP; (B) Excluded from GDP, and correctly so; (C) Excluded from GDP, but ideally should be included.

(a) the transfer from Burke to Solomon of shares in a mining company

(b) gardening services that Slade performs in his own backyard

(c) the increase in inventories at Zellers stores

(d) health care provided in a provincially-funded hospital in Prince Edward Island

(e) construction services provided in Indonesia by a Canadian-based firm

(f) Wilson's purchase of a second-hand radio from Pickett

8. In each case below, explain whether it is real GDP or nominal GDP that the speaker is discussing.

(a) "Last year the nation's GDP rose by 3.5%, but this did not translate into much growth since the Consumer Price Index was up 2.8%."

(b) "If GDP begins growing faster than population there will be more goods and services per capita, tending to improve our standard of living."

■ **TRUE-FALSE**

Circle T if the statement is true, F if it is false.

1. Gross domestic product measures the total market value of all final goods and services produced in the economy in one year. (T) F

2. Both the nominal GDP and the real GDP of the Canadian economy are measured in constant dollars. T (F)

3. Value added is the market value of a firm's output less the value of the inputs it has purchased from others. (T) F

4. If the value added by all firms in an economy were summed, the resulting figure would be equal to gross domestic product. (T) F

5. The gross domestic product would be understated if intermediate goods were included in its calculation. T (F)

6. Goods purchased with public transfer payments are not included in the gross domestic product. (T) F

7. If a car was produced in 1991 and sold in 1992, it would be included in 1992's gross domestic product. T (F)

8. The expenditure approach to computing GDP is also known as the factor payment approach. T (F)

9. The expenditure made by a household to have a new home built is a personal consumption expenditure. (T) F

10. In national income accounting any increase in the inventories of business firms is included in gross investment. (T) F

11. The revenue from the sale of new issues of stocks is included in gross investment but not in net investment. T (F)

12. Gross investment cannot be a negative amount. T (F)

13. The net exports of an economy equal its exports of goods and services less its imports of goods and services. (T) F

14. Dividends are the only part of corporate profits that are included in calculating gross domestic product by the income approach. T (F)

Use the data in the following table to answer true-false questions 15 to 17 and multiple-choice questions 10 to 16. There is no statistical discrepancy.

	Billions
Personal consumption expenditure	$50
Net investment	10
Capital consumption allowance	7
Government purchases of goods and services	31
Exports	8
Imports	6
Wages, salaries, and other labour income	40
Interest	9
Corporation income taxes	8
Dividends	11
Undistributed corporation profits	3
Net farm incomes	2
Net nonincorporated business incomes	12
Inventory evaluation adjustment	-1
Indirect taxes less subsidies	8
Government transfers to households	9
Personal taxes	20

15. The stock of capital goods in the economy has expanded. (T) F

16. Gross investment is $17 billion. (T) F

17. Net exports are equal to $2 billion. (T) F

18. A price index measures the combined price of a particular set of goods and services in a given period relative to the combined price of identical or similar goods and services in a base period. T F

19. A GDP value that reflects current prices is called current dollar or nominal GDP. T F

20. Comparison of a gross domestic product with the gross domestic product of an earlier year when the price level has risen between the two years necessitates the "inflation" of the GDP figure in the later year. T F

21. In a year when nominal GDP rises, real GDP must also rise, though not necessarily by the same percentage. T F

22. If the price index for 1990 is 126 and the price index for 1991 is 130, the price level rose by 4% between 1990 and 1991. **T F**

23. The inflation rate calculated from the consumer price index tends to overstate the increases in the cost of living. **T F**

24. Nominal GDP figures are adjusted for price changes over time by expressing each year's price index in hundredths and dividing it into the nominal GDP of that year. **T F**

25. GDP is an accurate measure of the social welfare of society. **T F**

26. The presence of an underground economy results in an overstatement of the GDP value. **T F**

■ **MULTIPLE-CHOICE**

Circle the letter that corresponds to the best answer.

1. Which of the following is not an important purpose for national income accounting?
(a) to provide a basis for the formulation and application of policies designed to improve the economy's performance
(b) to permit the measurement of the amount of unemployment in the economy
(c) to permit the estimation of the output of final goods and services in the economy
(d) to enable the economist to chart the growth of the economy over a period of time

2. In the computation of GDP, to include both the value of a loaf of bread and the value of the flour that goes into the bread would be an example of:
(a) including a nonmarket transaction
(b) including a nonproductive transaction
(c) including a noninvestment transaction
(d) multiple counting

3. In the definition of GDP the term "final goods and services" refers to:
(a) goods and services that are in the final stage of production
(b) goods and services that have been produced and purchased this year
(c) goods and services produced this year for final use and not for resale or further processing

(d) goods and services produced in prior years and finally sold this year

4. Excluded from the measurement of GDP are all of the following with the exception of:
(a) government transfer payments
(b) purchases of stocks and bonds
(c) second-hand sales
(d) investment expenditures by business firms

5. Net investment equals gross investment less:
(a) gross national product
(b) net inventory change
(c) capital consumption allowances
(d) government investment expenditure

6. Which is the correct equation for calculating GDP?:
(a) GDP = C + Ig + G + Xn
(b) GDP = C + Ig + G - Xn
(c) GDP = C + I + G + Xn
(d) GDP = C + Ig + G + X

7. If net investment is a positive value, a nation's stock of capital is:
(a) increasing
(b) declining
(c) staying constant
(d) not enough information provided to reach a conclusion

8. Which of the following does not represent investment?
(a) an increase in the quantity of shoes on the shelves of a shoe store
(b) the construction of a condominium
(c) the purchase of newly issued shares of stock in Canadian Pacific Limited
(d) the construction of a factory building using money borrowed from a bank

9. A refrigerator is manufactured in 1991, sold during 1991 to a retailer, and sold by the retailer to a final consumer in 1992. The refrigerator is:
(a) counted as consumption in 1991
(b) counted as investment in 1992
(c) counted as investment in 1991
(d) not included in the gross domestic product of 1991

10. The income approach to GDP sums the total income earned by resource suppliers and adds two nonincome charges:
(a) saving and investment

(b) depreciation and indirect taxes less subsidies
(c) indirect business taxes and dividends
(d) depreciation and net investment

Questions 11 to 17 use the national income accounting data in the table in the true-false section.

11. Gross domestic product is equal to:
(a) $90 billion
(b) $100 billion
(c) $107 billion
(d) $109 billion

12. Corporate profits are equal to:
(a) $15 billion
(b) $17 billion
(c) $19 billion
(d) $22 billion

13. Net exports are equal to:
(a) $3 billion
(b) $2 billion
(c) -$32 billion
(d) $32 billion

14. The net domestic income is equal to:
(a) $70 billion
(b) $75 billion
(c) $80 billion
(d) $85 billion

15. Personal income is equal to:
(a) $70 billion
(b) $74 billion
(c) $77 billion
(d) $83 billion

16. Personal disposable income is equal to:
(a) $50 billion
(b) $54 billion
(c) $57 billion
(d) $63 billion

17. Personal saving is equal to:
(a) -$3 billion
(b) $5 billion
(c) $8 billion
(d) $13 billion

18. In national income accounting personal income is:
(a) income earned by the factors of production for their current contribution to production

(b) income received by households before personal taxes
(c) income received by households less savings
(d) income received by households less personal consumption expenditure

19. If both nominal GDP and the level of prices are rising, it is evident that:
(a) real GDP is constant
(b) real GDP is rising but not as rapidly as prices
(c) real GDP is declining
(d) no conclusion can be drawn concerning the real GDP of the economy on the basis of this information.

20. Over a decade a nation's nominal GDP rose by 40%, its price level rose by 25%, and its population rose by 5%. Approximately how much did its per capita real GDP change?:
(a) -10%
(b) -5%
(c) 10%
(d) 20%

21. The real GDP in Canada in 1989 was $566 billion and in 1991 it was $553 billion. It can be concluded that:
(a) the price level in Canada declined between 1989 and 1991
(b) the price level in Canada rose between 1989 and 1991
(c) the quantity of goods and services produced in Canada fell between 1989 and 1991
(d) the quantity of goods and services produced in Canada increased between 1989 and 1991

22. In an economy, the total expenditure for a market basket of goods in year 1 (the base year) was $400 million. In year 2, the total expenditure for the same basket of goods was $450 million. What was the GDP price index for year 2?
(a) 88
(b) 112.5
(c) 188
(d) 103

23. Changes in the real GDP from one year to the next do not reflect:
(a) changes in the quality of goods produced
(b) changes in the nation's population
(c) changes in the average length of the work week

(d) any of the above changes

24. A price index one year was 145 and the next year it was 167. What is the approximate percentage change in the price level from one year to the next as measured by that index?
- **(a)** 12%
- **(b)** 13%
- **(c)** 15%
- **(d)** 22%

25. GDP is deficient as a measure of social welfare because GDP does not reflect:
- **(a)** increased leisure enjoyed by members of society
- **(b)** the composition and distribution of output
- **(c)** transactions in the underground economy
- **(d)** all of the above

26. Which of the following is **not** another term for nominal GDP?
- **(a)** current dollar GDP
- **(b)** unadjusted GDP
- **(c)** real GDP
- **(d)** money GDP

27. The CPI tends to overstate the rate of inflation because:
- **(a)** the quality of products tends to increase over time
- **(b)** consumers switch their purchases in favour of goods that have become relatively less expensive
- **(c)** consumers tend to buy more from those stores that offer special sale prices
- **(d)** all of the above reasons

■ **DISCUSSION QUESTIONS**

1. Of what use are national income accounts to the economist and to the government's economic policy makers?

2. Why must GDP be measured in monetary terms, and what problem does this cause?

3. Why does GDP exclude nonproductive transactions? What are the two principal types of nonproductive transactions? List some examples of each.
4. Why are there two ways, both of which yield the same answers, of computing GDP?

5. Why are transfer payments excluded from GDP but included in Personal Income?

6. Is residential construction counted as investment or consumption? Why? Why is a change in inventories counted as an investment?

7. Why do economists find it necessary to inflate and deflate GDP when comparing GDP in different years? How do they do this?

8. Why is GDP not a good measure of the well-being of a society? Are there any omissions from GDP that are likely to be particularly problematic if you are trying to use GDP data to compare well-being in the Bahamas with well-being in Canada? What if you want to compare social well-being in modern day Canada with Canada a century ago?

■ **ANSWERS**

FILL-IN QUESTIONS

1. gross domestic product, value, produced, market

2. national, 530, 540

3. multiple counting

4. output, purchases, market price, GDP

5. expenditures, income

6. (a) personal consumption expenditure; (b) gross investment; (c) government current purchase of goods and services; (d) net exports

7. C, I_g, G, X_n

8. capital, construction, inventories

9. negative, declining

10. produced

11. exports, imports

12. unincorporated

13. (a) corporation income tax; (b) dividends; (c) undistributed corporate profits

14. personal, taxes, transfers

15. GDP price index, constant, divide

16. (a) nonmarket, leisure; (b) quality, output, environment, underground

17. rise, 2.5, rising

PROBLEMS AND PROJECTS

1. (a) $22; (b) $-1; (c) $63; (d) expenditures approach: 398 + 139 + 133 + (-1) = $669; (e) income approach: 371 + 46 + 59 + 4 + 36 + 75 + 76 + 2 = $669

2. (a) Wood producer: $84; 0; $84; Toy manufacturer: $110; $84; $26; Toy retailer: $150; $110; $40; Totals: $344; $194; $150; (b) 111; 39; 150; (c) Total incomes = total expenditures

3. (a) 100 + 113 + (520 - 482) = $151 million; (b) 151 - 30 = $145 million

4. 1984: $467.1; 1985: 97.6; 1986: $505.7; 1987: 104.7; 1988: $553.3; 1989: $649.9

5. (a) index = 100 in 1939; (b) (1) deflation, (2) inflation; (c) 86, 62, 91; (d) (1) deflated, (2) inflated, (3) neither; (e) (1) 24.8, (2) 9.9

6. (a) (20 x 10) + (1000 x 1) + (8 x 20) + (100 x 2) = $1560; (b) $1614; (c) (20 x 8) + (1000 x 1) + (8 x 15) + (100 x 2) = $1480; (d) $1386; (e) ($1560/$1480) x 100 = 105.4; (f) 116.4; (g) inflation, (116.4-105.4)/105.4 x 100% = 10.4%; (h) less (because real GDP fell)

7. (a) A – nonproductive transaction; (b) B – a nonmarket, but productive, activity; (c) C – included in investment; (d) C – included in government expenditures; (e) B – production is outside Canada; (f) B – nonproductive transaction

8. (a) Most of the 3.5% increase in **nominal** GDP is caused by price increases; (b) **Real** GDP must grow faster than population for output per capita to increase.

TRUE-FALSE

1. T

2. F   only real GDP is in constant dollars

3. T

4. T

5. F   it would be overstated by multiple counting

6. F   transfer payments themselves aren't counted, but goods are counted if they are final goods produced in the country in this year

7. F   it would be included in 1991 GDP

8. F   the factor payment approach is also known as the income approach

9. F   construction of housing counts as investment

10. T

11. F   financial transactions are not counted in GDP

12. T   net investment can be, but gross investment cannot

13. T

14. F   all corporate profits are included

15. T   because net investment is positive

16. T   net investment + capital consumption allowance

17. T   exports - imports

18. T

19. T

20. F   the later figure needs to be "deflated"

21. F   if real GDP falls, but prices rise by a larger percentage, nominal GDP can rise

22. F   ((130-126)/126) x 100%

23. T   for several reasons

24. T

25. F

26. F   understatement (because some production is excluded from the GDP accounts)

MULTIPLE-CHOICE

1. (b)

2. (d)   include only the final product

3. (c)   the goods need not have been purchased this year, but they must have been produced this year

4. (d)   the others are not directly productive transactions

5. (c)   this is the same thing as depreciation

6. (a)

7. (a)   net investment represents the addition to the capital stock

8. (c)   this is purely a financial transaction

9. (c)   it is added to the retailer's inventories in 1991

10. (b)

11. (b)   50 + (10 + 7) + 31 + (8 – 6)

12. (d)   8 + 11 + 3

13. (b)   8 - 6

14. (d)   (50 + (10 + 7) + 31 + (8 – 6)) - 8 - 7

15. (d)   85 - (8 + 3) + 9

16. (d)   83 - 20

17. (d)   63 - 50

18. (b)

19. (d)   it depends whether or not prices are rising faster than nominal GDP

20. (c)   40% - 25% - 5%

21. (c)   since both figures are for real GDP we can infer nothing about how prices changed

22. (b)   (450/400) x 100

23. (d)   hence GDP is a flawed indicator of well-being

24. (c)   ((167-145)/145) x 100%

25. (d)

26. (c)

27. (d)

CHAPTER 7

Introduction to Economic Growth and Fluctuations

In the previous chapter you learned how to define and how to compute the nominal and real value of GDP. This chapter provides an introductory look at the growth of real GDP over the long run, and short run macroeconomic fluctuations in real GDP, unemployment, and inflation. The chapters that follow will provide fuller explanations for how these variables are determined, why they are subject to fluctuation, and what policies may be used to control them for the benefit of society.

Economic growth is measured as either increasing real GDP, or increasing real GDP per capita. Either way, growth is an important goal because it lessens the burden of scarcity. The basic sources of growth are increases in the supply of resource inputs and increases in the productivity of these inputs. Over the long haul, Canada's real GDP has shown a clear trend of growth (giving us a rising standard of living), but we see continual short-run deviations from the long-run trend. Sometimes we enjoy the prosperity that comes with rapidly growing output and employment, while at other times we suffer through hard times of shrinking output and employment. We refer to such periodic fluctuations in output, employment, and price levels as "business cycles." Different industries and areas of the country can be impacted quite differently by the business cycle.

Unemployment is divided into three main types: frictional, structural, and cyclical. The first two are present even when the economy is at "full employment," giving rise to the concept of the natural rate of unemployment. Currently, economists estimate that the Canadian economy reaches full employment when the unemployment rate is around 6 to 7%. Unemployment in excess of this rate is cyclical unemployment that usually arises in the recession phase of the business cycle. Careful examination of how unemployment is defined and measured reveals several problems that may lead to overstate-

ment or understatement of the unemployment problem. As well as the hardship experienced by unemployed workers themselves, unemployment costs society the lost output that the unemployed could have produced. The relationship between unemployment and lost production is captured in Okun's Law. The burden of unemployment is not borne equally: unemployment rates vary between men and women, between provinces, between younger and older workers, and between occupations.

Inflation is a second problem that can result from economic instability. The inflation rate is the annual percentage increase in the general level of prices in an economy. For the last decade Canada has experienced mild inflation, but we experienced inflation of over 10% per year as recently as the early 1980s. Inflation can be caused by factors on either the demand side or the supply side of the economy. If inflation is not extreme, its most significant effects are arbitrary redistributions of income and wealth, particularly when the inflation is unanticipated. Some individuals suffer while others benefit. But inflation may not only affect how the pie is divided, it may also affect the size of the pie. The fear of inflation is rooted in the lesson of history that extremely rapid inflation can lead to a severe breakdown in the economy which can devastate almost everyone's standard of living.

■ CHAPTER LEARNING OBJECTIVES

In this chapter you will learn:
☐ The definition and causes of economic growth.
☐ The nature and causes of the business cycle.
☐ The nature of unemployment and its measurement.
☐ The definition of inflation and how it is measured.
☐ The redistribution effects of inflation.

☐   The output effects of inflation.

■ CHAPTER OUTLINE

1. Canada has experienced a long-run trend of growth in real output. Economic growth is defined in two different ways:
   (a)   Increase in real GDP over some period.
   (b)   Increase in real GDP per capita over some period.

2. Growth is a widely held economic goal because it lessens the burden of scarcity. Even a small improvement in the annual growth rate of the economy can over a number of years imply a dramatic change in the standard of living.

3. The main sources of growth are increases in the supply of resource inputs, and increases in the productivity of these inputs. Over the last fifty years Canada has averaged about 4% per year growth in real GDP. This figure must be qualified because some of this measure does not reflect the impacts of improved products, increased leisure time, and increased environmental damage that have accompanied this growth.

4. Around the long-run trend of economic growth we experience business cycles (periods of short-term economic instability).
   (a)   A business cycle entails alternating periods of prosperity and recession (or depression). Cycles are of irregular duration and intensity but typically follow a four-phase pattern: peak, recession, trough, and recovery to the next peak.
   (b)   The most important cause of fluctuations in the levels of output and employment is fluctuation in the level of total spending or demand.
   (c)   The business cycle affects the entire economy, but it does not affect every industry or province in the same way or to the same degree.
   (d)   During a cycle, the output of capital goods and consumer durables fluctuates more than the output of services and consumer nondurables because the purchase of capital and durable goods can be postponed.

5. The measurement of unemployment starts with the definition of three groups in the Canadian population: (1) those not eligible to work (too young or institutionalized), (2) those eligible but not in the labour force (homemakers, full-time students, retired people), and (3) the labour force (those eligible and available to work – whether employed or unemployed).

6. The unemployment rate is defined as the percentage of the labour force represented by people who are not working but are actively seeking work. This definition tends to understate unemployment because: (1) part-time workers are counted as employed, even though many consider themselves largely unemployed because they desire full-time work, and (2) some workers have become so discouraged by looking for work that they are no longer seeking work and therefore not counted as unemployed.

7. There are three kinds of unemployment:
   (a)   Frictional unemployment arises when workers are "between jobs": searching for jobs, or are waiting to take jobs very soon. Such unemployment is inherent in a dynamic economy and is generally desirable for workers and society as a whole.
   (b)   Structural unemployment results from changes in technology or consumer demands. A mismatch between the skills or location of workers compared to the skills or location required for available jobs makes structural unemployment a serious and longer term problem.
   (c)   Cyclical unemployment is the result of insufficient aggregate spending in the economy.

8. Even when the economy is "fully employed" there is some frictional and structural unemployment. The natural rate of unemployment (NRU), or full-employment unemployment rate, is the sum of frictional and structural unemployment. It is achieved when cyclical unemployment is zero.
   (a)   The economy does not usually operate at full employment, so the unemployment rate is usually above the natural rate, but can be below.
   (b)   Canada's current NRU is estimated to be around 6 to 7 percent. Demographic and institutional changes can shift the NRU.

9. The economic cost of unemployment is measured by the GDP gap (or foregone output) that results during a recession.
   (a)   The GDP gap is the amount by which actual GDP falls short of potential GDP.
   (b)   Okun's law indicates that for every 1% which the actual unemployment rate exceeds the natural rate of unemployment, there is a GDP gap of about 2%.

(c) The burden of unemployment is unequally distributed among different groups in the labour force. Younger workers, blue-collar workers, less-educated workers, and workers in the Maritimes and Quebec have suffered higher than average unemployment rates in recent years.

(d) Unemployment also has non-economic costs. It has been shown to be a cause of a number of serious social problems.

(e) In the last decade, as compared to the United States, United Kingdom, France, Japan, and Germany, Canada's unemployment rate has improved significantly.

10. Inflation is a rise in the general level of prices, and is measured by the annual percentage rise in the Consumer Price Index (CPI).

(a) Since 1960, the general level of prices in Canada has risen every year. Inflation was highest in the 1970s and 1980s, while inflation was very mild during the 1960s and 1990s.

(b) The rule of 70 can be used to calculate how many years it would take for the price level to double at any given rate of inflation.

(c) Canada's inflation rate is now low relative to rates in other industrialized countries.

11. As a provisional theory of inflation, we distinguish between demand-pull inflation, which results from an excess aggregate demand for goods compared to the economy's capacity to produce, and cost-push inflation, which results from increasing per unit production costs. Demand-pull inflation can continue indefinitely whereas cost-push inflation is self-limiting.

12. Even if the total output of the economy is constant, *unanticipated* inflation arbitrarily redistributes real income and wealth, benefiting some people and hurting others.

(a) The percentage change in real income can be approximated by subtracting the percentage change in the price level from the percentage change in nominal income.

(b) Unanticipated inflation redistributes income away from fixed-income receivers. Flexible-income receivers (e.g. those whose incomes are subject to automatic cost-of-living adjustment) are not harmed by inflation.

(c) Unanticipated inflation injures savers because it decreases the real value of any savings, the nominal value of which is fixed.

(d) Unanticipated inflation benefits debtors and hurts creditors because it lowers the purchasing power or the real value of the debt when it is repaid.

(e) When the inflation is anticipated, and people can adjust their nominal incomes to reflect the expected rise in the price level, the redistribution of income and wealth is lessened. This occurs with COLA clauses in labour agreements and with adjustments to nominal interest rates in financial agreements.

(f) The nominal interest rate equals the real interest rate plus the premium for the expected inflation rate.

13. Three final points about the redistribution effects of inflation:

(a) The results of unanticipated deflation are exactly the opposite of unanticipated inflation.

(b) Most people experience mixed effects from inflation because most of us have several roles (e.g. wage earner, borrower, and saver).

(c) Inflation wreaks its effects in a purely arbitrary (and unfair) manner.

14. In some situations the inflation rate and the real output level are related.

(a) Sharp increases in the cost of resources (such as energy) can cause cost-push inflation, reduce the demand for goods, causing lower GDP and higher unemployment.

(b) Some economists stress that even mild inflation inflicts a cost on the economy as households and businesses spend time and other valuable resources trying to minimize the impact of inflation. Other economists believe that mild demand-pull inflation may a necessary side effect of maintaining sufficient demand in the economy to maintain full employment.

(c) Very rapid inflation (hyperinflation) will lead people to expect yet further price increases, so they will accelerate their spending in order to stay ahead of the anticipated price increases. Speculative behaviour of all sorts will ensue, and money eventually becomes worthless. Complete economic and social collapse is a possibility (such as in Weimar Germany). Hyperinflations have occurred recently in South America and Africa.

15. Major increases or decreases in prices on the stock market can create some macroeconomic instability. For example, stock price shifts alter the wealth of investors and may therefore alter their consumption spending. Sometimes stock prices seem to predict business cycles, but this does not imply that they cause recessions.

■ TERMS AND CONCEPTS

anticipated inflation
business cycle
cost-of-living
  adjustment (COLA)
cost-push inflation
cyclical unemployment
deflation
demand-pull inflation
discouraged workers
economic growth
frictional
  unemployment
GDP gap
hyperinflation
inflation
labour force

natural rate of unem-
  ployment (NRU)
nominal income
nominal interest rate
Okun's law
peak
potential output
productivity
real income
real interest rate
recession
recovery
rule of 70
structural
  unemployment
trough
unanticipated inflation
unemployment rate

■ HINTS AND TIPS

1. The term business cycle is misleading if it implies to you a sense of regularity or predictability. Neither the duration nor the depth of a recession is likely to be consistent from one recession to the next. Therefore, some economists prefer to use the term "business fluctuations" rather than "business cycles."

2. Even when the economy is at full employment there is some unemployment; this is the natural rate of unemployment. Therefore, it is also possible — such as occurred during World War II — for the economy to exceed its full employment level of output for a period of time.

3. Many people falsely assume that the categories of "the employed" and "the unemployed" account for everyone. In fact, some people are in neither category and therefore are not counted as members of the labour force. Movements in and out of the labour force can explain many otherwise puzzling changes in labour market statistics. For example, with a fixed population of adults, it is possible for both unemployment and employment to rise if the labour force grows.

4. How inflation affects the distribution of wealth and income depends crucially on whether or not the inflation is correctly anticipated. Learn to ask, whenever you are confronted with an inflation scenario: "what level of inflation had been anticipated?"

■ FILL-IN QUESTIONS

1. The main sources of economic growth are increases in the _____ or _____ of resource inputs.

2. The term "business cycle" refers to the recurrent _____ in the level of business activity around the long-run growth trend in the economy. The four phases of a typical business cycle are _____, _____, _____, and _____. The duration and magnitude of the fluctuation in output during the cycle (are, are not) _____ much the same from one cycle to another.

3. Production and employment in industries that produce consumer _____ goods and capital goods are especially susceptible to fluctuation during the business cycle because the purchase of these goods can be _____.

4. The three types of unemployment are:
  (a) _____
  (b) _____
  (c) _____

5. Frictional unemployment refers to that group of workers who are _____ for jobs or _____ to take jobs in the near future. Structural unemployment means the lack of job opportunities due to changes in product _____ or _____. Cyclical unemployment arises in the _____ - phase of the business cycle.

6. Full employment (does, does not) _____ - mean a zero unemployment rate. The full-employment unemployment rate is: (a) sometimes called the _____ rate of unemployment; (b) equals the total of the _____ and the _____ unemployment in the economy; (c) realized when the _____ unemployment in the economy is equal to zero and when the _____ output of the economy is equal to its _____ output; and (d) currently estimated to be about _____ to _____% in Canada.

7. When the economy achieves its natural rate of unemployment, the number of job seekers is (greater than, less than, equal to) _____ the number of job vacancies.

8. The unemployment rate is found by dividing _____ by the _____, and multiplying by 100%.

9. The cost to society of unemployment is the lost _____ that the unemployed resources could have produced. The GDP gap is equal to _____ GDP minus _____ GDP; and for every percentage point the unemployment rate rises above the natural rate of unemployment, the GDP gap will, according to Okun's law, (increase, decrease) _____ by _____%.

10. (a) An unemployed worker who is searching for work (is, is not) _____ classified as unemployed, and (is, is not) _____ classified as a member of the labour force. (b) An unemployed worker who has no job prospects and who is not actively seeking work (is, is not) _____ classified as unemployed, and (is, is not) _____ classified as a member of the labour force.

11. The burdens of unemployment are borne more heavily by (adult, teenage) _____ and (blue-collar, white-collar) _____ workers.

12. Inflation means a _____ in the general level of _____ in the economy. The rate of inflation in year 2001 is equal to the price index for year _____ less the price index for year _____ all divided by the price index for year _____, and multiplying by 100%.

13. If one's (real, nominal) _____ income rises by 10% over the same period that the price level rises by 7%, the percentage increase in _____ income would be 3%.

14. Inflation:
(a) hurts those whose money incomes are relatively (fixed, flexible) _____;
(b) penalizes savers when the inflation is (anticipated, unanticipated) _____, and benefits (borrowers, lenders) _____.

15. The redistributive effects of inflation are less severe when it is (anticipated, unanticipated) _____.

(a) Clauses in labour contracts that call for automatic adjustments of workers' income from the effects of inflation are called _____.
(b) The percentage increase in purchasing power that the lender receives from the borrower is the (real, nominal) _____ rate of interest; the percentage increase in money that the lender receives is the _____ rate of interest.

16. Real income measures the _____ power of nominal income. To obtain real income for a year divide the _____ income by a _____ index (expressed in hundredths) for that year. If nominal income increases at a faster rate than the price index, real income will _____; if the price index is increasing at a faster rate, real income will _____.

■ **PROBLEMS AND PROJECTS**

1. The solid line in the graph below shows twenty years of history of real output for some nation. The points labelled as years refer to the beginning of the years. The broken line shows potential real output for this nation.

Real GDP

(a) During this period the nation experienced six full business cycles. Identify the six peaks that marked the beginnings of these cycles.
(b) Which cycle lasted the longest from peak to peak?
(c) In which recession did real output fall the farthest?

(d)   Which recovery was the quickest?
(e)   What does the slope of the broken line indicate?
(f)   In what year was the output gap the largest? What does this indicate?
(g)   Were there any years when the output gap was negative? What does this indicate?
(h)   In what year was the level of cyclical unemployment probably highest? Why?

2. In the following table are Canadian labour force statistics for 1989 and 1990. (Numbers of persons are in thousands.)

	Year	
	1989	1990
Noninstitutionalized population (15+)	20,141	20,430
Labour force	13,503	13,688
Not in labour force	_____	_____
Employed	_____	12,486
Unemployed	1,108	_____
Unemployment rate (%)	_____	_____

(a)   Fill in the missing entries in the table.
(b)   How is it possible that both employment and unemployment increased in 1990?
(c)   Which year, 1989 or 1990, seems more likely to have been a year of recession?
(d)   Why is the task of maintaining full employment over the years more than just a problem of finding jobs for those who happen to be unemployed at any given time?

3. Janice consumes only one good, "Pepsi," and measures her purchasing power in terms of litres of "Pepsi."
(a)   At the beginning of the year when "Pepsi" was $1 a litre Janice loaned $100 interest free for one year to a friend. During the course of the year the price of "Pepsi" increased to $1.25.
(1) How many litres of "Pepsi" did Janice lend to her friend?
(2) How many litres of "Pepsi" were returned to Janice when the loan was paid back?
(3) By how much did the unanticipated inflation reduce Janice's wealth?
(b)   Suppose that Janice knew that the price of "Pepsi" would increase to $1.25. What nominal interest rate would she charge in order to keep the purchasing power of the loan constant?
(c)   Suppose that Janice wants to receive a 3% increase in purchasing power from the loan.

Given that she knows that the price of "Pepsi" will increase to $1.25, how much money must she receive when the loan is repaid? What nominal interest rate will she charge?

4. The nation whose GDP data appears in the following table had a natural rate of unemployment of 5% throughout the three years shown.

Year	Potential Real GDP	Actual Real GDP	Real GDP Gap
1994	600	600	_____
1995	618	_____	28
1996	630	_____	_____

(a)   In 1994 the nation's real GDP gap was ___, and the unemployment rate was _____%.
(b)   In 1995 actual real GDP was _____, and the unemployment rate must have been (above, below) _____ the natural rate of 5%.
(c)   Suppose that in 1996 the nation had 7% unemployment. By Okun's law, actual real GDP must have been approximately _____% below potential real GDP. Therefore, the real GDP gap was about _____, and actual real GDP was about _____.

5. The following table shows the price index in the economy at the end of four different years.

Year	Price Index	Rate of Inflation
1	100.00	
2	112.00	12 %
3	123.20	10 %
4	129.36	5 %

(a)   Compute and enter in the table the rates of inflation in years 2, 3, and 4.
(b)   Employing the "rule of 70," how many years would it take for the price level to double at each of these three inflation rates?
(c)   If nominal income increased by 15% from year 1 to year 2, what was the approximate percentage change in real income?
(d)   If nominal income was $25,000 in year 2, what was real income (measured in year 1 $)?
(e)   If the nominal interest rate was 14% to borrow money from year 1 to year 2, what was the approximate real rate of interest over that period?

6. Mr. Diamond drove a milk truck for Island Dairies from 1963, when his wage was $1.50 per hour, until his retirement in 1991, when his wage rate was $10.00 per hour. If the CPI was 25 in 1963 and 125 in 1991, did his real wage increase or decrease over these years, and by how much?

7. The Atlantic Bank lends Ms. Theberge $100,000 at a nominal interest rate of 11%. Both she and the bank expect that this will yield a real interest rate of 8%.
 (a) What inflation rate do the bank and Theberge expect?
 (b) Suppose that inflation turns out to be 5%. What is the error in the inflation prediction, what does the error do to the real interest rate, and to whose benefit is this surprise?

■ **TRUE-FALSE**

$8\% = 11\% - 3\%$

Circle T if the statement is true, F if it is false.

1. The long-term trend of economic growth in Canada has been interrupted by periods of unemployment and recession. **(T)** F

2. The business cycle is best defined as alternating periods of increases and decreases in the rate of inflation in the economy. T **(F)**

3. Individual business cycles tend to be of roughly equal duration and intensity. T **(F)**

4. Not all changes that occur in output and employment in the economy are due to the business cycle. T F

5. One reason for structural unemployment is a mismatch between worker skills and the skills required to fill vacant jobs. **(T)** F

6. Frictionally unemployed workers find it difficult to relocate or retrain to qualify for available jobs. T **(F)**

7. Cyclical unemployment is sometimes termed deficient-demand unemployment. **(T)** F

8. Full employment means zero unemployment. T **(F)**

9. The full-employment unemployment rate is equal to the total of the frictional and structural unemployment rates. T **(F)**

10. If unemployment in the economy is at its natural rate, the actual and potential outputs of the economy are equal. **(T)** F

11. The natural rate of unemployment in the Canadian economy has remained a constant 6% of the labour force since the 1950s. T **(F)**

12. At the natural rate of unemployment, the number of job vacancies is equal to the number of job seekers. **(T)** F

13. It is possible for the unemployment rate and the number of people employed to rise at the same time. **(T)** F

14. By not counting discouraged workers as unemployed, the official unemployment data tends to overstate the unemployment rate. T F

15. If some people who report themselves as "unemployed" are employed in the underground economy, the reported unemployment rate may be overstated. T **(F)**

16. The economy's GDP gap is measured by deducting actual GDP from potential GDP. T F

17. An economy cannot reach an actual real GDP level higher than its potential real GDP. T **(F)**

18. Teenagers, because they will work for lower wages, have a lower unemployment rate than persons 25 years of age and older. T **(F)**

19. The economic costs of cyclical unemployment are the goods and services that are not produced. T F

20. If over a one year interval the consumer price index rises from 114.0 to 119.5, the rate of inflation is 5.5%. T F

21. If the price level increases by 10% each year, the price level will double every ten years. T F

22. If the rate of inflation exceeds the percent rise in nominal income, real income will drop. T F

$$\frac{119.5 - 114.0}{114.0}$$

23. Inflation lowers the living standard of those individuals living on a fixed nominal income. **T F**

24. Unanticipated deflation would benefit creditors (lenders) and hurt debtors (borrowers). **T F**

25. The real interest rate equals the nominal interest rate plus the expected rate of inflation. **T F**

26. Whether the inflation is anticipated or unanticipated, the effects of inflation on the distribution of income are much the same. **T F**

27. The redistribution impact of inflation is somewhat reduced by the fact that many individuals simultaneously gain and lose from inflation. **T F**

■ **MULTIPLE-CHOICE**

Circle the letter that corresponds to the best answer.

1. Which one of the following is not one of the four phases of an idealized business cycle?
  (a) inflation
  (b) recession
  (c) recovery
  (d) trough

2. At an average annual growth rate of 4%, the Canadian economy would double its real GDP in about:
  (a) 10 years
  (b) 12 years
  (c) 18 years
  (d) 25 years

3. Which of the following factors must be considered when interpreting real GDP growth rates?
  (a) improved products and services
  (b) increased leisure time
  (c) increased environmental degradation
  (d) all of the above

4. Since 1945, the deepest recession experienced in Canada occurred in:
  (a) 1954
  (b) 1973
  (c) 1982
  (d) 1991

5. Production and employment in which of the following industries would be least affected by a recession?
  (a) dairy products
  (b) furniture
  (c) factory equipment
  (d) construction

6. A worker who loses her job because her job is computerized is an example of:
  (a) frictional unemployment
  (b) structural unemployment
  (c) cyclical unemployment
  (d) disguised unemployment

7. A worker who has quit one job and is taking two weeks off before reporting to a new job is an example of:
  (a) frictional unemployment
  (b) structural unemployment
  (c) cyclical unemployment
  (d) disguised unemployment

8. Insufficient aggregate demand results in:
  (a) frictional unemployment
  (b) structural unemployment
  (c) cyclical unemployment
  (d) disguised unemployment

9. The unemployment rate is computed as a ratio of the number unemployed over:
  (a) the labour force population
  (b) the labour force
  (c) the number employed
  (d) total population

10. If there are 150 people in the labour force, and the unemployment rate is 10%, the number of employed workers in the economy is:
  (a) 120
  (b) 135
  (c) 125
  (d) 130

11. The labour force data collected by Statistics Canada have been criticized because:
  (a) part-time workers are counted as if they are fully-employed
  (b) discouraged workers are treated as a part of the civilian labour force
  (c) part-time workers are not included in the labour force
  (d) none of the above

12. The full-employment unemployment rate in the economy has been achieved when:
(a) frictional unemployment is zero
(b) structural unemployment is zero
(c) cyclical unemployment is zero
(d) the natural rate of unemployment is zero

13. Which of the following could increase Canada's natural rate of unemployment?
(a) increased participation of women and teenagers in the Canadian labour force
(b) increases in employment insurance benefits in Canada
(c) increases in the legal minimum wage
(d) all of the above

14. What does an increase in the GDP gap indicate?
(a) potential output has decreased
(b) real output has fallen compared to nominal output
(c) the natural rate of employment has decreased
(d) actual output has decreased compared to potential output

15. Okun's law predicts that when the actual unemployment rate is two percentage points above the natural rate of unemployment, the GDP gap will equal:
(a) 1% of the potential GDP
(b) 3% of the potential GDP
(c) 4% of the potential GDP
(d) 5% of the potential GDP

16. If the GDP gap were equal to 6% of the potential GDP, the actual unemployment rate would exceed the natural rate of unemployment by:
(a) two percentage points
(b) three percentage points
(c) four percentage points
(d) five percentage points

17. The rate of unemployment is lowest among the following groups:
(a) the uneducated
(b) teenagers
(c) workers 15-24 years of age
(d) workers 25 years of age and older

18. During periods of inflation the purchasing power of money:

(a) rises
(b) falls
(c) stays constant
(d) could rise or fall

19. If a person's nominal income increases by 8% while the price level increases by 10%, the person's real income will have:
(a) increased by 2%
(b) increased by 18%
(c) decreased by 18%
(d) decreased by 2%

20. If no inflation were anticipated, a bank would be willing to lend a business firm $10 million at an annual interest of 8%. If the rate of inflation were expected to be 6%, the bank would charge the firm an annual interest rate of:
(a) 2%
(b) 6%
(c) 8%
(d) 14%

21. Of the following, who would not be hurt by inflation?
(a) those living on company pensions that are fixed in money terms
(b) those who find prices rising more rapidly than their money incomes
(c) those who have loaned money at fixed interest rates
(d) those who took out mortgage loans prior to the inflation

22. A cost-of-living adjustment clause (COLA) in a union contract:
(a) states that the last worker hired will be the first one fired in a cyclical downturn
(b) guarantees a worker a stated percentage of regular income during layoffs
(c) adjusts worker incomes automatically to inflation
(d) provides early retirement benefits for long-term employees in case of permanent layoffs

23. Which of the following is not often associated with hyperinflation?
(a) war or its aftermath
(b) rising output in the economy
(c) the hoarding of goods and speculation
(d) a halt to the use of money as both a medium of exchange and a standard of value

24. Which of the following is not among the inefficiencies caused by even a mild inflation?

(a) households spend more time acquiring information about prices

(b) businesses incur more costs in updating their prices

(c) households begin holding larger quantities of cash

(d) all of the above are among the inefficiencies created by inflation

■ DISCUSSION QUESTIONS

1. During the last four decades, what is the historical record of the Canadian economy with respect to economic growth, full employment, and price-level stability?

2. Define the business cycle. Why do some economists prefer the term "business fluctuation" to "business cycle"? Describe the four phases of an idealized cycle.

3. What, in the opinion of most economists, is the main cause of most business cycles?

4. Why are some industries particularly susceptible to downturn when the economy goes into recession? Can you give an example of an industry in your area that would be hit particularly hard, and one that would be affected only slightly?

5. Distinguish between frictional, structural, and cyclical unemployment.

6. When is there full employment in the Canadian economy? (Answer in terms of the unemployment rate, the actual and potential output of the economy, and the markets for labour.)

7. How is the unemployment rate measured in Canada? What criticisms have been made of Statistics Canada's method of determining the unemployment rate?

8. What is the economic cost of unemployment, and how is the cost measured? What does Okun's law say is the relationship between the unemployment rate and the cost of unemployment?

9. What groups in the economy tend to bear the burdens of unemployment, and what do you think are the reasons for their high unemployment rates?

10. What is inflation and how is the rate of inflation measured? If the price of gasoline rises, is this inflation? If the price of computers falls, is this deflation?

11. What is real income and how can real income be obtained from nominal income figures?

12. What groups benefit from and what groups are hurt by inflation? How do the effects of inflation depend on whether it is anticipated or unanticipated?

13. What are the different ways in which inflation can affect the level of real output?

14. How have Canada's unemployment rate and inflation rate compared with those for other industrialized nations in the 1990s?

15. When there is a sharp rise or fall in the average price of stocks, what does this imply for the economy as a whole?

■ ANSWERS

FILL-IN QUESTIONS

1. supplies, productivity

2. fluctuations, recession, trough, recovery, peak, are not

3. durable, postponed

4. (a) frictional unemployment; (b) structural unemployment; (c) cyclical unemployment

5. searching, waiting, demand, technology, recession

6. does not; (a) natural; (b) frictional, structural; (c) cyclical, actual, potential; (d) 6 to 7

7. equal to

8. the number of persons unemployed, labour force

9. output, potential, actual, increase, 2

10. (a) is, is; (b) is not, is not

11. teenage, blue-collar

12. rise, prices, 2001, 2000, 2000

13. nominal, real

14. (a) fixed; (b) unanticipated, borrowers

15. anticipated; (a) cost-of-living adjustments (COLA); (b) real, nominal

16. purchasing, nominal, price, increase, decrease

PROBLEMS AND PROJECTS

1. (a) 1981, 1984, 1988, 1991, 1994, 1996, 1999; (b) 1984 to 1988; (c) 1994 to 1996; (d) 1994 to 1996; (e) trend of growth in potential GDP; (f) 1995; economy was very far below potential; (g) parts of each year from 1996 to 1999; economy was temporarily operating above its normal full employment potential; (h) end of 1995 when the gap was the largest.

2. (a) The following figures complete the table:
1989: 6638, 12,395, 8.2%; 1990: 6742, 1202, 8.8%;
(b) The labour force increased more than employment increased; (c) Probably 1990. Because the unemployment rate was higher than in 1989, the output gap was likely also larger, unless the NRU had increased substantially from 1989 to 1990; (d) The number of people looking for work is continually expanding, and the structure of the demand for labour is continually changing.

3. (a) (1) 100 litres; (2) $100/$1.25 per litre = 80 litres: (3) 20 litres; (b) 25%; (c) $128.75; 28.75%

4. (a) 0, 5% (the natural rate); (b) 590, above; (c) 4; 25.2, 604.8

5. (a) 12, 10, 5; (b) approximately: 6, 7, 14; (c) 3%; (d) $22,321 (in year 1 $); (e) 2%

6. His real wage in 1963 was $1.50/.25 = $6.00 (in base year $). His real wage in 1991 was $10/1.25 = $8.00 (in base year $). His real wage increased by $2.00, or 33%.

7. (a) 3%; (b) the prediction is low by 2%; the effective real interest rate falls by 2%, to 6%; Ms. Theberge (the borrower) benefits.

TRUE-FALSE

1. T
2. F the increases and decreases are in real GDP, not the inflation rate
3. F they vary significantly
4. T some is the underlying long-run growth trend
5. T

6. F workers in this situation are suffering structural unemployment
7. T there is not enough demand during a recession
8. F there is always some frictional and structural unemployment
9. T this is also known as the natural rate (NRU)
10. T
11. T it has not remained constant over that period
12. T in other words, there is not a shortage of jobs
13. T with an expansion in the labour force
14. F for this reason, it tends to understate the problem
15. T there would be less unemployed than reported
16. T
17. F it can for brief periods (WWII, for example)
18. F they have a higher rate of unemployment
19. T
20. F a rise of 5.5 from a starting point of 114.0 is an increase of only 4.8%
21. F by the rule of 70, it would take about 7 years
22. T
23. T
24. T the creditors would be repaid money that has a higher purchasing power than expected
25. F the nominal interest rate minus the expected inflation rate
26. F when inflation is anticipated people take steps to hedge (protect themselves)
27. T for example, some people may lose as wage-earners, but gain as debtors

MULTIPLE-CHOICE

1. (a)
2. (c) 70/4 = approx 18
3. (d)
4. (c)
5. (a) purchases of consumer nondurables are not easily postponable
6. (b) there is no longer a match between her skill and the skill demanded in the labour market
7. (a)
8. (c)
9. (b)
10. (b) 150 - 15
11. (a) when, in fact, many part-time workers desire full-time work
12. (c)
13. (d) all would tend to make jobs harder to find, or make people able to remain unemployed longer
14. (d)
15. (c) 2% of GDP per 1% of unemployment
16. (b)
17. (d)
18. (b)
19. (a)
20. (d) the real interest rate plus the expected inflation premium

21. (d) these people would benefit from mortgage payment of lower real value than expected because their nominal interest rate did not include the correct inflation premium

22. (c)

23. (b) hyperinflation invariably reduces output

24. (c) if anything, people hold less cash in order to avoid the loss of purchasing power caused by inflation

CHAPTER 8

Building the Aggregate Expenditures Model

Chapter 7's discussion of business cycles covered the consequences of fluctuations in output and employment, but said very little about how the level of GDP is determined in the first place, and why the GDP fluctuates. This chapter tackles these remaining questions using the aggregate expenditures model, beginning first with the very simplified "private closed economy" model. Later in the chapter, an international sector and a government sector are added to complete the model.

The basic premise of the aggregate expenditures model is that the economy's output level depends only on the demand for output because the economy is assumed to have enough excess production capacity and unemployed workers to increase real output without driving prices up. In the "private closed economy" model demand has only two components: consumption and investment. The main determinant of consumption spending is the level of disposable income. The consumption schedule shows a positive relationship between consumption and disposable income, with the slope defining the marginal propensity to consume. Changes in the level of wealth, expectations, taxation, or household debt can shift the consumption schedule.

Investment expenditures (or purchases of capital goods) depend on the rate of return that business firms expect from investment projects and on the real rate of interest they have to pay for the use of money. Firms strive for profits, so they undertake only those investments having expected rates of return at least as high as the real rate of interest. This rule implies that the lower the real rate of interest, the larger will be the level of investment expenditures. The inverse relationship between the real interest rate and the level of investment spending is called the investment demand curve. Several other determinants of investment spending can shift the investment demand curve and cause investment expenditures to be a relatively volatile component of GDP.

The equilibrium level of output is that output the production of which will create planned aggregate spending just sufficient to purchase that much output. At this point, the total of consumption and planned investment equals the amount of real GDP. This equilibrium point can be located using either a table or a graph.

If demand for output does not match the level of output produced, the economy is in disequilibrium. Individual businesses will experience undesired changes in inventory levels, causing them to change their production levels, in turn leading to a change in the nation's aggregate output.

A shift in the consumption schedule or the investment schedule will lead to a change in equilibrium GDP, and the change in GDP is larger than the initial expenditure change itself! This is the multiplier effect. An initial change in spending by households or firms causes incomes to change for others in the economy; this in turn leads them to alter their expenditures, etc. The smaller is the marginal propensity to save, the larger is the multiplier, and therefore the change in GDP.

The closed economy model is extended to an open economy model by adding exports and imports. Exports are treated as a constant addition to the demand for Canada's output, whereas imports reduce the demand for our output because they represent expenditures on goods produced in other countries. Usually we think in terms of net exports (X_n), calculated as exports minus imports. The X_n schedule depends on the exchange rate between the Canadian currency and foreign currencies, tariffs, and on GDP levels in Canada and abroad.

Equilibrium GDP in the open economy model is found as in the closed economy model: where real GDP is equal to aggregate expenditures. The difference is that aggregate expenditures now include net exports; so equilibrium real GDP will equal $C + I_g + X_n$. The multiplier effect is also different in this version of the model. Because import spending is a leakage from the flow of domestic income, the open-economy multiplier is smaller than the simple multiplier in the closed economy model.

The final extension of the model takes us from a private (no government) open economy to a mixed open economy that has a public sector. This change is made in two steps. First, government spending (G) is added as an extra injection of aggregate expenditures. Second, taxes (T) are added as a new leakage from spending. The leakage of income into taxes reduces disposable income, consumption, saving, and imports. The revised expression for equilibrium, where aggregate expenditures equal output, is: $GDP = C + I_g + X_n + G$. If, as we assume in this chapter, taxes are levied as a lump sum, the open economy multiplier applies to this model also.

The economy's equilibrium GDP level need not match the full-employment level of GDP. Typically the economy will have either a recessionary gap (GDP is below full employment and there is cyclical unemployment) or an inflationary gap (GDP is above full employment and unemployment is below the natural rate). This insight was at the heart of John Maynard Keynes' *General Theory*, an important economics book written in response to the Great Depression. Prior to that time, economists believed that the economy was inherently stable, with market forces ensuring that the economy would automatically reach its output potential and provide employment for all those who were willing and able to work. This conclusion was based on Say's Law which held that supply creates its own demand. However, very high unemployment and very large recessionary gaps suffered by many nations during the Great Depression cast severe doubt on the market economy's self-regulating forces and opened the door for new theories, such as Keynes' aggregate expenditures model.

■ CHAPTER LEARNING OBJECTIVES

In this chapter you will learn:
□ The factors that determine consumption expenditure and saving.
□ The factors that determine investment spending.

□ How equilibrium GDP is determined in a closed economy without a government sector.
□ About the effects of the multiplier on changes in equilibrium GDP.
□ How international trade affects equilibrium output.
□ How adding the public sector affects equilibrium output.
□ The distinction between equilibrium versus full employment GDP.
□ The limitations of the aggregate expenditures model.

■ CHAPTER OUTLINE

1. Our initial aggregate expenditures model for "a private closed economy" is based on several assumptions: (1) the economy is closed (no imports or exports); (2) there is no government sector involved in spending or taxation; (3) all saving is personal saving by households; (4) depreciation is zero. Under these assumptions: (1) consumption and investment are the only expenditure components in the model, and (2) all income or output measures (GDP, NI, PI, DI) are equivalent.

2. Output and employment are directly related to the level of aggregate expenditures because the economy has excess production capacity and unemployed labour. The level of total expenditures is determined by the levels of consumption and investment expenditures.

3. Consumption is the largest component of aggregate expenditures; saving is disposable income not spent on consumer goods.
   (a) Disposable income, which equals GDP in this chapter, is the main determinant of both consumption and saving; both consumption and saving increase as income increases.
   (b) The consumption schedule shows the amounts households plan to spend for consumer goods at various levels of income, given a price level.
   (c) The saving schedule indicates the amounts households plan to save at different income levels, given a price level.
   (d) The average propensities to consume and to save and the marginal propensities to consume and to save can be computed from the consumption and saving schedules.

(1) The APC and the APS are the percentages of income spent for consumption and saved; and their sum is equal to 1.

(2) The MPC and the MPS are the percentages of **additional** income spent for consumption and saved; and their sum is equal to 1.

(e) Aside from income, several other determinants of consumption and saving can cause the consumption and saving schedules to change: wealth, expectations, household debt, and taxation.

(f) A change in the amount consumed (or saved) refers to a move from one point to another on a stable schedule, due to a change in disposable income. A change in consumption (or saving) refers to a shift in the schedule, due to a change in one of the non-income determinants. When these two schedules change, they normally change in opposite directions. These two schedules are normally very stable.

4. The two key determinants of the level of investment spending are the expected rate of return from the purchase of additional capital goods and the real rate of interest.

(a) The expected rate of return is higher the more revenues are expected to increase due to an investment, and lower the greater the cost of making an investment in capital goods.

(b) The rate of interest is the price paid for the use of the money capital needed to buy real capital. When the expected rate of return is greater (less) than the real rate of interest, a business will (will not) invest because the investment will be profitable (unprofitable).

(c) Therefore, the lower (higher) the real rate of interest, the greater (smaller) will be the level of investment spending in the economy; and the investment demand curve indicates this inverse relationship.

(d) Several non-interest-rate determinants of investment demand are: acquisition, maintenance, and operating costs; business taxes; technological change; the stock of capital goods on hand; and expectations. A change in any of these factors will shift the investment demand curve.

(e) The model in this chapter assumes investment to be independent of income, so the investment schedule is horizontal when plotted against real GDP.

(f) Because the five non-interest-rate determinants of investment are subject to sudden changes, investment spending fluctuates signifi-cantly. Shifts in any of these variables will shift the horizontal investment schedule.

5. The equilibrium level of real GDP can be determined and understood in several different ways.

(a) The equilibrium real GDP is the real GDP at which aggregate expenditures (consumption plus planned investment) equal the real GDP.

(b) In a graph, equilibrium is where the aggregate expenditures curve cuts the 45 degree line.

(c) Equilibrium is at the output level where saving and planned investment are equal.

(d) Equilibrium is at the output level where there are no unplanned changes in inventories.

6. If the GDP level is not at the equilibrium, market forces will tend to push the GDP back to equilibrium.

(a) If the level of GDP is below equilibrium:

(1) $C + I_g$ will exceed GDP, so planned spending exceeds production, causing a depletion of inventories.

(2) Planned investment will exceed saving, causing unplanned inventory decreases (so that actual investment equals saving).

(3) The unintended disinvestment through shrinking inventories will cause firms to increase production (up to equilibrium GDP).

(b) If the level of GDP is above equilibrium:

(1) GDP will exceed $C + I_g$, so production exceeds planned spending, causing an accumulation of inventories.

(2) Saving will exceed planned investment, causing unplanned inventory increases (so that actual investment equals saving).

(3) The unintended investment in rising inventories will cause firms to reduce output (until equilibrium GDP is reached).

7. A shift in the investment schedule or the consumption schedule will cause the equilibrium real GDP to change in the same direction, and by a larger amount than the initial change in spending. This is called the multiplier effect.

(a) The multiplier is equal to the ratio of the change in real GDP to the initial change in spending.

(b) The multiplier effect occurs because a change in spending by one person causes another person's income to change by the same amount. The initial rise in income causes the first person to spend a fraction, causing yet another person's income to rise, and their consumption to rise, and so on.

(c) The value of the simple multiplier is equal to the reciprocal of the marginal propensity to save: 1/MPS. A larger propensity to save implies a smaller multiplier.

(d) The significance of the multiplier is that small changes in the spending plans of business firms or households can trigger larger changes in equilibrium real GDP.

(e) If the economy has leakages other than savings, the simple multiplier is not applicable; we must use the complex multiplier which takes into account all leakages (such as taxes and imports).

8. In an open economy, exports (X) add to the nation's aggregate expenditures, and imports (M) subtract from the nation's aggregate expenditures.

(a) Aggregate expenditures now equal the sum of consumption spending, planned investment spending, and net exports (X_n) with $X_n = X - M$.

(b) Canada's imports are positively related to Canada's GDP, whereas our exports are positively related to GDP in other countries.

(c) An appreciation of the Canadian dollar will lead to increased imports and decreased exports. A depreciation of our dollar relative to foreign currencies will have the opposite effect.

(d) The net export schedule is a decreasing function of domestic GDP, with the marginal propensity to import (MPM) controlling the rate at which X_n falls as GDP rises.

(e) Because imports are related to the level of our GDP, the open economy multiplier will be smaller than the closed economy multiplier and its value equals 1/(MPS + MPM).

9. Equilibrium real GDP in an open economy occurs where the real GDP is equal to consumption plus planned investment plus net export spending: GDP = $C + I_g + X_n$

(a) By the leakages-injections approach, equilibrium occurs where $I_g + X = S + M$

(b) If net exports are negative (positive), the effect of net exports is to reduce (increase) Canada's equilibrium GDP.

(c) Any increase (decrease) in Canada's X_n will increase (decrease) our equilibrium real GDP with a multiplier effect.

(d) In the open economy model, Canada's GDP can change due to changes in prosperity levels abroad, changes in tariffs or quotas, or changes in exchange rates.

10. A public sector is added to the aggregate expenditures model under the following assumptions:

(a) Investment remains independent of GDP.

(b) Government spending levels do not affect private spending levels.

(c) Government's net tax revenues are derived entirely from personal taxes, so disposable income is less than GDP (though GDP = PI).

(d) The amount of taxes collected is fixed, regardless of GDP.

(e) The price level is constant.

11. Government purchases of goods and services (G) are an injection of spending that add to the aggregate expenditures schedule and increase equilibrium real GDP (with a multiplier effect).

12. Taxes (T) are a leakage of spending that reduce the aggregate expenditures schedule and decrease equilibrium real GDP. A change in the level of lump-sum taxes has a multiplier effect on GDP. Taxes cause disposable income (DI) to fall short of GDP, forcing households to reduce consumption, saving, and imports below what they would be in the absence of taxes.

13. Equilibrium real GDP in an open mixed economy occurs where real GDP equals the sum of consumption, planned investment, net export spending, and government purchases: GDP = $C + I_g + X_n + G$.

(a) By the leakages-injections approach, equilibrium is found where $I_g + X + G = S + M + T$.

(b) If G and T rise an equal amount, equilibrium GDP will rise by that same amount. Changes in government spending *directly* change aggregate expenditures by the full amount, whereas changes in taxation change aggregate expenditures only *indirectly* through the impact on disposable income. And because part of the change in DI is absorbed by changes in saving and imports, consumption changes by only a portion of the tax change.

(c) The balanced budget multiplier measures the ratio of the change in equilibrium real GDP to the change (in equal amounts) to both G and T. This multiplier equals 1.

14. The equilibrium level of real GDP can be below, above, or equal to, full-employment GDP.

(a) If equilibrium GDP is less than full-employment GDP, there is a recessionary gap.

The size of this gap is the amount by which the actual GDP is short of full-employment GDP.

(b) If equilibrium GDP is greater than full-employment GDP, there is an inflationary gap. The size of this gap is the amount by which the actual GDP exceeds full-employment GDP.

15. The concept of a recessionary gap can be illustrated with recent developments in the Japanese economy. In the 1980s the economy grew rapidly, and unemployment was exceptionally low. In the 1990s the Japanese saving rate remained high, but a collapse of investment spending meant that the injection of investment spending was insufficient to offset the leakage of saving. Thus, aggregate expenditures fell, and Japan's output dipped below its full-employment potential, creating cyclical unemployment and opening a recessionary gap.

16. The aggregate expenditures model has two key limitations (that will be dealt with in Chapter 10):

(a) The model does not show price-level changes.

(b) The model does not address cost-push inflation.

17. The Great Depression led to a revolution in macroeconomic theory.

(a) Classical economists believed that an economy in depression would automatically return to equilibrium of full employment, without any need for government policy intervention. These conclusions were based on Say's Law which states that supply creates its own demand. If there were an oversupply of goods (and an oversupply of labour), prices (and wages) would drop until the equilibrium was restored at full employment and potential output.

(b) During the Great Depression unemployment was so high and persistent that the classical conclusions were thrown into question.

(c) In his book, *The General Theory of Employment, Interest and Money*, John Maynard Keynes developed the aggregate expenditures model which rejected Say's Law and the classical theories. Keynes argued that while output creates enough income to purchase all of the output, there is no guarantee that all of the income will be spent on the current output because savings and investment decisions are not necessarily coordinated. Secondly, wages and prices are downwardly inflexible, so recessions may be deep and prolonged. Overall, Keynes did not believe the market economy to be capable of stabilizing itself.

■ TERMS AND CONCEPTS

actual investment	investment demand curve
aggregate expenditures schedule	investment schedule
average propensity to consume	leakage
	lump-sum tax
average propensity to save	marginal propensity to consume
balanced-budget multiplier	marginal propensity to import
break-even income	marginal propensity to save
consumption schedule	
equilibrium GDP	multiplier
expected rate of return	planned investment
45-degree line	recessionary gap
inflationary gap	saving schedule
injection	unplanned changes in inventory
	wealth effect

■ HINTS AND TIPS

1. Practise working with the concepts of this chapter from a variety of angles: drawing graphs, explaining in words, working with numerical tables. If your instructor favours a more algebraic approach than this text presents, then he/she may also give you some additional algebraic examples.

2. A key feature of the graphs for the aggregate expenditures model is the "45 degree line." The line is actually 45 degrees only if the measurement scale is identical on both the vertical and horizontal axes. If the scales differ, the line showing points where expenditures equal GDP will have a different angle.

3. The distinction between actual and planned investment is key to understanding equilibrium. Actual investment includes both planned and unplanned investment. Unplanned investment refers to unplanned changes in inventories when businesses have based their production plans on faulty forecasts of what amounts their customers will buy.

4. Although the model becomes more complex as the international sector and then the public sector is added, the basic mechanics of the model do not change. Equilibrium GDP is always found where

aggregate expenditures equal output, and there is always a multiplier effect when any of the expenditures schedules shift.

5. The multiplier is a crucial concept. It is simply the ratio of the change in equilibrium real GDP to the initial change in expenditures that caused the equilibrium to change. Play with numerical examples until you have a good grasp. Be sure you understand intuitively why a higher rate of leakages creates a smaller multiplier.

6. When faced with questions about the aggregate expenditure model — whether in this study guide or on an exam! — take time to assess which version of the model is indicated by the question. Is the economy open or closed? Is there a government sector? Are taxes fixed relative to income?

■ **FILL-IN QUESTIONS**

1. The first model in this chapter is based on four assumptions: a(n) (open, closed) _____ economy; no _____ or _____ by government; all saving is (personal, business) _____; and depreciation is _____. These assumptions imply that: the only relevant expenditure components are _____ and _____; and different measures of _____ can be treated as equivalent.

2. Because there is assumed to be _____ production capacity and _____ labour, the level of output in the economy depends directly on the level of _____ expenditures, and changes in the level of output (do, do not) _____ change the price level.

3. The most important determinant of consumption and of saving is the level of _____; and both consumption and saving are (directly, inversely) _____ related to this determinant.

4. A shift of the entire consumption schedule is referred to as a change in _____; but a movement from one point on a given consumption schedule to another point on the schedule is referred to as a change in _____.

5. Investment is defined as spending for additional _____ goods. The amount of investment spending depends on the expected rate of _____ and on the real rate of _____.

6. A firm will invest in more real capital if the expected rate of return on the investment project is (greater, less) _____ than the real rate of interest the firm must pay for the use of money capital.

7. Five non-interest-rate determinants of investment demand are: (a) _____, _____, and _____ costs; (b) _____ taxes; (c) _____ change; (d) stock of _____; and (e) _____.

8. The demand for new capital goods tends to fluctuate considerably because of the _____ of capital goods and the variability of _____ of profits.

9. In a private closed economy, the equilibrium level of real GDP is the real GDP at which:
(a) aggregate _____ equal real _____; (b) real GDP equals _____ plus _____; (c) the aggregate expenditures schedule or curve intersects the _____ line.

10. If:
(a) aggregate expenditures exceed real output, saving is (greater, less) _____ than planned investment, there is unplanned (investment, disinvestment) _____ in inventories, and real GDP will (rise, fall) _____.
(b) aggregate expenditures are less than real output, savings is _____ than planned investment, there is unplanned _____ in inventories, and real GDP will _____.
(c) aggregate expenditures are equal to real output, saving is _____ planned investment, unplanned investment in inventories is _____, and real GDP will _____.

11. The multiplier is the ratio of the change in _____ to an initial change in spending. When the initial change in spending is multiplied by the multiplier, the value equals the change in _____.

12. The multiplier effect rests on two facts:
(a) an initial increase in spending will increase the _____ of households in the economy; and
(b) this results in an increase in households' _____ spending equal to some _____ of the increase in income.

13. When a nation is able to export and import goods and services, but there is no government sector:

   (a) its net exports equal its _____ minus its _____.

   (b) In an open economy:

     (1) aggregate expenditures are equal to consumption plus planned investment plus _____;

     (2) the equilibrium real GDP is found where output equals _____.

14. The demand abroad for Canadian exports depends upon the GDP in (Canada, other countries) _____, whereas the demand for Canadian imports depends upon the GDP in _____.

15. An appreciation of the Canadian dollar generally causes Canada's imports to (increase, decrease) _____, and causes Canada's exports to _____.

16. The marginal propensity to import is defined as the ratio of the change in _____ over the change in _____.

17. If exports are constant and imports increase with an increasing domestic GDP, the open economy multiplier will be (greater than, less than) _____ the closed economy multiplier and is given by 1/(_____ + _____).

18. Equal increases in taxes and government purchases will (increase, decrease) _____ real GDP by an amount (greater than, less than, equal to) _____ the change in taxes and government purchases. This result is called the _____ multiplier, and the value of this multiplier is _____.

19. According to classical economic theory, if the economy were in recession, wages and prices of goods and services would tend to (rise, fall) _____ and thereby automatically restore the economy to the _____ level of output.

20. Another element of classical economics was _____ Law, which stated that _____ creates its own _____.

■ **PROBLEMS AND PROJECTS**

1. Following is a consumption schedule. Assume taxes and transfers are zero and that all saving is personal saving.

GDP	C	S	APC	APS
$1500	$1540	$ -40	1.027	-0.027
1600	1620	-20	1.03	-0.013
1700	1700	0	1.00	0
1800	1780	20	0.989	0.011
1900	1860	40		

   (a) Compute saving at each of the first three levels of GDP listed.

   (b) Compute consumption at GDP = $1800.

   (c) The break-even level of income (GDP) is: $ 1700 .

   (d) The marginal propensity to consume (MPC) between GDP = $1500 and $1600 equals $ 80 divided by $ 100 = 0.80 . Between GDP = $1600 and $1700 MPC equals $ 20 divided by $ 100 = .20 .

   (e) The marginal propensity to save (MPS) between GDP = $1500 and $1600 equals $ 20 divided by $ 100 = .20 . Between GDP = $1600 and $1700 MPS equals $ 20 divided by $ 100 = .20 .

   (f) Since the MPC is constant, the consumption level at GDP = $1900 is $ 1860 , and saving level is $ 40 .

   (g) Given the value of APC at GDP = $1500, APS at this level of income is -0.027 .

   (h) Given the value of APS at GDP = $1600, APC at this level of income is 1.013 .

   (i) Compute the APC and APS values for the remaining income levels.

   (j) As income rises, the APC (rises, falls) _____, and the APS _____.

2. This question is based on the data plotted in the graph that follows.

   (a) When GDP = 0, the level of consumption is _____.

   (b) The MPC = _____.

   (c) The break-even level of income is at GDP = _____.

   (d) When GDP = 0, the level of saving is ____.

   (e) The MPS = _____.

   (f) At the break-even level of income, the level of saving is _____.

(g) Plot the savings schedule in the lower panel of the following graph.

(h) Based on your answers in (a) through (g), fill in the parameters in the consumption and saving equations shown below the graphs.

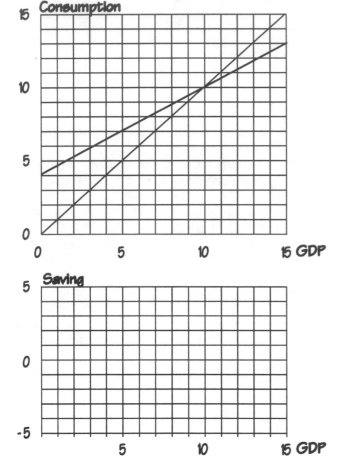

C = ___ + ___ GDP

S = ___ + ___ GDP

3. Indicate in the space next to each of the following events whether the event will increase (+), decrease (−), or not change (0) the consumption schedule and the saving schedule.

(a) Consumers begin to expect that prices will be higher in the future.   **c:** ☐ **s:** ☐

(b) Falling real estate prices reduce households' wealth.   **c:** ☐ **s:** ☐

(c) A rise in the actual level of disposable income.   **c:** ☐ **s:** ☐

(d) The government suddenly increases income tax rates.   **c:** ☐ **s:** ☐

(e) A rise in the level of household credit card debt.   **c:** ☐ **s:** ☐

4. A corporation's investment opportunities are shown in the following schedule. (In the economy as a whole, each firm has a similar schedule of its own.) For each project is given the dollar cost, and the expected rate of return.

Project	Investment Amount ($)	Expected Rate of Return
A: new warehouse	12 million	8%
B: new delivery vehicles	10 million	9%
C: computer upgrades	3 million	11%
D: office expansion	5 million	10%
E: retail store renovation	8 million	7%

(a) From the data indicate (by letters) which projects are profitable for the firm to invest in at each possible real interest rate, and then find the total amount of investment spending that would be undertaken at each of the real interest rates given.

Real Interest Rate (%)	Profitable Projects	Investment Amount (million $)
12	_____	_____
11	_____	_____
10	_____	_____
9	_____	_____
8	_____	_____
7	_____	_____

(b) Graph the data in the table completed in (a) as an investment demand curve. Plot the real rate of interest on the vertical axis and the amount of planned investment on the horizontal axis.

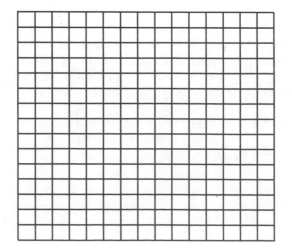

(c) The graph and the table show that the relation between the real rate of interest and the amount of investment spending is _____. When the real rate of interest increases, investment will (increase, decrease) _____.

5. Indicate in the box to the right of each event whether the event would tend to increase (+) or decrease (-) the investment demand curve. If the event does not shift the curve, indicate (0).

(a) An increase in the price of energy used for operating factory machinery. ☐

(b) A new expectation of higher taxes on business profits. ☐

(c) A mild recession. ☐

(d) A belief that the economy is due for a period of "slow" consumer demand. ☐

(e) Decreasing costs in the construction industry. ☐

(f) A period of a high level of investment spending that has resulted in productive capacity in excess of the current demand for goods and services. ☐

6. (a) The table below shows consumption and saving at some levels of real GDP. The equation for the consumption schedule is: $C = 10 + .80$ GDP. Planned investment expenditures are fixed at $I_g = 20$. Complete the table that follows, indicating consumption (C), saving (S), investment (I_g), aggregate expenditure ($C+I_g$), unplanned investment (UI) with unplanned accumulation shown by + and unplanned disinvestment by -, and the tendency of GDP to rise (+) or fall (-).

Real GDP	C	S	I_g	$C+I_g$	UI	GDP Change (+/-)
0	___	___	___	___	___	___
50	___	___	___	___	___	___
100	___	___	___	___	___	___
150	___	___	___	___	___	___
200	___	___	___	___	___	___
250	___	___	___	___	___	___

(b) The equilibrium real GDP will be $_____, because at this income level, real GDP and _____ are equal, or savings and _____ are equal.

(c) For the given data, the value of the MPC = _____ and the value of MPS = _____.

7. Assume a closed economy with no public sector. The marginal propensity to consume is 0.6. Suppose that this economy experiences an increase of $10 in planned investment because businesses become more optimistic about future profits. Work through the rounds of the multiplier effect to fill in the table below.

	Change in income	Change in C	Change in S
Increase in I_g	$10	____	____
2nd round	____	____	____
3rd round	____	____	____
4th round	____	____	____
5th round	____	____	____
all other rounds	____	____	____
Total	____	____	____

8. The table below shows consumption levels for various GDP levels in an economy that has no foreign trade or government sector. The table shows two columns of values for planned investment: (I_g and I_g^*).

GDP	C	I_g	AE	I_g^*	AE*
100	120	30	150	55	175
200	195	30	225	55	250
300	270	30	300	55	325
400	345	30	375	55	400
500	420	30	450	55	475
600	495	30	525	55	550

(a) Assuming planned investment is equal to I_g, complete the aggregate expenditures column labeled AE.

(b) Equilibrium GDP for this investment level is 300.

(c) Assuming planned investment is equal to I_g^*, complete the aggregate expenditures column labeled AE*.

(d) Equilibrium GDP for this investment level is 400.

(e) When planned investment rises by 25, equilibrium GDP changes by 100. Therefore the simple multiplier is $100 / 25 = 4$.

9. Suppose that households spend 80% of each dollar of disposable income on consumption goods, imports are 10% of disposable income, and personal taxes take 25% of each dollar of personal income.

(a)   For each $100 of new personal income, $_____ goes to taxes, and the other $_____ goes to new disposable income.
(b)   Of the $_____ in new disposable income, $_____ goes to consumption, and the other $_____ goes to saving.
(c)   Of the $_____ in new consumption, $_____ is spent on imported goods.
(d)   In summary, of the $100 of new income, the total new leakages is $_____ + $_____ + $_____ = $_____.
(e)   The fraction of the new $100 that leaks is _____, so the complex multiplier is 1/_____ = _____.
(f)   Given this multiplier value, a new injection of $1 would raise equilibrium GDP by $_____.

10. The tables below pertain to an open economy with a public sector. The full-employment level of GDP is $450. The consumption and import data are shown in the tables. At all GDP levels, taxes are $50, exports are $50, and government purchases are $55. Planned investment is given by the equation $I_g = 60 - i$, where i is the interest rate in percent. At present $i = 20$.
(a)   Complete the blank columns in the first table.
(b)   Find the equilibrium GDP by finding where GDP equals aggregate expenditures.
(c)   Confirm your result in (b) by proving that leakages equal injections at this GDP level.
(d)   At the equilibrium, does this economy have a recessionary gap or an inflationary gap, and what size is the gap?
(e)   What is the value of the multiplier for this economy?
(f)   If the interest rate falls from 20% to 14%, what is the change in I_g, and according to the multiplier effect, what is the change in GDP?
(g)   If foreigners decreased by $12 their purchases from this economy, what will be the impact on equilibrium income, according to the multiplier value found in (e)?
(h)   What will the new gap be after the change in interest rate, and after the drop in purchases by foreigners?
(i)   How much, and in what direction, would government purchases need to change in order to close the gap calculated in (h)?
(j)   Confirm your conclusion in (i) by completing the second table. To start, remember to change Ig and X from their values in the original table.

GDP	T	DI	C	S	Ig	X	M	Xn	G	AE
$400			$340					$40		
450			380					45		
500			420					50		
550			460					55		
600			500					60		

GDP	T	DI	C	S	Ig	X	M	Xn	G	AE
$400			$340					$40		
450			380					45		
500			420					50		
550			460					55		
600			500					60		

11. Indicate whether each of the following will increase (+) or decrease (-) an open economy's equilibrium real GDP.
(a)   An increase in its imports ☐
(b)   An increase in its exports ☐
(c)   An increasing level of national income among trading partners ☐
(d)   An increase in trade barriers imposed by trading partners ☐
(e)   A depreciation in the value of the economy's currency ☐

■   **TRUE-FALSE**

Circle T if the statement is true, F if it is false.

1. In the model in this chapter the price level remains constant so any change in GDP is a change in real output.   **T F**

Questions 2 through 5 are based on the data in the following table. Assume that there is no government and no business saving, so GDP and disposable income (*DI*) are equal.

GDP	Consumption
160	168
200	196
240	224
280	252
320	280

2. When the GDP is 240, the average propensity to consume is 0.95.   **T F**

3. At a GDP level of 320 there is dissaving.   **T F**

4. The break-even level of GDP is below 240. **T F**

5. The marginal propensity to consume in the table is 0.95 at all income levels.   **T F**

6. The level of saving depends primarily upon the level of disposable income.   **T F**

7. Other things equal, a rise in wealth will shift the consumption schedule upward and result in an increase in saving out of any given level of *DI*.   **T F**

8. An increase in the taxes paid by consumers will decrease both their consumption and their saving.
T F

9. The consumption schedule and the saving schedule tend to be more stable over time than the investment schedule.   **T F**

10. The APC is relatively high in Canada and the United States, as compared to other major industrialized nations.   **T F**

11. A business firm will purchase additional capital goods if the real rate of interest exceeds the expected rate of return from the investment.   **T F**

12. A decrease in the corporate profits tax will shift the investment demand curve to the left.   **T F**

13. In this chapter it is assumed that planned investment is independent of the level of GDP.   **T F**

14. The equilibrium level of output is that output level that generates planned spending exactly equal to the value of production.   **T F**

15. At the equilibrium level of income, potential and actual GDP are equal.   **T F**

16. The equilibrium level of GDP is that GDP that corresponds to the intersection of the aggregate expenditure schedule and the 45-degree line.   **T F**

17. The actual amounts saved and invested are always equal by definition, but only at the equilibrium level of GDP are planned investment and saving equal.   **T F**

18. The investment schedule is a schedule of actual investment rather than a schedule of planned investment.   **T F**

19. If the multiplier is 2.5, and planned investment spending drops by 10, equilibrium real GDP will increase by 25.   **T F**

20. If the GDP in the United States is growing, we can expect an increase in Canadian GDP, *ceteris paribus*.   **T F**

21. If the price of a U.S. dollar has risen from $1.40 Canadian to $1.50 Canadian, an increase in Canadian exports to the United States can be expected.
T F

22. A higher marginal propensity to import in Canada means that Canadian households are spending a larger percentage of their disposable income on foreign produced goods.   **T F**

23. Import spending, like investment spending, is an injection into the spending flow.   **T F**

24. Net exports will be equal to zero at the economy's equilibrium level of real GDP.   **T F**

25. If MPC is 0.3 and MPM is 0.2, the open-economy multiplier is 2.   **T F**

26. If the open-economy multiplier is 1.6, and the MPS is 1/4, then MPM must equal 3/8.   **T F**

27. A recessionary gap is the amount by which full-employment GDP falls short of actual GDP.   **T F**

28. When the economy is in a recessionary gap, unemployment is above its natural rate.   **T F**

29. The collapse of Japan's once exceptionally high growth rate was largely due to the very high rate of saving in Japan.   **T F**

30. Classical economists thought that the economy had enough wage and price flexibility to restore full employment equilibrium.   **T F**

■ **MULTIPLE-CHOICE**

Circle the letter that corresponds to the best answer.

1. Which of the following is **not** one of the assumptions made in developing the aggregate expenditure model in this chapter?
(a)   the price level is constant
(b)   business saving is zero
(c)   there is no government sector
(d)   investment spending is related to the level of income

2. In the aggregate expenditure model, output and employment depend:
(a)   directly on the level of total expenditures
(b)   inversely on the quantity of resources available
(c)   directly on the level of saving
(d)   directly on the rate of interest

3. As disposable income decreases, *ceteris paribus*:
(a)   both consumption and saving increase
(b)   consumption increases and saving decreases
(c)   consumption decreases and saving increases
(d)   both consumption and saving decrease

4. If consumption spending increases from $358 to $367 when disposable income increases from $412 to $427, then the MPC must be:
(a)   0.4
(b)   0.6
(c)   0.8
(d)   0.9

5. If when disposable income is $375 billion the average propensity to consume is 0.8, then:
(a)   the MPC is also 0.8
(b)   consumption is $325 billion
(c)   saving is $75 billion
(d)   the marginal propensity to save is 0.2

Use the following graph to answer questions 6 through 9.

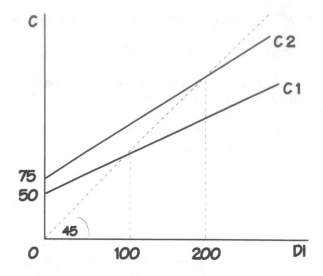

6. Which of the following could **not** cause the consumption curve to shift from C1 to C2?
(a)   a decrease in the level of income taxes on households
(b)   an increase in consumers' ownership of financial assets
(c)   a decrease in the amount of consumers' indebtedness
(d)   an increase in the income received by consumers

7. Which of the following is a true statement concerning the shift from C1 to C2?
(a)   the marginal propensity to consume has increased
(b)   the marginal propensity to save has increased
(c)   the break even level of income has decreased
(d)   the average propensity to save has decreased

8. What is the equation of consumption curve C2?
(a)   C = 75 + 0.50 DI
(b)   C = 50 + 0.50 DI
(c)   C = 75 + 0.625 DI
(d)   C = 50 + 0.625 DI

9. What are the marginal propensities to consume for the C1 and C2 consumption curves?
(a)   0.50 for C1 and 0.625 for C2
(b)   0.50 for C1 and 0.375 for C2
(c)   0.25 for C1 and 0.75 for C2
(d)   0.25 for both C1 and C2

10. Which of the following relationships is an inverse one in the aggregate expenditure model?
  (a) the relationship between consumption spending and disposable income
  (b) the relationship between investment spending and the rate of interest
  (c) the relationship between saving and the level of income
  (d) the relationship between investment spending and GDP

11. A leftward shift of the investment demand curve could be caused by:
  (a) a decline in the rate of interest
  (b) a decline in the level of wages paid
  (c) a decline in business taxes
  (d) a pessimistic outlook on the part of business owners

Questions 12 and 13 are based on the consumption schedule below and assume a closed economy with no government sector.

Real GDP	Consumption
$350	$320
400	360
450	400
500	440
550	480
600	520

12. If planned investment is $60, what is equilibrium real GDP?
  (a) $400
  (b) $450
  (c) $500
  (d) $550

13. If planned investment is $60, and GDP is $450, unplanned investment is:
  (a) -$20
  (b) -$10
  (c) $0
  (d) $10

The next graph is the basis for questions 14 through 16. The equation for the consumption is $C = 50 + .50$ GDP.

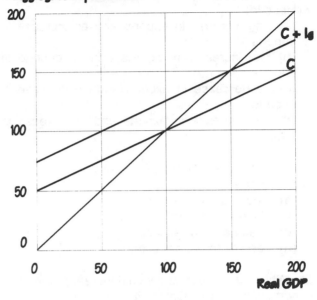

14. The level of planned investment is
  (a) $15
  (b) $25
  (c) $40
  (d) $50

15. The equilibrium level of real GDP is:
  (a) $120
  (b) $150
  (c) $175
  (d) $200

16. At a GDP level of $200, unintended investment is:
  (a) $25
  (b) $50
  (c) $75
  (d) cannot be calculated with the information supplied

17. If GDP is below equilibrium:
  (a) inventories will be zero
  (b) inventories will be diminishing
  (c) inventories will be increasing
  (d) inventories will be stable

18. The volume of Canada's exports depends on:
  (a) the price in foreign currency of a Canadian dollar
  (b) the level of Canadian prices relative to the price level abroad
  (c) the level of GDP in foreign countries
  (d) all of the above

19. Generally, a depreciation of the Canadian dollar will lead to:
- **(a)** an increase in exports and an increase in imports
- **(b)** an increase in exports and no change in imports
- **(c)** a decrease in exports and an increase in imports
- **(d)** an increase in exports and a decrease in imports

20. An increase in GDP in Canada will increase our imports and:
- **(a)** increase our exports
- **(b)** increase our net exports
- **(c)** decrease our exports
- **(d)** decrease our net exports

21. Which of the following would increase Canadian imports of fruits from California?
- **(a)** an increase in the price of Canadian fruit
- **(b)** an appreciation of the U.S. dollar relative to the Canadian dollar
- **(c)** an increase in the price of fruit in California
- **(d)** all of the above

22. A movement along Canada's net export schedule would be caused by:
- **(a)** an increase in export demand
- **(b)** an increase in our marginal propensity to import
- **(c)** an increase in the foreign exchange rate for our dollar
- **(d)** an increase in Canada's income

23. What is the correct formula for the open economy multiplier?
- **(a)** 1/MPS
- **(b)** 1/MPM
- **(c)** 1/MPS + MPM
- **(d)** 1/(MPS + MPM)

The following table of data represents the situation of an open economy with no government sector. Use the data to answer questions 24 through 27.

GDP	S	Ig	M	X
1000	200	150	150	340
1100	220	150	165	340
1200	240	150	180	340
1300	260	150	195	340
1400	280	150	210	340

24. For the economy in this table:
- **(a)** MPC = 0.80 and MPM = 0.15
- **(b)** MPS = 0.80 and MPM = 0.15
- **(c)** MPC = 0.20 and MPM = 0.10
- **(d)** MPS = 0.20 and MPM = 0.10

25. Equilibrium GDP is:
- **(a)** 1100
- **(b)** 1200
- **(c)** 1300
- **(d)** 1400

26. The open economy multiplier is:
- **(a)** 0.95
- **(b)** 2.86
- **(c)** 3.50
- **(d)** 4.32

27. If export expenditures fall by 35, equilibrium GDP will:
- **(a)** decrease by 35
- **(b)** increase by 35
- **(c)** decrease by 100
- **(d)** increase by 100

28. Other things remaining constant, which of the following would decrease an economy's real GDP and employment?
- **(a)** the imposition of tariffs on goods imported from abroad
- **(b)** an increase in the level of national income among the trading partners for this economy
- **(c)** a decrease in the marginal propensity to consume
- **(d)** a decrease in the marginal propensity to import

29. The effect of an increase in exports on GDP is similar to the effect of an increase in:
- **(a)** interest rates
- **(b)** saving
- **(c)** investment
- **(d)** business taxes

The data in the following table relate to an open economy with no public sector. Use the data to answer questions 30 through 33.

GDP	C + Ig	Xn
$900	$913	$3
920	929	3
940	945	3
960	961	3
980	977	3
1000	993	3
1020	1009	3

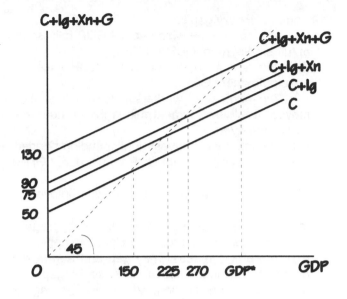

30. The equilibrium real GDP is:
   (a) $960
   (b) $980
   (c) $1000
   (d) $1020

31. If net exports are increased by $4 at each level of GDP, the equilibrium real GDP would be:
   (a) $960
   (b) $980
   (c) $1000
   (d) $1020

32. The multiplier in this economy is:
   (a)   2
   (b)   3
   (c)   4
   (d)   5

33. In the complete model with both government and foreign trade sectors, what is the proper expression of where equilibrium output is found?
   (a) $GDP = C + I_g + G + X$
   (b) $GDP = C + I_g + G + X_n$
   (c) $GDP = C + I_g + G + X + M$
   (d) $GDP = C + I_g + G + X_n - M$

Questions 34 through 37 are based on the following graph.

34. The multiplier in this economy is:
   (a)   2
   (b)   2.5
   (c)   3
   (d)   3.5

35. This diagram assumes that government purchases, net exports, and planned investment total:
   (a)   130 and are constant at all levels of GDP
   (b)   80 and are constant at all levels of GDP
   (c)   130 and increase as GDP increases
   (d)   80 and increase as GDP increases

36. What is the equilibrium level labelled GDP*?
   (a)   300
   (b)   390
   (c)   420
   (d)   450

37. If full-employment GDP happens to be 400, then what is the gap at GDP*?
   (a)   recessionary gap of 10
   (b)   inflationary gap of 10
   (c)   recessionary gap of 30
   (d)   none of the above

38. A change in which variable would change the slope of the $C+Ig+Xn+G$ curve?
   (a)   the level of planned investment
   (b)   the level of lump-sum taxes
   (c)   the level of government purchases
   (d)   the marginal propensity to import

39. An inflationary gap is:
(a)   the amount by which actual GDP falls short of full-employment GDP
(b)   the amount by which actual GDP exceeds full-employment GDP
(c)   the number of workers that would be employed at full employment minus the number actually employed
(d)   the increase in investment spending needed to reach full-employment GDP from present GDP

40. If equilibrium real GDP is below full-employment GDP:
(a)   there is a recessionary gap and aggregate expenditures must increase to close the gap
(b)   there is a recessionary gap and aggregate expenditures must decrease to close the gap
(c)   there is an inflationary gap and aggregate expenditures must increase to close the gap
(d)   there is an inflationary gap and aggregate expenditures must decrease to close the gap

41. A nation that enters a free trade agreement can expect that:
(a)   their multiplier will decrease because their MPM will rise
(b)   their multiplier will increase because their MPM will decrease
(c)   their multiplier will increase because their exports will increase
(d)   their multiplier will be unaffected

42. Classical economics suggests that in a market economy:
(a)   unemployment is a persistent problem
(b)   market forces will ensure full employment
(c)   a recession will cause automatic increases in prices and wages
(d)   demand creates its own supply

■   **DISCUSSION QUESTIONS**

1. Define aggregate expenditures and explain why, in a market economy, aggregate expenditures determine the level of output and income.

2.   Describe the relation between consumption and disposable income, and the relation between saving and disposable income; and then define the two average propensities and the two marginal propensities. Why does APC + APS always equal 1? Why does MPC + MPS always equal 1?

3. Determine how a change in each of the four non-income determinants will affect the consumption schedule and the saving schedule, and for each case explain concisely why consumption and saving change as you have indicated.

4. Explain: (a) when a business firm will or will not purchase additional capital goods; (b) how changes in the five non-interest-rate determinants of investment spending will affect the investment demand curve; (c) why investment spending tends to rise when the rate of interest falls; and (d) how changes in GDP might affect investment spending.

5. Why does the level of investment spending tend to fluctuate much more than the level of consumption spending?

6. What is meant by a leakage and by an injection? Which leakages and injections are considered in the different versions of the aggregate expenditures model? Why is the output at which leakages equals injections the equilibrium level of real GDP?

7. For investment, what is the distinction between the planned level and the actual level? Is the investment schedule planned or actual investment? What adjustment causes planned and actual investment to become equal?

8. What is the multiplier effect? Why is there such an effect, and what determines how large it will be? Why is the open economy multiplier smaller than the closed economy multiplier?

9. How does a change in the volume of exports and the volume of imports affect real GDP and the level of employment in an economy?

10. How would Canada's economy be affected by increased spending by the United States government to combat an American recession?

11. If taxes and government expenditures increase by equal amounts, what will happen to real GDP? Why?

12. Explain what a recessionary gap and an inflationary gap mean. What economic conditions are present in the economy when each of these gaps exists? How is the size of each of these gaps measured?

13. What are the limitations of the aggregate expenditures model?

14. What aspects of classical macroeconomic thinking did J.M. Keynes disagree with, and why? How did his criticisms of classical economics affect the aggregate expenditures model?

■ ANSWERS

FILL-IN QUESTIONS

1. closed, purchases, taxes, personal, zero, consumption, investment, income

2. excess, unemployed, aggregate, do not

3. income, directly

4. consumption schedule, amount consumed

5. capital, return, interest

6. greater

7. (a) acquiring, maintaining, and operating; (b) business; (c) technological; (d) capital goods on hand; (e) expectations

8. durability, expectations

9. (a) expenditures, output; (b) consumption, planned investment; (c) 45-degree

10. (a) less, disinvestment, rise; (b) greater, investment, fall; (c) equal to, zero, neither rise nor fall

11. equilibrium real GDP, equilibrium real GDP

12. (a) income; (b) consumption, fraction

13. (a) exports, imports; (b) (1) net exports; (2) aggregate expenditures

14. other countries, Canada

15. increase, decrease

16. imports, GDP

17. less than, MPS + MPM

18. increase, equal to, balanced budget, 1

19. fall, full employment

20. Say's, supply, demand

PROBLEMS AND PROJECTS

1. (a) S: -40, -20, 0; (b) 1780; (c) 1700; (d) 80, 100, 0.80; 80, 100, 0.80; (e) 20, 100, 0.20; 20, 100, 0.20; (f) 1860, 40; (g)-0.027; (h) 1.013; (i) APC: 1.000, 0.989, 0.979, APS: 0, 0.011, 0.021; (j) falls, rises

2. (a) 4; (b) 0.6; (c) 10, (d) -4; (e) 0.4; (f) 0; (h) C = 4 + 0.6 GDP; S = -4 + 0.4 GDP

3. (a) spending rises before prices rise: C+, S-; (b) wealth effect: C-, S+; (c) movement along C and S schedules, but no shift: 0; (d) taxes are financed partly from consumption and partly from saving: C-, S-; (e) C-, S+

4. (a) 12%: none, 0; 11%: C, 3; 10%: C, D, 8; 9%: C, D, B, 18; 8%: C, D, B, A, 30; 7%: all, 38; (c) inverse; decrease.

5. (a) - higher operating cost; (b) - lower after tax profitability in future; (c) – in short run, stock of capital on hand is high relative to what is needed; (d) - lower expected profitability in the short term; (e) + lower acquisitions costs; (f) - too much capital on hand in relation to needs in the short term

6. (a) C: 10, 50, 90, 130, 170, 210; S: -10, 0, 10, 20, 30, 40; I_g: 20 at all GDP values; $C+I_g$: 30, 70, 110, 150, 190, 230; UI: -30, -20, -10, 0, 10, 20; GDP Change: +, +, +, equilibrium, -, -; (b) 150; $C + I_g$, planned investment; (c) 0.80, 0.20

7. Because the MPC = .6, MPS = .4, and the multiplier = 1/.4 = 2.5. Therefore, the total change in income must be 2.5 x 10 = 25. Hence, to fill the table: Changes in income: $10, 6.00, 3.60, 2.16, 1.30, 1.94, 25.00; changes in C: $6.00, 3.60, 2.16, 1.30, 0.78, 1.16, 15.00; changes in S: $4.00, 2.40, 1.44, 0.86, 0.52, 0.77, 10.00

8. (a) 150, 225, 300, 375, 450, 525; (b) 300; (c) 175, 250, 325, 400, 475, 550; (d) 400; (e) 25, 100, 100, 25, 4

9. (a) 25, 75; (b) 75, 60, 15; (c) 60, 7.5; (d) 25, 15, 7.5, 47.5; (e) .475, .475, 2.11; (f) 2.11

10. (a) T: $50 at all GDP levels; DI: $350, 400, 450, 500, 550; S: $10, 20, 30, 40, 50; Ig: $40 at all levels; X: $50 at all levels; Xn: $10, 5, 0, -5, -10; G: $55 at all levels; AE: $445, 480, 515, 550, 585; (b) $550 (c) S+T+M = Ig+G+X: $145=145 (d) inflationary gap of $100 (e) MPS = 0.2, MPM = 0.10; 1/(MPS+MPM) = 3.33 (f) $6; 6 x 3.33 = $20 (g) -12 x 3.33 = decrease of $40 (h) inflationary gap of $80 (i) -80/3.33 = decrease by $24 (j) T: $50 at all GDP levels; DI: $350, 400, 450, 500, 550; S: $10, 20, 30, 40, 50; Ig: $46 at all levels; X: $38 at all levels; Xn: $-2, -7, -12, -17, -22; G: $31 at all levels; AE: $415, 450, 485, 520, 555

11. (a) - (net exports decrease); (b) + (net exports increase); (c) + (exports increase, and therefore net exports increase); (d) - (exports decrease, and therefore net exports decrease); (e) + (imports decrease and exports increase, and therefore net exports increase)

TRUE-FALSE

1. T
2. F $224/240 = 0.93$
3. F $S = 40$
4. T   at GDP = 240, C > GDP
5. F $28/40 = 0.70$
6. T
7. F   S decreases
8. T
9. T
10. T
11. F   real rate of interest must be below the expected rate of return
12. F   investment shifts to the right
13. T   so the investment schedule is horizontal
14. T
15. F   actual GDP can be more or less than potential GDP
16. T
17. T   at other GDP levels there is unplanned investment or disinvestment
18. F   it is a schedule of planned investment
19. F   GDP will decrease by 25
20. T   our X and AE will increase as GDP rises in US
21. T   our products would now be relatively less expensive for American buyers
22. T
23. F   investment is an injection, but imports are a leakage
24. F Xn could be positive or negative at equilibrium GDP
25. F   MPS = 1 - .3 = .7; multiplier = 1/(.7 + .2) = 1.11
26. T   multiplier = 1.6 = 1/(1/4 + MPM); solving for MPM yields 3/8
27. F   the amount by which actual GDP falls short of potential GDP
28. T
29. T   and therefore aggregate expenditures were not sufficient to buy Japan's potential output
30. T

MULTIPLE-CHOICE

1. (d)   we assume investment is independent of GDP
2. (a)
3. (d)   because both MPC and MPS are positive

4. (b) $9/15 = 0.6$
5. (c)   .8 x 375 = 300; 375 – 300 = 75
6. (d)   this is a movement along a C schedule, not a shift
7. (a)   C2 is steeper than C1
8. (c)   the intercept is 75, and the value of C = DI at DI = 200
9. (a)   50/100 and 125/200
10. (b)   the investment demand curve is downward-sloping
11. (d)   the others cause investment demand to shift rightward, or cause a movement along the curve
12. (c)   440 + 60 = 500
13. (b)   at GDP = 450, C = 400, so S = 50. Actual I = S = 50, so unplanned I = -10
14. (b)   at GDP = 150, C = 125, and C + Ig = GDP
15. (b)   where C + Ig = GDP
16. (a)   output exceeds AE by 25
17. (b)   there is excess demand in this amount
18. (d)
19. (d)   Canadians and foreigners tend now to buy more Canadian produced goods and services
20. (d)   imports are deducted to get net exports
21. (a)   relative price change favours California fruits
22. (d)   all of the others shift this schedule
23. (d)   note the placement of the brackets
24. (a)   MPC = 1 - MPS
25. (d)   S + M = Ig + X = 490
26. (b)   1/.35 = 2.86
27. (c)   2.86 x -35 = -100
28. (c)   the AE schedule shifts downwards, intersecting the 45 degree line at a lower GDP level
29. (c)   both are spending injections
30. (b)   977 + 3 = 980
31. (c)   993 + 7 = 1000
32. (d)   (1000-980)/(7-3) = 20/4 = 5
33. (b)   remember that $Xn = X - M$
34. (c)   for $1 injected in spending on Ig or X, there is a $3 increase in GDP
35. (b)   130 - 50
36. (b)   by the multiplier of 3
37. (a)   actual GDP is below potential GDP by 10
38. (d)   changes in the others would shift the intercept
39. (b)
40. (a)
41. (a)   assuming that the agreement increases the percentage of expenditures on imported goods
42. (b)   because wages and prices were believed to be very flexible

CHAPTER 9

Aggregate Demand and Aggregate Supply

The aggregate expenditures model from the previous chapter has an important limitation: it holds the price level fixed. Therefore, that model cannot explain how macroeconomic events affect the price level. This chapter introduces the aggregate demand-aggregate supply model, which overcomes this problem, and allows us to explain simultaneously the determination of real GDP and the price level.

The aggregate demand curve (AD) shows the total amounts of goods and services demanded in the economy at each possible price level. Plotted on the price level vs. real output axes, AD is downsloping because less is demanded at higher price levels. Movements along a given AD curve are caused by three consequences of price changes: the real-balances effect, the interest-rate effect, and the foreign-trade effect. The determinants of the AD curve (or aggregate demand shifters) are summarized in Figure 9-2, and include a variety of factors that shift consumer spending, investment spending, government spending, and net export spending. The appendix to this chapter shows how the AD curve can be derived from the aggregate expenditures model.

The short-run aggregate supply (AS) curve shows the level of real domestic output which will be produced at each price level, *if input prices remain fixed*. A rising price level implies greater profits for producers, and an incentive to produce and sell more output. But, as output expands and full capacity is approached, increasing shortages of inputs and various inefficiencies in production raise the per unit costs of production and the selling prices. When the economy is far below capacity output, these problems are minor, so the AS curve is quite flat. But, as output rises, these problems become more severe, so the curve eventually be-

comes steeper, until it becomes nearly vertical as the economy nears its short-run full capacity output. In most instances the economy is operating in the intermediate range of the short-run AS curve where the curve is upward sloping (meaning that the economy is neither in deep recession, nor at full-capacity production). Figure 9-4 lists the factors that affect the per-unit production costs, and therefore act as aggregate supply shifters.

The intersection of the AD and AS curves determines equilibrium real domestic output and price level. If the determinants of these curves do not change, competitive pressures will tend to keep the economy at this equilibrium. If any of the determinants of AD or AS changes, one of the curves will shift, and typically both equilibrium real GDP and the equilibrium price level will be affected. An increase in the AD curve will increase real GDP, as in the aggregate expenditures model, but with a smaller multiplier effect because some of the impact is absorbed in rising prices. The steeper the AS curve, the smaller the multiplier effect on real GDP.

If AS increases, the market forces tend to increase real GDP and put downward pressure on the price level. Recently, Canada has experienced strong growth in both AD and AS. This combination has allowed for the expansion of output and employment, but without inflation.

We define the short run as a period when nominal wages and other input prices are fixed. The long run is a period when nominal wages and other input prices are fully responsive to changes in the price level. Starting from a full-employment equilibrium, an increase in the price level will raise employment and production. Because nominal wages are fixed, firms' profit margins rise and they gain from hiring more labour and producing more output. However, nominal wages will eventually catch up to the price increases, eliminating the improvement in profit margins and the impetus for higher than normal employment and output. So the short-run AS curve slopes upward, but the long-run AS curve is vertical. After long-run adjustments in nominal wages, real GDP is equal to potential GDP, regardless of the specific price level.

If the short-run equilibrium in the AD-AS model is not at full-employment GDP, there will be an inflationary gap or a recessionary gap. Adjustments in nominal wages will eventually shift the short-run AS until it intersects AD and the long-run AS which is vertical at the full-employment equilibrium. Because this adjustment may be unacceptably slow, fiscal and monetary policies may be used to keep the economy at or near a noninflationary, full-employment equilibrium. These policies are examined in the next few chapters.

■ **CHAPTER LEARNING OBJECTIVES**

In this chapter you will learn:
□ Why the aggregate demand curve is downward sloping, and what factors shift the entire curve.
□ What determines the shape of the short-run aggregate supply curves, and what factors shift the entire curve.
□ How the equilibrium price level and real GDP are determined.
□ The distinction between the short-run and long-run supply curve.
□ The nature and causes of recessionary and inflationary gaps.

■ **CHAPTER OUTLINE**

1. The aggregate expenditures model is a fixed-price-level model in which real GDP is determined by demand side factors. The aggregate demand and aggregate supply model is more satisfactory because it includes the supply side of the economy, and it explains the determination of both real GDP and the price level.

2. Aggregate demand (AD) is a curve which shows an inverse relationship between the total quantity of goods and services that will be purchased by households, firms, foreigners, and government and the price level. There are three reasons why the AD curve is downward sloping:
   (a)   A higher price level reduces the purchasing power of financial assets, making asset holders feel less wealthy and causing them to reduce their spending. This is the real-balance effect.
   (b)   A higher price level causes people to demand more money to hold. With a fixed supply of money, the interest rate will rise, reducing interest-sensitive expenditures (by consumers and businesses). This is the interest-rate effect.
   (c)   A higher price level, when foreign prices are unchanged, will increase the relative price of goods produced in the domestic economy, reducing purchases of domestic output and increasing purchases of foreign output. This change in net export demand is the foreign-trade effect.

3. When changes in spending are caused by factors other than price level changes, the AD curve will shift. The determinants of AD discussed below are also summarized in Figure 9-2 in the textbook. Note that an increase in AD is a rightward shift; a decrease in AD is a leftward shift.
   (a)   Consumption spending will increase if domestic consumers experience: increases in wealth, improved expectations, reductions in indebtedness, or lower taxes.
   (b)   Investment spending — purchases of capital goods — will increase if businesses experience: lower interest rates or improved expected returns due to better expected business conditions, improved technology, less excess capacity, or lower business taxes.
   (c)   Government spending will increase if government purchases more goods and services, assuming that tax collections and interest rates do not change as a result.
   (d)   Net export spending will increase if the national incomes of our trading partners rise, or if our dollar depreciates and makes our goods relatively less expensive.

4. The short-run aggregate supply (AS) curve shows the level of real domestic output that will be produced at each price level, holding constant the prices of labour and other inputs. Higher price levels create incentives for firms to produce more output, so the curve is upward sloping. The steepness of AS depends on capacity utilization.
   (a)   When the economy is already at its short-run capacity output, as firms try to produce more output they will simply bid resources away from one another without producing any more. Prices rise, but output does not, so AS is vertical.

(b) When there is enough slack in the economy that output can expand without creating input shortages or production bottlenecks, there is no reason to raise prices when more is produced, so AS is horizontal.

(c) In most instances, the AS is upward sloping because the economy is neither in severe recession nor at full-capacity, so more can be produced, but not profitably at the same price level. As bottlenecks and inefficiencies begin to occur as output expands, per unit production costs rise, so the extra output will be produced only if prices are higher.

5. When per-unit production costs change for reasons other than a change in real output, firms collectively alter the amount of output they produce at each price level, so the AS curve shifts. The determinants of aggregate supply (or AS shifters) discussed below are also summarized in Figure 9-4 in the textbook. An increase (a decrease) in AS is a rightward (leftward) shift.

(a) Higher input prices increase per-unit production costs and decrease AS. Input prices could rise because of reductions in the availability of resources (land, labour, capital, and entrepreneurial ability), because of depreciation of the domestic currency that raises the price of imported resources; or because of an increased market power of resource suppliers.

(b) An increase in the amount of output per unit of input means that productivity increases, and that AS increases. Note that productivity increase is the same as decrease in per-unit production costs.

(c) Increases in taxes, reductions in subsidies, or increased regulation of business will tend to raise per-unit costs of output and decrease the AS curve.

6. The equilibrium real GDP and the equilibrium price level occur at the intersection of the AD and AS curves.

(a) If the price level were above the equilibrium level, the amount of output produced would exceed the amount demanded, so competition among sellers would drive the price level down to equilibrium to avoid an inventory buildup.

(b) If the price level were below the equilibrium level, the amount of output demanded would exceed the amount supplied, so competition among buyers would drive the price level up to equilibrium to avoid a depletion of inventories.

7. Any increase in aggregate demand leads to both inflation and increased output. To the extent that inflation results, the multiplier impact on real output is reduced. If AD increases:

(a) Equilibrium real output and price level both rise in the normal case where AS is upward sloping. Part of the multiplier effect is dissipated in inflation.

(b) Equilibrium real output rises and the price level is unchanged if AS is perfectly horizontal. The multiplier effect is maximized.

(c) The equilibrium price level rises and real output is unchanged if the AS is vertical. There is no multiplier effect.

8. In 2000 Canada experienced full employment, strong economic growth, and very low inflation. The underlying conditions that caused desirable combination of events can be understood with the AD-AS model. AD was growing, which alone would have increased real output and employment, but also the price level. However, productivity growth in the New Economy was also increasing the AS curve, further contributing to employment and output growth, and offsetting the inflationary effects of the AD shift.

9. The effects of many macroeconomic events differ between the short run and the long run because of the difference between short-run and long-run aggregate supply.

(a) The short run is a period in which nominal wages (and other input prices) remain fixed as the price level changes. Nominal wages may remain fixed temporarily either because workers are not immediately aware of the change in their real wages, or because they are employed under fixed-wage contracts that are set for a certain period of time.

(b) The long run is a period in which nominal wages (and other input prices) are fully responsive to changes in the price level. Given enough time, nominal wage changes will match price level changes so that real wages are unchanged.

10. Given these definitions of the short run and long run, we can be specific about the shape of the AS curve over these two periods.

(a) In the short run a price increase pushes real wages down because nominal wages are fixed. This raises profit margins for producers, creating an incentive to hire more labour (and other inputs) and produce more real output. AS in the short run is upward sloping.

(b) In the long run, workers eventually realize that their real wages have fallen, and fixed-wage contracts come up for renewal. Therefore, the price increase will be matched by a nominal wage increase, so real wages are returned to their original level. There is no longer any incentive to produce more than usual. The price level increase has no effect on real output, so the aggregate supply in the long run (AS_{LR}) is vertical.

11. Long-run equilibrium in the AD-AS model must be at the intersection of AD and AS (where demand for output and supply of output are equal), but it must also be on the vertical AS_{LR} curve (where nominal wages have adjusted to accommodate the price level and maintain the real wage). The AS_{LR} is vertical at the economy's full employment or potential GDP, and is consistent with the natural rate of unemployment.

12. The equilibrium level of real GDP in the short run need not be at full employment; it could be at a point with higher than natural unemployment, or at a point with inflation.

(a) A recessionary gap is the amount by which equilibrium GDP falls short of full-employment GDP. In the absence of any policy action to combat the problem, prices and nominal wages will eventually fall until the economy returns to full-employment GDP, but this is likely to take an unacceptably long time.

(b) An inflationary gap is the amount by which equilibrium GDP exceeds full-employment GDP. In the absence of any policy action, prices and nominal wages will rise far enough to reduce output until it returns to full-employment GDP. This will add to the inflation, and will also take some time.

13. European unemployment rates in recent years typically have been higher than rates in Canada and the United States. Competing theories view this high unemployment as the result of either: (a) high natural rate of unemployment, or (b) deficient aggregate demand.

■ **TERMS AND CONCEPTS**

aggregate demand
aggregate demand-

aggregate supply
  model

foreign-trade effect
inflationary gap
  interest-rate effect
long-run aggregate
  supply curve

determinants of
  aggregate demand
determinants of
  aggregate supply
equilibrium price level
equilibrium real
  domestic output

real-balances effect
recessionary gap
short-run aggregate
  supply

■ **HINTS AND TIPS**

1. You must recognize a key difference between the AD-AS model and the microeconomic model of supply and demand. In the aggregate model the price level measures the average of prices overall, and the aggregate quantity of all goods, rather than the price and quantity of any particular good.

2. Figures 9-2 and 9-4 list the determinants that cause shifts in the AD and AS curves, respectively. Study these tables carefully.

3. A common mistake when working with AS curves is to shift the curve in the wrong direction. If supply is increasing, the curve shifts rightward. It is easy to see how this leads to **more** output and **lower** prices.

■ **FILL-IN QUESTIONS**

1. In the AD-AS model the price level is _____, whereas in the aggregate expenditures model it is _____.

2. The graph for the AD-AS model plots _____ on the vertical axis, and _____ on the horizontal axis.

3. The AD curve shows the quantity of goods and services that will be _____ at various price _____. It slopes (upward, downward) _____ because of the _____, the _____, and the _____ effects.

4. (a) A change in one of the determinants of AD will cause a (movement along, shift of) _____ the AD curve.

(b) A change in the price will cause a (movement along, shift of) _____ the AD curve.

5. List the determinants of AD that affect consumption spending:
(a) _____
(b) _____

(c) _____

(d) _____

6. List the determinants of AD that affect investment spending:

(a) _____

(b) (1) _____

    (2) _____

    (3) _____

    (4) _____

7. List the determinants of AD that affect net export spending:

(a) _____

(b) _____

8. The AS curve shows the quantity of goods and services that will be _____ at various _____ levels. At all points along a given AS curve we assume that (input, output) _____ prices are constant.

9. The AS curve is _____ sloping because of the (increase, decrease) _____ in the per-unit costs of producing goods and services as output expands.

10. List the determinants of short-run aggregate supply:

(a) Change in input prices:

(1) Domestic resource availability of:

    (i) _____

    (ii) _____

    (iii) _____

    (iv) _____

(2) _____

(3) _____

(b) Change in _____

(c) Change in the legal-institutional environment:

(1) _____

(2) _____

11. Were AD to increase,

(a) the flatter the AS curve, the (greater, smaller) _____ is the multiplier effect on the real equilibrium GDP and the _____ is the effect on the equilibrium price level; and

(b) the steeper the AS curve, the _____ is the multiplier effect on the equilibrium real GDP and the _____ is the effect on the equilibrium price level.

12. Along the long-run aggregate supply curve, prices and (real, nominal) _____ wages change, but _____ wages are constant, and therefore so are producers' _____ margins, the level of _____ of labour, and the level of real output.

13. The economy can reach a (short, long) _____ run equilibrium at an output level below potential GDP. Such a situation is termed a(n) _____ gap. Eventually the gap would be resolved automatically by (rising, falling) _____ prices and nominal wages.

■ **PROBLEMS AND PROJECTS**

1. The amounts of real output demanded at different price levels are given as follows:

Price: 150 100 50

Real GDP: $4 $8 $12

(a) Use this data to plot the AD curve in the graph below.

(b) Plot the AS curve from the data shown in the next table.

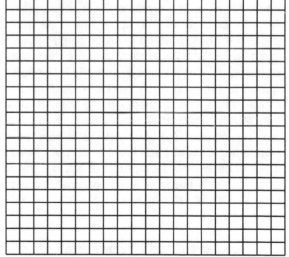

Price level	Real GDP
50	2
50	4
75	6
100	8
125	9
150	9

(c) The short-run equilibrium price level is $_____, and the short-run equilibrium real GDP is $_____.

(d) Assuming that potential GDP is $7, draw in the long-run aggregate supply curve (AS_LR) on the graph.

(e) At the short-run equilibrium in (b), there is a _____ gap of $_____.

2. The data below show relationships between the real domestic output and the quantity of input resources needed to produce each level of output.

GDP	Input	Productivity		Per-unit cost		
		(1)	(2)	(3)	(4)	(5)
2500	500	____	____	____	____	____
2400	400	____	____	____	____	____
2100	300	____	____	____	____	____
1600	200	____	____	____	____	____

(a) In column (1) compute the level of productivity at each level of GDP.

(b) In column (2) compute the level of productivity if now there is a doubling in the quantity of inputs required to produce each level of output.

(c) In column (3) compute per-unit production cost at each level of output, if each unit of input costs $3, given the productivity in column (1).

(d) In column (4) compute the new per-unit production cost at each level of output given that input price is $3, given that there has been a doubling in the required quantity of inputs required to produce each level of output as shown in column (2). What happens to the AS curve if this situation occurs?

(e) In column (5), compute the new per-unit production cost at each level of output, given that input price is now $2 instead of $3, but the level of productivity stays as it was originally, as in column (1). What will happen to the AS curve if this situation occurs?

3. For each event listed below, what is the most likely effect on Canada's: (1) aggregate demand; (2) aggregate supply; (3) the equilibrium price level, and; (4) equilibrium real GDP? Assume that all other things are equal, and that the AS curve is upward sloping. Use the following symbols to indicate the expected effects: I = increase; D = decrease; S = remains the same; and U = uncertain. (You are also encouraged to sketch out these situations on your own graphs.)

(a) A decrease in labour productivity:
AD _____ AS _____ P _____ Q _____

(b) A drop in interest rates:
AD _____ AS _____ P _____ Q _____

(c) Consumers' indebtedness increases to record high levels:
AD _____ AS _____ P _____ Q _____

(d) Energy prices increase, raising production costs for businesses:
AD _____ AS _____ P _____ Q _____

(e) The Canadian dollar appreciates:
AD _____ AS _____ P _____ Q _____

(f) Personal income tax rates increase:
AD _____ AS _____ P _____ Q _____

(g) Technological change improves productivity:
AD _____ AS _____ P _____ Q _____

4. Wimpyland produces nothing but hamburgers. The price level is therefore in $ per burger, nominal wages are in $, and real wages are in burgers. The initial nominal wage rate is $12. The current situation in Wimpyland is depicted by AS, AD_1, and AS_LR on the following graph.

(a) The short-run equilibrium price level is $_____ per burger, and the equilibrium output level is _____ burgers.

(b) Why is this equilibrium both a short-run equilibrium and a long-run equilibrium?

(c) In this equilibrium, the real wage rate is $_____/$_____ per burger = _____ burgers.

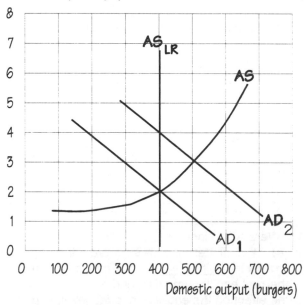

Price level ($ / burger)

(d) If AD_1 shifts up to AD_2, the new short-run equilibrium price level is $_____ per burger, and the output level is _____ burgers. There is a(n) _____ gap of 100 burgers.

(e)　At this new short-run equilibrium, the real wage is \$_____ ÷ \$_____ per burger = _____ burgers. Therefore, the real wage is now (above, below) _____ the long-run equilibrium real wage.

(f)　This disequilibrium will cause the AS curve to shift (rightward, leftward) _____ until a new long-run equilibrium is reached where the price level is \$_____ per burger, and the equilibrium output level is _____ burgers.

(g)　At this new equilibrium, the real wage will have returned to _____ burgers. Given the new price level, this implies that the nominal wage must have risen to \$_____.

■ TRUE-FALSE

Circle T if the statement is true, F if it is false.

1. An aggregate demand schedule shows the amounts of domestically produced goods and services that consumers, businesses, governments, and foreigners collectively wish to purchase at different price levels.　**T F**

2. The AD curve slopes downward.　**T F**

3. A change in aggregate demand is caused by a change in the price level, other things equal.　**T F**

4. A fall in the price level increases the real value of financial assets with fixed money value and, as a result, increases spending by the holders of these assets.　**T F**

5. A fall in the price level reduces the demand for money in the economy, pushes interest rates upward, and decreases investment spending.　**T F**

6. A rise in the price level of an economy (relative to foreign price levels) tends to increase that economy's net exports.　**T F**

7. According to the wealth effect, when the price level rises, households feel wealthier, and increase their spending.　**T F**

8. A decrease in the degree of excess capacity in the economy will retard the demand for new capital goods and therefore reduce AD.　**T F**

9. A high level of consumer indebtedness will tend to increase consumption spending and AD.　**T F**

10. Depreciation in the Canadian dollar would shift the AD curve for Canada to the right.　**T F**

11. The steepness of the AS curve depends on the degree of capacity utilization.　**T F**

12. Lower prices for land, labour, or capital will tend to shift the AS to the left.　**T F**

13. Productivity can be defined as the ratio of input divided by real output.　**T F**

14. Increased government regulation tends to decrease the AS curve.　**T F**

15. An increase in the short-run aggregate supply increases both the equilibrium real GDP and the potential output of the economy.　**T F**

16. A decrease in AS is "doubly good" because it increases the real domestic output and prevents inflation.　**T F**

17. Changes in the determinants of AS alter the per-unit production cost and shift AS.　**T F**

18. An increase in productivity will shift the aggregate supply curve rightward.　**T F**

19. A recessionary gap is the amount by which full-employment GDP falls short of actual GDP.　**T F**

20. When the AS curve is upward sloping, the multiplier effect of a change in spending on real output is less than in the aggregate expenditure model of the previous chapter.　**T F**

■ MULTIPLE-CHOICE

Circle the letter that corresponds to the best answer.

1. When the price level rises:
(a)　holders of financial assets with fixed money values increase their spending
(b)　the demand for money falls
(c)　interest rates rise and investment expenditures fall
(d)　exports increase and imports fall

2. The downward slope of the AD curve is the result of:
(a)　the real-balance effect

(b) the interest-rate effect
(c) the foreign-trade effect
(d) all of the above effects

3. Which of the following does not increase as a result of a decrease in the price level?
(a) consumption
(b) planned investment
(c) net exports
(d) government spending

4. The AS curve is the relationship between the:
(a) price level and the real domestic output purchased
(b) price level and the real domestic output produced
(c) price level producers are willing to accept and the price level purchasers are willing to pay
(d) real domestic output purchased and the real domestic output produced

5. The AS curve is upward sloping in the short run due to:
(a) increased input prices as output rises
(b) decreased input prices as output rises
(c) rising per-unit production costs as output rises
(d) a shortage of domestic resources

6. Which of the following is held constant when moving from one point on an AS curve to another point on the same curve?
(a) the price level
(b) the prices of inputs
(c) the per unit cost of production
(d) none of these are held constant

7. The AD curve will tend to be increased (shifted to the right) by:
(a) a decrease in the price level
(b) an increase in the price level
(c) an increase in the excess capacity of factories
(d) a depreciation in the Canadian dollar

8. An increase in business taxes will tend to:
(a) decrease AD but not change AS
(b) decrease AS but not change AD
(c) decrease AD and AS
(d) decrease AS and increase AD

9. An increase in AS will:
(a) reduce the price level and real domestic output

(b) reduce the price level and increase the real domestic output
(c) increase the price level and real domestic output
(d) reduce the price level and decrease the real domestic output

10. Why are nominal wages fixed in the short run, even when prices rise?
(a) workers may not immediately be aware of the price increases
(b) workers' wages may be fixed by contracts
(c) both of the above
(d) none of the above

11. If Parliament passed much stricter laws to control the air pollution from business, then this action would tend to:
(a) increase per-unit production costs and shift the AS curve to the right
(b) increase per-unit production costs and shift the AS curve to the left
(c) increase per-unit production costs and shift the AD curve to the left
(d) decrease per-unit production costs and shift the AS curve to the left

Suppose that real domestic output in an economy is 50, the quantity of inputs is 10, and the price of each input is $2. Answer questions 12 through 15 on the basis of this information.

12. The level of productivity in this economy is:
(a) 5
(b) 4
(c) 3
(d) 2

13. The per unit cost of production is:
(a) $0.40
(b) $0.50
(c) $0.75
(d) $1.00

14. If real domestic output in the economy rose to 60 units, then per-unit production costs would:
(a) remain unchanged and AS would remain unchanged
(b) increase and AS would decrease
(c) decrease and AS would increase
(d) decrease and AS would decrease

15. All else equal, if the price of each input increases from $2 to $4, productivity would:

  (a) decrease from $4 to $2 and AS would decrease

  (b) decrease from $5 to $3 and AS would decrease

  (c) increase from $4 to $2 and AS would increase

  (d) remain unchanged and AS would decrease

16. In the AD-AS model, an increase in the price level will:

  (a) shift the AD curve

  (b) shift the AS curve

  (c) shift both AD and AS curves

  (d) shift neither AD nor AS curve

17. When the economy is in deep recession, an increase in AD will:

  (a) increase the price level without affecting real output much

  (b) increase real output without affecting the price level much

  (c) substantially increase input prices

  (d) lead to widespread shortages of labour and raw materials

18. Which of the following statements is true in the aggregate demand-aggregate supply model?

  (a) there is no multiplier effect in this model

  (b) the effective multiplier is lower the steeper the aggregate supply curve

  (c) the multiplier effect is strengthened by price level changes

  (d) none of the statements is true

19. A decrease in the price of imported productive resources will:

  (a) expand output and lower the price level

  (b) expand output and raise the price level

  (c) contract output and lower the price level

  (d) contract output and raise the price level

■ **DISCUSSION QUESTIONS**

  1. Define the AD and AS curves.

  2. Explain why (a) the interest-rate effect, (b) the real-balance effect, and (c) the foreign-trade effect cause the AD curve to be downsloping.

  3. What factors that affect investment spending would cause the AD curve to shift to the left? What factors affecting consumption spending would move the AD curve to the left?

  4. Why does the AS curve slope upward in the short run? What happens to per-unit costs of production as we move along the curve?

  5. Explain how a change in input prices affects the AS curve. Define productivity and explain the effect on AS of an improvement in productivity.

  6. What is the long-run aggregate supply curve? Why is it vertical, and at what level of real output is it located?

  7. How is the equilibrium real domestic output determined? Why will domestic producers reduce or expand their production when they find themselves producing more or less than the equilibrium output?

  8. How are real domestic output and the price level affected when AD increases, and how do these effects depend on the slope of the AS curve? How are real domestic output and the price level affected when the AS decreases?

  9. What are the characteristics of long-run equilibrium? What roles do the adjustments in nominal wages and real wages play in restoring the economy to a long-run equilibrium?

  10. What is a recessionary gap, and an inflationary gap, and what economic conditions are present when each of these gaps exists? How is the size of each of these gaps measured? What changes in the economy would be needed to resolve an inflationary gap, or a recessionary gap?

■ **ANSWERS**

FILL-IN QUESTIONS

  1. variable, fixed

  2. price level, real GDP

  3. demanded (purchased), levels, downward, real-balance, interest-rate, foreign-trade

  4. (a) shift of; (b) movement along

  5. consumer wealth, consumer expectations, household indebtedness, taxes

6. (a) interest rates; (b) expected future business conditions, technology, degree of excess capacity, business taxes

7. national income of other nations; exchange rates

8. produced, price, input

9. upward, increase

10. (a) (1) land, labour, capital, entrepreneurial ability; (2) prices of imported resources; (3) market power; (b) productivity; (c) (1) business taxes and subsidies; (2) government regulation

11. (a) greater, smaller; (b) smaller, greater

12. nominal, real, profit, employment

13. short, recessionary, falling

PROBLEMS AND PROJECTS

1. (c) 100, 8; (d) vertical at GDP = 7; (e) inflationary, 1

2. (a) 5, 6, 7, 8; (b) 2.5, 3, 3.5, 4; (c) 0.60, 0.50, 0.43, 0.38; (d) 1.20, 1.00, 0.86, 0.75; AS shifts leftward; (e) 0.40, 0.33, 0.29, 0.25; AS shifts rightward

3. (a) S, D, I, D; (b) I, S, I, I; (c) D, S, D, D; (d) S, I, D, I; (e) D, I, D, U; (f) D, S, D, D; (g) S, I, D, I

4. (a) 2, 400; (b) AS = AD = AS_{LR}; (c) 12, 2, 6; (d) 3, 500; inflationary; (e) 12, 3, 4; below; (f) leftward, 4, 400; (g) 6; 24

TRUE-FALSE

1. T
2. T
3. F   price changes cause movements along AD, not shifts in AD
4. T   this is the real balance effect
5. F   interest rate will decrease and investment will increase
6. F   net exports will decrease
7. F   this describes the real-balance effect
8. F   demand for capital is increased
9. F   decreased consumption and AD
10. T   net exports increase
11. T   as capital utilization increases, AS becomes steeper
12. F   AS increases, which is a rightward shift
13. F   output divided by input
14. T   by raising the cost per unit of production
15. F   potential output is unaffected by AS shifts
16. F   an increase in AS would be "doubly good" for these reasons

17. T
18. T
19. F   actual GDP is less than full-employment GDP
20. T   part of the multiplier effect is dissipated in price increases

MULTIPLE-CHOICE

1. (c)   all of the others are backwards
2. (d)
3. (d)   all of the others depend on the price level
4. (b)
5. (c)   as capacity utilization rises
6. (b)
7. (d)   because net exports rise as goods from Canada drop in relative price
8. (b)   per unit costs of production increase
9. (b)
10. (c)
11. (b)
12. (a)   50/10
13. (a) $20/50
14. (c)
15. (d)   costs per unit increase, though productivity is constant
16. (d)   change in price level causes movements along AD and AS
17. (b)   AS is horizontal
18. (b)
19. (a)   AS shifts rightward

Connecting the Aggregate Expenditures Model and the AS-AD Model

This appendix shows how the flexible-price aggregate demand and aggregate supply model of Chapter 9 is related to the fixed-price aggregate expenditures model of Chapter 8. The specific connection is found in deriving the AD curve by varying the price level and observing the effect on the aggregate expenditures curve and the equilibrium level of real domestic output.

If, for example, the price level increases, this will decrease the level of aggregate expenditures (AE) through the interest-rate, real-balance, and foreign-trade effects. The result is a downward shift in the AE schedule, and therefore a lower equilibrium level of real domestic output. For each price level there is a unique position for the AE schedule and equilibrium real GDP. The AD curve plots all of the combinations of price level and real domestic output level where the production of goods equals the demand for goods.

The AD curve is shifted by the same factors that shift the AE schedule. Holding the price level constant, if something changes to increase the level of consumption, investment, government spending, or net exports, it will shift the AE schedule upward, and shift the AD curve rightward.

From the aggregate expenditures model we are familiar with the multiplier effect whereby a shift in the AE leads to a larger increase in the equilibrium real GDP. Because of this multiplier effect, when the AE shifts vertically, the horizontal shift in the AD curve is a multiple of the AE shift.

■ CHECKLIST

When you have studied this appendix, you should be able to:

□ Derive an aggregate demand curve using the aggregate expenditures model.
□ Explain how AE shifts lead to AD shifts.
□ Explain how the multiplier effect in the aggregate expenditures model affects the AD curve.

■ APPENDIX OUTLINE

1. The aggregate expenditures model is normally used as a fixed-price model, but if the price level does change, the AE schedule will shift due to the interest-rate, real-balance, and foreign-trade effects.
   (a) An increase in the price level will shift AE downward.
   (b) A decrease in the price level will shift AE upward.

2. A shift in the AE schedule due to a price level change will change the equilibrium level of real GDP.
   (a) If AE shifts up, real GDP increases.
   (b) If AE shifts down, real GDP decreases.

3. The aggregate demand (AD) curve is downward sloping and plots all combinations of different price levels and the corresponding equilibrium real GDP level. Price level is on the vertical axis, and real GDP on the horizontal.

4. Any change in one of the determinants of the components of AE will horizontally shift the AD curve. The AD shift will be a multiple of the initial shift in expenditures due to the same multiplier effect discussed in Chapter 8.

■ HINTS AND TIPS

1. Remember that a price level change shifts the AE curve upwards or downwards, but causes only a movement along the AD curve.

2. The size of the multiplier in the aggregate expenditures model dictates the extent of the horizontal shift in the AD curve when there a change in one of the determinants of expenditures. For example, if the multiplier is 3 and investment increases by $1 billion, the AD curve will shift rightward by $3 billion. In the AD-AS model the equilibrium GDP does not change by as much as this shift in the AD curve because there is also the AS curve to consider.

■ FILL-IN QUESTIONS

1. In the aggregate expenditure model, a price increase will shift the aggregate expenditure curve (up, down) _____, and the equilibrium level of real GDP will (increase, decrease) _____. This (direct, inverse) _____ relationship between the price level and the amount of output demanded can be used to derive the _____ curve (or schedule).

2. An event that shifts the aggregate expenditures curve upward will cause the (AD, AS) _____ curve to shift to the (left, right) _____ by (the same, a larger, a smaller) _____ amount. This is the _____ effect.

3. The variables plotted on the axes of the AD curve are _____ on the vertical, and _____ on the horizontal.

■ PROBLEMS AND PROJECTS

1. This question involves the derivation of a downsloping AD curve from the aggregate expenditure model. Suppose the equation for aggregate expenditures is given by: C+Ig+Xn+G = 4 + 0.5 GDP when the price level is 100. If the price level falls to 50, the intercept of this function rises by 2, whereas if the price level increases to 150 the intercept falls by 2.

(a) In the upper panel of the graph plot the aggregate expenditure functions pertaining to three price levels: 50, 100, 150, and determine the equilibrium level of GDP that would correspond to each.

(b) Use your findings in (a) to plot three combinations of price level and equilibrium GDP. Join these points to form the AD curve.

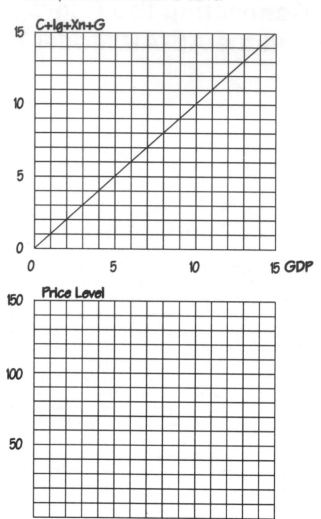

2. This question continues with the data from question 1.

(a) Plot a new aggregate demand curve, AD', that results from a $1 increase in investment spending. (Hint: the increase in investment will shift all three aggregate expenditures curves in the top panel upward by 1.)

(b) Given the horizontal shift from AD to AD', the size of the multiplier for this economy is equal to _____.

(c) The actual effective multiplier effect will be the value found in (b) if the AS curve is (horizontal, vertical, upward sloping) _____; it will be positive but smaller than this if the AS curve is

_____; and it will be zero if the AS curve is

_____.

■ TRUE-FALSE

Circle T if the statement is true, F if it is false.

1. An increase in government purchases will shift the aggregate expenditures curve upwards, and shift AD leftward. **T F**

2. If the AE schedule shifts up by $1 million, the AD curve will shift right by $1 million. **T F**

3. The AE curve is used in the derivation of both the AD and AS curves. **T F**

4. If the AD curve shifts $9 billion to the right when government spending rises by $2 billion, the aggregate expenditures model multiplier is 4.5. **T F**

■ MULTIPLE-CHOICE

Circle the letter that corresponds to the best answer.

1. In the aggregate expenditures model, a drop in the price level will lead to:
(a) a lower aggregate expenditures curve and a lower multiplier
(b) a higher aggregate expenditures curve and a higher multiplier
(c) a lower aggregate expenditures curve and a lower equilibrium real output
(d) a higher aggregate expenditures curve and a higher equilibrium real output

2. A decrease in the price level will shift the:
(a) consumption, investment, and net exports curves downward
(b) consumption, investment, and net exports curves upward
(c) consumption and investment curves downward and the net exports curve upward
(d) consumption and net exports curves upward, but the investment curve downward

3. An upward shift in aggregate expenditures in the aggregate expenditure model shifts the AD curve to the:
(a) right by the amount of the increase in aggregate expenditure

(b) right by the amount of the increase in aggregate expenditure times the multiplier
(c) left by the amount of the increase in aggregate expenditure
(d) left by the amount of the increase in aggregate expenditure times the multiplier

4. A rise in prices will:
(a) shift the AE curve down and shift the AD curve to the left
(b) shift the AE curve down and shift the AD curve to the right
(c) shift the AE curve up and shift the AD curve to the left
(d) shift the AE curve down and not shift the AD curve

5. Which of the following will shift the AD curve to the right?
(a) a decrease in investment spending
(b) a decrease in government spending
(c) a decrease in export spending
(d) a decrease in import spending

6. The extent to which a $10 increase in government spending will shift the AD curve depends on what?
(a) the marginal propensity to consume
(b) the marginal propensity to import
(c) both of the above
(d) none of the above

■ DISCUSSION QUESTIONS

1. Explain the difference between the AE schedule and the AD curve.

2. How is the AD curve derived from the aggregate expenditure model?

3. What determines how far the AD shifts when there is a change in one of the components of aggregate expenditures?

■ ANSWERS

FILL-IN QUESTIONS

1. down, decrease, inverse, AD

2. AD, right, a larger, multiplier

3. price level, real domestic output (GDP)

PROBLEMS AND PROJECTS

1. (b) three points: P = 150, GDP = 4, P = 100, GDP = 8, P = 50, GDP = 12

2. (a) three points: P = 150, GDP = 6, P = 100, GDP = 10, P = 50, GDP = 14; (b) 2; (c) horizontal; upward sloping; vertical

TRUE-FALSE

1. F   AD would shift rightward
2. F   AD would shift more than this because of the multiplier effect
3. F   the AE schedule has no relevance for the AS curve
4. T   4.5 x $2 billion

MULTIPLE-CHOICE

1. (d)
2. (b) by the interest-rate, real-balance, and foreign-trade effects
3. (b)
4. (a)
5. (d) because imports are deducted from net exports
6. (c) because both MPC and MPM affect the multiplier

CHAPTER 10

Fiscal Policy

This chapter is concerned with fiscal policy, which is the federal government's use of its spending and taxation powers to help achieve full-employment GDP, price level stability, and a high rate of economic growth. The business cycle is one of the major problems for our economy, and since 1945 Canadian governments have used fiscal policy in an effort to prevent or smooth out macroeconomic fluctuations.

Fiscal policy can be discretionary or non-discretionary. Discretionary fiscal policy occurs when Parliament decides to make deliberate changes in taxes and/or government spending with the goal of shifting the aggregate demand curve (AD). In a recession, expansionary fiscal policy is called for because AD is insufficient to produce equilibrium at full-employment GDP. To expand AD, the appropriate policy is to: (1) increase government spending; (2) reduce taxes (so that households have more disposable income and will consume more); or (3) a combination of the two. An expansionary fiscal policy pushes the government's budget towards a deficit. An inflationary gap calls for a contractionary policy (which requires a cut in AD, and therefore opposite changes in government spending and taxation from an expansionary policy). A contractionary policy pushes the government's budget towards surplus. Whether the gap is recessionary or inflationary, the government could wait for full employment equilibrium to be restored through wage and price adjustments stemming from the supply side, but these automatic changes are bound to be slow and painful.

Non-discretionary fiscal policy does not require deliberate government action to change tax laws or government spending plans. Instead, non-discretionary fiscal policy relies on built-in stabilizers that automatically increase government deficits during recessions and increase government surpluses during inflation. These changes occur automatically because most taxes vary directly with GDP, and many transfer payments are inversely related to GDP. The advantage of built-in stabilizers is that they do not have to wait for Parliament's decisions. Unfortunately, non-discretionary fiscal policy alone is not enough to eliminate all recessions and inflations that occur in Canada, so full-employment GDP and price stability cannot be restored quickly without discretionary fiscal policy.

How do we evaluate whether discretionary fiscal policy is contractionary, expansionary, or neutral at a given time? We cannot tell simply from the government's actual budget. Built-in stabilizers cause the actual budget to fluctuate whenever GDP does, even when the government has made no decision to change fiscal policy. Such illusions created by the built-in stabilizers forced economists to develop the "cyclically adjusted budget" to measure the budget balance at a standardized point: the full-employment level of real GDP. This budget measure changes only when there is a discretionary policy change.

Fiscal policy is subject to various problems. Time lags prevent the policy from working immediately when it is needed, and political constraints often make it impossible or unpalatable for the federal government to take the necessary policy actions. Increased government spending may lead to crowding-out of private investment spending, thus offsetting some of the intended stimulus to aggregate expenditures. When the economy is in the upward sloping section of the aggregate supply curve, some of the impact of expansionary fiscal policy will be dissipated in inflation instead of raising real GDP and employment. Canada's growing trade with foreign countries makes it more difficult to know what fiscal policy to use because unpredictable AD disturbances abroad can be transmitted to Canada, and because the net export effect weakens the impact of fiscal policy.

Some economists tout supply-side fiscal policy by which tax changes directly affect the aggregate supply curve. Reductions in tax rates may induce higher levels of investment, work effort, risk-taking, and other decisions that improve productivity.

■ **CHAPTER LEARNING OBJECTIVES**

In this chapter you will learn:
□ What fiscal policy is and what it is used for.
□ What discretionary fiscal policy is and its function.
□ About the economy's built-in stabilizers.
□ What a cyclically adjusted budget is.
□ The problems, criticisms, and complications of fiscal policy.

■ **CHAPTER OUTLINE**

1. Since World War II, when unemployment insurance was introduced, the Canadian government has held a legislative mandate to use stabilization policy to counter unemployment and inflation.

2. Fiscal policy can be either discretionary or non-discretionary. Discretionary fiscal policy is the deliberate manipulation of taxes and government spending to offset cyclical fluctuations. Its goals are: full employment, price stability, and steady growth.
   (a) Two assumptions simplify our analysis of the effects of fiscal policy: that government purchases do not affect private spending, and that fiscal policy does not shift the aggregate supply curve.
   (b) Government purchases of goods and services increase the AD curve and increase equilibrium real GDP and employment.
   (c) Taxes decrease disposable income, and therefore decrease consumption and the AD curve.

3. The elimination of an inflationary (recessionary) gap is accomplished by contractionary (expansionary) fiscal policy, which is composed of an increase (decrease) in taxes, a decrease (increase) in government purchases, or a combination of both. Contractionary (expansionary) fiscal policy moves the government's budget towards a surplus (deficit). If a discretionary policy is not adopted, the market forces will eventually shift the AS curve enough to

restore full employment, but that could take too long.

4. Whether government spending or taxes should be altered to reduce recession and inflation depends to a large extent upon whether an expansion or a contraction of the public sector is desired.
   (a) Some economists believe that government should play a larger role in addressing social and infrastructure issues. In a recession, these economists would favour an increase in government spending (tending to make the public sector grow); in an inflationary period, they would prefer a tax increase (tending again to make the public sector grow).
   (b) Other economists believe that government is currently too large. In a recession, they would favour a cut in taxes (making the public sector shrink); in an inflationary period, they would favour a cut in government spending (tending again to shrink the public sector).

5. Non-discretionary fiscal policy continually provides some built-in stability for the economy.
   (a) Net tax revenues (tax receipts minus government transfers and subsidies) increase as the GDP rises and decrease as the GDP falls.
   (b) This net tax system serves as a built-in stabilizer of the economy because it reduces purchasing power when there is an inflationary gap and expands purchasing power when there is a recessionary gap.
   (c) As GDP increases, the average tax rates will increase in progressive systems, remain constant in proportional systems, and decrease in regressive tax systems, so there is more built-in stability with a more progressive tax system.
   (d) Built-in stabilizers can reduce, but cannot fully eliminate, economic fluctuations.

6. Built-in stabilizers cause the actual budget deficit or surplus to automatically fluctuate as GDP fluctuates. Therefore, movements in the actual budget deficit or surplus do not indicate whether the government's fiscal policy has become more expansionary or contractionary.
   (a) The cyclically adjusted budget is a better fiscal policy indicator than the actual budget because it measures what the federal budget deficit or surplus would be if the economy had achieved its full employment GDP level.
   (b) If the cyclically adjusted deficit as a percentage of GDP increases (decreases), then the

stance of fiscal policy has become more expansionary (contractionary).

(c) If the cyclically adjusted surplus as a percentage of GDP increases (decreases), then the stance of fiscal policy has become more contractionary (expansionary).

(d) A cyclical deficit occurs when the economy is operating below full employment and is computed as the difference between the actual budget deficit and the cyclically adjusted budget balance.

7. In the 1990s Canada consistently had substantial actual and cyclically adjusted budget deficits until 1997. Since then we have had budget surpluses – both actual and cyclically adjusted. The trend in the cyclically adjusted budget shows that fiscal policy became substantially more contractionary during the 1990s. This trend ended in the end of the decade: for 1997, 1998, and 1999 the cyclically adjusted surplus remained about 1% of GDP.

8. Certain problems and complications arise in the use of fiscal policy. Timing problems create three lags: a recognition lag, an administrative lag, and an operational lag.

9. Political problems arise because the government has other objectives besides economic stability. The desire to maximize voter support may even create a political business cycle if government increases spending and cuts taxes whenever an election is near. Another political constraint is that provincial and municipal governments often pursue policies that don't coordinate easily with federal policies and may even be pro-cyclical.

10. An expansionary fiscal policy may raise the interest rate and crowd out private spending, weakening the effect of the fiscal policy stimulus on real GDP. The increased demand from the government is offset by decreased demand from the private sector. But this crowding-out effect may be small, especially when there is a large recessionary gap or if the Bank of Canada increases the supply of money to prevent interest rates from rising.

11. The effect of an expansionary fiscal policy on real GDP will also be weakened when it results in a rise in the price level (inflation). The closer the economy is to full employment, the steeper the AS curve, and the greater is this concern.

12. Other complications for fiscal policy arise because Canada is an open economy.

(a) We are vulnerable to demand shocks from abroad that could shift our exports in a way that offsets our domestic fiscal policy.

(b) When expansionary fiscal policy raises our interest rates, the Canadian dollar will appreciate against other currencies, causing a drop in the demand for our net exports, cancelling some of the fiscal stimulus. This net export effect is very similar to the crowding-out effect.

13. Supply-side fiscal policy is another option. Tax cuts can increase the incentives to save, invest, work, and take risks. Such changes in behaviour will shift the AS curve to the right, increasing real GDP and reducing inflation. Critics of such policies claim that the incentive effects are not very strong, and take a long time to take effect.

14. Policy-makers use a set of "leading indicators" to forecast fluctuations in real GDP. These are variables that have historically changed prior to GDP fluctuations, so they provide some advance warning.

■ **TERMS AND CONCEPTS**

budget deficit	fiscal policy
budget surplus	net export effect
built-in stabilizer	political business
contractionary fiscal	cycle
policy	progressive tax
crowding-out effect	proportional tax
cyclical deficit	regressive tax
cyclically adjusted	supply-side fiscal
budget	policy
expansionary fiscal	
policy	

■ **HINTS AND TIPS**

1. Discretionary fiscal policy occurs when government deliberately chooses to change taxes or spending. Non-discretionary fiscal policy occurs when automatic stabilizers are at work. Using the analogy of your car, discretionary fiscal policy operates like brakes: unless you decide to step on the brake pedal, the brakes cannot slow you down. Non-discretionary fiscal policy operates like shock absorbers: they work automatically when you go over a bump, whether or not you noticed the bump, and without you taking any action.

2. The most difficult concept in this chapter is the cyclically adjusted deficit. This measure was designed because the government budget can fluctuate either because government makes deliberate policy changes or because GDP fluctuations automatically cause fluctuations in net tax revenues. The cyclically adjusted deficit is calculated at a constant real GDP (the full employment level). If this number as a percentage of GDP changes then we know the government has changed fiscal policy.

3. If you have studied Chapter 8, remember that multiplier effects are at work when the government changes its fiscal policy by raising or lowering its expenditures on goods and services, or its tax collections.

■ **FILL-IN QUESTIONS**

1. To increase real GDP during a recession, taxes should be (increased, decreased) _____ and government spending should be _____. If fiscal policy is not employed, the (AD, AS) _____ curve will (soon, eventually) _____ shift to the right to close the gap.

2. If fiscal policy is to help offset business cycles, it will probably be necessary for the government to incur a budget (surplus, deficit) _____ during a recession and a budget _____ during inflation.

3. A contractionary fiscal policy is composed of (1) decreased _____, or (2) increased _____, or (3) a combination of both.

4. If Parliament votes to increase tax revenues by raising income tax rates, it is using (discretionary, nondiscretionary) _____ fiscal policy, whereas when income tax revenues increase only because the GDP rises, this is _____ fiscal policy.

5. A leading indicator is an economic variable that has traditionally reached its peak or trough (after, before) _____ the corresponding turns in the business cycle.

6. Those who favour growth in the public sector would, during a period of inflation, advocate a(n) (increase, decrease) _____ in government (spending, taxes) _____; and those who wish to contract the public sector during a recession would advocate a(n) _____ in _____.

7. Net taxes equal _____ minus _____ and _____.

8. When net tax revenues are directly related to the GDP the economy has some _____ stability because:
(a) when the GDP rises, tax revenues (increase, decrease) _____, helping to curb spending.
(b) when the GDP falls, tax revenues _____, helping to cushion the drop in spending.

9. As GDP increases, the average tax rate will increase in (progressive, proportional, regressive) _____ systems, remain constant in _____ systems, and decrease in _____ systems. Economies with more progressivity of taxes have (more, less) _____ built-in stability.

10. The cyclically adjusted budget balance:
(a) indicates what the federal _____ would have been if the economy had operated at _____ during the year; and (b) tells us whether the fiscal policy has become more _____ or _____ during the year.

11. A timing problem in the use of discretionary fiscal policy stems from the _____, _____, and _____ lags.

12. When the federal government employs an expansionary fiscal policy, it usually has a budget (surplus, deficit) _____ and normally (lends, borrows) _____ funds in the money market.
(a) This will (raise, lower) _____ interest rates in the economy and (contract, expand) _____ investment spending.
(b) This change in investment is called the _____ effect, and it tends to (weaken, strengthen) _____ the impact of the expansionary fiscal policy on real GDP and employment.

13. In an economy with an upward sloping AS curve, an expansionary fiscal policy will raise the real GDP and (raise, lower) _____ the price level. This change in the price level will (weaken, strengthen) _____ the impact of the expansionary fiscal policy on output and employment.

14. A contractionary fiscal policy will tend to (raise, lower) _____ the interest rate. In an open economy this will create capital (inflows, outflows) _____ that will lead to (appreciation, depreciation) _____ of the domestic currency. This currency value change will cause net exports to (increase, decrease) _____, which will (reinforce, offset) _____ part of the intended contraction in AD. This phenomenon is known as the _____ effect.

■ PROBLEMS AND PROJECTS

1. Columns A, B, and C in the table show levels of taxes at different income levels, under three tax systems.

Income	A:_____	B:_____	C:_____
1000	200	200	100
2000	375	400	300
3000	525	600	600
4000	625	800	1000

(a) Indicate in the blanks whether each system is progressive, regressive, or proportional.
(b) In which system is there the greatest degree of built-in stability? _____ The least? _____

2. The next table shows a nation's fiscal situation in each of five different years. The budget amounts shown are measured in billions of $.

Year	1	2	3	4	5
Actual budget (surplus +, deficit -)	-40	-90	-60	-28	-50
Cyclically adjusted budget (surplus +, deficit -)	-20	-61	-60	-16	+4
GDP	600	630	660	630	600
Cyclically adjusted budget as % of GDP	-3.3	-9.7	-9.1	-2.5	+1.7
Direction of fiscal policy		—	—	—	—

(a) Starting with year 2, determine for each year whether fiscal policy became more expansionary (E), more contractionary (C), or neutral (N), as compared to the previous year.
(b) The full-employment GDP level in this economy is _____ and occurs in year _____.
(c) In which years was there a cyclical deficit, and what was the size of the cyclical deficit in each of those years?_____

3. The equation representing the economy's taxes (net of transfers) is $T = 20 + 0.25$ GDP. The level of government purchases is constant: $G = 90$. Full employment real GDP is 300, but the current equilibrium GDP is 260.
(a) What is the current actual deficit or surplus?
(b) What is the current cyclically adjusted budget balance?
(c) What is the current cyclical deficit or surplus?

4. This question uses the analysis of Chapter 8, and shows that an economy with a proportional tax system is more stable than an economy without taxes that vary with income. Assume the economy is closed. Initially assume no taxes or government spending. The consumption schedule is given by the equation: $C = 80 + 0.8$ GDP, and planned investment is constant at $I = 40$.
(a) Fill in the C and AE columns in the table below.
(b) The equilibrium GDP is _____.

GDP	C	I	I'	C+I = AE	C+I' = AE'
500	—	40	30	_____	_____
550	—	40	30	_____	_____
600	—	40	30	_____	_____
650	—	40	30	_____	_____
700	—	40	30	_____	_____

(c) Column I' shows a drop of 10 in investment spending. Fill in column AE' accordingly.
(d) After the drop in investment, the new equilibrium GDP is _____.
(e) The multiplier in this model is = change in GDP / initial change in spending = _____/_____ = _____.

Now we introduce a public sector. Taxes (T) are 10% of GDP. The consumption function is as before, except the relevant income measure is disposable (after-tax) income (DI): $C = 80 + 0.80\ DI$. Government purchases are constant at 48. Again, investment is initially 40.
(f) Fill in the table below.
(g) The equilibrium GDP is _____.

GDP	T	DI	C	I	G	C+I+G = AE
500	—	—	—	40	48	—
550	—	—	—	40	48	—
600	—	—	—	40	48	—
650	—	—	—	40	48	—
700	—	—	—	40	48	—

(h) Suppose that planned investment drops by 14. Fill in the table below.

GDP	T	DI	C	I'	G	C+I+G = AE'
500	—	—	—	26	48	—
550	—	—	—	26	48	—
600	—	—	—	26	48	—
650	—	—	—	26	48	—
700	—	—	—	26	48	—

(i) After investment falls, equilibrium GDP becomes _____.

(j) The multiplier in this model is = change in GDP / initial change in spending = _____ / _____ = _____.

(k) Because the multiplier is (larger, smaller) _____ in the economy with taxes that depend on income, this economy is (less, more) _____ stable in the face of shifts in expenditures.

■ **TRUE-FALSE**

Circle T if the statement is true, F if it is false.

1. A major goal of fiscal policy is to stabilize economic activity at some desired level of employment. **T F**

2. A decrease in taxes will cause an upward shift in the consumption schedule and an increase in equilibrium GDP. **T F**

3. Fiscal policy is contractionary whenever it results in an actual deficit on the government's budget. **T F**

4. To stabilize the economy, the government should move their budget toward a surplus during the recession phase of the business cycle. **T F**

5. Built-in stabilizers are not sufficiently strong to prevent recession or inflation, but they can reduce the severity of a recession or of inflation. **T F**

6. Built-in stabilizers operate automatically to increase the government's deficit during inflation and increase its surplus during recessions. **T F**

7. The cyclically adjusted budget balance compares government spending to the tax revenue that would be forthcoming at full employment. **T F**

8. Macroeconomic stabilization is the sole goal of the federal government's spending and taxing policies. **T F**

9. Economists who see evidence of a political business cycle argue that the government tends to increase taxes and reduce expenditures before elections. **T F**

10. If financing a deficit results in increased interest rates, investment spending will be reduced and the expansionary effect of the deficit on aggregate demand reduced. **T F**

11. When a given increase in government spending is applied, the ultimate effect on real GDP is less if the AS curve is steeper. **T F**

12. The greater the percentage of demand for our goods that comes from foreign countries, the more vulnerable Canada is to AD fluctuations that arise from events abroad. **T F**

■ **MULTIPLE-CHOICE**

Circle the letter that corresponds to the best answer.

1. Fiscal policy influences the level of economic activity by manipulating:
   (a) the interest rate
   (b) the money supply
   (c) the foreign exchange rate
   (d) government spending and tax rates

2. Contractionary fiscal policy is composed of:
   (a) a reduction in government expenditure and the money supply or some combination of both
   (b) an increase in government expenditure and taxes or some combination of both
   (c) a reduction in government expenditure and increase in taxes or some combination of both
   (d) a reduction in taxes and the money supply or some combination of both

3. In the aggregate expenditure model, taxes:
(a) are paid out of savings and have no effect on equilibrium output
(b) reduce consumption at each level of GDP by an amount equal to the amount of the tax
(c) reduce both consumption and saving at each level of GDP
(d) are an injection into the spending flow

4. During which Prime Minister's term was unemployment insurance introduced in Canada?
(a) Louis St. Laurent
(b) Mackenzie King
(c) Pierre Trudeau
(d) John Diefenbaker

5. If the government wishes to increase the level of real GDP, it might:
(a) reduce taxes
(b) reduce its purchases of goods and services
(c) reduce transfer payments
(d) reduce the size of the budget deficit

6. For the economy to have built-in stability, when real GDP falls:
(a) tax receipts and government transfer payments should fall
(b) tax receipts and government transfer payments should rise
(c) tax receipts should fall and government transfer payments should rise
(d) tax receipts should rise and government transfer payments should fall

7. A direct relation between taxes and real GDP:
(a) automatically produces budget surpluses during a recession
(b) makes it easier for discretionary fiscal policy to move the economy out of a recession and toward full employment
(c) makes it easier to maintain full employment in a growing economy
(d) reduces the effect of a change in planned investment spending on GDP and employment

8. Why is Canada's employment insurance system considered a type of automatic stabilizer?
(a) approximately the same amount of employment insurance benefits are paid out each year
(b) the employment insurance system has the effect of stabilizing the unemployment rate
(c) employment insurance benefits paid out increase every year

(d) employment insurance benefits paid out increase when the economy is in recession

9. Which of the following is not an automatic stabilizer in the Canadian economy?
(a) GST
(b) CPP deductions
(c) income taxes
(d) all of these are automatic stabilizers

10. The crowding-out effect of expansionary fiscal policy results from government borrowing that:
(a) increases interest rates and investment spending
(b) increases interest rates and decreases investment spending
(c) decreases interest rates and increases investment spending
(d) decreases interest rates and investment spending

11. Which of the following is not an example of a discretionary fiscal policy action?
(a) a new plan to spend $100 million on child-birth centres
(b) an increase in the number of people on welfare because of rising unemployment
(c) a 10% cut in the rate of income tax
(d) a change in the maximum benefits available under employment insurance

Answer questions 12 through 15 on the basis of the following diagram:

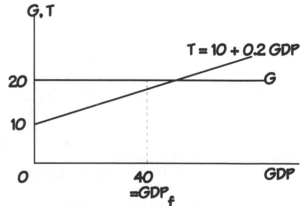

12. If GDP$_f$ signifies full-employment real GDP, then the cyclically adjusted deficit is:
(a) 0
(b) 2
(c) 4
(d) 6

13. If actual GDP is at 35, then the actual budget deficit or surplus will be:
  (a) a surplus of 1
  (b) a deficit of 1
  (c) a deficit of 3
  (d) a deficit of 5

14. If the government employs an expansionary fiscal policy by increasing government purchases by 2, and this moves equilibrium real GDP from 35 to 39, then:
  (a) the cyclically adjusted deficit rises by 2, and the actual deficit rises by 1.2
  (b) the cyclically adjusted deficit rises by 1.2, and the actual deficit drops by 0.8
  (c) the cyclically adjusted deficit falls by 2, and the actual deficit rises by 1.2
  (d) the cyclically adjusted deficit does not change, and the actual deficit rises by 1.2

15. If the T line had a steeper slope, there would be:
  (a) more built-in stability for the economy
  (b) less built-in stability for the economy
  (c) no change in the built-in stability in the economy
  (d) a need for more emphasis on discretionary fiscal policy

Questions 16 through 18 pertain to the next graph.

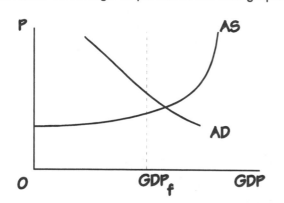

16. Given the current position of AD and AS, what is the situation in this economy?
  (a) there is an inflationary gap and contractionary fiscal policy is needed
  (b) there is an inflationary gap and expansionary fiscal policy is needed
  (c) there is a recessionary gap and contractionary fiscal policy is needed
  (d) there is a recessionary gap and expansionary fiscal policy is needed

17. In the neighbourhood of the current equilibrium, an expansionary fiscal policy will change:
  (a) the price level, but not output
  (b) output, but not the price level
  (c) both output and the price level
  (d) neither output nor the price level

18. If the government does not take any fiscal policy action, how will the economy shown in the graph adjust?
  (a) wages and input prices will eventually rise enough to shift the AS upward until it intersects AD at GDP_f
  (b) wages and input prices will eventually fall enough to shift the AS upward until it intersects AD at GDP_f
  (c) expenditures will eventually fall enough that AD will shift left until it intersects AS at GDP_f
  (d) none of the above

19. During the 1990s, Canada had a trend of:
  (a) decrease in the actual annual federal deficit
  (b) increase in the cyclically adjusted annual deficit
  (c) increasingly expansionary fiscal policy
  (d) all of the above

20. The phenomenon where government generates an economic boom when an election is approaching, and a recession shortly after an election, is known as:
  (a) stabilizing fiscal policy
  (b) cyclically adjusted fiscal policy
  (c) Keynesian economics
  (d) a political business cycle

21. The length of time it takes for the fiscal action taken by the federal government to affect output, employment, or the price level is called the:
  (a) administrative lag
  (b) operational lag
  (c) recognition lag
  (d) fiscal lag

22. The length of time it takes for government to decide what policy to adopt to address a recessionary or inflationary gap is called the:
  (a) administrative lag
  (b) operational lag
  (c) recognition lag
  (d) fiscal lag

23. If there is an inflationary gap, those who favour smaller government would advocate that fiscal policy take the form of:
  (a) increased taxes and government spending
  (b) decreased taxes and government spending
  (c) decreased government spending
  (d) increased taxes

24. The crowding-out effect may be lessened if:
  (a) the Bank of Canada increases the supply of money when government increases its borrowing
  (b) the economy is already near full employment when government spending increases
  (c) the profit expectations of businesses weaken when government spending increases
  (d) all of the above

25. Suppose that the economies of Canada's trading partners improved substantially and at the same time Canada had adopted an expansionary fiscal policy. What would most likely happen in Canada?
  (a) there would be a rise in net exports, a rise in aggregate demand, and the potential for inflation
  (b) there would be a fall in interest rates, a rise in aggregate demand, and the potential for a recession
  (c) there would be a rise in the incomes of trading partners, less demand for Canadian goods, and the potential for a recession
  (d) there would be a rise in the employment in other nations, a fall in net exports, and the potential for inflation

26. The effect of an expansionary (deficit) fiscal policy on the real GDP of an economy with an upward sloping aggregate supply curve is lessened by:
  (a) increases in aggregate supply
  (b) the crowding-out effect
  (c) increases in the price level
  (d) both (b) and (c)

27. A change in the government's fiscal policy stance is best measured by changes in:
  (a) equilibrium real GDP
  (b) the actual deficit or surplus as a percentage of GDP
  (c) the cyclical deficit or surplus as a percentage of GDP
  (d) the cyclically adjusted deficit or surplus as a percentage of GDP

28. If expansionary fiscal policy is adopted in an open economy, the resulting increase in interest rates will tend to raise demand for the nation's currency, causing currency appreciation and reduction in the demand for the nation's exports. This is termed the:
  (a) net export effect
  (b) crowding-out effect
  (c) exchange rate effect
  (d) interest rate effect

29. A supply-side fiscal policy intended to close a recessionary gap might be a tax cut intended to increase incentives to:
  (a) invest
  (b) work
  (c) save
  (d) all of the above

30. Skeptics of supply-side fiscal policy argue that:
  (a) the AS curve shifts only relatively slowly
  (b) incentive effects of tax cuts are greater than assumed by advocates of these policies
  (c) tax cuts usually end up creating budget surpluses for governments
  (d) tax cuts cause crowding-out

■ **DISCUSSION QUESTIONS**

1. What is meant by fiscal policy? When would expansionary (contractionary) fiscal policy be used? What options are open to the government when it applies expansionary (contractionary) fiscal policy?

2. What are the effects of different policy options on the federal budget?

3. Explain, for both a recession and an inflation, what kind of fiscal policy would be advocated (a) by those who prefer an expanded role for the public sector and (b) by those who wish to contract the influence of government in our lives.

4. What is the difference between discretionary and nondiscretionary fiscal policy? How do the built-in stabilizers work to reduce fluctuations in the level of nominal GDP?

5. Define progressive, proportional, and regressive tax systems. Explain which system leads to the most built-in stability for the economy.

6. How is the cyclically adjusted budget defined? For what purpose did economists define this measure? Under what circumstances will the cyclically adjusted deficit change, and under what circumstances will the actual deficit change?

7. Explain the three kinds of time lags that make it difficult to use fiscal policy to stabilize the economy.

8. How is the federal government's use of fiscal policy for stabilization purposes complicated by the fact that municipal and provincial governments also have large budgets and priorities of their own?

9. Explain how the following reduce the effectiveness of fiscal policy: (a) crowding-out effect, (b) inflation, and (c) net export effect.

10. Why does Canada's close trading relationship with the United States complicate the job of fiscal policy-makers in Canada?

11. How does supply-side fiscal policy work? What advantages and disadvantages does it have as compared with traditional fiscal policy, which works on the AD side?

■ ANSWERS

FILL-IN QUESTIONS

1. decreased, increased, AS, eventually

2. deficit, surplus

3. (1) government spending, (2) taxes

4. discretionary, nondiscretionary

5. borrowing

6. increase, taxes; decrease, taxes

7. taxes, transfers, subsidies

8. built-in; (a) increase; (b) decrease

9. progressive, proportional, regressive; more

10. (a) budget balance, full employment GDP; (b) expansionary, contractionary

11. recognition, administrative, operational

12. deficit, borrows; (a) raise, contract; (b) crowding-out, weaken

13. raise, weaken

14. lower; outflows, depreciation, increase, offset, net export

PROBLEMS AND PROJECTS

1. (a) A: regressive (taxes as % of income falls as income rises); B: proportional (taxes as % of income rises); C: progressive (taxes remain constant % of income); (b) C; A

2. (a) judging by change in cyclically adjusted deficit as % of GDP: E, C, C, C; (b) 660; 3 (because in this year the actual budget balance and cyclically adjusted balance are equal).

3. (a) G – T = 90 – 85 = deficit of 5; (b) G – T at full employment = 90 – 95 = surplus of 5; (c) cyclical deficit of 10 (difference between cyclically adjusted and actual budget balance).

4. (a) *C*: 480, 520, 560, 600, 640; *AE*: 520, 560, 600, 640, 680; (b) 600 (where GDP = *AE*); (c) *AE'*: 510, 550, 590, 630, 670: (d) 550; (e) -50, -10, 5; (f) *T*: 50, 55, 60, 65, 70; *DI*: 450, 495, 540, 585, 630; *C*: 440, 476, 512, 548, 584; *AE*: 528, 564, 600, 636, 672; (g) 600; (h) *T*: 50, 55, 60, 65, 70; *DI*: 450, 495, 540, 585, 630; *C*: 440, 476, 512, 548, 584; *AE'*: 514, 550, 586, 622, 658; (i) 550; (j) -50, -14, 3.57; (k) smaller; more

TRUE-FALSE

1. T   in other words, at full employment GDP
2. T
3. F   whether contractionary or expansionary is judged by the change in the cyclically adjusted balance
4. F   towards a deficit
5. T   thus the term "stabilizers"
6. F   surplus increases during inflations, deficits increase during recessions
7. T
8. F   other objectives, including political ones, also exist
9. F   taxes decrease and expenditures rise
10. T   this is the crowding-out effect
11. T   the remainder of the effect is dissipated in inflation
12. T

MULTIPLE-CHOICE

1. (d)
2. (c)   both will reduce AD

3. (c) because both C and S depend on disposable (after-tax) income
4. (b)
5. (a) in order to increase households' disposable income so that they can increase C
6. (c) to increase disposable income and C
7. (d) increased leakage means a smaller multiplier, and more built-in stability
8. (d) thus replacing some of the household income lost when workers are laid off
9. (d)
10. (b)
11. (b) all of the others require a deliberate action by the government; this one occurs automatically
12. (b) G = 20, and at GDPf, T = 18
13. (c) G = 20, T = 17
14. (a G rises by 2, but T rises by .8
15. (a)
16. (a) AD = AD at GDP > GDPf
17. (c) because AS is upward sloping
18. (a)
19. (a) the cyclically adjusted balance moved toward surplus and policy became more contractionary
20. (d)
21. (b)
22. (a)
23. (c) cutting spending would reduce the size of government; increasing taxes would increase the size of government
24. (a) this would prevent interest rates from rising
25. (a) the overall increase in AD would be too great
26. (d) if the AS were to increase, this would help
27. (d)
28. (a)
29. (d) all of these would shift the AS to right to some extent
30. (a)

CHAPTER 11

Deficits, Surpluses, and the Public Debt

The federal government can operate with a budget deficit, budget surplus, or balanced budget. After more than twenty consecutive years of deficits, Canada has had a budget surplus each year since 1997. The accumulation of past deficits has created a large public debt which stood at about $650 billion at the end of 2000. This chapter examines the economic impacts of deficits, surpluses, and the public debt.

A deficit occurs whenever the government's revenues fall short of their spending for the same period. Whenever a deficit occurs it adds to the total stock of the government's debt (public debt). A surplus exists if revenues exceed spending, and a surplus can be applied to reduce the debt.

There are three fundamental philosophies on how the government should manage its budget: annually balanced budgets; cyclically balanced budgets (by which the budget is balanced on average over the whole business cycle); and functional finance (by which fiscal policy is used to balance the economy, not the budget).

Canada's public debt has been caused by wars (which required high government expenditures), by recessions (which cut government tax revenues and necessitated increased transfer payments and spending), and lack of political will to make unpopular spending cuts or tax increases.

To get the best perspective on the debt, we examine: the debt as a ratio to GDP; Canada's debt compared to the debt of other major nations; the burden of interest payment obligations; the ownership of the debt; and the effects of inflation and accounting practices on the debt. All told, these considerations indicate that Canada's debt situation has improved and is quite manageable, despite the enormous total of $650 billion. Two of the most common concerns – that Canada may become bankrupt, and that an enormous burden is being imposed on future generations – are shown to be false.

However, there are some substantive issues with the debt, including the following: (1) increased inequality of incomes; (2) reduced incentives for work and production (because of higher taxes); (3) decreased standard of living when repayments must be made on external debt; and (4) crowding out of capital investment.

The crowding-out effect is likely the most serious of these problems, and may arise when increased government spending is financed by selling bonds. By competing with private firms for loanable funds, the government drives up the interest rate and reduces private sector investment in capital goods. This imposes a burden on future generations by reducing the growth of the nation's capital stock, and its future output potential. Note, however, that the problem of crowding out is offset if the government's spending is used to create public capital such as highways or universities.

With government running surpluses for the past few years, the current debate concerns what to do with the surpluses. The basic options are: (1) pay off debt; (2) cut taxes; (3) increase public spending; or (4) a combination of these. Each alternative has merits, and people's preferences are likely to be influenced by their views on the relative value and efficiency of goods and services provided by government as compared to the private sector.

■ **CHAPTER LEARNING OBJECTIVES**

In this chapter you will learn:
☐ What a budget deficit and a budget surplus are, and their connection to the public debt.

☐ About the recent history of Canada's budget surpluses, deficits, and public debt.
☐ The misconceptions about budget deficits and the public debt.
☐ The substantive issues about budget deficits and the public debt.
☐ The effect of the recent budgetary surplus.

■ **CHAPTER OUTLINE**

1. A budget deficit of a government is the amount by which its expenditures exceed its revenues in any year. A budget surplus is the amount by which its revenues exceed expenditures in a year. The public debt is the total accumulation of deficits and surpluses through time, and represents the total amount owed at a particular point in time.

2. If the government uses discretionary fiscal policy to combat recession and inflation, their budget will not usually be balanced. Three budgetary philosophies may be adopted by government as they approach the trade-off between full-employment and budget balance.

(a) The "annually balanced budget" philosophy requires government to balance expenditures and tax revenues each year. Such a budget is pro-cyclical, meaning that the government's actions will intensify the business cycle. The government is unable to use fiscal policy to counter the business cycle. This philosophy is favoured by some who see it as a way to control undesirable expansion of the public sector.

(b) The "cyclically balanced budget" philosophy requires government to run surpluses in years of prosperity, and deficits in recession years. The effect is counter-cyclical because the output swings in the business cycle are dampened by the government's actions. Ideally, over a period of years, surpluses will equal the deficits, so that the budget is balanced on average. This will not work so smoothly if upswings and downswings in the economy are not of equal magnitude and duration.

(c) The "functional finance" philosophy requires government to choose fiscal policies that will achieve the goal of non-inflationary full employment, regardless of the effects upon the deficit and the debt.

3. The three principal reasons for Canada's debt are: wars (World War I and World War II); recessions (including major recessions in 1981-82 and

1990-91); and a lack of political will to cut spending or to raise taxes as needed to eliminate deficits. By 2000, the gross federal debt was about $650 billion.

4. To properly assess Canada's debt situation a number of aspects must be considered.

(a) The debt to GDP ratio is important because the nation's GDP is a measure of its ability to carry debt. Canada's debt as a percentage of GDP fell from the end of World War II until 1975. It then rose until the mid-1990s, and has fallen since. In 2000 the debt was 62.6% of GDP.

(b) Canada's total public debt to GDP ratio is one of the highest among major industrialized countries.

(c) Starting in the late 1970s, a mushrooming debt and higher interest rates pushed up the ratio of interest payments to GDP. This trend subsided in the 1990s as the debt to GDP ratio fell and lower inflation allowed for lower interest rates.

(d) About 8% of the public debt is held by the Bank of Canada and 92% by private households, companies, and financial institutions. More importantly, about 20% is held by foreigners.

(e) Because the accounting system used by the federal government does not record public assets, the debt gives an overly negative picture of the government's financial position. Also, because the debt is expressed in nominal terms, the effects of inflation exaggerate the growth of the debt.

5. Concerns that a large debt may bankrupt the government and pass the cost onto future generations are largely false.

(a) Debt does not threaten to bankrupt the federal government because:
(1) it can refinance its debt
(2) it has the constitutional authority to levy and collect taxes.

(b) Deficit financing does not necessarily shift the burden of the debt to future generations.
(1) About 80% of the debt is held by Canadians, so any repayment of principal or interest creates a transfer of wealth between Canadians, not a reduction of wealth for Canadians collectively.
(2) Though a great deal of debt was incurred in World War II, the burden of the war was borne mainly by those whose standard of living was sharply reduced while the economy's energy was focused on producing military goods instead of consumer goods.

(3) The burden imposed on future generations is lessened if the increase in government expenditures is for real or human capital or if the economy were initially operating at less than full employment (and it stimulates an increase in investment demand).

(4) Debt held in foreign countries is a burden because both interest and debt repayment require a transfer of real output to other nations.

6. Public debt does pose several substantive problems.

(a)   The payment of interest on the debt probably increases the extent of income inequality.

(b)   Economic growth is reduced because the taxes levied to finance the debt reduce incentives to bear risks, to innovate, to invest, and to work.

(c)   The 20% of Canadian bonds owned by foreigners represent claims on Canada's future GDP. That is, we will have to give up some of our output to foreigners instead of consuming it ourselves.

(d)   Government borrowing to finance the debt tends to increase interest rates and reduce private investment spending. This "crowding-out effect" leaves future generations with a smaller stock of capital goods and a less productive economy. This concern is tempered by the fact that much government spending is on public investment that also improves the economy's productivity (roads, hospitals, airports, etc.), and the fact that there are often complementarities between public and private investments.

7. From the mid-1970s to the mid-1990s, the federal government had a deficit every year, with the deficit hitting a high of $40 billion in 1993. This produced massive growth in the accumulated debt. Fiscal policy then turned to deficit elimination in order to promote a reverse crowding-out effect.

8. Having turned the corner by eliminating deficits, the government now faces choices about what to do with the annual budgetary surplus. There are three main options (and combinations of these):

(a)   Paying down the debt would create a reverse crowding-out effect, but there are questions about how significant this effect would be. There is also concern that reducing the stock of government securities in circulation might cause problems in financial markets.

(b)   Cutting taxes (by reducing rates or increasing tax deductions and credits) could even-

tually stimulate economic growth, and (say some advocates) prevent undesirable growth of the public sector. This alternative may be inflationary if it expands the AD curve when we are already at or close to full employment.

(c)   Increasing public expenditures would enable us to address various needs for public capital and social programs. This alternative may also be inflationary, and critics fear that additional government spending programs may quickly become institutionalized and difficult to scale back later.

9. Lotteries are now a significant, but controversial, source of revenues for provincial governments. Some people consider lotteries to be a regressive tax preying on lower income individuals, and exposing people to serious problems of gambling addiction. Others do not consider lottery revenues to be taxes because purchasing lottery tickets is a voluntary choice. Given the need for public revenues, and the fact that consumers spend vast amounts on various forms of gambling, they argue that government might as well tap this revenue source.

■   **TERMS AND CONCEPTS**

annually balanced budget	**functional finance**
cyclically balanced budget	**public debt**
external public debt	**public investments**

■   **HINTS AND TIPS**

1.   Media reports sometimes use the terms debt and deficit interchangeably. Don't make the same mistake. A deficit is a flow variable: so many dollars *per year*. A debt is a stock variable: so many dollars. The two are related: the larger the deficit flows the larger the stock of debt.

2.   The most meaningful measure of how the debt problem is changing over time is the debt to GDP ratio. Inflation affects both the numerator and denominator, so it washes out of the ratio. The ratio also incorporates real output growth in the economy which improves our ability to "carry" the debt.

3.   Whether, and how, the debt creates a burden on our society is the most interesting and controversial issue in the chapter. It is worth studying especially carefully this section of the chapter, because some of the points are subtle, and they don't always match what you read or hear from the media or the politicians.

■ **FILL-IN QUESTIONS**

1. The budget deficit of the federal government in any year is equal to its (expenditures, revenues) _____ less its _____ in that year; and the public debt is equal to the sum of the federal government's past budget _____ less its budget _____.

2. An annually balanced budget is (pro-, counter-) _____ cyclical because when a recession sets in, tax revenues tend to (fall, rise) _____ so government must (cut, increase) _____ its spending to keep the budget balanced. This ends up (increasing, reducing) _____ AD at a time when the opposite is needed to stabilize the economy at full-employment output.

3. A cyclically balanced budget suggests that, to ensure full employment without inflation, the government should incur deficits during periods of _____ and surpluses during periods of _____, with the deficits and surpluses balancing out over the business cycle.

4. The principal causes of Canada's public debt are _____, _____, and lack of _____.

5. At the end of 2000 Canada's public debt was:
   (a) about $_____ billion and about _____% of the GDP;
   (b) about _____% of this debt was held by foreigners, and about _____% was held by Canadians.

6. The accounting procedures used by the federal government reflect its (assets, debts) _____ but do not reflect its _____.

7. The possibility that the federal government will go bankrupt is a false issue because the government can retire maturing securities by _____ them; and it has the constitutional authority to _____ and _____ taxes.

8. The public debt is a burden on an economy if it is (internally, externally) _____ held. The debt and the payment of interest on it may, however, (increase, decrease) _____ income inequality in the economy; dampen the _____ to work, take

risks, save, and invest; and have a _____ effect on investment.

9. A public debt that is internally held will burden future generations if the borrowing done to finance an increase in government expenditures (increases, decreases) _____ interest rates, _____ investment spending, and leaves future generations with a smaller stock of _____ goods.
   (a) But if the increased government expenditures are financed by an increase in the taxes on personal income, the present generation will have fewer _____ goods and the burden of the increased government expenditures will be on the _____ generation.
   (b) The burden on future generations of increased government expenditures financed by borrowing is reduced if the government expenditures pay for public _____.

10. Alternatives for disposing of budgetary surpluses include:
   (a) _____ the debt;
   (b) cutting _____; or
   (c) increasing _____.

■ **PROBLEMS AND PROJECTS**

1. Suppose that a nation's full-employment level of output is $500 billion per year. Over the course of a business cycle the nation's average output would be $450 billion per year. Government spending has already been determined, and is $100 billion for the current year.
   (a) If the nation pursues a cyclically balanced budget, how much tax revenue should be collected per year (on average) and what tax rate would generate this much revenue? Revenue = $_____ billion, Tax rate = _____%
   (b) In order to have an annually balanced budget, how would taxes have to change from your result in (a), assuming that government spending is constant at $100 billion per year?
   (c) If the government follows the functional finance philosophy, how would taxes have to change from your result in (a), again assuming government spending is held at $100 billion?

2. The table below shows data for four years for some country.
   (a) Fill in the table assuming that: (1) all income is taxed at a 20% rate; (2) the government annually pays 6% interest on the debt owing at the

beginning of the year. Round the numbers to the nearest integer.

(b) Because there is a deficit every year, the debt _____ each year.

(c) In years 1 and 2 there would be no deficit were it not for the _____ on debt from previous years.

(d) Though the debt increases each year, the country's debt situation improves in year _____ as measured by the _____.

Years	1	2	3	4
GDP ($)	1000	1100	1200	1300
Government purchases ($)	200	220	250	300
Tax revenues ($)	____	____	____	____
Interest on debt ($)	____	____	____	____
Debt at Jan 1 ($)	300	____	____	____
Deficit ($)	____	____	____	____
Debt at Dec 31 ($)	____	____	____	____
Debt at Dec 31 / GDP (%)	____	____	____	____

■ **TRUE-FALSE**

Circle T if the statement is true, F if it is false.

1. The budget deficit in any year is equal to the amount by which the government's revenues exceed its expenditures. **T F**

2. A budget surplus will reduce the public debt. **T F**

3. A nation will not be able to use fiscal policy both to promote full employment and balance its budget annually. **T F**

4. Proponents of functional finance argue that a balanced budget, whether it is balanced annually or over the business cycle, is less important than the objective of full employment without inflation. **T F**

5. Interest payments on the debt must be included in the calculation of government expenditures. **T F**

6. About half of Canada's public debt is currently held by foreigners. **T F**

7. The main contributing factor to Canada's large public debt is social programs spending. **T F**

8. Inflation increases the real value of the nominal public debt. **T F**

9. Selling government securities to foreigners to finance increased expenditures by the government imposes a burden on future generations. **T F**

10. The crowding-out effect of borrowing in the money market to finance an increase in government expenditures results from a rise in interest rates. **T F**

11. The crowding-out effect shifts the investment demand curve to the left. **T F**

12. Surpluses can produce a reverse crowding-out effect. **T F**

13. If the government pays off its debt, investors would no longer have the option of holding Canada government bonds. **T F**

14. Canada's public debt is higher than any other major industrialized country. **T F**

15. If lottery revenues are considered a tax, then they are a progressive tax. **T F**

■ **MULTIPLE-CHOICE**

Circle the letter that corresponds to the best answer.

1. Canada's public debt is the sum of all previous:
   (a) expenditures of the federal government
   (b) budget deficits of the federal government
   (c) budget deficits less the budget surpluses of the federal government
   (d) budget deficits less the budget surpluses of the federal and provincial governments

2. Which of the following would involve cutting government expenditures and raising tax rates during a recession?
   (a) an annually balanced budget policy
   (b) functional finance
   (c) a cyclically balanced budget policy
   (d) a policy employing built-in stability

3. Which is the most likely consequence for a nation following a cyclically balanced budget philosophy, if that nation's recessions are of greater magnitude and longer duration than its booms?
   (a) the nation will have a deficit every year
   (b) the nation will have surpluses more often than deficits

(c)   the nation's surpluses will tend to be bigger than their deficits

(d)   the nation's debt will rise

4. Which is a true statement about the recent trends in Canada's debt situation?

(a)   interest payments are growing as a percentage of GDP

(b)   interest payments are growing in absolute terms

(c)   the debt continues to increase in absolute terms

(d)   the debt is now falling as a percentage of GDP

5. The accounting procedures used by the federal government record:

(a)   only its assets

(b)   only its debts

(c)   both its assets and debts

(d)   its net worth

6. Inflation is a tax on:

(a)   the holders of the public debt and reduces the real size of the debt

(b)   the holders of the public debt and expands the real size of the debt

(c)   the federal government and reduces the real size of the debt

(d)   the federal government and expands the real size of the debt

7. The public debt cannot bankrupt the federal government because the federal government:

(a)   need not reduce the size of the debt

(b)   is able to refinance the debt

(c)   can levy and collect taxes to repay the debt and pay the interest on it

(d)   all of the above

8. Which one of the following is not a way for the government to finance its budget deficit?

(a)   sale of bonds to the Canadian public

(b)   sale of bonds to the Canadian central bank

(c)   sale of bonds to foreign investors

(d)   sale of common stock to Canadian investors

9. Canada's public debt is mainly held by:

(a)   the Bank of Canada

(b)   the Government of Canada

(c)   private households and financial institutions

(d)   foreign investors

10. Incurring internal debts to finance a war does not pass the cost of war on to future generations because:

(a)   the opportunity cost of the war is borne by the generation that fights it

(b)   the government need not pay interest on internally held debts

(c)   there is never a need for government to refinance the debt

(d)   war-time inflation reduces the relative size of the debt

11. If the government elects to pay down the public debt, what exactly would they do?

(a)   transfer money to foreign governments

(b)   send tax rebates to Canadian citizens

(c)   transfer money to the International Monetary Fund

(d)   buy back government bonds and Treasury bills

12. Which of the following would be a consequence if the government pays off debt held by Canadians?

(a)   a reduction in the nation's productive capacity

(b)   a reduction in the nation's standard of living

(c)   a redistribution of the nation's wealth among its citizens

(d)   an increase in aggregate expenditures in the economy

13. Which of the following is a consequence of the public debt of Canada?

(a)   it increases incentives to work and invest

(b)   it transfers a portion of the Canadian output of goods and services to foreign nations

(c)   it reduces income inequality in Canada

(d)   it leads to greater saving at every level of disposable income

14. The crowding-out effect of borrowing in the money market to finance an increase in government expenditures:

(a)   increases the interest rate and reduces current private investment expenditures

(b)   decreases the interest rate and increases private investment expenditures

(c)   allows for an increase in government and private borrowing

(d)   places the burden of the debt on today's generation

15. The crowding-out effect of government borrowing to finance its increased expenditures is reduced:
(a) when the economy is operating at or near full employment
(b) when there are complementarities between public investments and private investments
(c) when the interest rate is increased
(d) all of the above

16. What is an argument against tax reductions as a way to dispose of a federal budget surplus?
(a) the surplus may be temporary, so taxes should not be reduced permanently
(b) tax reductions may be inflationary if the economy is already near full employment
(c) there may be important needs for increases in government spending
(d) all of the above

17. Which of the following strategies for disposing of a surplus might create a reverse crowding-out effect?
(a) increasing public expenditures
(b) cutting taxes
(c) paying off debt
(d) none of the above

■ **DISCUSSION QUESTIONS**

1. What is the difference between the government's budget deficit and the public debt?

2. Explain the three different budget philosophies, and explain whether each one tends to intensify or reduce the fluctuations of GDP during the business cycle.

3. How big is the public debt of Canada, absolutely and relatively? How large are the interest charges on the debt, absolutely and relatively? What has happened to the size of the debt and interest charges since 1926, between 1975 and 1997, and since 1997? Why did these changes occur?

4. How could the accounting procedures of the federal government be changed to better represent the government's actual financial position (its net worth)? How does inflation affect the real size of the public debt and the real size of the federal government's budget deficits?

5. Why can't the public debt bankrupt the federal government? Are the same arguments true for provincial government debts?

6. Explain the difference between an internally held and an externally held public debt. If the debt is internally held, government borrowing to finance a war does not pass all the cost of the war on to future generations. Why? Why does the portion of the public debt externally held impose a burden on the economy?

7. How does the public debt and the payment of interest on the debt affect the income distribution and incentives?

8. Under what conditions will deficits impose a burden on future generations? Why don't increases in government expenditures financed by increased personal taxes impose the same burden on future generations? What will lessen the burden of deficit financing on future generations?

9. What circumstances would help Canada to continue to have budget surpluses? What are the options for what should be done with the surpluses? What might be the consequences for you of each of these options?

10. What are the arguments for and against governments raising revenues from lotteries instead of regular taxes?

■ **ANSWERS**

FILL-IN QUESTIONS

1. expenditures, revenues, deficits, surpluses

2. pro-, fall, cut, reducing

3. recession, inflation

4. wars, recessions, political will

5. (a) 650, 63; (b) 20, 80

6. debts, assets

7. refinancing, levy, collect

8. externally, increase, incentives, crowding-out

9. increases, decreases, capital; (a) consumer, present; (b) capital

10. (a) paying down; (b) taxes; (c) public expenditures

PROBLEMS AND PROJECTS

1. (a) 100, 100/450 = 22; (b) higher in recession years, lower in inflation years; (c) lower taxes to expand AD to move GDP to full-employment

2. (a) Tax revenues: 200, 220, 240, 260; Interest on debt: 18, 19, 20, 22; Debt at Jan 1: 300, 318, 337, 367; Deficit: 18, 19, 30, 62; Debt at Dec 31: 318, 337, 367, 429; Debt/GDP: 32, 31, 31, 33; (b) increased; (c) interest; (d) 2, Debt/GDP ratio.

TRUE-FALSE

1. F the amount by which expenditures exceed revenues
2. T debt increases when there is a deficit and decreases when there is a surplus
3. T an annually balanced budget is pro-cyclical
4. T
5. T
6. F the ratio is only about 20%
7. F wars, recessions, and lack of political will are the main reasons
8. F inflation decreases the real value
9. T foreigners have a claim on some of the nation's future output
10. T investment falls when interest rates rise
11. F it causes a movement along the investment demand curve
12. T if they result in lower interest rates, investment will increase
13. T these bonds are the government's main debt instrument
14. F several countries have larger debts, even on a debt to GDP ratio basis
15. F the lottery "tax" is regressive

MULTIPLE-CHOICE

1. (c)
2. (a) which would tend to deepen the recession
3. (d) because deficits will occur more frequently than surpluses, and will usually be larger
4. (d)
5. (b) therefore the debt situation looks worse because public assets are not taken into account
6. (a) the value of the money owed to bondholders is falling
7. (d)
8. (d) stocks are sold by corporations, not governments
9. (c)
10. (a)

11. (d) in simple terms, bonds and Treasury bills are the government's "IOUs"
12. (c) the bonds are the liability of the government (and indirectly taxpayers at large), but are the assets of bondholders (most of whom are Canadians)
13. (b) to the extent that the debt is held externally
14. (a)
15. (b) these complementarities could increase private investment, offsetting the drop in private investment created by higher interest rates
16. (d)
17. (c) because this could reduce the interest rate

CHAPTER 12

Money and Banking

This chapter explains the nature and functions of money and identifies the basic institutions in Canada's banking system. This information will prepare you for the discussion in later chapters of how banks can change the money supply, and how the Bank of Canada uses monetary policy to promote macroeconomic stability.

Anything that performs the functions of money is considered to be money. The most important function of money is to serve as a medium of exchange. Money also serves as a unit of account and a store of value. So, in Canada, which assets meet these criteria? Because there is no single best answer to this question, there are several definitions of the money supply. The narrowest, M1, includes currency (coins and paper money) outside chartered banks, and demand deposits (funds held in chequing accounts at chartered banks). The broadest, M2+, which includes the assets in M1 plus various "near-monies": savings and notice deposits at chartered banks, deposits at near banks (trust companies, mortgage companies, credit unions, and *caisses populaires*), and money market mutual funds. Most of the analysis in this text relies on the M1 definition.

What "backs" the money supply? Nothing tangible backs the money; it is backed simply by the government's ability to keep the value of money fairly stable. Currency is the debt of the Bank of Canada, and deposits are the debts of chartered banks. The chartered banks are obligated to redeem deposits with currency, but ultimately, the Bank of Canada has nothing with which to redeem the currency for which it is responsible. Given this, why does money have value? First, by social convention, we all accept money in exchange for goods and services (so these goods and services back the money, in a sense). Second, government has de-

clared currency to be legal tender. Third, the value of money depends on its relative scarcity (both for currency and bank deposit money). Many historical cases have shown that when money suddenly becomes much more plentiful, prices rise and money loses its value. In cases of hyperinflation, people may cease to accept currency as a medium of exchange and revert to transacting business by barter, or substitute a more stable foreign currency.

The last part of the chapter outlines the Canadian banking system, an industry dominated by a few major players. Chartered banks are businesses that seek to maximize profits for their shareholders, mainly by lending at interest rates higher than the rates paid to depositors. They try to create as many interest-earning loans as possible, while keeping enough currency to meet the needs of depositors who wish to withdraw funds from their accounts. From a macroeconomic perspective, the key aspect of bank activities is the creation of money by creating new loans and deposits. The next chapter analyses this in depth.

Many changes are underway in the banking industry: restructuring through mergers and acquisitions, globalization of financial markets, innovations in services, and increased use of electronic transactions are some. The biggest recent issue has been proposed mergers between major chartered banks. Government blocked two such mergers out of concern for competition in the industry, but did permit the Toronto-Dominion Bank and Canada Trust to merge in 2001.

■ CHAPTER LEARNING OBJECTIVES

In this chapter you will learn:
- ☐ The definition and function of money.
- ☐ What constitutes the supply of money.

☐   What backs Canada's money supply.
☐   About the structure of the Canadian financial system.

■ CHAPTER OUTLINE

1. Money is whatever performs the three basic functions of money: a medium of exchange, a standard of value, and a store of value. Historically, many different items have been used in different societies.

2. In Canada, currency (coins and paper money) outside the chartered banks and demand deposits (chequing account funds in chartered banks) are accepted media of exchange and constitute M1, which is the narrowest measure of the money supply.
   (a)   Coins are token money because their intrinsic value is below their face value.
   (b)   Paper currency is in the form of Bank of Canada notes.
   (c)   Demand deposits, which are bank-created money, account for about two-thirds of M1. ·
(Currency and deposits owned by the federal government and the banks are not included in the money supply.)

3. Other highly liquid financial assets (such as savings account funds) are so easily converted into media of exchange that they are called near-monies, and are included in broader measures of the money supply.
   (a)   M2 adds personal savings deposits and non-personal (business) notice deposits to M1.
   (b)   M2+ adds deposits at near banks to M2.

4. Credit cards are not included in the money supply because they are not money. A credit card is a vehicle for gaining short term credit, not a method of making final payment. Use of credit cards does, however, allow individuals and businesses to hold less money than they would otherwise.

5. What "backs" the money supply in Canada?
   (a)   In Canada, money is debt owed by chartered banks (demand deposits) or the Bank of Canada (currency).
   (b)   Currency has no significant intrinsic value, and cannot be redeemed for anything of tangible value.

   (c)   Money has value only because people can exchange it for desirable goods and services. This occurs because of:
   (1) a general social consensus to accept money as payment;
   (2) the government's declaration that currency is legal tender (which makes currency fiat money);
   (3) the relative scarcity of money.

6. The value of money is determined by its purchasing power in terms of real goods and services.
   (a)   The value of a dollar is inversely related to the price level.
   (b)   In a hyperinflation money can lose value so quickly that people become unwilling to hold money or to accept it as a medium of exchange. Then society reverts to barter or switches to a more stable money such as a foreign currency.
   (c)   Accordingly, it is vital that the supply of money be controlled: both in the Bank of Canada's issuance of currency and the chartered banks' creation of deposits.

7. In Canada, chartered banks are privately-owned firms that Parliamentary has granted charters to operate as banks.
   (a)   There are numerous banks in Canada, but about 90% of deposits are held by the six largest chartered banks.
   (b)   All of our largest banks are Canadian-owned. Many foreign banks operate here, but their market shares will always remain small because the Bank Act places legal restrictions on their growth.
   (c)   The banks perform the two essential functions of holding deposits and making loans. They strive to make profits for shareholders by making as many loans as prudently possible, and by charging higher interest rates on loans than they pay on deposits.

8. In addition to chartered banks, financial intermediaries include trust companies, loan companies, credit unions, *caisses populaires*, and insurance companies. All of these institutions act as intermediaries by accepting deposits from savers and lending to investors.

9. The Canadian Payments Association provides an inter-bank cheque clearing system between the chartered banks and near-banks.

10. The banking industry is undergoing many changes as a result of competition, globalization of financial markets, and technological progress:

(a) Banks are offering new products (different kinds of deposit accounts and loans) and expanded services (more branches, ATMs);

(b) Banks are competing more than ever in international markets for both deposit and loan customers;

(c) Internet banking, and e-business generally, are growing in popularity, and other innovations in how the public makes payments (such as smart cards) seem likely to gain popularity.

11. In numerous countries around the world the American dollar is the unofficial currency of choice. Some dollar holding is fuelled by black market activity, but much of the demand stems from a desire for a currency more stable than the local currency.

■ **TERMS AND CONCEPTS**

Bank of Canada notes	M2+
chartered bank	medium of exchange
demand deposit	near-monies
electronic transactions	prime rate
financial intermediary	store of value
legal tender	token money
M1	unit of account
M2	

■ **HINTS AND TIPS**

1. Money is not defined by its physical attributes; nor does something become money solely because the government declares that it is. The public must accept it as a medium of exchange.

2. Rapid inflation causes money to become a poor store of value (because monetary assets erode in value), and a poor unit of account (because the prices of goods and services are constantly changing). These problems can be so severe that people seek alternative forms of money, or even resort to barter. In either case, the original money loses its status as the unquestioned medium of exchange.

■ **FILL-IN QUESTIONS**

1. Three functions of money are
(a) _medium of exchange_
(b) _store of value_
(c) _unit of account_

2. The supply of money, M1, in Canada consists of currency (_coins_ and _paper $_) outside chartered banks and _deposits_ in chartered banks.

3. Financial intermediaries channel funds from _____ to _____.

4. Near-monies are highly _____ financial assets that do not directly function as a medium of _____ but can be readily converted in _____ or _____ deposits. Near-monies (are, are not) _____ counted in the M1 measure of the money supply.

5. Paper money is the debt of the _____, and demand deposits are the debts of _____.

6. Money has value because it can be exchanged for _____. Its value varies (directly, inversely) _____ with changes in the _____ level.

7. In Germany, after World War I, a rapid expansion in the _____ led to rapidly rising _____. In recent times, some nations with similar experiences have found their own currency being replaced by a more _____ currency such as the American dollar.

8. To operate as a bank in Canada, a financial institution requires a _____ granted by the (federal, provincial) _____ government.

■ **PROBLEMS AND PROJECTS**

1. With the information given below, determine M1, M2 and M2+.

Currency outside financial institutions:	$ 39
Currency at chartered banks:	17
Demand deposits at chartered banks:	60
Nonpersonal notice deposits at chartered banks:	205
Personal savings deposits at chartered banks:	112
Deposits at trust and mortgage companies, credit unions, and *caisses populaires:*	240

M1 = $_____
M2 = $_____
M2+ = $_____

2. Complete the following table showing the relationship between the percentage change in the price level and the percentage change in the value of money. Calculate to one decimal place.

Change in the Price Level	Change in the Value of Money
(a) Rise by:	
5%	- _____ %
10%	- _____ %
20%	- _____ %
(b) Fall by:	
5%	+ _____ %
10%	+ _____ %
20%	+ _____ %

3. Indicate which money supply measure(s) include each of the following items. Check off as many as apply. If an item is not included in any of the money supply measures, indicate "none."

	M1	M2	M2+	none
(a) Currency in your pocket	☐	☐	☐	☐
(b) A savings deposit in a credit union	☐	☐	☐	☐
(c) Currency in the vault of a bank	☐	☐	☐	☐
(d) A savings account in a bank	☐	☐	☐	☐
(e) Money market mutual funds	☐	☐	☐	☐
(f) A Canada Savings bond	☐	☐	☐	☐

4. Match the term on the left with the appropriate description on the right.

(a) paper money 2

(b) token money 4

(c) near money (1)

(d) chequebook money

(1) demand deposits (b)

(2) declared by government to be legal tender (a)

(3) readily convertible into medium of exchange (d)

(4) intrinsic value is less than face value (b)

Circle T if the statement is true, F if it is false.

1. All money in Canada is issued by the Bank of Canada or the federal government. **(T) F**

2. Money, by providing a convenient way to exchange goods and services, promotes specialization. **T F**

3. What we employ as money in Canada are actually debts of the chartered banks and the Bank of Canada. **T F**

4. Money serves as a store of value when it is used for measuring the worth of goods. **T F**

5. When a person writes a cheque on a deposit in a chartered bank to pay for groceries, money is being used as a medium of exchange. **T F**

6. Currency includes both coins and paper money. **T F**

7. A loonie is "token money" because its face value is less than its intrinsic value. **T F**

8. Canadian paper money can be converted into gold at a rate fixed by the Bank of Canada. **T F**

9. The Bank of Canada is our "central bank" and is owned by the federal government. **T F**

10. The most inclusive measure of money discussed in the chapter is M2+. **T F**

11. The fastest growing part of the Canadian money supply is credit card money. **T F**

12. Currency and chequable deposits are money because they are acceptable to sellers in exchange for goods and services. **T F**

13. If money is to have a fairly stable value, its supply must be limited relative to the demand for it. **T F**

14. If the price level triples, the value of one unit of currency will be only one-third of what it was previously. **T F**

15. Hyperinflation can cause money to fall out of use.   **T F**

16. Appropriate fiscal policy is one way for the government to maintain stability in the value of money.   **T F**

17. The Royal Bank of Canada is one of the ten largest banks in the world.   **T F**

18. The Canadian government has placed certain restrictions on the conditions under which banks may merge.   **T F**

19. A "smart card" is a new device that can store electronic money.   **T F**

20. The U.S. dollar is the official currency in some Latin American nations.   **T F**

■   **MULTIPLE-CHOICE**

Circle the letter that corresponds to the best answer.

1. Which of the following has been used as money?
   (a) circular stones
   (b) furs
   (c) cigarettes
   (d) all of the above

2. Which of the following is not one of the functions of money?
   (a) a factor of production
   (b) a medium of exchange
   (c) a store of value
   (d) a unit of account

3. Which of the following best expresses how the use of money benefits our society?
   (a) money is intrinsically valuable
   (b) money creates wealth by generating interest income
   (c) money creates wealth by facilitating specialization
   (d) the larger the money supply the larger the economy's output

4. Which of the following makes up the biggest share of Canada's M1 money supply?
   (a) coins

   (b) paper money
   (c) term and notice deposits
   (d) demand deposits

5. Demand deposits are money because they are:
   (a) legal tender
   (b) fiat money
   (c) accepted as a medium of exchange
   (d) fully guaranteed by the chartered banks

6. The supply of money, M1, consists of the debts of:
   (a) the federal government
   (b) the Bank of Canada
   (c) chartered banks
   (d) the Bank of Canada and chartered banks

7. Which of the following best describes the "backing" of money in Canada?
   (a) the gold bullion stored in the Bank of Canada's vaults
   (b) the belief of holders of money that it can be exchanged for desirable goods and services
   (c) the willingness of banks and the government to surrender something of value in exchange for money
   (d) the faith and confidence of the public in the ability of government to pay its debts

8. Bank of Canada notes are:
   (a) "backed" by gold
   (b) counted as part of the money supply when held by the chartered banks
   (c) legal tender in Canada
   (d) circulating assets of the Bank of Canada

9. Whenever a person withdraws $100 cash from a demand deposit at a chartered bank, the M1 money supply has:
   (a) increased
   (b) decreased
   (c) stayed the same
   (d) not enough information provided to tell

10. If a person closes her personal chequing account at the Bank of Montreal and deposits the balance in her personal chequing account at Vancouver City Savings Credit Union, then:
   (a) M1 falls, M2 falls, and M2+ rises
   (b) M1 is unchanged, M2 rises, and M2+ rises
   (c) M1 falls, M2 is unchanged, and M2+ rises
   (d) M1 falls, M2 falls, M2+ is unchanged

11. Pre-1967 dimes and quarters with high silver content have nearly disappeared from circulation, whereas pre-1967 pennies and nickels still circulate. Why?

(a) the quarters and dimes wore out

(b) the token value of quarters and dimes exceeds the intrinsic value

(c) more pennies and nickels were issued to begin with

(d) the intrinsic value of quarters and dimes exceeds the token value

12. The purchasing power of money decreases whenever:

(a) the unemployment rate rises

(b) the GDP price index falls

(c) the Consumer Price Index rises

(d) the interest rate falls

13. Which of the following is **not** an example of a financial intermediary?

(a) a credit union

(b) a *caisse populaire*

(c) a trust company

(d) the Bank of Canada

14. The Canadian Payments Association:

(a) represents the Canadian chartered banks in discussions with the government

(b) helps restructure loans for individuals and institutions that are unable to repay borrowings from the banks

(c) operates the inter-bank cheque clearing system

(d) determines the prices to be charged for different banking services

15. The prime rate of interest is:

(a) the interest rate paid on Canada Savings Bonds

(b) the interest rate on Government of Canada bonds

(c) the interest rate charged by the chartered banks to their best corporate customers

(d) the interest rate charged by the chartered banks for home mortgages

16. Identify the *false* statement:

(a) banking is a more concentrated industry in Canada than in the United States

(b) in the Canadian market, foreign-owned banks are larger and more powerful than domestically-owned banks

(c) foreign banks have entered the Canadian market, but the impact on competition has been limited

(d) the Canadian financial system is restructuring to permit greater competition between different sectors of the industry

17. Which is not among the "Four Pillars" of the Canadian financial system?

(a) insurance companies

(b) banks

(c) securities dealers

(d) Bank of Canada

18. When banks work on the "fractional reserve system" it means that:

(a) they pay only a small interest rate to their depositors

(b) a fraction of their borrowers default on their bank loans

(c) they keep only a small fraction of deposits to meet cash withdrawals

(d) they lend out only a small fraction of the funds deposited with them

19. Many transactions in Russia now occur in American dollars rather than in rubles because:

(a) Russian people are beginning to support capitalism

(b) there is a severe shortage of rubles

(c) there is an oversupply of dollars

(d) the value of the dollar is much more stable than the ruble

■ **DISCUSSION QUESTIONS**

1. How would you define money? Why are credit cards not counted as money?

2. At the University of B.C., plastic tokens redeemable for beer at the student pub were routinely accepted instead of currency in card games in the student residences. To what extent were these tokens considered to be money, and why did they function as such?

3. What are the components of M1? What are some examples of near-monies?

4. Suppose that you spend the summer working on a grain farm to earn money for school. Why would you rather be paid in money instead of in grain of equivalent market value? In responding, consider the three functions of money.

5. What "backs" the money used in Canada? What determines the value of money?

6. Why do you think that cigarettes came to be used as money in World War II prisoner-of-war camps?

7. Explain the relationship between the value of money and the price level. If prices are rising rapidly, what happens to the usefulness of currency in serving the three functions of money?

8. What roles do financial intermediaries play in a modern economy? How are chartered banks different from other financial intermediaries, and how are they similar? Where do you have your "bank" account; at a chartered bank, or at a near bank? Why did you choose that one?

9. Banks are firms that seek to maximize profits for their shareholders. How do they go about doing this? What risks are there to the public?

10. Should the government permit mergers between chartered banks that already have large market shares in the Canadian banking industry?

11. How is the growing use of debit cards (and perhaps "smart cards") affecting the public's use of currency and cheques? How are these new instruments different from credit cards?

■ **ANSWERS**

FILL-IN QUESTIONS

1. (a) medium of exchange; (b) unit of account; (c) store of value

2. coins, paper money, demand deposits

3. savers, borrowers (or investors)

4. liquid, exchange, currency, demand, are not

5. Bank of Canada, chartered banks

6. goods and services, inversely, price

7. money supply, prices, stable

8. charter, federal

PROBLEMS AND PROJECTS

1. M1 = 99; M2 = 416; M2+ = 656 (note that currency at chartered banks is not included in any money supply definition)

2. (a) 4.8, 9.1, 16.7; (b) 5.3, 11.1, 25.0

3. (a) M1, M2, M2+; (b) M2+; (c) none; (d) M2, M2+; (e) M2+; (f) none

4. (a)(2); (b)(4); (c)(3); (d)(1)

TRUE-FALSE

1. F   chartered banks are responsible for issuing chequing deposits
2. T   without money, exchange would be by the inefficient barter system
3. T   demand deposits are debts of chartered banks and currency is the debt of the Bank of Canada
4. F   this is its "unit of account" role
5. T   because chequing deposits at banks **are** money
6. T
7. F   its face value exceeds its intrinsic value (the worth of the metal)
8. F   in Canada paper money is not redeemable into anything at all
9. T   its role will become clearer in later chapters
10. T   it includes everything in M1, M2, and other near-monies
11. F   credit cards are not money
12. T
13. T
14. T
15. T   causing society to resort to barter
16. T
17. F   no Canadian bank is among the 10 largest in the world
18. T   any thereby prevented some proposed mergers
19. T
20. T   for example: Ecuador and Panama

MULTIPLE-CHOICE

1. (a)   in different times and societies
2. (a)
3. (c)   a specialized economy is not viable without the means for efficient exchange of goods and services
4. (d)   in other words, chequing accounts at banks
5. (c)
6. (d)
7. (b)   this social confidence is vitally important
8. (c)   though not backed by anything tangible, they are the debts of the Bank of Canada

9. (c) currency has increased $100, and demand deposits have decreased $100, so the total is unchanged

10. (d) M1 and M2 fall because they only include chartered bank deposits; M2+ is unchanged because the total deposits are unchanged (despite the transfer)

11. (d) so these coins were presumably melted down

12. (c)

13. (d) the Bank of Canada does not deal with regular firms and households

14. (c) for both chartered banks and certain other financial institutions

15. (c)

16. (b) we have many foreign banks, but they are smaller and less powerful than our domestic banks

17. (d)

18. (c) implications of this are discussed in the next chapter

19. (d)

CHAPTER 13

How Banks Create Money

The previous chapter showed that demand deposits at chartered banks are money. This chapter explains how the chartered banks can create these deposits – and thereby create money! The fundamental principles behind this seemingly mysterious process are laid bare by the brief history of goldsmiths. Goldsmiths evolved from providers of simple safe-keeping services to lenders who could issue paper money based on the gold stored in their vaults.

To explain banking operations we use the very simple device of the balance sheet, showing how each action changes the balance sheet. Accounts listed on the left side of a balance sheet are the firm's assets, and on the right side are the claims on those assets: liabilities and net worth. Based on accounting principles, the assets must equal liabilities plus net worth. The balance sheet for Canadian chartered banks was shown in Table 12-2. There we see that (aside from foreign-currency assets and liabilities) loans represent the majority of bank assets, and various kinds of deposits represent the majority of bank liabilities.

As you read this chapter, you must analyze the effect upon the balance sheet of each and every banking transaction discussed. The most important items in the balance sheet are deposits and reserves, because deposits are money, and a bank's ability to create new deposits is limited by the amount of its reserves. Only when they have excess reserves can a chartered bank expand the money supply. Excess reserves are not listed separately in the balance sheet, but can be inferred because excess reserves equal actual reserves less desired reserves.

The money creation process is explained in two scenarios: a single chartered bank, and the banking system (all banks as a group). The key difference is that the money-creating ability of the banking system as a whole is subject to a multiplier effect because the system as a whole does not lose reserves, whereas the money-creating ability of a single bank is not, because the bank must account for loss of reserves to other banks in the system.

The equilibrium level of deposits in the banking system is achieved through banks balancing the conflicting goals of profit and liquidity. Banks wish to create loans (and buy securities) in order to earn interest, but they also want to have enough liquidity (e.g., cash reserves) to be able to meet obligations to depositors. When a bank temporarily has excess reserves it may compromise by lending those funds to another bank on a day-to-day basis at the overnight loans rate.

The Last Word tells the story of how bank panics in the United States during the Great Depression led to a drastic multiple contraction of the money supply. This illustrates how the money creation process works in reverse.

■ CHAPTER LEARNING OBJECTIVES

In this chapter you will learn:
☐ How a single chartered bank can create (or destroy) money through loans to the public.
☐ About the multiple-deposit expansion of the entire chartered banking system.
☐ What the monetary multiplier is and how to calculate it.

■ CHAPTER OUTLINE

1. The balance sheet of a chartered bank is a statement of the assets and claims on assets at a specific time. Claims on assets consist of claims by non-owners (liabilities) and claims by owners (net

worth). Always, assets must equal liabilities plus net worth.

2. Medieval goldsmiths operated like modern banks.

(a) Traders deposited gold with a goldsmith in exchange for receipts which began to circulate in place of gold; in effect, the receipts became paper money.

(b) Eventually goldsmiths realized that little of the gold deposited with them was ever withdrawn, so they began to create interest-earning loans by creating additional gold receipts.

(c) Once loans were created, even though the receipts (paper money) remained redeemable for gold, these receipts were only fractionally backed by gold. Thus, there was always some risk of a bank panic.

(d) Goldsmiths' receipts (and gold in their vaults) are analogous to chartered banks' demand deposits (and cash reserves).

3. By examining how the balance sheet of the chartered bank is affected by various transactions, one can understand how a single chartered bank in a multibank system can create money.

(a) Initial transactions in the formation of a bank include capitalization by sale of shares, acquisition of property and equipment, and the acceptance of initial deposits from customers.

(b) The chartered bank desires to keep some cash reserves for depositor withdrawals (usually as vault cash), and for cheque clearing (usually as deposits at the Bank of Canada). These reserves are referred to as desired reserves.

(c) When a cheque is drawn against an account in one bank and deposited to an account at a second bank, the first bank loses reserves and deposits, and the second bank gains reserves and deposits.

4. There are several key points about reserves.

(a) Desired reserves are usually some percentage of deposits; this can be expressed as the desired reserve ratio.

(b) Actual reserves of vault cash and deposits at the Bank of Canada may not equal desired reserves.

(c) Excess reserves equal actual reserves less desired reserves.

(d) Money creation depends upon the presence of excess reserves.

(e) The Bank of Canada (as we learn more about in the next chapter) can influence the lending ability of chartered banks changing the amount of excess reserves.

5. The next transactions are crucial for understanding money creation and destruction.

(a) When a single bank extends loans or buys securities, it increases its own deposit liabilities (and, therefore, the supply of money) by the amount of the loan or security purchase. But the bank will lend or buy securities in an amount no more than its excess reserves because it anticipates a loss of reserves to other banks.

(b) When a single bank receives loan payments or sells securities, its deposit liabilities decrease (and the money supply shrinks) by the same amount.

(c) A bank balances its desire for profits (from interest earned on loans and securities) with its desire for liquidity or safety (which it achieves by having reserves). A bank may compromise somewhat when it temporarily has excess reserves by lending these funds to another bank at the overnight loans rate.

6. The banking system taken as a whole can create an amount of new loans and deposit money greater than its excess reserves. The maximum amount is equal to the excess reserves in the system multiplied by the monetary multiplier.

(a) Even though no single bank ever lends an amount greater than its excess reserves, the banking system as a whole **can** because, unlike a single bank, it does not lose reserves.

(b) The monetary multiplier is equal to the reciprocal of the desired reserve ratio; the maximum expansion of demand deposits is equal to the excess reserves in the system times the monetary multiplier.

(c) The banking system reaches equilibrium when it is "loaned up" such that actual reserves equal desired reserves.

(d) The multiplier process applies to money destruction as well as money creation.

(e) Less new money will be created than the monetary multiplier suggests if there are leakages because borrowers choose to have additional currency or if bankers choose to have excess reserves.

7. If bankers lend the maximum during periods of prosperity and less than the maximum during recessions, they add to the instability of the economy. To reduce the instability, the Bank of Canada must use monetary policy tools to control the money supply in a countercyclical way.

8. Bank panics in the United States during the Great Depression illustrate many of the principles in this chapter. The trouble started when depositors at banks in financial difficulty chose *en masse* to withdraw their funds rather than risk losses should their banks go bankrupt. Given the fractional reserve nature of banking, this virtually guaranteed that the banks **would** end up bankrupt. As the panic spread, thousands of banks failed between 1930 and 1933. The mass conversion of deposits into currency reduced bank reserves and, with the multiplier effect, led to a huge contraction in the supply of money. Ultimately, a system of deposit insurance was created (also in Canada) to protect public confidence in banks and prevent a problem at one bank from being contagious.

■ **TERMS AND CONCEPTS**

actual reserves	fractional reserve
balance sheet	monetary multiplier
desired reserve ratio	overnight loans rate
desired reserves	vault cash
excess reserves	

■ **HINTS AND TIPS**

1. The story of the goldsmith is superbly instructive because the scenario is easily understood, and parallels very closely our current system of banking which is more difficult to understand.

2. A balance sheet must balance. A bank's assets are either claimed by owners (net worth) or by non-owners (liabilities). Assets = liabilities + net worth. Use this principle to check both your calculations and your intuition when you work with balance sheets.

3. A chartered bank can be considered to be in equilibrium when it has zero excess reserves, because at this point it has precisely balanced the conflicting goals of profit and liquidity. A bank is said to be "loaned up" when it has no excess reserves. If we know a bank's desired reserve ratio, we can determine how many reserves a bank will desire for a given level of deposits, *or* we can determine how many deposits a bank can support with a given level of actual reserves.

4. Using balance sheets, it is common to confuse two very different concepts of "balance." Since assets must *always* equal liabilities + net worth, the accounts will always balance, but this does not imply balance in the sense of equilibrium. That is, the bank is not necessarily satisfied with its present ratio of reserves to demand deposits just because its balance sheet is balanced.

■ **FILL-IN QUESTIONS**

1. The balance sheet of a chartered bank is a statement of the bank's _____, _____, and _____ at some specific point in time.

2. Medieval goldsmiths issued receipts that could be redeemed for _____ but were also used as a medium of exchange. Therefore these receipts served as _____.

3. Like modern banks, the medieval goldsmiths operated on a _____ reserve system. Under such a system, banks (or medieval goldsmiths) are able to _____ money.

4. A bank _____ can occur when many depositors lose confidence in banks and decide to _____ large amounts of deposits.

5. Banks hold vault cash to meet the needs of depositors who wish to _____ cash.

6. The goal of _____ motivates banks to keep their reserves to a minimum, while the goal of _____ motivates banks to hold a prudent amount of reserves.

7. The excess reserves of a chartered bank equal its _____ reserves less its _____ reserves.

8. When a cheque is drawn upon bank X, deposited in bank Y, and cleared, the reserves of bank X are (increased, decreased, not changed) _____ and the reserves of bank Y are _____; deposits in bank X are _____, and deposits in bank Y are _____.

9. A single bank in a multibank system can safely make loans or buy securities equal in amount to their own _____.

10. When a chartered bank sells a $2,000 government bond to a securities dealer, the supply of money (increases, decreases) _____ by $_____.

11. The banking system can make loans (or buy securities) and create money in an amount equal to its excess reserves multiplied by the _____. Its lending potential per dollar of excess reserves is greater than the lending potential of a single bank because it does not lose _____ to other banks.

12. If the desired reserve ratio is 5%, the banking system is $6 million short of reserves, and the banking system is unable to increase its reserves, the banking system must _____ the money supply by $_____. This can be accomplished by customers making _____ payments totalling this amount, or by banks selling this amount of _____ to the public. In either case, we assume that payments would be made by writing _____ that would result in an (increase, decrease) _____ in the banks' _____ liabilities.

13. The money-creating potential of the chartered banking system is lessened by the withdrawal of _____ from banks and by the decision of bankers to keep _____ reserves.

14. Chartered banks, in the past, (a) have kept considerable excess reserves during periods of (prosperity, recession) _____ and have kept few or no excess reserves during periods of _____; (b) and by behaving in this way have made the economy (more, less) _____ unstable.

15. Bank _____ in the Great Depression caused a large (expansion, contraction) _____ in the money supply, and led to the creation of a deposit _____ program to protect bank customers.

■ **PROBLEMS AND PROJECTS**

1. Indicate whether each item following would be listed under the assets (A) or under the liabilities + net worth (L) of a bank's balance sheet.

(a) A government bond held by the bank A
(b) A mortgage loan to a homeowner A
(c) The computer owned by the bank L
(d) Demand deposits L
(e) Cash held in a bank vault A
(f) A government deposit held in the bank L
(g) Reserves held at the Bank of Canada A
(h) Common stock issued by the bank A

2. Following is the simplified balance sheet of a chartered bank. Assume that the figures given show the bank's situation prior to each of the following four transactions. Fill in the blanks in each column to show the balance sheet effects of the corresponding transaction. For each transaction, start from the "initial" figures.

	Initial	(a)	(b)	(c)	(d)
Assets					
Reserves	$100	$150	$160	$160	$200
Loans	700	100	740	70	
Securities	200	200	200	20	100
Liabilities & net worth					
Deposits	900	950	940	960	
Capital	100	100	100	100	100

(a) A cheque for $50 is written by a depositor of the bank, and given to a person who deposits it in another bank, and then cleared.
(b) The bank loans $40 to a customer, and deposits the $40 into the customer's account.
(c) A cheque for $60 drawn on another bank is deposited in this bank and cleared.
(d) The bank sells $100 of government bonds to the Bank of Canada.

3. In the table below are four balance sheets for a single chartered bank [columns (1)-(4)]. The desired reserve ratio is 20%.
(a) In the opening situation shown in column (1), compute the following amounts: desired reserves = $_____, excess reserves = $_____, and new loans that can be extended = $_____
(b) Fill in column (2) showing the bank's new balance sheet after the bank has extended the maximum amount of new loans, and has deposited the funds in borrowers' deposit accounts.
(c) Fill in column (3) showing the bank's new balance sheet after the borrowers have spent the funds just borrowed, assuming that they do so by writing cheques to people who are customers of other banks.
(d) Given the situation shown in column (3), confirm that the bank is "loaned up" and incapable of further expansion deposits and loans.

	(1)	(2)	(3)
Assets			
Reserves	$50	$____	$____
Loans	100	____	____
Securities	50	____	____
Liabilities & net worth			
Deposits	175	____	____
Capital	25	____	____

	initial	(1)	(2)	(3)	(4)	(5)	(6)
Assets:							
Reserves	$25	$__	$__	$__	$__	$__	$__
Loans	425	__	__	__	__	__	__
Securities	100	__	__	__	__	__	__
Liabilities & net worth							
Deposits	500	__	__	__	__	__	__
Capital	50	50	50	50	50	50	50

4. Suppose that banks desire a 4% reserve ratio.
(a) What is the value of the monetary multiplier? _____
(b) What is the maximum amount of new loans and deposits that a single bank could create if they had $1 of excess reserves? $_____
(c) What is the maximum amount of new loans and deposits that the whole banking system could create if one bank had $1 of excess reserves? $_____
(d) How many excess reserves would have to exist in the banking system to make possible the creation of $75 of new loans and deposit money? $_____

5. Following is the simplified consolidated balance sheet for all chartered banks in the economy. Assume that the figures given show the bank's assets and liabilities prior to each of the following three transactions, and that the desired reserve ratio is 5%. For each of the three transactions ((a), (b), and (c)), start with the figures in the "initial" column.
(a) The public deposits $5 in cash in the banks, and the banks keep the cash in their vaults. Fill in column 1. Fill in column 2 on the assumption that the banking system extends the maximum amount of new loans.
(b) The banking system sells $8 worth of securities to the Bank of Canada in exchange for new reserves. Complete column 3. Assuming the system extends the maximum amount of loans that it can, fill in column 4.
(c) The Bank of Canada sells $1 worth of securities to the chartered banks. Complete column 5. Complete column 6 showing the condition of the banks after they have contracted their loans by the amount necessary to meet the desired reserve ratio.

6. Imagine a banking system with only three chartered banks: the Bank of Charlottetown, Newfoundland Marine Bank, and the Moncton Bank. Through the Canadian Payments Association, the three banks settle claims against one another as follows:
Charlottetown depositors wrote cheques to Newfoundland depositors = $20
Charlottetown depositors wrote cheques to Moncton depositors = $80
Newfoundland depositors wrote cheques to Charlottetown depositors = $50
Newfoundland depositors wrote cheques to Moncton depositors = $60
Moncton depositors wrote cheques to Charlottetown depositors = $30
Moncton depositors wrote cheques to Newfoundland depositors = $70.
(a) How much do the inter-bank clearing settlements increase or decrease each bank's reserves: Bank of Charlottetown: $_____; Newfoundland Marine Bank: $_____; Moncton Bank: $_____
(b) How much will each bank expand or contract their deposits (and loan or security holdings), assuming the maximum effects?
Bank of Charlottetown: $_____
Newfoundland Marine Bank: $_____
Moncton Bank: $_____
(c) Ultimately, what is the net effect on the money supply of this shuffling of reserves among the three banks? $_____

■ TRUE-FALSE

Circle T if the statement is true, F if it is false.

1. The balance sheet of a chartered bank shows the transactions which the bank has undertaken in a given year. T **F**

2. A chartered bank's assets plus its net worth equal the bank's liabilities. **T** F

3. Banks, operating under a fractional reserve system, can create money.   **T F**

4. Goldsmiths increased the money supply when they made loans and issued paper receipts that were not fully backed by gold in their vaults.   **T F**

5. Chartered banks hold their reserves either as deposits in the Bank of Canada or as government bonds in their own vaults.   **T F**

6. If the office owned by a bank increases in value, this will increase the bank's assets and owners' net worth.   **T F**

7. A goldsmith might experience a bank panic if customers began to doubt whether the goldsmith would be able to redeem gold receipts.   **T F**

8. An increase in a bank's deposit liabilities will increase the bank's desired reserve ratio.   **T F**

9. The actual reserves of a chartered bank equal excess reserves plus desired reserves.   **T F**

10. Chartered banks are required by law to hold a certain percentage of their deposits in reserves.   **T F**

11. A cheque for $1,000 drawn on bank X by a depositor and deposited in bank Y will increase the excess reserves of bank Y by $1,000.   **T F**

12. If the banking system has $10 million in excess reserves and if the reserve ratio is 5%, it can increase its loans by $200 million.   **T F**

13. When a borrower repays a loan of $500, either in cash or by cheque, the supply of money is reduced by $500.   **T F**

14. The granting of a $5,000 loan and the purchase of a $5,000 government bond from a securities dealer by a chartered bank have the same effect on the money supply.   **T F**

15. The monetary multiplier effect is reduced if the public wishes to hold more currency when their deposit balances increase.   **T F**

16. The monetary multiplier is increased if banks are content to hold excess reserves.   **T (F)**

17. The monetary multiplier is also known as the demand-deposit multiplier.   **T F**

18. Historically, banks have tended to create more new money when the economy is booming, and this adds to macroeconomic instability.   **T F**

19. A chartered bank seeks both profits and liquidity, but these are conflicting goals.   **T F**

■ **MULTIPLE-CHOICE**

Circle the letter that corresponds to the best answer.

1. The fundamental balance identity is:
 (a) assets = liabilities - net worth
 (b) assets = liabilities + net worth
 (c) assets = liabilities
 (d) assets + liabilities = net worth

2. On a bank's balance sheet, loans are recorded as:
 (a) part of net worth
 (b) an asset
 (c) a liability
 (d) none of the above

3. The entry on the balance sheet of a bank that counts as part of the money supply is:
 (a) cash held by the bank
 (b) bank loans
 (c) reserves held at the central bank
 (d) demand deposits

4. On a bank's balance sheet, the entry for capital stock represents:
 (a) cash reserves
 (b) bank loans
 (c) owners' equity
 (d) government securities

5. The goldsmiths became bankers when:
 (a) they accepted deposits of gold for safe storage
 (b) they issued receipts for the gold stored with them
 (c) their receipts for deposited gold were used as paper money
 (d) they issued paper money in excess of the amount of gold stored with them

6. The immediate effect when cash is deposited in a deposit account in a chartered bank is:
  (a)   a decrease in the money supply
  (b)   an increase in the money supply
  (c)   no change in the composition of the money supply
  (d)   a change in the composition of the money supply

7. A chartered bank has actual reserves of $2,000 and deposit liabilities of $30,000; the desired reserve ratio is 5%. Excess reserves of the bank are:
  (a) $500
  (b) $0
  (c)   minus $1,000
  (d) $1,500

8. The basic reason that a chartered bank chooses to hold reserves is:
  (a)   to protect the chartered bank against losses from unpaid loans
  (b)   to maximize the bank's interest income
  (c)   to meet the Bank of Canada's regulations
  (d)   to provide liquidity for the chartered bank and protect it against a "run" on the bank

9. A depositor places $1,000 in cash in a chartered bank, which has a desired reserve ratio of 5%. As a result, the reserves and excess reserves of the bank have been increased, respectively, by:
  (a) $1,000 and $50
  (b) $1,000 and $950
  (c) $1,000 and $1,000
  (d) $500 and $500

10. A chartered bank has no excess reserves, but then a depositor places $600 in cash in the bank, and the bank adds the $600 to its reserves. The bank then loans $300 to a borrower. The net effect is that the money supply has:
  (a)   not been affected
  (b)   increased by $300
  (c)   increased by $600
  (d)   increased by $900

11. A chartered bank has excess reserves of $500 and desires a reserve ratio of 10%; it grants a loan of $1,000. If the borrower writes a cheque for $1,000, which is deposited in another chartered bank, the first bank will be short of reserves, after the cheque has been cleared, in the amount of:
  (a) $100
  (b) $700

  (c) $500
  (d) $1,000

12. A chartered bank sells a $1,000 government security to a broker. The broker pays for the bond in cash, which the bank puts in its vault. Strictly by this transaction alone, the money supply has:
  (a)   not been affected
  (b)   decreased by $1,000
  (c)   increased by $1,000
  (d)   increased by $1,000 multiplied by the monetary multiplier

13. If the desired reserve ratio were 4%, the value of the monetary multiplier would be:
  (a)   16
  (b)   20
  (c)   24
  (d)   25

14. A chartered bank has deposit liabilities of $100,000, reserves of $37,000, and a desired reserve ratio of 25%. The amount by which a single chartered bank and the amount by which the banking system can increase loans are, respectively:
  (a) $12,000 and $48,000
  (b) $17,000 and $68,000
  (c) $12,000 and $60,000
  (d) $17,000 and $85,000

15. By making new loans of $7,000 the banking system eliminates its excess reserves of $700, and becomes "loaned up." The desired reserve ratio for this banking system must be:
  (a)   5%
  (b)   6.25%
  (c)   8%
  (d)   10%

16. The chartered banking system finds that its desired reserve ratio has risen from 5% to 6.25%, with the result that it is $100 million short of reserves. If it is unable to obtain any additional reserves, it must decrease its money supply by:
  (a) $100 million
  (b) $125 million
  (c) $1,600 million
  (d) $2,000 million

17. The money-creating potential of the banking system is reduced when:
  (a)   bankers choose to have excess reserves

(b) borrowers choose to hold none of the funds they have borrowed in currency
(c) bankers borrow from the Bank of Canada
(d) banks reduce their loan interest rates

18. The excess reserves held by banks tend to:
(a) rise during periods of prosperity
(b) fall during periods of recession
(c) rise during periods of recession
(d) fall when interest rates in the economy fall

19. Unless controlled, the money supply will:
(a) fall during periods of prosperity
(b) rise during periods of recession
(c) change in a fashion that reinforces cyclical fluctuations in the economy
(d) change in a fashion that counters cyclical fluctuations in the economy

Use the following balance sheet for the Maple Leaf Bank for questions 20 through 22. Assume the desired reserve ratio is 20%.

Assets		Liabilities and Net Worth	
Reserves	$50,000	Demand deposits	$150,000
Loans	70,000	Capital stock	100,000
Securities	30,000		
Property	100,000		

20. Maple Leaf Bank has excess reserves of:
(a) $10,000
(b) $20,000
(c) $30,000
(d) -$20,000

21. Maple Leaf Bank can safely expand its loans by a maximum of:
(a) $50,000
(b) $40,000
(c) $30,000
(d) $20,000

22. If the original bank balance sheet was for the chartered banking system, rather than just for Maple Leaf Bank, loans and deposits could have been expanded by a maximum of:
(a) $50,000
(b) $100,000
(c) $150,000
(d) $200,000

23. The overnight loans rate is:
(a) the interest rate on short term cash advances on credit cards
(b) the interest rate banks charge one another for short term loans of cash reserves
(c) the interest rate the Bank of Canada charges banks
(d) the percentage of cash reserves which chartered banks are willing to lend out

24. A bank is said to be "loaned up" when:
(a) it has no excess reserves
(b) it can find no more willing borrowers to take out new loans
(c) when all of its assets are invested in loans
(d) when all of its loans have been repaid

Questions 25 and 26 are based on the following consolidated balance sheet for the banking system. All figures are in billions. The desired reserve ratio is 12.5%.

Assets		Liabilities and Net Worth	
Reserves	$20	Demand deposits	$200
Loans	95	Capital stock	120
Securities	120		
Property	85		

25. This banking system will have to contract deposits by how much?
(a) $5 billion
(b) $20 billion
(c) $25 billion
(d) $40 billion

26. The required contraction of deposits could be accomplished by:
(a) calling in loans
(b) buying government securities
(c) reducing reserves
(d) any of the above

27. The formula for the monetary multiplier is given by $m = 1/R$, where R stands for:
(a) excess reserves
(b) the desired reserve ratio
(c) the marginal propensity to save
(d) the interest rate

28. The maximum deposit expansion for the whole banking system is found by multiplying the volume of excess reserves by:
(a) the desired reserve ratio

(b)   1 minus the desired reserve ratio
(c)   the monetary multiplier
(d)   the reciprocal of the interest rate

29. Why did the money supply in the United States shrink drastically in the early 1930s?
(a)   the government restricted how much banks could loan out
(b)   banks increased their desired reserve ratios
(c)   bank panics caused bank reserves to shrink drastically
(d)   the public deposited most of its currency in banks

■ DISCUSSION QUESTIONS

1. List and explain each category of assets and liabilities in the simplified balance sheet of a bank.

2. How did the early goldsmiths come to issue paper money and then become bankers? Explain the difference between 100% and a fractional reserve system of banking, and why the latter system is subject to bank panics and may require public regulation.

3. Chartered banks seek both profits and liquidity. Why are the two objectives in conflict?

4. Why does it work for banks to hold only fractional reserves? What might be some reasons that the desired reserve ratio might change from time to time?

5. Why does the granting of a loan by a chartered bank increase the supply of money? Why does the repayment of a loan decrease the money supply?

6. The owner of a ski shop writes a cheque on his account in a Banff bank and sends it to one of his suppliers, who deposits it in a different bank in Calgary. How does the Calgary bank obtain payment from the Banff bank? How are the reserves of the two banks affected?

7. Why is a single bank able to loan safely an amount equal to only its excess reserves, while the banking system as a whole can extend loans and expand the money supply by an amount that is a multiple of the system's excess reserves? How does such a multiple expansion of deposits (that is, money) take place?

8. What are two reasons why the potential expansion of the money supply – as according to the monetary multiplier -- may not be fully achieved?

9. Why is there a "need for monetary control" in the Canadian economy?

10. Why is there a need for deposit insurance?

■ ANSWERS

FILL-IN QUESTIONS

1. assets, liabilities, net worth

2. gold, money

3. fractional, create

4. panic (failure), withdraw

5. withdraw

6. profitability, liquidity

7. actual, desired

8. decreased, increased, decreased, increased

9. excess reserves

10. decreases, 2,000

11. monetary multiplier, reserves

12. decrease, 120 million, loan, securities, cheques, decrease, deposit

13. currency, excess

14. (a) recession, prosperity; (b) more

15. panics (failures), contraction, insurance

PROBLEMS AND PROJECTS

1. (a) A; (b) A; (c) A; (d) L; (e) A; (f) L; (g) A; (h) L

2.	(a)	(b)	(c)	(d)
Assets:				
Reserves	50	100	160	200
Loans	700	740	700	700
Securities	200	200	200	100
Liabilities and net worth:				
Deposits	850	940	960	900

3. (a) 35, 15, 15; (b) entries down column (2): 50, 115, 50, 190, 25; (c) entries down column (3): 35, 115, 50, 175, 25; (d) Deposits = 175, and Reserves = 35 = 20% of 175.

4. (a) 25; (b) 1; (c) 25; (d) 3

5.

	(1)	(2)	(3)	(4)	(5)	(6)
Assets:						
Reserves	$30	$30	$33	$33	$24	$24
Loans	425	520	425	585	425	405
Securities	100	100	92	92	101	101
Liabilities and net worth:						
Deposits	505	600	500	660	500	480

6. (a) Charlottetown pays $50 to Moncton, and receives $30 from Newfoundland = net reserve decrease of $20; Newfoundland pays $30 to Charlottetown, and receives $10 from Moncton = net reserve decrease of $20; Moncton: receives $50 from Charlottetown, and pays $10 to Newfoundland = net reserve increase of $40;
(b) Charlottetown: contract by $20; Newfoundland: contract by $20; Moncton: expand by $40;
(c) No change, since the banking system as a whole experiences neither loss nor gain of reserves.

TRUE-FALSE

1. F   it shows the situation at a point in time
2. F   assets = liabilities + net worth
3. T
4. T
5. F   government bonds are not considered reserves; only cash and deposits at the Bank of Canada qualify
6. F
7. T
8. F   this would increase the amount of reserves, but not the desired reserve ratio
9. T
10. F   this was once true, but no longer
11. F   bank Y will have excess reserves but only $1,000 less whatever the desired reserves are for the added $1,000 in deposits
12. T   1/.05 = 20 = monetary multiplier
13. T   either currency in circulation or demand deposits decrease by $500
14. T   in both cases the bank will create $5,000 in new deposit money
15. T   currency drain is a leakage from the monetary multiplier
16. F   it decreases because excess reserves are a leakage from the monetary multiplier process
17. T
18. T   their lending behaviour tends to be procyclical
19. T

MULTIPLE-CHOICE

1. (b)
2. (b)   the loans are owed to the bank
3. (d)
4. (c)   the owners' claims on the firm's assets
5. (d)   this represents fractional reserve banking
6. (d)   the total money supply does not change, but the composition (deposits vs. currency) does
7. (a)   30,000 x .05 = 1,500; 2,000 − 1,500 = 500
8. (d)   they must be able to meet depositors' demands for withdrawals
9. (b)   because $50 of the $1,000 is desired reserves against the new deposit
10. (b)   the initial deposit had no net effect on the money supply, but the loan increases it
11. (c)   the bank loses $1,000 in reserves
12. (b)   currency in circulation has decreased by $1,000
13. (d)   1/.04 = 25
14. (a)   R = 25%, so the monetary multiplier is 4
15. (d)   if excess reserves can be turned into 10 times as much in new loans and deposits
16. (c)   1/.0625 = 16
17. (a)   excess reserves are a leakage from the multiplier process
18. (c)   because there are less qualified borrowers
19. (c)   this procyclical tendency creates a need for monetary control by the Bank of Canada
20. (b)   150,000 x .20 = 30,000; 50,000 − 30,000
21. (d)   the amount of their excess reserves
22. (b)   excess reserves x monetary multiplier
23. (b)
24. (a)   its actual reserve ratio = its desired reserve ratio
25. (d)   shortage of reserves x monetary multiplier
26. (a)   borrowers will use up demand deposits to make loan payments
27. (b)
28. (c)
29. (c)   depositors panicked and withdraw funds *en masse*

CHAPTER 14

The Bank of Canada and Monetary Policy

This, the last of three chapters on money and banking, explains how the Bank of Canada uses monetary policy — the control of the money supply — to fight macroeconomic fluctuations. The objective of monetary policy is much the same as that of fiscal policy: to attain a full employment GDP without inflation.

The Bank of Canada has five functions: (1) serve as a "bankers' bank" when chartered banks need to borrow extra reserves; (2) to issue paper currency; (3) to act as fiscal agent for the federal government; (4) to supervise the chartered banks; and (5) to regulate the supply of money. The last of these functions is the most important from a macroeconomic standpoint, and is the focus of the chapter.

About 80% of the Bank of Canada's assets are held in various forms of Government of Canada securities, such as Treasury bills and bonds. Another important asset is advances to chartered banks (IOUs for reserves that chartered banks have borrowed temporarily). The Bank of Canada's liabilities consist of notes in circulation (such as the $5 bill in your pocket), chartered bank deposits held at the Bank of Canada, and Government of Canada deposits held at the Bank of Canada.

The central bank implements monetary policy by influencing short-term interest rates. This is done mainly by changing the reserves of chartered banks (because the amount of deposit money depends on the amount of reserves chartered banks have). There are two main instruments used by the Bank of Canada to alter reserves: open-market operations and government deposit switching. In open-market operations the Bank of Canada buys or sells securities in the open market (from the chartered banks, or the public). For example, if the goal is to expand the money supply, the Bank of Canada will buy securities, paying for these securities by creat-

ing deposits at the Bank of Canada. These newly created deposits are reserves for the chartered banks, and enable them to make new loans and deposits that expand the money supply. If the Bank of Canada switches some of the government's deposits from itself to chartered banks, the result will be the same. A third method of influencing the money supply is to change the bank rate — the interest rate that the Bank of Canada charges chartered banks for advances of reserves. Since 1996 the bank rate has been based on the upper limit of its target band for the overnight loans rate.

The next section turns to the demand for money. Money's role as a medium of exchange creates the transactions demand for money, and its role as a store of value creates the asset demand for money. The transactions demand varies directly with nominal GDP, and the asset demand varies inversely with the rate of interest, so the total demand for money depends on these two variables in the same way. At the interest rate where the demand for money is equal to the supply of money, the money market is in equilibrium. A shift in the money supply will change the equilibrium. For example, if the Bank of Canada decreases the money supply, there will be a shortage of money which people will try to make up by selling financial assets (bonds). The price of bonds will fall, and the interest rate on bonds will rise. Money market equilibrium is restored when the interest rate has increased enough that people are once again satisfied with their money balances relative to their holdings of bonds.

The cause-effect chain from money supply changes to changes in employment, output, and inflation, is called the transmission mechanism. Consider the case of an expansionary monetary policy. When chartered banks get new excess reserves they will create new deposit money, leading to a surplus of money and shortage of bonds. As people try to buy more bonds, bond prices rise and interest rates fall. Lower interest rates stimulate investment spending, causing AD to expand, and the equilibrium levels of employment, output, and prices to rise. A contractionary monetary policy would trigger opposite effects, but the transmission mechanism is otherwise similar.

The effectiveness of monetary policy in expanding real GDP depends on a number of factors. As with fiscal policy, how the effects of an expansionary policy are divided between real GDP growth and price increases depends on where the economy is along the short-run aggregate supply curve. There are time lags and political constraints on the use of monetary policy, but less so than for fiscal policy. Concerns about the effectiveness of monetary policy include fears that financial innovations have reduced the Bank of Canada's control over the money supply; that fluctuations in the velocity of money's circulation weaken the link between AD and the money supply; and that monetary policy is more effective for stemming inflationary pressures than for pulling the economy out of recession.

Linkages between Canada and foreign economies also pose complications. An expansionary monetary policy will lower domestic interest rates, and thereby reduce capital inflows. Less financial investment from abroad means less demand for the Canadian dollar, so the dollar will depreciate. The depreciation will raise net exports (our exports increase and our imports fall). This net export effect reinforces the demand stimulus intended by the expansionary monetary policy. However, we may also desire a balance between our exports and imports. If so, the expansionary monetary policy intended to boost our domestic economy may either help or hinder us in achieving our goal of balance in our foreign trade.

The chapter ends with a schematic diagram (Figure 14-6) summarizing the theories from Chapters 6 through 14. This key graph provides a compact overview of many important models, and highlights how the principles are connected parts of an overall theory. It also highlights the range of policies available for achieving the goals of economic stabilization and growth.

■ **CHAPTER LEARNING OBJECTIVES**

In this chapter you will learn:
☐ The main functions of the Bank of Canada.
☐ How the Bank of Canada can expand or contract the money supply.
☐ The components of money demand.
☐ How the equilibrium interest rate is determined in the money market.
☐ The mechanism by which the interest rate affects GDP.

■ **CHAPTER OUTLINE**

1. The objective of monetary policy is full employment without inflation. The Bank of Canada can achieve this objective by controlling the level of excess reserves held by the chartered banks, thereby influencing the size of the money supply, the interest rate, and the level of aggregate expenditures and demand.

2. The Bank of Canada has five functions:
   (a)   to serve as the "bankers' bank";
   (b)   to supply paper currency to the economy;
   (c)   to act as fiscal agent for the federal government;
   (d)   to supervise chartered banks;
   (e)   to regulate the supply of money.

3. To understand how monetary policy works, it is necessary to understand the assets and liabilities on the balance sheet of the Bank of Canada.
   (a)   The relevant assets are Government of Canada securities (bonds and Treasury bills), and advances (normally very short-term loans) to chartered banks.
   (b)   The relevant liabilities are bank notes in circulation (currency), reserve deposits of chartered banks, and Government of Canada deposits.

4. The Bank of Canada employs two main instruments to control the reserves of banks and the size of the money supply: open-market operations and switching government deposits between itself and chartered banks.
   (a)   In order to increase bank reserves and the money supply, the Bank of Canada could:
   (1) Buy bonds or other government securities from banks or the public in the open market.
   (2) Switch government deposits from the Bank of Canada to chartered banks.
   (b)   In order to decrease bank reserves and the money supply, the Bank of Canada could:
   (1) Sell bonds or other government securities to banks or the public in the open market.

(2) Switch government deposits from chartered banks to the Bank of Canada.

5. As "lender of last resort" the Bank of Canada occasionally makes short-term loans of reserves to chartered banks. The interest rate on such loans is the bank rate.

(a) Since 1996 the bank rate has been set at 1/2% above the prevailing overnight loans rate in the money market. The Bank of Canada publicizes a target range for the overnight loans rate.

(b) When the Bank of Canada lends and borrows in the overnight loans market, it affects the availability of reserves, and the opportunity cost of these reserves, for the chartered banks, thus influencing monetary conditions.

6. The public (firms and households) holds money for two reasons:

(a) The transactions demand stems from money's use as a medium of exchange. The higher nominal GDP is, the more transactions are made, and the greater the transactions demand for money.

(b) The asset demand stems from money's function as a liquid store of value. The higher is the interest rate on bonds and other interest-bearing assets, the greater the opportunity cost of holding money, and the less the asset demand for money.

(c) The total demand for money is found by adding the asset demand horizontally to the transactions demand. There is an inverse relation between the quantity of money the public wants to hold and the interest rate. Increases in nominal GDP shift the money-demand curve to the right.

(d) The supply of money can be determined by the Bank of Canada, and does not vary with the interest rate.

(e) Equilibrium in the money market occurs at the interest rate where the downsloping money-demand curve and the vertical money-supply curve intersect.

(f) If there is a shortage of money, the public will attempt to sell bonds and financial assets to restore their desired money balances. These transactions will decrease the prices of existing bonds and increase the interest rate. This interest rate adjustment continues until the amount of money demanded falls enough to match the fixed supply of money.

(g) If there is a surplus of money, the public will attempt to purchase bonds and other interest-bearing financial assets. This will drive up the prices of bonds, and drive down the interest rate. This continues until the interest rate is low enough to induce the public to willingly hold the amount of money that exists.

7. The cause-effect chain from monetary policy changes to changes in equilibrium GDP and price level is known as the transmission mechanism, and is summarized as follows:

(a) In the money market the demand curve and the supply curve determine the equilibrium interest rate; the investment-demand curve and the equilibrium rate of interest determine planned investment; and planned investment helps determine the level of the aggregate demand curve (and the aggregate expenditures curve); the intersection of aggregate supply and aggregate demand determines the equilibrium GDP and price level.

(b) In the case of a recessionary gap, the Bank of Canada increases the money supply, causing the interest rate to fall and investment spending to increase, thereby increasing real GDP by a multiple of the increase in investment.

(c) In the case of an inflationary gap, the Bank of Canada decreases the money supply, causing the interest rate to rise and investment spending to decrease, thereby reducing inflation.

8. As was true with fiscal policy, the impact of a particular monetary policy will depend on the aggregate supply conditions. The flatter the aggregate supply curve is, the greater is the effect of a change in the money supply on real GDP and the smaller is the effect on the price level. If there is no monetary policy (or fiscal policy) action when there is a recessionary or inflationary gap, the short-run aggregate supply curve will eventually shift to close the gap.

9. The effectiveness of monetary policy depends on certain strengths and shortcomings.

(a) Its strengths are that:

(1) it can be more quickly changed than fiscal policy;

(2) it is more isolated from political pressure than fiscal policy;

(3) it has been successful in recent years in reducing inflation and in pulling the economy out of recession.

(b) Its five shortcomings or problems are that:

(1) it may be losing effectiveness because innovations in banking practices may be weakening

the Bank of Canada's control over the money supply;

(2) it is subject to the cyclical asymmetry of being more effective in fighting inflation than in curbing recession;

(3) it can be offset by changes in the velocity of money.

10. The Bank of Canada has, since 1996, set the bank rate based on the upper level of its operating band for the overnight loans rate. For example, when the Bank of Canada sells bonds (through sale and repurchase agreements) or switches government deposits out of the chartered banks, the increased scarcity of reserves will drive up the overnight loans rate. The increase in this rate, and thus the bank rate, signals a tighter monetary policy.

11. Linkages with foreign economies complicate the effects of monetary policy.

(a) Expansionary monetary policy will decrease Canadian interest rates, thereby decreasing the amount of capital inflows from abroad. Demand for the Canadian dollar will fall, and the dollar will depreciate, causing increased demand for Canada's exports, and decreased demand for imports. In summary, this net export effort will reinforce the expansionary effect on AD of an expansionary monetary policy.

(b) A widely held economic goal is that Canada should balance its exports and imports. A monetary policy appropriate for alleviating a domestic stabilization problem could either complement or conflict with the goal of balanced trade.

12. To sum up the models presented in Chapters 6 through 14, the equilibrium levels of real GDP, employment, and prices are determined by aggregate supply and aggregate demand.

(a) There are four expenditure components of AD: consumption, planned investment, government, and net exports.

(b) The three major determinants of AS are: input prices, productivity, and legal-institutional environment.

(c) Fiscal, monetary, or other government policies may effect either AD or AS, and thereby influence the level of real GDP, employment and prices.

■ TERMS AND CONCEPTS

asset demand for money	sale and repurchase agreements (SRA)
bank rate	special purchase and
government deposit switching	resale agreement (SPRA)
monetary policy	total demand for money
money market	transactions demand
open-market operations	velocity of money

■ HINTS AND TIPS

1. To understand how open-market operations and switching of government deposits works, it is important to have mastery of the balance sheets of the Bank of Canada and the chartered banks.

2. If you find counterintuitive the concept of a "surplus" of money, you may be confusing money and assets. A person with a surplus of money does not have too many assets; they are simply holding too large a portion of their assets in the form of money. They prefer less money and more bonds (or other interest-bearing financial assets).

3. The transmission mechanism is crucial. Be sure that you can explain it thoroughly, and that you can draw the three graphs that illustrate all of the linkages: the money market graph, the investment-demand graph, and the aggregate supply and aggregate demand graph.

4. Figure 14-6 is an excellent tool for preparing for the final exam. It is a comprehensive diagram of all of the macroeconomic models and theories from previous chapters

■ FILL-IN QUESTIONS

1. The objective of monetary policy in Canada is to help achieve and maintain a _____, _____ level of total output. The institution responsible for these monetary policies is the _____.

2. The Bank of Canada has five major functions:
(a) _____
(b) _____
(c) _____
(d) _____
(e) _____

3. As fiscal agent for the federal government, the Bank of Canada helps the government collect _____, and administers the sale and redemption of government _____.

4. In open-market operations, the Bank of Canada buys and sells _____ in the open market in order to change the level of chartered banks' _____, and therefore influence the amount of new _____ that chartered banks can create.

5. The total demand for money is the sum of:
(a) the _____ demand, which relates to money's function as a medium of exchange, and which depends (directly, inversely) _____ upon the _____;
(b) and the _____ demand, which relates to money's function as a store of value, and which depends _____ upon the _____.

6. The equilibrium real interest rate is determined by the money _____ and money _____ curves. This equilibrium interest rate and the _____ curve determine the level of planned investment. The level of investment helps to determine the level of aggregate _____.

7. There is a(n) (direct, inverse) _____ relation between interest rates and the price of existing bonds.

8. If the Bank of Canada sells $10 million in government bonds to the public, who pays for them by cheque, and the desired reserve ratio is 5%, the supply of money is immediately reduced by $_____, the reserves of the chartered banks are immediately reduced by $_____, and the excess reserves of the banks are immediately reduced by $_____. But if these bonds are sold to the chartered banks instead, the supply of money is immediately reduced by $_____, the reserves of the banks are immediately reduced by $_____, and the excess reserves of the banks are immediately reduced by $_____. In either case, the final net effect on the money supply will be a reduction of $_____ if the maximum money multiplier effects take place.

9. Suppose that the Bank of Canada buys government securities in the open market. Complete the chain of effects by indicating increase (+) or decrease (-) in each case:

(a)   chartered bank reserves ☐
(b)   chartered bank deposit liabilities ☐
(c)   money supply ☐
(d)   interest rate ☐
(e)   planned investment ☐
(f)   aggregate demand ☐
(g)   price level and real GDP level ☐

10. Beginning from an equilibrium in the money market, a decrease in the supply of money will cause a (surplus, shortage) _____ of money, and a _____ of bonds and other interest-bearing assets. This causes the prices of bonds to be bid (down, up) _____, and interest rates to (fall, rise) _____. The change in interest rates causes the public to adjust its (transactions, asset) _____ demand for money until money demand and supply are once again _____.

11. To eliminate inflationary pressures in the economy, the Bank of Canada should (increase, decrease) _____ the reserves of chartered banks; this would tend to _____ the money supply and to _____ the rate of interest; and this, in turn, would cause investment spending, aggregate demand, and output to _____. This action by the Bank of Canada would be considered a(n) _____ monetary policy.

12. Expansionary monetary policy will push interest rates (down, up) _____, which in turn (increases, decreases) _____ the demand for the domestic currency. Therefore, the currency will (appreciate, depreciate) _____, leading net exports to (increase, decrease) _____. This net export effect (reinforces, counteracts) _____ the intended expansionary effect of the monetary policy.

■ **PROBLEMS AND PROJECTS**

1. The consolidated balance sheet of the chartered banks and the balance sheet of the Bank of Canada are shown below. The chartered banks have a desired reserve ratio of 10%.
(a)   Initially, demand deposits are $_____ and the currency in circulation is $_____, so the money supply is $_____.
(b)   Suppose that the Bank of Canada conducts open-market operations by purchasing $10 in government securities directly from chartered banks. In the (b) columns of the two balance sheets show the immediate results — prior to the

chartered banks making any adjustments to re-store their desired reserve ratio.

CHARTERED BANKS		(b)	(d)
Assets			
Reserves	$50	___	___
Government Securities	100	___	___
Loans	350	___	___
Liabilities			
Demand deposits	500	___	___

BANK OF CANADA		(b)	(d)
Assets			
Government Securities	$300	___	___
Liabilities			
Reserves of banks	50	___	___
Government deposits	100	___	___
Bank of Canada Notes	150	___	___

(c)   The money supply immediately after the open-market operation is $___.

(d)   In the (d) columns, show the balance sheet entries after the chartered banks create as many new loans and deposits as they can, consistent with their desired reserve ratio.

(e)   The money supply after this is $___.

(f)   Since an increase of $___ in bank reserves increased the money supply by $___, the monetary multiplier in this case is ___.

2. Below are balance sheets for the Bank of Canada and the chartered banks. Suppose the Bank of Canada wants chartered bank reserves cut by $5.

CHARTERED BANKS		(a)	(b)
Assets			
Reserves	$25	___	___
Government Securities	50	___	___
Loans	250	___	___
Liabilities			
Demand deposits	325	___	___

BANK OF CANADA		(a)	(b)
Assets			
Government Securities	$80	___	___
Liabilities			
Reserves of banks	25	___	___
Government deposits	15	___	___
Bank of Canada Notes	40	___	___

(a)   In the (a) columns show how this could be accomplished by an open-market operation.

(b)   In the (b) columns show how this could be accomplished by switching government deposits. Start this part using the original data.

3.   The two graphs following show the money market and the demand for investment. The money demand curve is given by the equation: $D_m = 400 - 50\,i$ where D_m is the quantity of money demanded in billion $, and i is the interest rate in percent. Planned investment spending is given by $I_g = 80 - 10\,i$ where I_g is spending in billion $.

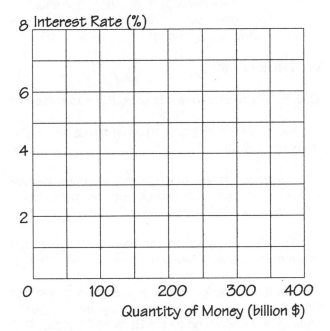

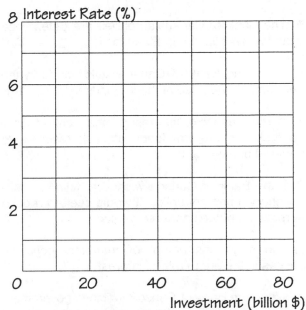

(a)   Graph the D_m function and the I_g function.

(b)   The current money supply is $200 billion. Graph this, labelling the line S_{m0}.

(c)   The equilibrium interest rate is _____%.

(d)   The level of planned investment at the equilibrium interest rate is $_____ billion.

(e)   If the Bank of Canada increases the money supply by $100 billion, will there be a surplus or a shortage of money?

(f)   The new equilibrium interest rate is _____%.

(g)   The new level of investment demand is $_____ billion.

(h)   If the expenditures multiplier in this situation is 3, the money supply increase will shift the AD curve (leftward, rightward) _____ by $___ billion.

■   TRUE-FALSE

Circle T if the statement is true, F if it is false.

1. Paper currency is among the main assets of the Bank of Canada.   **T F**

2. Evidence shows that countries whose central banks are more independent tend to have lower inflation rates.   **T F**

3. The federal government has a chequing account at the Bank of Canada.   **T F**

4. Chartered banks' deposits held at the Bank of Canada are counted as assets by the chartered banks and as liabilities by the Bank of Canada.   **T F**

5. The Bank of Canada's policies are determined by the federal Minister of Finance.   **T F**

6. When the Bank of Canada sells bonds in the open market, the price of these bonds falls.   **T F**

7. As the "lender of last resort," the Bank of Canada makes short-term loans of cash reserves to chartered banks.   **T F**

8. If the Bank of Canada wished to follow a contractionary monetary policy, it would seek to reduce the reserves of the chartered banks.   **T F**

9. The major instrument of monetary policy is changes in the prime rate of interest.   **T F**

10. When the Bank of Canada switches government deposits from itself to the chartered banks, the reserves of the chartered banks will be decreased. **T F**

11. The asset demand for money varies inversely with the rate of interest.   **T F**

12. An increase in the equilibrium GDP will shift the money demand curve to the left and increase the equilibrium interest rate.   **T F**

13. Monetary policy is more effective in fighting recession than it is in curbing inflation.   **T F**

14. An expansionary monetary policy shifts the aggregate demand curve to the right.   **T F**

15. A surplus of money will cause bond prices to rise.   **T F**

16. It is generally agreed that fiscal policy is more effective than monetary policy in controlling the business cycle because fiscal policy is more flexible.
                       T F

17. When the Bank of Canada enters into a special purchase and resale agreement (SPRA) it intends to put downward pressure on short-term interest rates.

                       T F

18. If no monetary policy or fiscal policy is initiated to close an inflationary gap, the AS curve will eventually shift leftward to close the gap.   **T F**

19. There is concern that changes in banking practices may eventually make monetary policy less effective.   **T F**

20. Monetary policy is weakened if the velocity of money's circulation decreases when the money supply is expanded.   **T F**

21. When the AS curve is very steep, expansionary monetary policy has more impact on real GDP than on prices.   **T F**

22. If the economy has a trade surplus and a recessionary gap, an expansionary monetary policy is compatible with both the domestic stabilization goal and the balance of trade goal.   **T F**

■ **MULTIPLE-CHOICE**

Circle the letter that corresponds to the best answer.

1. The agency directly responsible for monetary policy in Canada is:
- **(a)** the Canadian Bankers' Association
- **(b)** the Bank of Canada
- **(c)** the Parliament of Canada
- **(d)** the Department of Finance

2. The largest single asset on the Bank of Canada's balance sheet is:
- **(a)** government securities
- **(b)** loans
- **(c)** notes in circulation
- **(d)** chartered banks' deposits

3. All of the following are functions of the Bank of Canada with the exception of:
- **(a)** acting as fiscal agent of the government
- **(b)** holding deposits of the chartered banks
- **(c)** regulating the supply of money
- **(d)** determining the prime rate of interest

4. Open-market operations refer to:
- **(a)** the buying and selling of government bonds by the Bank of Canada
- **(b)** the buying and selling of government bonds by the chartered banks
- **(c)** the buying and selling of stocks and bonds by the Bank of Canada
- **(d)** the shifting of government deposits to and from the chartered banks by the Bank of Canada.

5. Which of the following is not one of the tools of monetary policy used by the Bank of Canada?
- **(a)** switching of government deposits
- **(b)** open-market operations
- **(c)** setting the bank rate
- **(d)** setting the required reserve ratio

6. Which of the following acts would not change the money supply in the same direction as the other three?
- **(a)** the Bank of Canada sells bonds to chartered banks
- **(b)** the Bank of Canada raises the bank rate
- **(c)** the Bank of Canada shifts government deposits to the chartered banks
- **(d)** the Bank of Canada sells bonds to the public

7. If the Bank of Canada sells $20 million in government securities to chartered banks who have a desired reserve ratio of 10%, then the potential change on the money supply is:
- **(a)** an increase of $20 million
- **(b)** an increase of $200 million
- **(c)** a decrease of $20 million
- **(d)** a decrease of $200 million

8. In the chain of cause and effect between changes in the excess reserves of chartered banks and the resulting changes in output and employment in the economy:
- **(a)** an increase in excess reserves will decrease the money supply
- **(b)** a decrease in the money supply will increase the rate of interest
- **(c)** an increase in the rate of interest will increase aggregate demand
- **(d)** an increase in aggregate expenditures will decrease output and employment

9. To contract the money supply, the Bank of Canada could:
- **(a)** buy bonds or switch government deposits away from chartered banks
- **(b)** sell bonds or switch government deposits away from chartered banks
- **(c)** buy bonds or switch government deposits into chartered banks
- **(d)** sell bonds or switch government deposits into chartered banks

10. There is an asset demand for money because money is:
- **(a)** a medium of exchange
- **(b)** a standard of value
- **(c)** a store of value
- **(d)** a standard of deferred payment

11. The transactions demand for money:
- **(a)** varies directly with nominal GDP
- **(b)** varies inversely with nominal GDP
- **(c)** varies directly with the interest rate
- **(d)** varies inversely with the interest rate

12. The total demand for money would shift to the left as a result of:
- **(a)** an increase in the interest rate
- **(b)** a decline in nominal GDP
- **(c)** a decrease in the interest rate

(d)   an increase in nominal GDP

13. The equilibrium interest rate is determined by:
(a)   the demand for money and the level of nominal GDP
(b)   the transactions demand for money and the supply of money
(c)   the total demand for money and the supply of money
(d)   the demand for money and the demand for bonds

14. An increase in the interest rate would increase:
(a)   the opportunity cost of holding money
(b)   the transactions demand for money
(c)   the asset demand for money
(d)   the price of bonds

15. Suppose the transactions demand for money is equal to 10% of the nominal GDP, the supply of money is $45 billion, and the asset demand for money is as shown in the following table. If nominal GDP is $300 billion, the equilibrium interest rate is:
(a)   14%
(b)   13%
(c)   12%
(d)   11%

Interest Rate (%)	Asset Demand (billions)
14	$10
13	15
12	20
11	25

16. Given the data in Question 15, what change in the money supply would be needed to lower the interest rate by 1%?
(a) $5 billion increase
(b) $5 billion decrease
(c) $10 billion increase
(d) $10 billion decrease

17. Which one of the following statements is true?
(a)   bond prices and the interest rates are directly related
(b)   a lower interest rate shifts the aggregate demand curve to the left
(c)   the supply of money is directly related to the interest rate
(d)   bond prices and interest rates are inversely related

18. A bond that pays fixed interest payment of $100 per year falls in price from $1,000 to $800. What happens to the interest rate on the bond?
(a)   increase by 1.25 percent per year
(b)   decrease by 1.25 percent per year
(c)   increase by 2.50 percent per year
(d)   decrease by 2.50 percent per year

19. If the Bank of Canada decides to buy government bonds, the demand for government bonds will:
(a)   decrease, bond prices will decrease, and the interest rate will decrease
(b)   increase, bond prices will increase, and the interest rate will decrease
(c)   increase, bond prices will increase, and the interest rate will increase
(d)   decrease, bond prices will increase, and the interest rate will decrease

20. Compared to fiscal policy, monetary policy is:
(a)   more subject to political interference
(b)   more direct in its effects on aggregate demand
(c)   used less frequently
(d)   more quickly altered

21. An expansionary monetary policy:
(a)   reduces the supply of money, increases the interest rate, reduces investment, and reduces the equilibrium GDP
(b)   increases the money supply, reduces the rate of interest, increases investment, and reduces the equilibrium GDP
(c)   reduces the money supply, reduces the rate of interest, increases investment, and increases the equilibrium GDP
(d)   increases the money supply, reduces the interest rate, increases investment, and increases the equilibrium GDP

22. The transmission mechanism through which monetary policy affects aggregate demand is primarily through:
(a)   consumption spending
(b)   investment spending
(c)   government spending
(d)   net exports

23. When the money supply expands, the net export effect:
(a)   increases AD, because the interest rate falls, leading to depreciation of the domestic currency

(b) increases AD, because the interest rate falls, leading to appreciation of the domestic currency

(c) decreases AD, because the interest rate falls, leading to depreciation of the domestic currency

(d) decreases AD, because the interest rate rises, leading to appreciation of the domestic currency

24. In which situation would a contractionary monetary policy help to resolve both the domestic stabilization problem and the balance of trade problem?
(a) inflationary gap and trade surplus
(b) inflationary gap and trade deficit
(c) recessionary gap and trade surplus
(d) recessionary gap and trade deficit

■ **DISCUSSION QUESTIONS**

1. Define monetary policy and state its basic objective.

2. Describe the five main functions of the Bank of Canada.

3. What are the principal assets and liabilities of the Bank of Canada?

4. What are the two main instruments of monetary control available to the Bank of Canada, and how do they work?

5. Using open-market operations, what would the Bank of Canada do to contract the money supply? Or to expand it?

6. Use a simplified balance sheet of the chartered banking system to explain the effect on reserves of switching government deposits between the Bank of Canada and the chartered banks.

7. Why does a change in the bank rate end up affecting interest rates and the money supply? How does the Bank of Canada set the bank rate?

8. For what two reasons do people wish to hold money? How are these two reasons related to the functions of money?

9. Explain the determinants of the two demands for money. Explain how changes in these determi-

nants will affect the amount of money people want to hold.

10. Explain how the demand for money and the supply of money determine the interest rate. Explain how the money market adjusts if there is a shortage or a surplus of money.

11. Describe the relationship between the changes in the interest rate and changes in the price of existing bonds.

12. Use a set of three graphs to explain what determines: (a) the equilibrium interest rate; (b) planned investment; and (c) the equilibrium GDP. Now employ these graphs to show the effects of a cut in the money supply on equilibrium GDP.

13. What are the strengths and shortcomings of monetary policy?

14. Why is monetary policy more effective in controlling inflation than in reducing unemployment?

15. Explain the net export effect caused by monetary policy.

16. Distinguish between fiscal and monetary policy and explain how each may be used to achieve reasonably full employment and relatively stable prices.

■ **ANSWERS**

FILL-IN QUESTIONS

1. full-employment, noninflationary, Bank of Canada

2. (a) bank for the chartered banks; (b) issuing currency; (c) fiscal agent for the government; (d) supervisor of chartered banks; (e) regulator of the supply of money

3. taxes, bonds

4. bonds, reserves, money (or deposits)

5. (a) transactions, directly, nominal GDP; (b) asset, inversely, rate of interest

6. supply, demand, investment-demand, demand

7. inverse

8. 10 million, 10 million, 9.5 million, 0, 10 million, 10 million, 200 million (10 million x (1/.05))

9. (a) +, (b) +, (c) +, (d) -, (e) +, (f) +, (g) +

10. shortage, surplus, down, rise, asset, equal

11. decrease, decrease, increase, decrease, contractionary (tight)

12. down, decreases, depreciate, increase; reinforces

PROBLEMS AND PROJECTS

1. (a) $500, $150, $650; (b) Chartered banks: $60, 90, 350, 500; Bank of Canada: $310, 60, 100, 150; (c) $650; (d) Chartered banks: $60, 90, 450, 600; Bank of Canada: $310, 60, 100, 150; (e) $750; (f) 10, 100, 10

2. (a) Chartered banks: $20, 55, 250, 325; Bank of Canada: $75, 20, 15, 40; (b) Chartered banks: $20, 50, 250, 320; Bank of Canada: $80, 20, 20, 40

3. (c) 4; (d) 40; (e) surplus of $100 billion; (f) 2; (g) 60; (h) rightward, 60 (20 x 3)

TRUE-FALSE

1. F   currency is a liability for the Bank of Canada
2. T
3. T   which the Bank of Canada can use in deposit switching to alter chartered bank reserves
4. T
5. F   the Bank of Canada is largely independent of the federal government
6. T   and the interest rate on them rises
7. T   not often, but when necessary
8. T   which would lead to a multiple contraction of deposit money
9. F   the Bank of Canada does not control the prime rate
10. F   the reserves would be increased, and most of the added reserves would be excess
11. T   the higher the opportunity cost of liquidity, the less liquidity is demanded
12. F   money demand shifts right, leading to an interest rate increase
13. F   the opposite is true
14. T   by cutting interest rates and stimulating investment spending
15. T   a surplus of money means a surplus of bonds
16. F   fiscal policy is less flexible than monetary policy
17. T   the Bank of Canada is expanding the reserves available to the chartered banks
18. T   with emphasis on the word "eventually"
19. T   as people substitute quickly between near-monies and other financial assets
20. T   the anticipated increase in spending due to increased supply of money would not occur
21. F   it has almost all of its effect on price level since the economy is already at or beyond normal capacity

22. F   the net export effect would tend to increase the size of the trade surplus

MULTIPLE-CHOICE

1. (b)
2. (a)   bonds and Treasury bills
3. (d)   this is determined by chartered banks and other lending institutions
4. (a)
5. (d)   the Bank of Canada cannot manipulate this ratio
6. (c)   this action is expansionary while all of the others are contractionary
7. (d)   reserves fall 20 million; multiplier is 10
8. (b)
9. (b)   both actions reduce reserves
10. (c)
11. (a)
12. (b)   due to transactions demand component
13. (c)
14. (a)   and therefore reduce amount demanded for asset purposes
15. (b)   transactions demand = 30, so asset demand must = 15 in order for total demand = supply = 45
16. (a)   asset demand must increase by the 5
17. (d)
18. (c)   100/1000 = 10%; 100/800 = 12.5%
19. (b)
20. (d)   it affects AD more indirectly, but can be changed quickly without a long political process, so it is used often
21. (d)
22. (b)   investment spending responds to interest rate changes
23. (a)
24. (a)   interest rate would rise, the currency appreciate, and net exports fall (reducing AD and the trade surplus)

CHAPTER 15

Long-Run Macroeconomic Adjustments

Previous chapters have focused mostly on short-run macroeconomic adjustments, with particular attention to the events and policies on the demand side. Macroeconomists are increasingly paying attention to long-run macroeconomic changes and to the supply side. This chapter examines new perspectives on aggregate supply, and applies the AD-AS model to analyze demand-pull inflation, cost-push inflation, and recession. We examine the relationship between inflation and unemployment, and the role of expectations in that relationship. Finally, we consider the ideas of supply-side economics.

In a situation of demand-pull inflation the economy can temporarily exceed its potential real GDP, but labour market adjustments will eventually restore real wages and return the economy to its long-run equilibrium at potential GDP. When the economy experiences cost-push inflation the real output drops below the potential level, posing a dilemma for policy-makers. They can wait for market forces to close the recessionary gap, but it may be a very long wait. Alternately, they can use expansionary fiscal or monetary policy, but this will push prices yet higher, running the risk of setting off an inflationary spiral of nominal wage increases followed by price increases. In a recession stemming from falling demand, output drops below potential but will eventually recover when prices and nominal wages fall far enough. Here the key question is how long the process will take.

These three cases support three generalizations about the long-run outcomes in the AD-AS model: (1) there is normally a short-run tradeoff between inflation and unemployment; (2) AS shocks can cause both higher inflation and higher unemployment; and (3) there is no significant lasting tradeoff between inflation and unemployment. The chapter then examines each of these generalizations.

In the 1960s economists accepted the Phillips Curve model which showed a trade-off between inflation and unemployment that fit the evidence from many countries during the 1960s. Policy-makers came to think that they could choose any inflation and unemployment combination on the Phillips Curve. For example, a lower rate of unemployment could be achieved, but only if the country was willing to tolerate the corresponding higher rate of inflation. By the 1970s and early 1980s the data no longer supported a stable Phillips Curve. Many economies, including Canada, had stagflation (simultaneously rising inflation rate and unemployment rate). The inflation during this period began as cost-push inflation, and since macroeconomic models of the time ignored the supply side, economists had work to do.

These events were caused by adverse supply shocks that shifted the AS curve to the left, and thus shifted the Phillips Curve outward, to combinations of higher unemployment and inflation. Under this interpretation there is still a Phillips Curve showing a trade-off, but it is a short-run tradeoff, and it shifts up or down as inflation expectations change. In the long-run there is no tradeoff, so the long-run Phillips Curve is a vertical line at the level of full-employment GDP. At this GDP level unemployment is at its natural rate. In other words, in the long run, the economy tends towards a natural rate of unemployment and this level of unemployment can exist at any level of inflation. Expectations are central to the process: when market participants react to their expectations about inflation, there is no lasting Phillips Curve tradeoff.

Along with this rethinking of the Phillips Curve, economists began to build the supply side into their macroeconomic models. A group known as supply-side economists emphasize that AS determinants

163

have important effects on inflation, real output, and economic growth. Taxation is their key concern. They argue that cutting marginal tax rates would substantially increase incentives to work, save, and invest, and thereby increase aggregate supply. A famous and controversial element of supply-side economics is the Laffer Curve theory which holds that lower tax rates would stimulate economic activity enough to generate more total tax revenue despite the cut in the percentage of income taken in tax. While this is a logical possibility, the evidence does not support this hopeful idea.

■ **CHAPTER LEARNING OBJECTIVES**

In this chapter you will learn:
□ To apply the long-run AD-AS model.
□ About the inflation-unemployment relationship.
□ About the effects of taxation on aggregate supply.

■ **CHAPTER OUTLINE**

1. If the economy begins at full employment, demand-pull inflation occurs when AD increases.
(a)   The short-run impact is an expansion in output and an increase in the price level. Because nominal wages are fixed over this period, real wages drop.
(b)   When workers' contracts expire, and when they realize that their real wages have fallen, workers demand and get higher nominal wages. This shifts the AS curve leftward until the inflationary gap is closed and the economy is back at full-employment equilibrium where real wages are restored to their original level.
(c)   Demand-pull inflation produces a lasting price level increase and a temporary real output increase.

2. If the economy begins at full employment, cost-push inflation occurs when per-unit production costs rise, and AS decreases.
(a)   The short-run impact is a drop in output and an increase in the price level.
(b)   If no government stabilization policy is used, input prices will eventually fall, shifting the AS back to the right until a long-run equilibrium is restored at full-employment output. This will be a very slow process, meaning a prolonged recession.
(c)   If government uses an expansionary monetary or fiscal policy, the AD curve could be

increased to meet the new AS curve at full-employment. However, this would drive prices even higher, and might ignite an inflationary spiral of further increases in wages and prices.

3. Starting from full employment, a recession that stems from falling expenditures will decrease the AD curve.
(a)   The short-run impact is a drop in output and a decrease in the price level. Because nominal wages are fixed, real wages rise, leading to employment losses.
(b)   Eventually nominal wages will fall to restore the previous real wage, employment, and output levels. This economy is likely to endure a prolonged recession before this adjustment process is complete.

4. From the analysis of the three scenarios above, we conclude that the long-run AD-AS model supports three generalizations:
(a)   Under normal circumstances, there is a short-run tradeoff between inflation and unemployment.
(b)   AS shocks can cause both higher inflation rates and higher unemployment rates.
(c)   There is no significant tradeoff between inflation and unemployment over longer periods.

5. If AS is upward sloping, the greater the rate of increase in AD the greater is the rate of increase in the price level and in real output, and the lower is the rate of unemployment (and vice versa).
(a)   This inverse relationship between the inflation rate and the unemployment rate is called the Phillips Curve.
(b)   According to the Phillips Curve theory, fiscal and monetary policy can be used to manage AD and to "choose" a combination of inflation and unemployment along this curve.
(c)   Data from the 1960s showed this inverse relationship between unemployment and inflation rates for many countries, including Canada.

6. Events of the 1970s and 1980s changed our understanding of the Phillips Curve. During this time Canada experienced "stagflation": higher rates of inflation **and** unemployment.
(a)   During these years a series of adverse supply shocks (especially a quadrupling of oil prices) decreased AS, and increased both inflation and unemployment in Canada.

(b)   Stagflation ended in the 1983-89 period because of various factors. Unemployment and inflation both decreased (instead of moving in opposite directions as predicted by the Phillips Curve theory).

(c)   This experience suggests that the Phillips Curve is not a stable relationship and cannot be used as the basis for economic policy. Instead, there seems to be a short-run tradeoff, but one shifts. Supply shocks shifted the short-run Phillips Curve rightward between 1971 and 1982, and other events shifted it leftward between 1983 and 1989.

7. The data from the 1960s to the present shows that in the long run the natural rate of unemployment can exist with any rate of inflation. Therefore, the long-run Phillips Curve is vertical at the natural rate of unemployment. The processes behind this involve the expectations of inflation and how the economy adjusts when the inflation rate is not what was expected.

(a)   Starting from full employment, with a certain expected rate of inflation, nominal wages will be set to increase at the same rate as prices, thus maintaining the real wage.

(b)   If inflation turns out to be higher than expected, firms enjoy higher than normal profit margins, because of lower than normal real wages. Accordingly, they hire more workers and produce more output. Unemployment drops below the natural rate. The result is higher inflation and lower unemployment: the Phillips Curve tradeoff!

(c)   The higher inflation rate is soon factored into nominal wage expectations, and real wage rates return to normal. Profit margins also return to normal, and so does the level of unemployment. Now unemployment is back to its natural rate, and the inflation rate is higher than before, so the short-run Phillips Curve has shifted upward.

(d)   The process is repeated if government tries again to reduce unemployment, and the inflation rate accelerates as the short-run Phillips Curve shifts upward. Expansionary policies generate accelerating inflation rather than lower unemployment.

(e)   In the long run, the Phillips Curve is stable only as a vertical line at the natural rate of unemployment. There is no trade-off between unemployment and inflation.

8. Supply-side economists argue that more attention should be paid to the effects of shifts in the aggregate supply, particularly in policy-making.

(a)   They argue for lower marginal tax rates on incomes from labour, savings, and investments. Lower taxes would increase incentives to work, save, and invest, thereby increasing the economy's productivity. This would shift both short-run and long-run AS curves to the right.

(b)   The Laffer Curve suggests that lower tax rates are compatible with constant or even larger tax revenues. If tax rates are cut, enough output and taxable income could be generated to increase the total tax revenue. Reduced tax avoidance and tax evasion would also result.

9. Critics of supply-side economics and the Laffer Curve question whether tax cuts would create such benefits for aggregate supply because:

(a)   The effects on incentives are small or uncertain.

(b)   Tax cuts would cause AD to increase, creating inflationary pressure.

(c)   Tax revenues will only increase if the economy is on the right section of the Laffer Curve, and there is no evidence that it is.

■   TERMS AND CONCEPTS

aggregate supply shocks	**Phillips Curve**
	stagflation
Laffer Curve	**supply-side economics**

■   HINTS AND TIPS

1.   This chapter provides a great example of how real world experience has changed our prevailing economic theories. Actual experience with inflation and unemployment from the late 1960s through the early 1980s dramatically changed theories of the Phillips Curve. In the 1960s, the orthodox position was one of a stable unemployment-inflation tradeoff, whereas by the 1980s, most economists believed that there is no stable or long-run tradeoff.

2.   The role of real and nominal wages is crucial in the explanation of how the economy moves away from the natural rate of unemployment, and then returns to the natural rate. Remember that decisions by workers and employers are ultimately based on real wages. Therefore, price level changes must ultimately be matched by nominal wage changes in order to keep real wages in equilibrium.

■ FILL-IN QUESTIONS

1. Demand-pull inflation is initiated by a shift to the (right, left) _____ of the (AD, AS) _____ curve. This will (decrease, increase) _____ the price level and temporarily _____ real output. As a consequence, the (short-run, long-run) _____ aggregate supply curve will shift left because of a rise in (real, nominal) _____ wages, producing a (lower, higher) _____ price level at the original level of real output. Eventually equilibrium is restored at the _____ level of output.

2. Cost-push inflation starts with a shift to the (right, left) _____ of the (AD, AS) _____ curve. Thus the price level will (increase, decrease) _____ and real output will temporarily _____. If government takes no action to counter the cost-push inflation, the resulting recession will _____ nominal wages, and shift the _____ curve back to its original position. If the government tries to counter the cost-push inflation and recession with an expansionary monetary or fiscal policy, the price level will move (back down, even higher) _____.

3. If the AS curve is upward sloping (and stable), the greater the increase in AD, the (greater, smaller) _____ will be the increase in the price level, the _____ will be the increase in real output, and the _____ will be the unemployment rate; and there will be a(n) (direct, inverse) _____ relationship between the inflation rate and the unemployment rate. This relationship is known as the _____ Curve.

4. According to the traditional Phillips Curve theory accepted in the 1960s, the policy dilemma faced by government policy-makers is that:
   (a) to have full employment we must also have _____, and to have stable prices we must tolerate _____;
   (b) to reduce the unemployment rate, the rate of inflation must (increase, decrease) _____; and to reduce the rate of inflation the unemployment rate must _____.

5. The expectation of inflation by workers and employers leads to (higher, lower) _____ nominal wage rates and in turn to a (rise, fall) _____ in per-unit production costs, to a(n) (increase, decrease) _____ in AS, to a

(higher, lower) _____ price level, and to a _____ rate of unemployment in the economy.

6. On the (long-run, short-run) _____ Phillips Curve, the unemployment rate will rise if inflation is (higher, lower) _____ than the expected inflation rate.

7. If inflation is lower than expected, and (real, nominal) _____ wage rates are temporarily fixed by labour contracts, then the (real, nominal) _____ wage will be (higher, lower) _____ than usual, causing profit margins to be (higher, lower) _____ than usual. Therefore, firms (hire, layoff) _____ workers, causing the unemployment rate to be (above, below) _____ the natural rate.

8. Supply-side economists believe that inflation has increased and growth slowed down because governments have: (1) set excessively high marginal tax rates that reduce _____ to work, save, invest, and take risks; (2) created too many and overly generous _____ payment programs; and (3) decreased productivity because of increased _____ of industry. These economists argue that the main remedy for stagflation is a substantial (increase, decrease) _____ in taxes, transfers, and regulation.

9. The _____ Curve is a relationship between the tax rate and tax _____. Supply-side economists believe that (higher, lower) _____ tax rates will increase tax _____. They also argue that lower tax rates will shift the (AD, AS) _____ to the right.

■ PROBLEMS AND PROJECTS

1. On the following page is a traditional Phillips Curve.
   (a) At full employment (8% unemployment), the price level would rise by _____ % each year.
   (b) If the price level were stable (increasing by 0% per year), the unemployment rate would be _____%.
   (c) Which of the combinations along the Phillips Curve would you choose for the economy? Why would you select this combination?

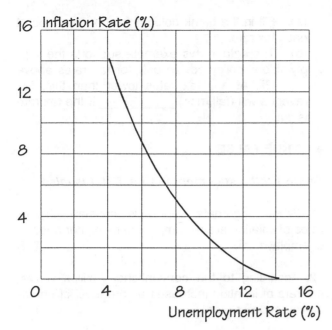

2. Following is a graph of the AD-AS model. Assume that the economy is initially in equilibrium at AD_1 and AS_1. The price level will be _____ and the real domestic output will be _____.

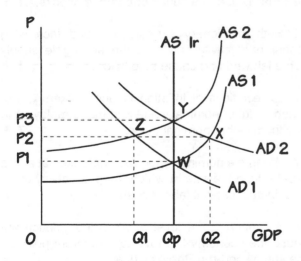

(a) If there is demand-pull inflation, then:

(1) in the short run, the new equilibrium is at point _____, with the price level at _____ and real output at _____;

(2) in the long run, nominal wages will rise so the aggregate supply curve will shift from _____ to _____. The equilibrium will be at point _____ with the price level at _____ and real output at _____; and so the increase in aggregate demand has only moved the economy along its _____ curve.

(b) Now assume that the economy is initially in equilibrium at point *W*, where AD_1 and AS_1 intersect. If there is cost-push inflation, then:

(1) in the short run, the new equilibrium is at point _____, with the price level at _____ and real output at _____.

(2) if the government tries to counter the cost-push inflation with expansionary monetary and fiscal policy, then AD shifts from _____ to _____, with the price level becoming _____ and real output _____. But this policy has a trap because the price level has shifted from _____ to _____ and the new level of inflation might shift _____ leftward.

(3) if government does not counter the cost-push inflation, the price level will eventually move to _____ and real output to _____ as the recession reduces nominal wages and shifts the AS curve from _____ to _____.

3. The next graph shows short-and long-run Phillips Curves.

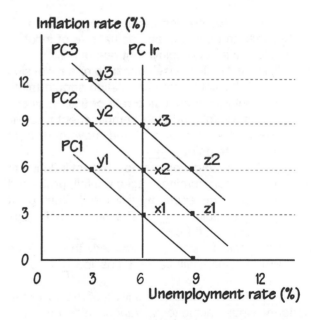

(a) The economy is initially at point X_1, with nominal wages currently being set on the expectation that a 3% rate of inflation will continue.

(1) If government uses expansionary fiscal or monetary policy to cut unemployment from 6% to 3%, the actual rate of inflation will move to _____%. The higher prices will lift firms' profits and they will hire more workers; thus moving the economy temporarily to point _____.

(2)   If workers now demand and receive higher wages to compensate for the loss of purchasing power from higher than expected inflation, then business profits will fall from previous levels and firms will reduce employment. Therefore, employment will move from point _____ to point _____ on the graph. The short-run Phillips Curve has shifted from _____ to _____.

(3) If government again tries to stimulate AD with monetary or fiscal policy to reduce the unemployment rate from 6% to 3%, then prices will rise before nominal wages, and output and employment will increase, causing a move from point _____ to point _____.

(4) But when workers get nominal wage increases, profits fall, and unemployment moves from point _____ at _____% to point _____ at _____ %. The short-run Phillips Curve has now shifted from _____ to _____.

(5) The long-run Phillips Curve is the line _____.

(b) Suppose now the economy begins at point X_3, with an expected and actual rate of inflation of 9% and an unemployment rate of 6%.

(1)   If AD decreases because of a recession and if the actual rate of inflation should fall to 6%, below the expected rate of 9%, business profits will fall and the unemployment rate will rise to 9% as shown by the movement from point X_3 to point _____.

(2) If firms and workers now expect inflation to be 6%, then nominal wages will fall, profits will rise, and the economy will move from point _____ to point _____. The short-run Phillips Curve will shift from _____ to _____.

(3) If this process is repeated, the long-run Phillips Curve will be traced as line _____.

4. The table below shows the level of real GDP the economy would achieve at various different marginal income tax rates.

Tax Rate	Level of GDP ($ billions)	Tax Revenue ($ billions)
20%	4,500	_____
30%	4,000	_____
40%	3,500	_____
50%	3,100	_____
60%	2,500	_____
70%	2,000	_____

(a)   Fill in the blank column for tax revenues at each tax rate.

(b)   The data in this example supports the supply-siders' policy advice only for tax rates above _____%. At any tax rates lower than this, tax revenue will (fall, rise) _____ if the tax rate is cut.

■   **TRUE-FALSE**

Circle T if the statement is true, F if it is false.

1. When aggregate supply is constant, higher rates of inflation are accompanied by higher rates of unemployment.   **T F**

2. According to the conventional Phillips Curve, the rate of inflation increases as the level of unemployment decreases.   **T F**

3. Stagflation refers to a situation in which both the price level and the unemployment rate are falling. **T F**

4. The stagflation of the 1970s and early 1980s was mainly due to a series of demand shocks.   **T F**

5. Both inflationary expectations and increasing labour productivity can shift the aggregate supply curve leftward and cause stagflation.   **T F**

6. Expectations of inflation induce workers to demand a higher nominal wage and their employers to pay them higher nominal wages.   **T F**

7. When the nominal wage rate increases at a rate greater than the rate at which the productivity of labour increases, unit labour costs will rise.   **T F**

8. A change in the level of expected inflation will cause the economy to move to a different point on the same short-run Phillips Curve.   **T F**

9. According to the long-run Phillips Curve theory, the economy's natural rate of unemployment can be achieved only if the rate of inflation is zero.   **T F**

10. When the actual rate of inflation is higher than the expected rate, the unemployment rate will fall.   **T F**

11. The short-run AS curve is upward sloping because nominal wages are considered variable and rise as prices rise.   **T F**

12. The long-run AS is vertical at the GDP level corresponding to the natural rate of unemployment.

T F

13. Demand-pull inflation will increase the price level and real output in the short run; but, in the long run, only the price level will increase. **T F**

14. An inflationary spiral is likely to result from the use of stabilization policies to maintain full employment when the economy is experiencing cost-push inflation. **T F**

15. The Laffer Curve proves that tax cuts would enable our government to collect more tax revenue.

T F

16. Tax avoidance is legal whereas tax evasion is illegal. **T F**

■ **MULTIPLE-CHOICE**

Circle the letter that corresponds to the best answer.

1. As long as AS remains constant and the economy operates along the upward sloping portion of AS, the greater the increase in AD:
  (a) the greater is the increase in the price level
  (b) the greater is the increase in the unemployment rate
  (c) the smaller is the increase in real output
  (d) the smaller is the increase in employment

2. The conventional Phillips Curve:
  (a) shows the inverse relation between the rate of increase in the price level and the unemployment rate
  (b) indicates that it is possible for the economy to achieve full employment and stable prices
  (c) indicates that prices do not rise until full employment has been achieved
  (d) slopes upward from left to right

3. The stabilization policy dilemma illustrated by a Phillips Curve is the mutual inconsistency of:
  (a) more employment and price stability
  (b) a higher unemployment rate and price stability
  (c) inflation and more employment
  (d) inflation and a lower unemployment rate

4. Stagflation is characterized by:
  (a) rising inflation and rising government deficits
  (b) rising unemployment and rising government deficits
  (c) rising taxes and rising government deficits
  (d) rising inflation and rising unemployment

5. Which of the following was a supply-side shock that affected Canada during the 1970s and early 1980s?
  (a) the imposition of wage and price controls
  (b) the appreciation of the dollar
  (c) the fall in the price charged by OPEC nations for oil
  (d) worldwide agricultural shortfalls

6. If productivity of labour rises by 2% and nominal wage rates rise 5%, the percentage change in unit labour costs is:
  (a) 1%
  (b) 3%
  (c) 7%
  (d) 10%

7. Which of the following factors contributed to the demise of stagflation in the 1983-1988 period?
  (a) lessening of foreign competition
  (b) strengthening OPEC's monopoly power
  (c) a recession caused by tight money policy
  (d) increased regulation of transportation industries

8. Our current theories of the Phillips Curve suggest that the economy is stable only in the:
  (a) short run at the natural rate of unemployment
  (b) short run at the natural rate of inflation
  (c) long run at the natural rate of unemployment
  (d) long run at the natural rate of inflation

9. An inflationary spiral is particularly a risk if:
  (a) there is cost-push inflation and government counters the recession with expansionary policy
  (b) there is demand-pull inflation and government counters the inflation with contractionary policy
  (c) there is cost-push inflation and government takes no policy action to counter the recession
  (d) there is demand-pull inflation and government takes no policy action to counter the inflation

10. Which of the following is an example of an adverse supply shock?

(a) falling oil prices
(b) mass crop failures
(c) productivity growth from computerization
(d) appreciation of the domestic currency

11. When the actual inflation rate falls below the expected inflation rate:

(a) real wages rise temporarily
(b) profit margins fall temporarily
(c) layoffs occur and unemployment temporarily exceeds the natural rate
(d) all of the above

12. In the short run, demand-pull inflation:

(a) is caused by a downward shift in the Phillips Curve
(b) is the result of a decrease in AD
(c) produces an increase in real output
(d) is caused by rising wage rates

13. In the long run, demand-pull inflation will:

(a) decrease the unemployment rate
(b) decrease the level of nominal wages
(c) increase the level of prices
(d) increase real national output

14. The short-run Phillips Curve will shift down if:

(a) actual inflation decreases
(b) expected inflation decreases
(c) unemployment goes down
(d) any of the above

15. Supply-side economists would argue for fighting stagflation with a policy of:

(a) tax cuts
(b) government regulation
(c) government spending
(d) monetary policy

16. What benefits would supply-side economists expect to see from a cut in the marginal tax rate on personal incomes:

(a) an increase in labour force participation
(b) an increase in personal saving
(c) an increase in investment
(d) all of the above

17. The Laffer Curve shows the relationship between:

(a) the rate of inflation and the rate of unemployment

(b) the rate of inflation and the rate of employment
(c) the tax rate and the budget deficit
(d) the tax rate and tax revenue

18. Which of the following is a criticism of the Laffer Curve as an argument for tax cuts?

(a) tax cuts have large effects on incentives to work, save and invest
(b) tax cuts reinforce inflation
(c) tax cuts will generate more tax revenue
(d) none of the above

19. Oil price increases in 2000 seemed to be less inflationary than oil price increases in the 1970s and 1980s. Which of the following is not among the possible reasons?

(a) in 2000 the Bank of Canada is more adept at maintaining price stability through monetary policy
(b) in 2000 favourable supply-side changes were taking place at the same time as the oil price increases
(c) in 2000 goods that are energy intensive to make and transport make up a much lower share of GDP
(d) in 2000 the Bank of Canada accommodated the oil price increases with expansionary monetary policy

■ **DISCUSSION QUESTIONS**

1. Describe the process of demand-pull inflation in the short run and in the long run. How does demand-pull inflation influence the AS curve?

2. Define cost-push inflation and describe how it comes about. How does the economy adjust to cost-push inflation in the short run? In the long run? What dilemma does cost-push inflation pose for macroeconomic policy-makers?

3. How does the economy recover in the long-run from a recession if: (a) the government uses no expansionary policy, and (b) the government uses expansionary policy when the recession is diagnosed?

4. What is a Phillips Curve? Explain how a Phillips Curve with a negative slope may be derived by holding AS constant and increasing AD.

5. What is the stabilization policy dilemma illustrated by the traditional Phillips Curve? Does the manipulation of AD through monetary and fiscal policy shift the Phillips Curve or cause a movement along the Phillips Curve?

6. Over what period(s) of Canada's history was our experience consistent with the conventional Phillips Curve explanation?

7. What supply-side shocks brought stagflation to the Canadian economy during the 1970s and early 1980s? How did these shocks affect aggregate supply and the short-run Phillips Curve? What factors contributed to stagflation's demise during the 1983-88 period?

8. What causes the short-run Phillips Curve to shift? What does the long-run Phillips Curve look like, and why?

9. Supply-side economists believe that there are significant tax and transfer payment disincentives in the economy. What are they, and what policies are suggested?

10. Draw a Laffer Curve. Explain the economic implications of the curve according to supply-side economists. Outline three criticisms of the ideas expressed by the Laffer Curve.

■ **ANSWERS**

FILL-IN QUESTIONS

1. right, AD, increase, increase, short-run, nominal, higher, full-employment

2. left, AS, increase, decrease, decrease, AS, even higher

3. greater, greater, smaller, inverse, Phillips

4. (a) inflation, unemployment; (b) increase, increase

5. higher, rise, decrease, higher, higher

6. short-run, lower

7. nominal, real, higher, lower, lay off, above

8. incentives, transfer, regulation, decrease

9. Laffer, revenues, lower, revenues, AS

PROBLEMS AND PROJECTS

1. (a) 5 (b) 14 (c) (it's your choice)

2. P_1, Q_p (a) (1) X, P_2, Q_2 (2) AS_1, AS_2; Y, P_3, Q_p, AS_{lr}; (b) (1) Z, P_2, Q_1 (2) AD_1, AD_2, P_3, Q_p; P_2, P_3, AS (3) P_1, Q_p, AS_2, AS_1

3. (a) (1) 6, Y_1 (2) Y_1, X_2; PC_1, PC_2, (3) X_2, Y_2 (4) Y_2, 3, X_3, 6, PC_2, PC_3 (5) PC_{lr}; (b) (1) Z_2 (2) Z_2, X_2, PC_3, PC_2, (3) PC_{lr}

4. (a) 900, 1200, 1400, 1550, 1500, 1400; (b) 50, fall

TRUE-FALSE

1. F   with AS fixed, higher inflation must be due to a rightward shift in AD; this would also imply lower unemployment

2. T   there is a tradeoff between the two in this view

3. F   both price level and unemployment are rising

4. F   supply shocks were the main reason

5. F   true for inflationary expectations, but false for productivity increases

6. T   thus maintaining real wage levels if nominal wage increases match price level increases

7. T   the two factors offset one another, so the AS will shift in the direction of the stronger effect

8. F   the short-run Phillips Curve shifts (e.g. upwards if expected inflation rises)

9. F   this unemployment rate is compatible with any rate of inflation

10. T   because real wages fall and profit margins improve, firms hire more workers

11. F   nominal wage rates, and other input prices, are fixed along a given short-run AS curve

12. T

13. T   the inflationary gap will eventually be resolved, returning the economy to full-employment GDP

14. T

15. F   the Laffer Curve suggests that this may be possible, depending which section of the curve we are currently on

16. T   investing in RSPs is an example of tax avoidance; failing to report income is an example of tax evasion

MULTIPLE-CHOICE

1. (a) AD shifts right against a static AS

2. (a)

3. (a)

4. (d)

5. (d) decreased productivity in food production

6. (b) 5% - 2%

7. (c) this took much inflationary pressure out of wages, etc.

8. (c)

9. (a) the leftward AS shift is countered by a rightward AD shift, perhaps triggering another leftward AS shift

10. (b)

11. (d) because nominal wages were based on the (higher) expected inflation

12. (b)

13. (c) prices (and nominal wages) will rise; there is no permanent effect on real output or unemployment

14. (b)

15. (a) to increase the AS curve

16. (d)

17. (d)

18. (b) by increasing disposable income, tax cuts are likely to cause AD to shift rightward

19. (a) accommodating the oil price increases would have fed the inflation

CHAPTER 16

Economic Growth and the New Economy

In the 20th century economic growth produced tremendous increases in the standard of living for Canadians. As we try to meet the challenge of producing enough goods for a continually growing population, and hopefully with an improving standard of living, it is important to understand the sources and consequences of growth.

There are six main ingredients in economic growth. Four supply factors determine the output potential of the economy: increases or improvements in: (1) the quantity and quality of natural resources; (2) the quantity and quality of human resources; (3) the stock of capital goods; and (4) production technology. These factors are often rolled into one equation in which real GDP is calculated as the product of worker-hours and labour productivity. Whether the economy's full potential is reached depends upon two other factors: the demand factor, and the efficiency factor. Two familiar models are applied to illustrate how the six factors determine growth: the production possibilities model and the aggregate demand-aggregate supply model. Economic growth requires that the production possibilities curve shift outward, but there must also be enough demand, and efficient use of the resources, in order for the expanded potential to be realized. Similarly, in the aggregate demand-aggregate supply model, growth requires shifts in both the long-run aggregate supply and aggregate demand curves.

Since 1926 Canada's real GDP has grown an average rate of 4% per year, and our per capita real GDP has grown an average of 2.1% per year. Growth was very weak in the early 1990s, but recovered from 1997 to 2000.

What accounts for Canada's growth? The amounts of labour and capital inputs have increased, and so has the productivity of these inputs.

These factors can be traced back to such things as: population growth and increased participation in the labour force, investment in capital goods, technological advances, improvements in education and training, economies of scale and reallocation of resources, a large endowment of natural resources, and a favourable social, cultural, and political environment. Complementing this, aggregate demand has expanded sufficiently to bring to fruition most of the potential output growth stemming from these factors on the supply side.

Over the long haul, the economy's labour productivity determines the average real wage rate per hour of work. The dominant source of growth today is the New Economy – the explosion of investment and entrepreneurial activity stemming from innovations with the microchip and information technology. Some of this activity is in existing industries (transportation, banking, etc.) where established firms are implementing the new technologies to reduce costs and improve products. Much of the activity is in start-up firms that have emerged strictly because of the new technologies. Such firms typically enjoy increasing returns (increasing efficiency as their output grows).

The productivity growth generated by the New Economy means that our long-run aggregate supply curve is increasing faster, allowing our demand and real output to grow with less inflationary pressure than in earlier decades. Innovations in information technology have improved the efficiency of labour markets, lowering frictional unemployment and dropping the natural rate of unemployment.

Skeptics question whether there really is a sustainable New Economy, or simply a temporary boom. They also doubt that the economy can continue to grow at this rate without inflationary pressures setting in soon. Whether growth is desirable and sustainable is also a serious question. Arguments against the pursuit of growth are numerous environment impacts and the sense that while growth may improve our material standard of living that it does little to improve the quality of individual lives as individuals, or the health of our society. Defenders of growth hold that most people desire higher incomes, and that increased material output is the most realistic source of solutions to poverty and various other social problems.

The Last Word discusses why wage and price controls, though a tempting and commonly used strategy, are not effective for controlling inflationary pressures.

■ CHAPTER LEARNING OBJECTIVES

In this chapter you will learn:
☐ About the ingredients of economic growth.
☐ About production possibility analysis.
☐ About Canada's economic growth rates.
☐ About productivity growth in the New Economy.

■ CHAPTER OUTLINE

1. The potential for economic growth is created by increasing the quantity of inputs, or by using inputs more efficiently, or a combination of both. Whether the potential growth will be realized depends upon demand factors and the efficient allocation of existing resources.

(a) Supply factors include increases in the quantity and quality of resources (human, natural, capital) and improvements in technology.

(b) Aggregate demand growth must be adequate to provide employment for all resources in the economy.

(c) Productive efficiency requires that goods be produced in the least costly way, and allocative efficiency requires that resources be used to produce goods that maximize society's well-being.

2. The production possibilities model and the AD-AS model can be used to analyze economic growth.

(a) Economic growth shifts the production possibilities curve outward because of improvement in supply factors that increase real output by increasing labour inputs or by increasing the productivity of labour (in equation terms: Total output = worker-hours × labour productivity). However, whether the economy operates on the curve depends on demand considerations as well as the efficient allocation of the inputs.

(b) In the AD-AS model supply factors that contribute to economic growth shift the long-run aggregate supply curve to the right. Assuming downward price and wage inflexibility, for growth to be realized the aggregate demand curve must also increase.

3. The growth record of the Canadian economy has been impressive, with real GDP increases averaging about 4% per year in the 20th century. On a per capita basis the growth rate has been about 2.1%. Our growth was especially strong in the 1960s, then slowed some in the 1970s and 1980s. In the first years of the 1990s growth was particularly weak, but the growth rate picked up significantly in the 1997-2000 period.

4. Output can increase due to an increase in resource inputs and/or an improvement in the output per unit of input. Between 1961 and 2000, growth in labour accounted for 30% of GDP growth, and growth in capital accounted for 36%, leaving a residual of about 33% of growth attributed to gains in multifactor productivity.

5. The following specific factors have contributed to real growth in the Canadian economy:

(a) labour force growth due to immigration and increased labour force participation by women;

(b) technological advances (including innovative production techniques, new managerial methods, and forms of business organization);

(c) capital accumulation through business investment in plant and equipment, and government investment in infrastructure;

(d) human capital accumulation through investment in education and training of workers;

(e) economies of scale from growing size of markets and firms;

(f) improved resource allocation through industrial restructuring, lessening of labour market discrimination, freer international trade;

(g) an abundant and varied endowment of natural resources; and

(h) a very favourable social-cultural-political environment.

6. Real output, real income, and real wages are determined by the productivity of labour. The New Economy has been an engine of productivity growth.

(a) The invention of the microchip, and its application to many industrial, commercial and household uses, created an explosion of entrepreneurial and investment activity. The information technology industry is the best example.

(b) The new technology has given birth to many start-up firms, many of which enjoy increasing returns and economies of scale for a number of reasons:

(1) they can use more specialized inputs;

(2) they can spread fixed development costs over more units as production increases;

(3) often their products can be consumed simultaneously by many consumers;

(4) often their products create network effects for consumers; and

(5) their operations become more efficient through learning-by-doing especially while firms are very new.

7. The acceleration in productivity increases due to the New Economy has macroeconomic implications.

(a) The long-run aggregate supply is shifting rightward faster than it otherwise would have, increasing our full-employment GDP level. Growth in this sector of the economy produces less inflationary pressure because increasing returns are common, and because of global competition.

(b) Labour market benefits in terms of both frictional and structural unemployment have reduced unemployment and lower the natural rate of unemployment.

(c) Government revenue from income taxes has grown quickly, helping to make possible the elimination of the federal government's habitual deficits.

8. Some people believe that the New Economy is too good: that it will turn out to have been a temporary boom, and that the New Economy will turn out to be like the old economy in the sense that capacity constraints will be met – sooner or later – and that traditional inflationary pressures are inevitable if the growth continues much longer.

9. Economists usually assume that growth is desirable and sustainable, but both of these assumptions are debatable.

(a) Opponents of economic growth contend that it pollutes the environment, creates poor-quality, alienating jobs, does little or nothing to solve social problems such as poverty or crime, and while providing more goods and services, it does not provide a better life.

(b) Advocates of growth argue that it results in a higher standard of living and lessens the burden of scarcity, thereby giving us the resources to fight social problems, pollution, etc. They argue that many problems are falsely blamed on growth.

10. Wage and price controls have been imposed in many different jurisdictions seeking solutions to inflation. Invariably such laws have failed to cure the problem. There are several reasons:

(a) Such laws attack symptoms, not the causes of the inflation.

(b) Enforcement and compliance represent enormous challenges because incentives are strong for market participants to engage in black market transactions at illegal prices.

(c) Because the controls interfere with the rights of individuals and businesses, and create shortages in many markets, governments cannot maintain long-term public support for controls.

(d) Where the controls are effective in restricting changes in prices and wages they also distort the allocation of resources and cause rationing problems: goods and services and resources are often not allocated to their highest value uses.

■ **TERMS AND CONCEPTS**

demand factor	**labour productivity**
economies of scale	**learning-by-doing**
efficiency factor	**network effects**
increasing returns	**New Economy**
information	**start-up firm**
technology	**supply factors**
labour force	
participation rate	

■ **HINTS AND TIPS**

1. The rate of economic growth depends on the rate of increase in the quantity and the quality of inputs, and on changes in technology (which represent our "know how" for turning inputs into outputs). However, these factors merely increase the potential output of the economy. For growth to occur, actual output must increase. That requires growth in demand as well as growth in supply.

2. Figure 16-2 is a nifty summary of how to think about the ingredients of growth. The focus is on labour. Real GDP is defined as the amount of labour employed times the productivity of labour. In this view, changes in capital, technology, education pro-

grams, etc. all impact real GDP through their effect on labour productivity.

■ FILL-IN QUESTIONS

1. Assume that an economy has a GDP of $800 billion. If the growth rate is 4%, GDP will increase by $_____ billion in one year; but if the rate of growth is only 2%, the year's increase in GDP will be $_____ billion. A two percentage point difference in the growth rate results in a $_____ billion difference in the year's increase in GDP. At a constant annual growth rate of 4%, real GDP will double in _____ years, whereas at a growth rate of 2%, it will take _____ years for real GDP to double. (Hint: recall the rule of 70).

2. Graphically, economic growth can be shown as a _____ shift of the production possibilities curve or as a combined shift to the right of the _____ and _____ curves.

3. In the production possibilities model, economic growth increases primarily because of (demand, supply) _____ factors, but the economy may not reach its full potential because there may be less than full _____ or full _____.

4. The four supply factors in economic growth are:
   (a)   increases in _____
   (b)   increases in _____
   (c)   increases in _____
   (d)   improvements in _____
The other two factors are the _____ factor and the _____ factor.

5. The real GDP of any economy in any year is equal to the _____ of labour employed multiplied by the _____ of labour.
   (a)   The former is measured by the number of _____.
   (b)   The latter is measured as _____ per _____.

6. In Canada between 1961 and 2000 about (1/3, 2/3) _____ of the economic growth was due to use of more inputs, and the remaining _____ was due to increase in _____.

7. Technological progress means that we learn how to employ given quantities of resources to obtain greater _____; and, more often than not, this progress requires _____ in new machinery and equipment.

8. The New Economy, developed since 1995, is characterized by applications of the microchip and _____ technology, and its fast growth in _____, for _____ returns in production, and _____ competition in its markets.

9. The macroeconomic benefits of the New Economy include faster shifting of the long-run (AD, AS) _____ curve, reduction in _____ pressures, and increased _____ for government.

■ PROBLEMS AND PROJECTS

1. The next table shows the quantity of labour (in hours) and the productivity of labour (in real GDP per hour) in a hypothetical economy in three different years.
   (a)   Compute the economy's real GDP in each of the three years and enter them in the table.
   (b)   Between years 1 and 2, the quantity of labour remained constant; but
   (1) labour productivity increased by _____%; and, therefore,
   (2) real GDP increased by _____%.
   (c)   Between years 2 and 3, labour productivity remained constant; but
   1) the quantity of labour increased by _____%; and, therefore,
   (2) real GDP increased by _____%.

Year	Quantity of Labour	Productivity of Labour	Real GDP
1	1000	$100	$_____
2	1000	105	_____
3	1100	105	_____

   (d)   Between years 1 and 3,
   (1) real GDP increased by _____%; and
   (2) this rate of increase is approximately equal to the sum of the rates of increase in the _____ and the _____ of labour.

2. An information technology company has developed a videoconferencing service for corporate subscribers. The service is able to connect only subscribers who join this particular service. The provider pays the initial development cost of $1,000,000 and a variable cost of $20,000 per subscriber. The value of the service to customers rises the more other subscribers are connected. This is reflected in the price schedule in the following table.

Subscribers	10	100	200
Development Cost	$___	$___	$___
Variable Cost	___	___	___
Total Cost	___		
ATC	___		
Price	$5000	$15000	$25000
Total Revenue	___	___	___
Profit	___	___	___

(a) Calculate and fill in the remaining values.

(b) That the videoconferencing provider experiences economies of scales is shown by the (rising, falling) _____ values for the _____ variable as the number of subscribers increases.

(c) That videoconferencing services are subject to network effects is shown by the (rising, falling) _____ values for the _____ variable as the number of subscribers increases.

(d) In order to break even the firm needs at least _____ subscribers.

(e) Why would increasing demand for this service not be likely to contribute to inflation?

■ **TRUE-FALSE**

Circle T if the statement is true, F if it is false.

1. An economy that expands its productive capacity will not realize its potential economic growth unless there is full employment of resources and full production in the economy. **T F**

2. The demand factor means that creating more demand for goods is a sufficient condition for growth to occur. **T F**

3. The efficiency factor in economic growth incorporates issues of productive efficiency and allocative efficiency. **T F**

4. Real GDP has tended to increase more rapidly than per capita GDP in Canada. **T F**

5. The real GDP is equal to input of labour divided by the productivity of labour. **T F**

6. The growth rate in Canada's real GDP fell throughout the 1990s. **T F**

7. A decline in the rate of increase of population may cause a decline in the rate of growth of real GDP, but may also raise the growth rate of real GDP per capita, especially if a larger percentage of the population is able to find employment. **T F**

8. Multifactor productivity measures the change in output not accounted for by changes in the quantity of inputs. **T F**

9. More often than not, technological progress requires the economy to invest in new machinery and equipment. **T F**

10. The Canadian social, cultural, and political environment has, in general, worked to slow Canadian economic growth. **T F**

11. The productivity of the nation's labour is affected by both the amount of education and quality of education received by workers. **T F**

12. Increases in labour productivity can, at least in the Canadian economy, be taken largely for granted, because the rate of increase has been nearly constant for much more than half a century. **T F**

13. The availability of natural resources in Canada has been a significant factor in the growth of the Canadian economy. **T F**

14. Critics of economic growth point to the negative consequences for the nature of work and the number of meaningful jobs in the economy. **T F**

15. Defenders of economic growth claim that most problems of pollution are due not to growth but to the "common property" nature of resources such as air and water. **T F**

16. A telephone system is an example of a good that has network effects in consumption, meaning that one user's value increases the more other users there are. **T F**

17. An economy restricted by wage and price controls can effectively reallocate resources in response to changing relative scarcities of different goods and services **T F**

■ MULTIPLE-CHOICE

Circle the letter that corresponds to the best answer.

1. If the real GDP of a nation increases from $2,000 billion to $2,100 billion in one year, the rate of growth of real GDP during that year would be:
(a) 0.5%
(b) 5%
(c) 10%
(d) 50%

2. Suppose an economy has a GDP of $700 billion and a steady annual growth rate of 5%. Over a two-year period, GDP will increase by:
(a) $14 billion
(b) $35 billion
(c) $70 billion
(d) $71.75 billion

The labour input in hours worked and the real GDP for a hypothetical economy are given in the table below. Use the data to answer questions 3 and 4.

Year	Hours Worked (Millions)	Real GDP (Billion $)
1990	150	30.0
1995	156	31.2
2000	160	32.4

3. From 1990 to 2000 the total growth in GDP was:
(a) 8%
(b) 2.4%
(c) 4%
(d) none of the above

4. Labour productivity was highest in:
(a) 1990
(b) 1995
(c) 2000
(d) labour productivity was constant

5. An outward shift of the entire production possibilities curve of an economy is most likely caused by:
(a) supply factors
(b) demand factors
(c) allocative factors
(d) efficiency factors

6. If a nation is presently operating at a point that lies inside its current production possibilities curve, the most likely reason is:
(a) supply and environmental factors
(b) demand and efficiency factors
(c) increased labour productivity
(d) increased total factor productivity

7. Which of the following is not a supply factor in economic growth?
(a) an expansion in purchasing power
(b) an increase in the economy's stock of capital goods
(c) more natural resources
(d) technological improvements

8. That Canada's real GDP growth has been accompanied by inflation is a sign that:
(a) AD and AS_{LR} have increased equally
(b) AD has increased relative to AS_{LR}
(c) AD has increased less than AS_{LR}
(d) AD has increased but the AS_{LR} curve has decreased

9. Which of the following is an accurate statement about the relationship between technological advance and investment spending?
(a) technological advances usually spur spending on new capital goods
(b) technological advances are not related to investment spending
(c) technological advances reduce the need for spending on new capital goods
(d) spending on technology and on capital goods are usually substitutes

10. Which types of capital contribute to economic growth?
(a) private capital such as factories
(b) public capital such as highways
(c) both private and public capital
(d) only financial capital

11. Concerns about the quality of Canadian education arise from:
(a) the fact that a smaller percentage of our population is attending college or university
(b) the fact that more students are attending college instead of university
(c) decreases in government expenditures on post-secondary education

(d) deterioration in the performance of Canadian students on standardized achievement tests

12. Which of the following has contributed to improved resource allocation in the Canadian economy?
(a) decline of discrimination against women in labour markets
(b) freer international trade
(c) the shift of labour out of the agricultural sector
(d) all of the above

13. Canada enjoys a social-cultural-political environment that is on the whole very favourable for growth. Which of the following does not contribute to this favourable environment?
(a) few taboos against work, production, and material progress
(b) strong personal and corporate incentives encouraging growth
(c) a stable rule of law and enforcement of contracts
(d) some social programs give incentives not to work

14. Increasing returns are common in information technology industries because of:
(a) network effects
(b) high fixed development costs
(c) products can be simultaneously consumed by many consumers
(d) all of the above

15. Which of the following goods is a prime example of simultaneous consumption?
(a) recorded music
(b) apples
(c) haircuts
(d) automobiles

16. How has expansion in the New Economy helped drive down the natural rate of unemployment?
(a) start-ups hired large numbers of unemployed people already trained for the high-tech sector
(b) many high-tech firms have been willing to hire and then train workers
(c) information technology has improved the flow of information between workers and employers, reducing frictional unemployment
(d) both (b) and (c)

17. Which is not among the reasons that skeptics doubt whether the "miracle" of the New Economy will endure?
(a) several other productivity booms have lasted a few years and then petered out
(b) even this sector will eventually reach capacity constraints if it grows long enough
(c) business cycles are likely to occur, even around a higher trend of productivity growth
(d) the New Economy has not actually raised our productivity so far

18. Which of the following is not a part of the case against economic growth?
(a) growth produces pollution
(b) growth impedes the increased production of consumer goods
(c) growth prevents the attainment of a better life
(d) growth is not needed to provide us with the means of solving domestic social problems

19. Which of the following is not a part of the case in favour of economic growth?
(a) growth lessens the scarcity problem
(b) growth lessens the extent of anxiety and insecurity
(c) growth is not the primary reason for pollution and environmental degradation
(d) growth is the only practical way to reduce poverty

20. The fact that natural resource prices have not generally risen is presented as an argument in support of the view that:
(a) growth is beneficial
(b) growth is sustainable
(c) growth allows us to escape the laws of economics
(d) all of the above

■ **DISCUSSION QUESTIONS**

1. How does economic growth affect the production possibilities curve? What demand and efficiency assumptions are necessary to achieve maximum productive potential?

2. Describe how economic growth can be illustrated in an aggregate demand-aggregate supply model.

3. What are the six basic ingredients of economic growth? What is the essential difference between the supply factors and the other two factors?

4. What is Canada's record on economic growth? During what periods did our economy grow particularly quickly or slowly?

5. What is the relationship between the annual real GDP, the quantity of labour employed, and the productivity of labour? What factors affect the productivity of labour?

6. What is the relationship between investment and the stock of capital? What is the connection between increases in the capital stock and the rate of economic growth?

7. If the quantity of the labour and capital inputs stayed constant from year to year what productivity measure would indicate how quickly production is growing? How much has this source of productivity contributed to Canada's economic growth since 1961?

8. What is the nature of the New Economy, and what are the reasons that businesses in this sector tend to have increasing returns?

9. Why, or under what conditions, would growth stemming from the New Economy be less inflationary than growth stemming from traditional industries such as manufacturing? Again, relative to growth in traditional sectors, why might growth in the New Economy lower the natural rate of unemployment?

10. What are the arguments for and against the desirability and the sustainability of economic growth in Canada?

11. How are wage and price controls supposed to work? What serious problems do such controls encounter in practice?

■ **ANSWERS**

FILL-IN QUESTIONS

1. 32, 16, 16, approx. 18, 35

2. rightward, AD, AS_{LR}

3. supply, employment, production

4. (a) quantity and quality of natural resources; (b) quantity and quality of human resources; (c) the supply or stock of capital goods; (d) technology; demand, efficiency

5. quantity, productivity; (a) worker hours; (b) output, worker hour

6. 2/3, 1/3, multifactor productivity

7. output (production), investment

8. information, productivity, increasing, global

9. AS, inflationary, tax revenues

PROBLEMS AND PROJECTS

1. (a) 100,000, 105,000, 115,500; (b) (1) 5, (2) 5; (c) (1) 10, (2) 10; (d) (1) 15.5, (2) quantity, productivity

2. (a) Development: $1.0 million all entries; Variable Cost: $0.2 million, 2.0 million, 4.0 million; Total Cost: $1.2 million, 3.0 million, 5,0 million; ATC: $120,000/subscriber, 30,000, 25,000; Total Revenue: $50,000, 1.5 million, 5.0 million; $-1.15 million; -1.50 million; 0; (b) falling, ATC; (c) rising, price; (d) 200; (e) increasing returns

TRUE-FALSE

1. T
2. F it is a necessary condition, not a sufficient condition
3. T
4. T population increases has diluted the per capita real GDP growth rate to some extent
5. F multiplied, not divided
6. F the growth rate recovered at the end of the 1990s
7. T
8. T
9. T
10. F these factor improve the general productivity of our economy, thus improved our growth rate
11. T
12. F this component of growth has fluctuated significantly
13. T
14. T
15. T
16. T
17. F with wage and price controls relative prices can't change properly, so resources not likely to be reallocated; misallocation of resources will result

MULTIPLE-CHOICE

1. (b) 100/2,000
2. (d) 5% of 700 + 5% of (700 + 5% of 700)
3. (a) 2.4/30
4. (c) real GDP/hours worked = .2025 in 2000
5. (a) such as more labour or other resources
6. (b)
7. (a) this is a demand factor
8. (b) whether long-run AS has increased or not, AD has increased more
9. (a) the Internet has necessitated huge spending on computers, fibre optics networks, etc.
10. (c)
11. (d) some example results are shown in the chapter
12. (d)
13. (d)
14. (d)
15. (a) any number of people can simultaneously listen to copies of the same piece of music
16. (d) the natural rate depends on both frictional and structural unemployment
17. (d) activity in the New Economy has raised productivity significantly
18. (b) economic growth leads to increased production of consumer goods
19. (b) unfortunately, problems of anxiety and insecurity may well worsen in a dynamic growing economy
20. (b) were natural resources becoming depleted, one would expect to see ongoing price rises on these commodities, but we haven't seen this happen

CHAPTER 17

The Gains from International Trade

This chapter builds on Chapter 5 which introduced you to Canada's connections with the global economy. After reviewing the key facts about world trade, the chapter examines the theory of comparative advantage. This theory provides the basis for international specialization and trade, by demonstrating that both nations in an export-import relationship can gain. Canada's economy has always been heavily dependent on international trade, exporting and importing with many different nations, and over an astonishing range of goods and services.

We trade because trade benefits us; so what is the source of these benefits? Economic resources (natural, human, and capital) are distributed unevenly between nations. Efficient production of various goods requires different technologies or combinations of resources. Therefore, some nations are well-suited to producing labour-intensive goods while others are well-suited to capital-intensive goods. The theory of comparative advantage predicts that each nation will specialize in producing those goods for which they have the lower opportunity cost. Production according to this principle will maximize the total output of goods, and through exports and imports, each nation will end up able to consume larger quantities than they could without free trade.

The standard supply and demand model can be adapted to find export supply and import demand curves. If the price in Canada is above (below) the world price, Canada will sell exports (demand imports) equal to our domestic surplus (shortage). In a two-country model, the world price for a product is found where one country's export supply curve intersects the other country's import demand curve.

Despite the strong case for specialization and free trade according to comparative advantage, virtually all nations have engaged in protectionism by erecting barriers to free trade: tariffs, quotas, and other restrictions on imports. Thus, the chapter looks at: (1) what techniques nations use to limit imports; (2) the economic impacts of trade barriers; and (3) the arguments in favour of protectionism. Though it is easy to understand why certain groups desire protection from competition with foreign producers, protectionism is costly to a nation overall.

The chapter closes with a description of the World Trade Organization (WTO), an international forum for planning and negotiating liberalization of trade around the world. While WTO agreements have the potential to expand world output by 8% by 2005, the organization faces opposition from a host of protest groups opposed to multinational corporations, loss of national sovereignty, environmental degradation, etc.

■ CHAPTER LEARNING OBJECTIVES

In this chapter you will learn:
☐ The facts about Canada's international trade.
☐ About specialization and comparative advantage.
☐ About supply and demand analysis of exports and imports.
☐ About trade barriers and their negative effects on nations' economic well-being.

■ CHAPTER OUTLINE

1. International trade is vital to the Canadian economy.
   (a) Canada is more trade dependent than most nations; exports are 40% of Canadian GDP.
   (b) Canada's principal commodity exports are automotive products, machinery and equipment,

and forestry products. Its main imports are machinery and equipment and automotive products.

(c) Most of Canada's trade is with other industrialized nations, particularly the United States, Japan, and Western European nations.

(d) Markets continue to become increasingly global, and international trade and financial relationships are important policy issues in Canada and nearly all other nations.

2. Specialization and trade between nations are advantageous because:

(a) Nations differ in their endowments of natural, human, and capital resources.

(b) Efficient production of different products requires different technologies and combinations of resources.

(c) Products are differentiated, and people may prefer certain imported goods over domestically produced varieties of the same good.

3. The basis for trade is the principle of comparative advantage. It states that the allocation of resources is most efficient, and total output is maximized, when each good is produced where its opportunity cost is lowest. A simple hypothetical example illustrates comparative advantage and the gains from trade.

(a) Suppose the world is composed of only two nations, each capable of producing two different commodities and having straight-line production possibilities curves with different slopes. That is, each country has a constant opportunity cost of producing each good, but this cost is different between the two countries.

(b) Given different opportunity costs, each nation has a comparative (cost) advantage in the production of one of the two goods. For the world to use its resources economically, each nation must specialize according to their comparative advantage.

(c) The ratio at which one product is traded for another is called the "terms of trade" and lies between the opportunity cost ratios of the two nations.

(d) Each nation can share in the gains from trade because specialization permits a greater total output from the same resources and a better allocation of the world's resources.

(e) If cost ratios in the two nations are not constant, specialization may not be complete.

(f) If opportunity cost ratios do not differ, there is no basis for mutually beneficial trade.

(g) In addition to improving efficiency and expanding output, free trade has side-benefits: it promotes competition and deters monopoly, offers consumers a wider range of product choices, and links national interest and makes nations more interested in cooperation as compared to conflict.

4. Supply and demand analysis can show how the equilibrium price and quantity of exports and imports for a product are determined in trade between two nations.

(a) Each nation has a domestic demand and a domestic supply. In the absence of international trade, the intersections of these curves establish the price in each nation.

(b) If there is trade, the export supply curve shows how much domestic producers are willing to sell abroad at each world price above the domestic (no-trade) equilibrium price. The import demand curve shows how much consumers are willing to buy from abroad at each world price below the domestic equilibrium price.

(c) The equilibrium world price and world levels of exports and imports are determined where one nation's import demand curve intersects the other nation's export supply curve.

5. Nations restrict international trade by imposing tariffs, import quotas, various non-tariff barriers, and voluntary export restrictions. Special-interest groups within nations benefit from protection and persuade their governments to erect trade barriers. The costs to consumers of this protection exceed the benefits to workers and shareholders, so the economy experiences a net cost.

6. The imposition of a tariff on a good imported from abroad has both direct and indirect effects on an economy.

(a) The tariff increases the domestic price of the good, reduces its domestic consumption, expands its domestic production, decreases foreign production, and transfers income from domestic consumers to producers and the government.

(b) The tariff also reduces the income of foreign producers and the ability of foreign nations to purchase goods and services in the nation imposing the tariff. Export industries in the nation imposing the tariff suffer a loss of sales, and must cut production and release resources, despite their efficiency (as proven by their comparative advantage).

(c)   Tariffs are like sales taxes. Therefore they are regressive taxes and affect low-income families proportionately more than high-income families.

7. An import quota is a legal limit on the amount of a product that may be imported each year. Its direct and indirect effects are similar to those of a tariff, except that what would otherwise be tariff revenue for the government ends up as revenue for foreign producers.

8. The military self-sufficiency argument for protectionism is questionable because it is difficult to say which industry is "vital" to national security and therefore must be protected. It would be more efficient economically to provide a direct subsidy to strategic industries.

9. Trade barriers are often implemented to protect jobs at home but, for several reasons, this strategy often fails.
(a)   Imports may eliminate some jobs, but they create others; therefore, imports may only change the composition of employment, not the overall level of employment;
(b)   There is a fallacy of composition problem: it is impossible for all nations to restrict imports, yet still maintain their exports. Trade barriers can be viewed as "beggar thy neighbour" policies;
(c)   Other nations are likely to retaliate with their own tariffs and quotas, leading to reduced national output and employment; and
(d)   Barriers reduce the efficiency of resource allocation by shielding domestic industries from competition.

10. Tariffs are sometimes advocated as devices to help diversify, and thereby stabilize, the economy. The Canadian economy is already quite diversified, so this justification has no merit here. In less-developed nations this strategy could have huge economic costs because it pushes nations to produce contrary to comparative advantage.

11. It is alleged that infant industries need protection until they are strong enough to compete. But the argument may not apply to developed economies: it is difficult to select which industries will prosper; protectionism tends to persist long after it is needed; and direct subsidies may be more economically efficient.

12. As instruments of strategic trade policy, tariffs may give domestic producers an advantage over foreign competitors, allowing them to grow more rapidly and achieve greater economies of scale. The protected firms can then dominate world markets because of lower costs. In other words, the goal is to acquire comparative advantage by strategic economic policies rather than depending solely on a country's resource allocation. Such strategies, however, tend to provoke retaliatory trade barriers by other nations.

13. Sometimes protection is sought against the "dumping" of foreign goods at a price below cost. Dumping is a legitimate concern and is restricted under Canadian trade law; but there are so few proven cases of dumping that this problem does not justify widespread tariff protection. If foreign companies are more efficient than our firms, what appears to be dumping may actually be the result of comparative advantage.

14. Protection is sometimes sought to shield Canadian workers from cheap foreign labour. In fact these differences in labour costs are the very basis for mutually beneficial trade. If countries with low wages cannot export labour-intensive goods to high-wage nations, their living standards, and our living standards, will be lower.

15. In summary, there are many arguments for protectionism, but most are fallacious or based on half-truths. The only points that have some validity, under certain conditions, are the infant-industry and military-sufficiency arguments, but both are subject to abuse. The historical evidence suggests that free trade promotes prosperity and growth in the world.

16. The inefficiencies of trade protectionism motivate nations to work together for freer trade. The World Trade Organization (WTO), consisting in 2000 of 138 member countries, agreed to trade liberalizations including: tariff reductions, rules to promote trade in services, reductions in agricultural subsidies, protections for property in intellectual property. The WTO has been heavily protested by groups concerned about globalization, environmental degradation, loss of sovereignty, etc.

17. Bastiat's petition of the candlemakers (1845) is a classic satire of the claims the producers make in search of protectionist policies. It shows their arguments to be self-serving and often fallacious.

■ TERMS AND CONCEPTS

capital-intensive goods
cost ratio
domestic price
dumping
equilibrium world price
export supply curve
gains from trade
import demand curve
import quotas
labour-intensive goods

land-intensive goods
non-tariff barriers
protective tariff
revenue tariff
strategic trade policy
tariff
trading possibilities line
voluntary export restrictions (VERs)
world price

■ HINTS AND TIPS

1. Spend time working numerical examples of the comparative advantage model. This is a very important model, but it can be tricky to master.

2. To understand why tariffs exist, even if the costs to consumers exceed the benefits to domestic producers, consider the following questions. Do you know whether or not Canada has a tariff on shoelaces, and if so, what is it? If you were a Canadian manufacturer of shoelaces, do you think that you would know more about the tariff? Why?

■ FILL-IN QUESTIONS

1. A nation with relatively low wages will tend to produce and export goods that are (capital, labour) _____ -intensive to produce.

2. Nations tend to trade among themselves because the distribution of economic resources among them is (even, uneven) _____ and because the efficient production of various goods and services necessitates (the same, different) _____ technologies or combinations of resources.

3. A nation will tend to specialize in and export those goods in the production of which they have a _____, and to import those goods in the production of which they do not have a _____.

4. If the opportunity cost of one banana in country X is four hats, while in country Y the opportunity cost of one banana is three hats:

(a) hats are relatively (more, less) _____ expensive in country X and bananas relatively _____ expensive;
(b) hats are relatively _____ expensive in country Y and bananas relatively _____ expensive;
(c) X has a comparative advantage and should specialize in the production of _____ and Y has a comparative advantage and should specialize in the production of _____.
(d) When X and Y specialize and trade, the terms of trade will be somewhere between _____ and _____ hats for each banana; and will depend upon world _____ and _____ for hats and bananas.
(e) If the terms of trade turn out to be 3.5 hats for one banana, the cost of obtaining one hat has been decreased from _____ to _____ bananas in Y, and the cost of one banana has been decreased from _____ to _____ hats in X.
(f) This international specialization will not be complete if the cost of producing either good (increases, decreases, remains constant) _____ as a nation produces more of it.

5. The basic argument for free trade is that it results in a better _____ of resources and a higher _____ of living.

6. The barriers to international trade include _____, _____ quotas, _____ barriers, and _____ restrictions.

7. A trade war can result if one nation's imposition of a tariff causes its trading partners to _____.

8. When Canada imposes a tariff on a good that is imported from abroad,
(a) the price of that good in Canada will (increase, decrease) _____;
(b) the total amount purchased of that good in Canada will _____;
(c) the output of:
(1) Canadian producers of the good will _____;
(2) foreign producers of the good will _____;
(d) the ability of foreigners to buy goods from Canada will _____, and, as a result, output and employment in Canadian industries that export will _____.

9. While a tariff generates revenue for the Canadian _____, an import quota transfers that revenue to _____.

10. List the six main arguments that protectionists use to justify trade barriers.
   (a) _____
   (b) _____
   (c) _____
   (d) _____
   (e) _____
   (f) _____

11. The only two arguments containing any reasonable justification for protection are the _____ and the _____ arguments.

12. WTO is the abbreviation for the _____.

■ **PROBLEMS AND PROJECTS**

1. Assume that labour is the only input. In England it takes six hours of labour to produce one unit of cloth and four hours to produce one unit of wine. There are a total of 60 hours of labour available in the English economy.

In Canada it takes 2.5 hours to produce one unit of cloth and two hours to produce one unit of wine. There are a total of 30 labour hours available in Canada.
   (a) Construct the production possibilities graphs for cloth and wine in England and Canada.
   (b) What does Canada have a comparative advantage in producing?
   (c) If trade takes place, what should Canada produce, export, and import?
   (d) Suppose that the number of labour hours available in England increases to 120. What does Canada now have a comparative advantage in producing?
   (e) If trade takes place, what should Canada produce, export, and import?

2. Below are the production possibilities curves for Canada and Chile. Suppose these two nations do not currently engage in international trade or specialization, and suppose that points A and a show the combinations of wheat and copper they now produce and consume.
   (a) The fact that the curves are straight lines indicates that the cost ratios in the two nations are (changing, constant) _____.

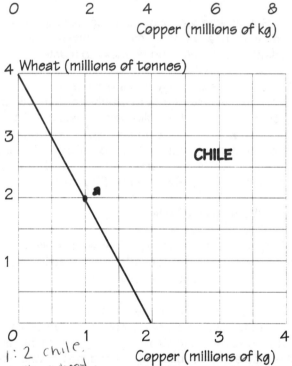

1 : 2 chile.
1 : ½. wheat.

(b) Examination of the two curves reveals that the cost ratio in
   (1) Canada is ____4____ million tonnes of wheat for one million kilograms of copper.
   (2) Chile is _____ million tonnes of wheat for one million kilograms of copper.
(c) If these two nations were to specialize and trade wheat for copper,
   (1) Canada would specialize in the production of _____ (Why?);

canada
¼ = .25   1 copper   4 wheat
chile.
1   1 copper   2 wheat.
2 = .50

(2) Chile would specialize in the production of

_____.

(d)   The terms of trade, if specialization and trade occur, will be greater than two and less than four million tonnes of wheat for one million kilograms of copper. Why?

(e)   Assume the terms of trade turn out to be three million tonnes of wheat for one million kilograms of copper. Draw in the trading possibilities lines for Canada and Chile.

(f)   With these trading possibilities lines, suppose Canada decides to consume five million tonnes of wheat and one million kilograms of copper, while Chile decides to consume three million tonnes of wheat and one million kilograms of copper. The gains from trade to:

   (1) Canada are _____ million tonnes of wheat and _____ million kilograms of copper.

   (2) Chile are _____ million tonnes of wheat and _____ million kilograms of copper.

3. Suppose that the Canadian demand for woven blankets is given in the table.

Price	Canadian Qd	Canadian Qs
21	62,000	42,000
22	59,000	44,000
23	56,000	46,000
24	53,000	48,000
25	50,000	50,000
26	47,000	52,000

(a)   The domestic equilibrium price is $_____, and quantity is _____.

(b)   Suppose that Canada can now import blankets. Foreign suppliers are willing to sell at a price of $22 as many blankets as Canada will buy. The new price in Canada will be $_____, and quantity consumed with be _____. Canadian producers will supply _____ and the remaining quantity of _____ will be imported.

(c)   If the Canadian government imposes an import tariff of $1 per blanket, the new price in Canada will be $_____, and quantity consumed with be _____. Canadian producers will supply _____ and the remaining quantity of _____ will be imported. The government will collect tariff revenue of $_____.

(d)   Of the following groups, who gains from the tariff, and who loses: Canadian blanket consumers, Canadian blanket producers, foreign blanket producers?

4. The following table shows demand and supply in two nations for some product.

(a)   In the absence of trade, the price in Nation 1 would be $_____, and the price in Nation 2 would be $_____.

(b)   Use the data to generate export supply and import demand curves for each nation, and plot these curves in the graph below.

Price	Nation 1		Nation 2	
	Qd	Qs	Qd	Qs
$8	2	10	4	8
7	3	9	5	7
6	4	8	6	6
5	5	7	7	5
4	6	6	8	4
3	7	5	9	3

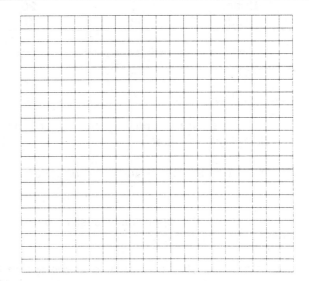

(c)   When trade occurs between the two nations, the equilibrium price in both nations will be $_____.

(d)   In equilibrium: Nation 1 produces _____ units, consumes _____ units, and (exports, imports) _____ the difference. Nation 2 produces _____ units, consumes _____ units, and (exports, imports) _____ the rest.

■ TRUE-FALSE

Circle T if the statement is true, F if it is false.

1. One reason for international trade is that some consumers prefer foreign-produced varieties of certain goods.　**T F**

2. A nation that is experiencing rising wages (relative to other input prices) will become less likely to export labour-intensive goods.　**T F**

Use the following production possibilities tables to answer true-false questions 3 through 8 and multiple-choice questions 4 and 5.

ADANAC		
Butter	0	20
Cloth	40	0

ZATELBA		
Butter	0	60
Cloth	60	0

3. In Adanac the opportunity cost of one unit of cloth is 1/4 unit of butter.　**T F**

4. In Adanac the opportunity cost of butter is constant.　**T F**

5. In Zatelba the opportunity cost of one unit of cloth is one unit of butter.　**T F**

6. Adanac has the comparative advantage in the production of cloth.　**T F**

7. Zatelba has the comparative advantage in the production of both goods.　**T F**

8. With specialization and trade, the trading possibilities line of both nations would move to the right of their production possibilities curve.　**T F**

9. Increasing production costs lead to incomplete specialization in production in trading nations.　**T F**

10. International trade tends to increase the efficiency of allocation of the world's resources and leads to a greater world output of goods.　**T F**

11. A tariff on coffee in Canada is an example of a protective tariff.　**T F**

12. When Canada places a tariff on an import, some groups in Canada gain and others lose.　**T F**

13. Direct subsidies to vital industries would be more effective than tariffs as a means to ensure military self-sufficiency.　**T F**

14. An import quota specifies the minimum price that can be charged for an imported good.　**T F**

15. Most of the economic consequences of tariffs and import quotas are similar.　**T F**

16. A significant difference between a tariff and an import quota is that a quota generates revenue for the government, whereas a tariff does not.　**T F**

17. One-crop economies may be able to make themselves more stable and diversified by imposing tariffs on goods imported from abroad; but these tariffs are apt also to lower the standard of living in these economies.　**T F**

18. The only argument for tariffs that has, in the appropriate circumstances, any economic justification is the argument of increasing domestic employment.　**T F**

19. If A and B are the only nations that produce and consume figs, and there is free trade between the two nations, an increase in the supply of figs in B will lower the price of figs in B and in A.　**T F**

20. A protective tariff generally conveys benefits on domestic producers that in total are more than the cost imposed on domestic consumers.　**T F**

21. Tariffs on specific goods can be a legitimate remedy for combating dumping.　**T F**

22. Canada's standard of living would increase if we stopped importing goods produced in countries with very low wages.　**T F**

23. A policy of free trade was one of the factors contributing to Great Britain's industrialization and rapid growth in the mid-nineteenth century.　**T F**

24. The basic goal of the WTO is liberalization of world trade.　**T F**

■ MULTIPLE-CHOICE

Circle the letter that corresponds to the best answer.

1. Nations would not need to engage in trade if:
(a) all products were produced from the same combinations of resources
(b) world resources were evenly distributed among nations
(c) consumers had no preference for imported brands over domestic brands of goods
(d) all of the above

2. Country A has a comparative advantage over country B in the production of sofas:
(a) when sofas are produced in both countries and wages are lower in country A
(b) when country A has an absolute advantage in the production of sofas
(c) when the opportunity cost of sofas is lower in country A than In country B
(d) when the opportunity cost of sofas is lower in country B than in country A

3. If country B has a comparative advantage over country A in the production of steel, then:
(a) country B has an absolute advantage in the production of steel
(b) the production of steel in country B uses less resources than in country A
(c) the opportunity cost of producing steel is less in country B than in country A
(d) inputs are more efficient in country B than in country A

Use the tables preceding true-false question 3 to answer the following two questions.

4. If Adanac and Zatelba engage in trade, the terms of trade will be:
(a) between one and two units of butter for one unit of cloth
(b) between 1/2 and one unit of butter for one unit of cloth
(c) between three and four units of butter for one unit of cloth
(d) between 1/8 and 1/4 unit of butter for one unit of cloth.

5. If, after trade starts, the exchange ratio was one cloth for 1/2 butter, the gains from trade would:

(a) all go to Adanac
(b) all go to Zatelba
(c) be equally distributed between Adanac and Zatelba
(d) be captured by the larger of the two countries

6. The terms of trade:
(a) are the reciprocal of the exchange rate
(b) measure the number of units of imports obtained per unit of export
(c) are given by the reciprocal of the foreign trade multiplier
(d) improve whenever the exchange rate depreciates

7. What does economic growth have in common with specialization and trade according to the principle of comparative advantage?
(a) both cause a nation's production possibilities curve to shift outward
(b) both permit a nation to consume combinations of goods that would otherwise not have been available
(c) both change the slope or steepness of the production possibilities curve
(d) both expand the supply of available resources

8. In the trade model, changing the assumption of constant costs to one of increasing costs results in:
(a) the principle of comparative advantage no longer holding
(b) only one of two trading partners gaining from trade
(c) a tendency towards incomplete specialization
(d) trade flows being greater than in the constant cost model

9. Which one of the following is a characteristic of tariffs?
(a) they legally prohibit the importation of goods from abroad
(b) they specify the maximum amounts of specific commodities that may be imported during a given period of time
(c) they often protect domestic producers from foreign competition
(d) they enable nations to reduce their exports and increase their imports during periods of depression

10. The motive for a nation to erect barriers to the importation of goods and services is to:
   (a) improve economic efficiency in that nation
   (b) protect and benefit special-interest groups in that nation
   (c) reduce the prices of the goods and services produced in that nation
   (d) expand the export of goods and services to foreign nations

11. Which of the following is the likely result of Canada employing tariffs to protect its high wages and standard of living from cheap foreign labour?
   (a) a decrease in the productivity of Canadian workers
   (b) an increase in Canadian exports
   (c) a rise in the Canadian real GDP
   (d) an improved standard of living for workers in low-wage country

12. Which of the following is a likely result of imposing tariffs to increase domestic employment?
   (a) a short-run increase in domestic employment
   (b) retaliatory increases in the tariffs of foreign nations
   (c) a long-run decline in exports
   (d) all of the above

13. Which of the following is not true of tariffs established to support an infant industry?
   (a) such tariffs tend to remain in place long after the industry has matured
   (b) it is difficult for government to determine which infant industries have potential to benefit from such a tariff
   (c) such tariffs may not be the best way to achieve the goal: direct subsidies might be more effective
   (d) all of the above are true

Answer the next four questions (14 through 17) on the basis of the following diagram, where *Sd* and *Dd* are the domestic supply and demand for a product and *Pw* is the world price of that product.

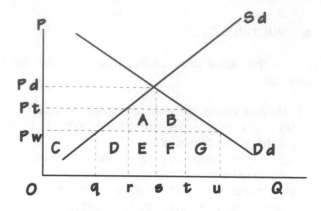

14. In a closed economy (without international trade), the equilibrium price would be:
   (a) *OPd*; but in an open economy, the equilibrium price will be *OPt*
   (b) *OPd*; but in an open economy, the equilibrium price will be *OPw*
   (c) *OPd*; but in an open economy, the equilibrium price will be *OPd*
   (d) *OPd*; but in an open economy, the equilibrium price will be *OPt*

15. If there were free trade in this economy and no tariffs, the total revenue going to the foreign producers is represented by:
   (a) area *C*
   (b) areas *A* and *B* combined
   (c) areas *A*, *B*, *E*, and *F* combined
   (d) areas *D*, *E*, *F*, and *G* combined

16. If a tariff was imposed in the amount of *PwPt* per unit imported, then domestic producers would supply:
   (a) *Oq* units and foreign producers would supply *qu* units
   (b) *Os* units and foreign producers would supply *su* units
   (c) *Or* units and foreign producers would supply *rt* units
   (d) *Ot* units and foreign producers would supply *tu* units

17. Given a per unit tariff in the amount of P_wP_t, the amount of the tariff revenue paid by consumers of this product is represented by:
   (a) area *A*
   (b) area *B*
   (c) areas *A* and *B* combined
   (d) areas *D*, *E*, *F*, and *G* combined

18. A tariff introduced to protect the Canadian furniture industry would create:

(a) benefits for shareholders, workers and consumers of the Canadian furniture industry

(b) benefits for shareholders and workers that exceed the costs to consumers

(c) costs to consumers that exceed the benefits for shareholders and workers

(d) costs to shareholders, workers and consumers

19. In Canada, a tariff on which good would be considered a revenue tariff (as opposed to a protective tariff)?

(a) wheat

(b) potatoes

(c) coffee

(d) apples

20. An example of a non-tariff barrier is:

(a) unreasonable labelling standards for food products imported from Brazil

(b) a quota on imported French wine

(c) voluntary export restriction by Toyota

(d) an export subsidy for Canadian book publishers

21. If Japanese manufacturers dump VCRs in Canada, they are:

(a) selling VCRs in Canada at a price less than the cost of production

(b) selling VCRs in Canada at a price less than the price in Japan

(c) selling VCRs in Canada at a price that is less than the price in Japan plus shipping cost

(d) selling VCRs in Canada that were produced in a foreign government-owned establishment

22. Which group would be unlikely to be in support of a Canadian tariff on foreign-recorded CDs?

(a) artists recording in Canada

(b) owners of recording studios in Canada

(c) employees in recording studios in Canada

(d) music retail stores in Canada

23. Strategic trade policy is a variant of which argument in favour of tariffs?

(a) infant-industry

(b) diversification for stability

(c) protection against dumping

(d) increased domestic employment

24. Which of the following is not among the initiatives of the World Trade Organization?

(a) reductions in tariffs worldwide

(b) rules to promote trade in services

(c) protections for intellectual property rights

(d) sanctions against nations who violate human rights

■ **DISCUSSION QUESTIONS**

1. Why do nations specialize in certain products and export their surplus production of these goods at the same time that they are importing other goods? Why not reallocate their resources to producing on their own the goods and services that they wish to consume?

2. What three facts provide the basis for trade among nations?

3. Explain: (a) the theory of comparative advantage; (b) what is meant by and what determines the terms of trade; (c) the gains from the trade.

4. What motivates nations to erect barriers to the importation of goods from abroad, and what types of barriers do they erect?

5. Suppose Canada were to increase the tariff on wine imported from Europe (and elsewhere). What would be the effect of this tariff-rate increase on

(a) the price of wines in Canada;

(b) the total number of bottles of wine sold in Canada during a year;

(c) the number of bottles of wine produced by and employment in the European wine industry;

(d) production and employment in the Canadian wine industry;

(e) European incomes obtained by selling wine in Canada;

(f) the European demand for goods produced in Canada;

(g) the production and employment in those Canadian industries that export goods to Europe;

(h) the standard of living in Canada and in Europe;

(i) the allocation of resources in the Canadian economy;

(j) the allocation of Europe's resources?

6. What is the "case for protection"? How valid and pertinent to Canada is each of the six basic arguments for protection?

7. If it is true that trade barriers impose greater costs on consumers than the benefits conferred on businesses and workers, why have trade barriers been so prevalent throughout our history?

8. What is the WTO, and what does this organization seek to achieve?

■ ANSWERS

FILL-IN QUESTIONS

1. labour

2. uneven, different

3. comparative advantage, comparative advantage

4. (a) less, more; (b) more, less; (c) hats, bananas; (d) 3, 4, demand, supply; (e) 1/3, 2/7, 4, 3.5; (f) increases

5. allocation, standard

6. tariffs, import, non-tariff, voluntary export

7. retaliate

8. (a) increase; (b) decrease; (c) (1) increase, (2) decrease; (d) decrease, decrease

9. government, foreign producers

10. (a) military self-sufficiency; (b) infant industry; (c) increase domestic employment; (d) diversification for stability; (e) cheap foreign labour; (f) protection against dumping

11. military self-sufficiency, infant-industry

12. World Trade Organization

PROBLEMS AND PROJECTS

1. (a) endpoints: England: 10 cloth and 0 wine, 0 cloth and 15 wine; Canada: 12 cloth and 0 wine, 0 cloth and 15 wine; (b) cloth; (c) cloth, cloth, wine; (d) cloth; (e) cloth, cloth, wine

2. (a) constant; (b) (1) 4, (2) 2; (c) (1) wheat; because its cost of producing 1 wheat is only 0.25 copper, compared to Chile's cost of 0.50 copper, (2) copper; (d) one of the two nations would be unwilling to trade if the terms of trade were outside this range; (f) (1) 1, 0, (2) 1, 0

3. (a) 25, 50,000; (b) 22, 59,000, 44,000, 15,000; (c) 23, 56,000, 46,000, 10,000, 10,000

4. (a) 4, 6; (c) 5; (d) Nation 1 produces 7, consumes 5, exports 2; Nation 2 produces 5, consumes 7, imports 2

TRUE-FALSE

1. T
2. T because their comparative advantage is eroding
3. F 1/2 unit of butter
4. T
5. T
6. T 1/2 butter is lower than one butter
7. F with only two goods, it's impossible to have comparative advantage over the other country in both goods
8. T the PPC becomes concave
9. T
10. T
11. F we don't produce coffee, so there are no domestic jobs to protect
12. T e.g., consumers lose and producers gain
13. T
14. F quota is a maximum amount that may be imported
15. T
16. F a tariff generates government revenue; a quota does not
17. T diversification goes against comparative advantage
18. F
19. T
20. F other way around
21. T but would not justify widespread, or permanent tariffs
22. F our standard of living would deteriorate
23. T
24. T

MULTIPLE-CHOICE

1. (d) if any of the three conditions hold, there is reason to trade
2. (c) comparative advantage is defined in terms of relative opportunity costs
3. (c) as for the previous question
4. (b) between the opportunity cost ratios of the two producers
5. (b) because the terms of trade simply match Adanac's opportunity costs along their PPC
6. (b)
7. (b) growth by shifting the PPC, and specialization and trade by creating a trading line outside the PPC
8. (c) specialization occurs only until the opportunity cost has reached the terms of trade
9. (c) typically, though some tariffs are exclusively revenue tariffs
10. (b) typically

11. (a) we make ourselves worse off by having to use some of our workers in industries where we do not have comparative advantage

12. (d)

13. (d) unfortunately!

14. (b)

15. (d) they sell quantity qu at a price of Pw

16. (c)

17. (c) $PtPw$ x import quantity (rt)

18. (c)

19. (c) because we don't produce coffee; we do produce the other goods

20. (a)

21. (a)

22. (d) stores sell predominantly music recorded elsewhere, so would lose sales; the other groups would gain income

23. (a) the idea is to create a comparative advantage where one would not otherwise exist

24. (d) all of the others are stated goals of the WTO

CHAPTER 18

Exchange Rates, and the Balance of Payments

This chapter is about the financial or monetary side of the international trade discussed in Chapter 17. The main topics are: (1) how nations using different currencies are able to trade with each other; (2) how transactions with non-residents are recorded in the balance of payments accounts; (3) how to interpret various balance of payments accounts and terminology; (4) how foreign exchange rates are determined in flexible rate and fixed rate systems; and (5) a brief outline of different exchange rate systems that have been used in recent times.

Given that countries use different currencies, when people in different countries trade, there must be a way to exchange currencies. When Canadian residents (e.g., consumers or firms) need to make payments to residents of, say, Mexico, they buy pesos. They pay for the Mexican pesos with Canadian dollars. And when, for example, French residents sell goods and receive payment from Canadian residents, and obtain Canadian dollars, they sell this foreign money — often called foreign exchange — in return for some francs (the French currency). The market where such trades take place is the foreign exchange market. The price paid (in one money) for a unit of another money is called the foreign exchange rate (or rate of exchange). Under the system in use in Canada, the exchange rate for any foreign currency is determined by the demand for and the supply of that currency. Exports from Canada create a demand for Canadian dollars (and a supply of foreign currency). Canadian imports create a supply of Canadian dollars (and a demand for foreign currency).

As Chapter 17 showed, large quantities of goods and services are traded internationally. There are also huge volumes of international transactions in financial assets (e.g., stocks and bonds), in real assets (e.g., land and capital goods); and there are gifts and other transfers. A nation summarizes its transactions with the rest of the world in its balance of payments: a record of how it obtained foreign money during the year and what it did with this foreign money. Of course, all foreign money obtained was used for some purpose — it did not evaporate — and consequently the balance of payments always balances. However, individual accounts (current account and capital account) need not balance.

Probably the most difficult section of this chapter is concerned with balance of payments deficits and surpluses, their causes, and their economic implications. A deficit (surplus) exists when the receipts of foreign money are less (greater) than the payments of foreign money and the nation's official international reserves are reduced (expanded). The discussion of these topics is linked with explanations of exchange-rate determination under flexible rate and fixed rate systems. How balance of payments deficits or surpluses are resolved depends on the type of exchange rate system in effect. This difference is an important element to consider in weighing the advantages and disadvantages of fixed versus flexible rates.

In the twentieth century three distinct exchange-rate systems were used: the gold standard, the Bretton Woods system, and the current managed floating rate. The gold standard and the Bretton Woods were fixed-exchange systems, while in the current system exchange rates are fixed in the short run (to get the advantages of fixed exchange rates) and flexible in the long run (to enable nations to correct balance of payments deficits and surpluses).

The Last Word points out that, contrary to popular belief, currency speculators play a socially valuable role in lessening exchange rate fluctuations and absorbing some of the risk inherent in these fluctuations.

CHAPTER LEARNING OBJECTIVES

In this chapter you will learn:
☐ What determines the supply of and demand for a nation's currency.
☐ About a nation's balance of payments.
☐ What a flexible exchange-rate system is and its effects on the domestic economy.
☐ What a fixed exchange rate system is and its effects on the domestic economy.
☐ About the history of the world's international exchange-rate systems.

CHAPTER OUTLINE

1. International trade differs from domestic trade because each nation uses a different currency. The problem is resolved with foreign exchange markets where money used by one nation can be traded for another nation's money.

(a) Canadian exports create a foreign demand for dollars, and the fulfillment of this demand increases the supply of foreign currency in the foreign exchange market. More foreign currency is now in Canadian banks and available to Canadian buyers.

(b) Canadian imports create a domestic demand for foreign currencies, and the fulfillment of this demand reduces the supply of foreign currency in the foreign-exchange market. Less foreign currency is now in Canadian banks and available to Canadian buyers.

2. A nation's balance of payments is an annual record of all transactions between its residents and residents of all other nations.

(a) The current account records trade in goods and services. Recorded as credits are: merchandise exports, exports of services, receipts of investment income, and receipts of transfers. Counted as debits are: merchandise imports, imports of services, payments of investment income, and transfers paid out.

(1) The trade balance is equal to the difference between the exports and imports of goods. A nation is said to have a favourable trade balance if exports exceed imports.

(2) The balance on current account is equal to the balance on goods and services plus the balance on investment income and transfers.

(b) The capital account records the nation's trade in real and financial assets. Sales are counted as credits, and purchases are debits.

(1) The balance on capital account is a surplus (deficit) if sales are greater (less) than purchases of real and financial assets.

(c) The current and capital accounts are inter-related. A nation with a current account deficit can finance the deficit by borrowing or selling assets abroad (with a capital account surplus), and a nation with a current account surplus can lend or buy assets abroad (incur a capital account deficit).

(d) The official settlement account refers to the movement of official international reserves. When Canada has a net surplus on its current and capital accounts combined, our reserves of foreign currency will increase, showing in the balance of payments as a negative value on the official settlements account. When our current and capital accounts combine for a deficit, we will have used up some international reserves, and the official settlements account will show a positive value.

(e) Whenever the balance of payments is said to be in surplus or deficit, this refers to the net surplus or deficit before including the official settlements account. Canada has a balance of payments surplus (deficit) when the current and capital account combined balance is positive (negative) and the official reserves increase (decrease).

(f) A balance of payments deficit is not necessarily a bad thing (nor is a surplus necessarily good). However, a persistent balance of payments deficit is undesirable because the nation's official international reserves are limited, and if they are exhausted the nation may be forced to take painful macroeconomic adjustments to correct the deficit.

3. These points can be illustrated using Canadian 2000 data shown in Table 18-1. We had a current account surplus of $18.9 billion, so we were able to lend or buy assets abroad to the extent of this excess of current account inpayments over outpayments. The capital account deficit of $16.6 billion reflects the net outflow of investment from Canada. Overall, there was a net inflow of foreign currency equal to $2.3 billion (+$18.9 - $16.6), and this was added to our official reserves. It was recorded as -$2.3 billion on the official settlements account.

4. For a nation with a flexible (floating) exchange rate, what causes the exchange to change, and how does the nation adjust to a balance of payments deficit or surplus?

(a)   With flexible rates, the demand for and the supply of foreign exchange determine exchange rates. The exchange rate for a currency is the price of that currency in terms of our dollars, and the equilibrium rate is found where the quantity demanded of that money is equal to the quantity supplied.

(b)   A change in the demand or supply of foreign money will cause the exchange rate for that money to rise or fall. When the dollar price of one unit of a foreign money rises (falls), it is said that the dollar has depreciated (appreciated) and that the foreign money has appreciated (depreciated).

(c)   Changes in the demand for or supply of a foreign currency are caused by changes in tastes, relative incomes, relative prices, relative interest rates, and by speculation.

(d)   The flexible-exchange rate system has the huge advantage of providing an automatic adjustment mechanism for payments imbalances. A balance of payments deficit (surplus), will cause its currency to depreciate (appreciate). This will make foreign goods and services more (less) expensive, decrease (increase) imports, make a nation's goods and services less (more) expensive for foreigners to buy, and increase (decrease) its exports. These adjustments correct the nation's payments deficit (surplus).

(e)   Flexible exchange rates have three disadvantages: currency fluctuations create uncertainties for international traders and therefore tend to discourage trade; exchange rate changes also change the terms of trade; and exchange rate fluctuations can destabilize economies (by creating inflation or unemployment).

5. How does a fixed-exchange rate system work, and how does it deal with balance of payments deficits or surpluses? When a nation fixes (or "pegs") its exchange rate, its government must somehow prevent shortages and surpluses of their currency in the foreign exchange market. There are several ways to do this.

(a)   With currency intervention a government can stabilize the exchange rate by selling (buying) foreign money in exchange for its own money when there is a shortage (surplus) of the foreign money.

(b)   With trade policies (such as import tariffs and quotas, and export subsidies) a nation with a payments deficit can discourage imports and encourage exports. Such tactics reduce the volume of trade and hamper efficient resource allocation.

(c)   With exchange controls a nation can deal with a payments deficit by requiring exporters who earn foreign exchange to sell it to the government. The government then rations available foreign exchange among importers to ensure that imports are not too high compared to exports.

(d)   Using domestic stabilization policies (monetary and fiscal policies) a nation with a balance of payments deficit can reduce its national income and price level to stimulate net exports, and raise interest rates to attract capital inflows.

6. In recent times major trading nations have employed three different exchange-rate systems. From 1879 to 1934 the gold standard system kept exchange rates fairly stable.

(a)   A nation was on the gold standard when it: defined its currency in terms of a quantity of gold; maintained a fixed relationship between its stock of gold and its money supply; and allowed gold to be freely exported and imported.

(b)   Because each currency had a fixed gold value, and gold could flow freely between countries, currencies also had fixed values (exchange rates) in terms of one another.

(c)   When a nation with a balance of payments deficit (surplus) began to lose (gain) gold, its money supply would shrink (grow). This would raise (lower) interest rates and reduce (expand) aggregate demand, domestic output, employment, and prices in that country; and the payments deficit (surplus) would be eliminated.

(d) The relative stability of exchange rates under the gold standard encouraged trade and automatically corrected payments deficits and surpluses. However, it required that a nation tolerate unpleasant domestic adjustments such as recession and inflation, because they had no independent control over their own money supply.

(e) During the worldwide Great Depression of the 1930s, many nations abandoned the gold standard, devaluing their currencies in hopes of selling more exports and boosting their employment and output.

7. From 1944 until 1971 most nations used an adjustable-peg system known as the Bretton Woods system. The International Monetary Fund

(IMF) was created to manage this system that kept exchange rates relatively stable.

(a) The system required each IMF member nation to define its currency in terms of gold or US dollars. This established fixed exchange rates.

(b) Each nation committed to use their international reserve, when necessary, to maintain their fixed exchange rate.

(c) Each nation could acquire reserves for protecting their exchange rates by selling foreign currencies, selling gold, or borrowing on a short-term basis from the IMF.

(d) A nation experiencing a fundamental imbalance (persistent and sizable balance of payments deficit) was permitted to address the problem by orderly devaluation of its currency (increasing its defined gold or dollar equivalent).

(e) Gold and US dollars came to be regarded as international reserves. Other nations accumulated vast quantities of US dollars, as the United States rain continual balance of payments. Because US gold reserves were limited, it eventual became unlikely that the United States would be able to maintain free convertibility of dollars into gold at $35 per ounce. The United States suspended convertibility of the dollar in 1971, ending the Bretton Woods system, and beginning the era of floating exchange rates.

8. Exchange rates today are managed by individual nations to avoid short-term fluctuations and they are allowed to float in the long term to correct fundamental payments imbalances. There is a loose agreement between major nations on this system. This new system of managed floating exchange rates is favoured by some and criticized by others.

(a) Proponents say that the managed float system has allowed trade to flourish and has enabled the world to adjust to severe economic shocks.

(b) Critics believe that the system has produced excessive volatility of exchange rates and has not reduced payments deficits and surpluses; that it reinforces inflationary pressures in a nation; and that it is a "nonsystem" that nations may use for their own domestic economic goals, and at the expense of international financial stability.

9. Many people blame fluctuations in exchange rates on speculators who try to profit from buying and selling currencies. It is true that speculative "bubbles" can occur, where expectations become self-fulfilling for a while, and an exchange rate moves for no good economic reason, but this is rare. More typically, speculation has two positive effects:

(a) Speculators help to lessen rate fluctuations because they buy currencies that are low (thus raising their value) and sell currencies that are high (thus dropping their value).

(b) Speculators bear some of the risk that most international traders want to avoid. They do this by participating in currency futures markets where traders wanting to avoid risk can "hedge" against adverse fluctuations.

TERMS AND CONCEPTS

balance of payments	flexible or floating exchange-rate system
balance of payments deficit	gold standard
balance of payments surplus	International Monetary Fund
balance on goods and services	managed floating exchange rates
Bretton Woods System	official international reserves
capital account	
currency intervention	purchasing power parity theory
current account	
devaluation	trade balance
exchange control	trade deficit
fixed-exchange rate system	trade surplus

HINTS AND TIPS

1. This chapter is relatively long and difficult, and filled with new terms. Allocate your time accordingly. Fortunately, some of the new terms are just special words used in international economics for economic concepts already familiar to you.

2. It can be difficult to think about the "price" of a unit of money, even when that money is a unit of foreign currency. It may be helpful to remember that a peso or a franc is much like a kilogram of coffee or a litre of milk whose market price is determined by the forces of demand and supply.

3. The terms *depreciate* and *appreciate* confuse many students. Here are some hints that may help. To depreciate means to decrease (and appreciate means to increase). If country A's currency depreciates, what decreases is the amount of country B's currency that a unit of A's currency will exchange for. If 1 dollar first bought 10 pesos, and later bought only 8 pesos, the dollar has depreciated.

4. Capital flows can be tricky to classify as debits or credits. To keep this straight, think of merchandise trade. When Canada exports a satellite dish, money comes in from abroad so that is a credit for Canada. Similarly, when Canada exports a government bond, or the title deed to an office building in Brampton, or shares in Nortel, money comes in from abroad so that is also a credit for Canada.

FILL-IN QUESTIONS

1. The rate of exchange for the French franc is the number of (francs, dollars) _____ that a Canadian must pay to obtain one (franc, dollar) _____.

2. When the rate of exchange for 1 Euro is 1.339 Canadian dollars, the rate of exchange for the Canadian dollar is _____ Euros.

3. Canadian:
(a) exports create a (demand for, supply of) _____ foreign money and generate a _____ dollars;
(b) imports create a _____ foreign money and generate a _____ dollars.

4. In addition to the demand for foreign exchange by Canadian firms that wish to import goods from foreign countries, Canadians also demand foreign money to purchase _____ and _____ and _____ services abroad and to pay _____ and _____ on foreign investments in Canada.

5. A balance of payments transaction that earns foreign exchange for a nation is a (debit, credit) _____ and is shown with a (+, -) _____ sign. In contrast, a transaction that uses up foreign exchange is a _____ and is shown with a _____ sign.

6. When a nation has a
(a) deficit trade balance, its exports of _____ are (greater, less) _____ than its imports of _____.
(b) current account deficit, its balance on goods and services plus its net _____ income and net _____ is (positive, negative) _____.

7. The capital account records the capital inflows and capital outflows of a nation.
(a) Capital inflows are the expenditures made (in that nation, abroad) _____ for _____ and _____ assets by residents of (that nation, other nations) _____; and capital outflows are the expenditures made _____ by residents of _____ for _____ and _____ assets.
(b) A nation has a capital account surplus when its capital inflows are (greater, less) _____ than its outflows.

8. A nation may:
(a) finance a current account deficit by (buying, selling) _____ assets or by (borrowing, lending) _____ abroad; and
(b) use a current account surplus to (buy, sell) _____ assets or to (borrow, lend) _____ abroad.

9. (a) The official international reserves of a nation are the quantities of _____ owned by its _____ bank.
(b) In the official settlements balance, if Canada has an entry with a + (plus) sign, this indicates that the Bank of Canada has (bought, sold) _____ foreign exchange reserves.
(c) Thus a + (plus) on the official settlements balance means Canada has had a balance of payments (surplus, deficit) _____; and a - (minus) sign would mean Canada has had a payments _____.

10. If our dollar is floating freely, so the Bank of Canada (is, is not) _____ intervening in the foreign exchange market, and Canada is tending towards a balance of payments deficit:
(a) our dollar will (appreciate, depreciate) _____; and
(b) this change in the exchange rate will cause our imports to (increase, decrease) _____, our exports to _____, and the size of our payments deficit will _____.

11. If the Canadian dollar appreciates relative to the US dollar, then the US dollar must _____ relative to the Canadian dollar.

12. The demand for US dollars in the foreign exchange market is downsloping because as the US dollar becomes less expensive, American goods become _____ in Canadian dollars, and

therefore Canadians will increase their purchases of these goods and services.

13. In general, the higher a nation's price level, the _____ is the amount of its currency that can be obtained for a unit of foreign currency. The _____ theory holds that exchange rates adjust to reflect differences in price levels in various countries.

14. There are three disadvantages of flexible exchange rates: (1) the risks and uncertainties associated with flexible rates tend to (expand, diminish) _____ trade between nations; (2) when a nation's currency depreciates, its terms of trade with other nations are (worsened, bettered) _____; and (3) fluctuating exports and imports can destabilize an economy and result in _____ or _____ in that economy.

15. To fix or "peg" the rate of exchange for the German mark when:
(a) the Canadian dollar is appreciating against the mark, Canada would (buy, sell) _____ marks in exchange for dollars;
(b) the Canadian dollar is depreciating against the mark, Canada would _____ marks in exchange for dollars.

16. A nation with a balance of payments deficit:
(a) might attempt to eliminate the deficit by (taxing, subsidizing) _____ imports or by _____ exports;
(b) might employ exchange controls and ration foreign exchange among those who wish to (export, import) _____ goods and services and require all those who _____ goods and services to sell the foreign exchange they earn to the _____.

17. A nation on the gold standard: (1) defines its money in terms of _____; (2) maintains a fixed relationship between its _____ supply and gold _____; and (3) allows gold to be freely _____ from and _____ into the nation.

18. When the gold standard was in effect:
(a) exchange rates were relatively (stable, unstable) _____;
(b) but when a nation had a payments deficit, gold flowed (into, out of) _____ the nation, its money supply and price level (increased, decreased) _____, and its interest rates _____. Thus, its payments deficit (rose,

fell) _____, but it suffered (inflation, recession) _____.

19. The Bretton Woods system was established to bring about a modified fixed exchange rate system; and, to accomplish this, it employed the _____ system of exchange rates. Under this system:
(a) each member nation defined its monetary unit in terms of _____ or _____;
(b) each member nation stabilized the exchange rate for its currency and prevented it from rising by (buying, selling) _____ foreign currency, by (buying, selling) _____ gold, or by (borrowing from, lending to) _____ - the International Monetary Fund;
(c) a nation with a fundamental payments deficit could (devalue, revalue) _____ its currency;
(d) it was hoped that exchange rates in the short run would be (stable, flexible) _____ enough to promote international trade and in the long run would be _____ enough to correct balance of payments imbalances.

20. The system of exchange rates that developed since 1971 has been labelled a system of _____ exchange rates.

PROBLEMS AND PROJECTS

1. A Canadian exporter sells $3 million worth of wheat to an importer in Colombia. If the exchange rate for the Colombian peso is $0.02 (two cents), the wheat has a total value of 150 million pesos.
(a) There are two ways the import firm might pay for the wheat. One way is to write a cheque for 150 million pesos drawn on its bank in Bogota and send it to the Canadian exporter.
(1) The Canadian exporter would then sell the cheque to its bank in Regina where its demand deposit would increase by $_____ million.
(2) This Regina bank branch sells the cheque for 150 million pesos to its main branch, that is, the head office branch of the bank that keeps an account in the Bogota bank. The Regina bank's account in the main branch increases by _____ million (dollars, pesos) _____; and the main branch's account in the Bogota bank increases by _____ million (pesos, dollars) _____.
(b) The second way for the importer to pay is to buy from its bank in Bogota a draft on a Canadian bank for $3 million, pay for this draft by writ-

ing a cheque for 150 million pesos drawn on the Bogota bank, and send the cheque to the Canadian exporter.

(1) The Canadian exporter would then deposit the draft in its account in the Regina bank and its demand deposit account there would increase by $_____ million.

(2) The Regina bank collects the amount of the draft from the Canadian bank on which it is drawn through the clearinghouse. The account at the Bank of Canada of the bank of which the Regina branch forms a part increases by $_____ million; and the account of the bank on which the draft was drawn decreases by $_____ million.

(c) Regardless of the method employed by the Colombian importer to pay for the wheat,

(1) the export of the wheat created a (demand for, supply of) _____ dollars and a _____ pesos;

(2) the number of dollars owned by the Canadian exporter has (increased, decreased) _____ and the number of pesos owned by the Colombian importer has _____.

2. In 2005 Canada has a current account surplus of $27 billion, and a capital account deficit of $23 billion.

(a) In 2005, Canada has a balance of payments (deficit, surplus) _____ of $_____ billion.

(b) Accordingly, the official settlements balance would show an entry of $_____ billion. (Hint: specify the sign + or -)

(c) This entry means that Canada has (gained, lost) _____ this amount of foreign reserves.

3. Below are the supply and demand schedules for the British pound.

Qs of Pounds	Price per Pound ($)	Qd of Pounds
400	5.00	100
360	4.50	200
300	4.00	300
286	3.50	400
267	3.00	500
240	2.50	600
200	2.00	700

(a) Assume that exchange rates are flexible.

(1) The rate of exchange for the pound will be $_____ per pound.

(2) The rate of exchange for the dollar will be _____ pounds per dollar.

(3) How many pounds will be purchased in the market? _____

(4) How many dollars will be purchased in the market? _____

(b) If the Bank of Canada wished to fix or "peg" the price of the pound at $5.00, it would have to (buy, sell) _____ (how many) _____ pounds for $_____.

4. The exchange rate between the Canadian dollar and the US dollar is floating. What effect, if any, is each of the following events likely to have on the exchange rate, other things being equal? In the blanks, indicate "A" for appreciation of the Canadian $, "D" for depreciation, and "N" for no change.

(a) ____ Canadian corporations make large payments to American bondholders.

(b) ____ The rate of inflation in Canada increases relative to the US inflation rate.

(c) ____ The Bank of Canada purchases Canadian dollars with US dollars to build its foreign exchange reserves.

(d) ____ The US enters the recovery stage of the business cycle, while Canada remains mired in recession.

(e) ____ The province of Ontario finances its deficit by borrowing in New York.

(f) ____ Interest rates fall in Canada and remain constant in the United States.

(g) ____ Falling unit labour costs in Canada increase the competitiveness of Canadian exports in the US market.

(h) ____ An American-owned firm reinvests in Canada profits that are earned in Canada.

(i) ____ Speculators anticipate a depreciation of the Canadian dollar relative to the US dollar.

(j) ____ The demand by Americans for Canadian-produced forest products diminishes sharply due to trade disputes.

TRUE-FALSE

Circle T if the statement is true, F if it is false.

1. The importation of goods by Canadians from abroad creates a supply of dollars in the foreign exchange market. **T F**

2. Canada's balance of international payments records all the payments its residents receive from and make to the residents of foreign nations. **T F**

3. Exports are credits and imports are debits in the balance of payments of a nation. **T F**

4. When a Canadian province sells bonds in Europe, the inflow of money shows up in the Canadian balance of payments in the capital account with a minus (-) sign attached. **T F**

5. A country will have a favourable balance of trade whenever the value of exported goods is greater than the value of imported goods. **T F**

6. If a resident of Germany buys a cottage on Salt Spring Island, B.C., this counts as a credit on Canada's capital account, and a debit on Germany's capital account. **T F**

7. If the current account balance is $5 billion and the official settlements balance is -$4 billion, the capital account must be in a deficit of $1 billion. **T F**

8. A nation running a balance of payments deficit is losing official international reserves. **T F**

9. Suppose that Canadian $1.35 = US $1.00. Then it must also be true that US $0.65 = Canadian $1.00. **T F**

10. The Canadian dollar has depreciated, relative to a foreign currency, whenever it takes more Canadian dollars to purchase a unit of the foreign currency. **T F**

11. In a system of managed floating exchange rates, the central bank sometimes intervenes in the foreign exchange market. **T F**

12. The quantity demanded of US dollars is downsloping because foreigners purchase greater quantities of American goods, and so require more US dollars, as the US dollar becomes less expensive in foreign currency terms. **T F**

13. When the Bank of Canada buys US dollars, it is putting upward pressure on the international value of the Canadian dollar. **T F**

14. An increase in the number of dollars earned as dividends by Japanese investors in Canadian corporations will increase the demand for dollars and the supply of yen, and the price of the dollar will appreciate in Japan. **T F**

15. Were Canada's terms of trade with Venezuela to worsen, Venezuela would obtain a greater quantity of Canadian goods and services for every barrel of oil it exported to Canada. **T F**

16. If Canada wishes to fix (or "peg") the value of the Canadian dollar in terms of the US dollar, the Bank of Canada must sell US dollars (in exchange for Canadian dollars) when the Canadian dollar is tending to depreciate. **T F**

17. Under the gold standard, if 1 franc is convertible for 5 grains of gold, and 1 pound is convertible for 15 grains of gold, then there will be a fixed exchange rate of 3 francs per 1 pound. **T F**

18. In the Bretton Woods system, a nation was permitted to devalue its currency by as much as 10% in order to address a fundamental balance of payments deficit. **T F**

19. A basic problem with the Bretton Woods system was its inability to bring about the changes in exchange rates needed to correct persistent payments deficits and surpluses. **T F**

20. Using the managed floating system of exchange rates, a nation with a persistent balance of payments surplus should allow the value of its currency to depreciate. **T F**

21. The adjustable-peg system was intended to keep exchange rates nearly fixed, but also to avoid painful macroeconomic adjustments. **T F**

MULTIPLE-CHOICE

Circle the letter that corresponds to the best answer.

1. If a Canadian could buy 25,000 British pounds for $100,000, the rate of exchange for the pound would be:
- **(a)** $40
- **(b)** $25
- **(c)** $4
- **(d)** $0.25

2. There is an increased demand for foreign currency (increased supply of Canadian dollars) when Canadians:

(a) pay for goods and services imported from abroad

(b) make payments of interest and dividends to foreign countries on their investments in Canada

(c) make real and financial investments abroad

(d) do all of the above

3. A nation's balance on the current account is equal to its:

(a) exports less its imports of merchandise (goods)

(b) exports less its imports of goods and services

(c) exports less its imports of goods and services plus its net investment income and net transfers

(d) exports less its imports of goods, services, and capital

4. Capital flows into Canada include the purchase by foreign residents of:

(a) a factory building owned by Canadians

(b) shares of stock owned by Canadians

(c) bonds owned by Canadians

(d) all of the above

5. A Canadian current account deficit may be financed by:

(a) borrowing abroad

(b) selling real assets to foreigners

(c) selling financial assets to foreigners

(d) any of the above

6. If Canada's official settlements balance is zero, and Canada has a capital account surplus, it must also have a:

(a) current account surplus

(b) current account deficit

(c) balance of payments surplus

(d) balance of payments deficit

7. A nation may be able to correct or eliminate a persistent balance of payments deficit by:

(a) lowering the barriers on imported goods

(b) reducing the international value of its currency

(c) expanding its national income

(d) reducing its official international reserves

8. If exchange rates float freely, the exchange rate for any currency is determined by:

(a) the demand for it

(b) the supply of it

(c) the demand for and the supply of it

(d) the official reserves that "back" it

9. Under a floating exchange rate system, an increase in Canadian interest rates relative to US interest will:

(a) appreciate the Canadian dollar relative to the US dollar

(b) depreciate the Canadian dollar relative to the US dollar

(c) raise the price of US goods in Canadian dollars

(d) appreciate the US dollar relative to the Canadian dollar

10. If a Canadian province finances a deficit by borrowing abroad:

(a) Canadian interest rates will rise

(b) the Canadian dollar will depreciate

(c) the Canadian dollar will appreciate

(d) there will be an outflow of capital from Canada

11. If a nation had a balance of payments surplus and a floating exchange rate:

(a) its currency would appreciate, its exports would increase, and its imports would decrease

(b) its currency would appreciate, its exports would decrease, and its imports would increase

(c) its currency would depreciate, its exports would increase, and its imports would decrease

(d) its currency would depreciate, its exports would decrease, and its imports would increase

12. If exchange rates are flexible, which of the following would increase the Canadian dollar price of the Swedish krona?

(a) a rate of inflation greater in Sweden than in Canada

(b) real interest-rate decreases greater in Sweden than in Canada

(c) national income increases slower in Sweden than in Canada

(d) expectations that the price of the krona will be lower in the future

13. Which of the following would be one of the results of using flexible exchange rates to correct a nation's balance of payments surplus?
(a) the nation's terms of trade with other nations would be worsened
(b) importers in the nation who had made contracts for the future delivery of goods would find that they had to pay a higher price than expected for the goods
(c) if the nation were at full employment, the decrease in exports and the increase in imports would be inflationary
(d) exporters in the nation would find their sales abroad had decreased

14. Disadvantages of a floating exchange rate system include all of the following except:
(a) uncertainty over future exchange rates
(b) instability in the macroeconomy caused by changing exchange rates
(c) decline in the terms of trade that accompany a currency depreciation
(d) an automatic adjustment mechanism for balance of payments problems

15. A nation with fixed exchange rates and a payments surplus might attempt to resolve the surplus by employing:
(a) import quotas
(b) higher tariffs
(c) subsidies on items the nation exports
(d) none of the above

16. Which one of the following was not among the conditions a nation was required to meet to operate under the gold standard?
(a) use only gold as a medium of exchange
(b) maintain a fixed relationship between its gold stock and its money supply
(c) allow gold to be freely exported from and imported into the nation
(d) define its monetary unit in terms of a fixed quantity of gold

17. If the nations of the world were on the gold standard and one nation had a balance of payments surplus:
(a) foreign-exchange rates in that nation would rise toward the gold import point
(b) gold would tend to be imported into that nation
(c) the level of prices in that nation would tend to fall

(d) employment in that nation would tend to fall

18. Under the gold standard, a nation with a balance of payments deficit would experience all but one of the following. Which one?
(a) gold would flow out of the nation
(b) the nation's money supply would contract
(c) interest rates in the nation would fall
(d) real domestic output, employment, and prices in the nation would decline

19. Which of the following was the principal disadvantage of the gold standard?
(a) unstable foreign-exchange rates
(b) persistent payments imbalances
(c) the uncertainties and decreased trade that resulted from the depreciation of gold
(d) domestic macroeconomic adjustments experienced by a nation with a payments imbalance

20. Which of the following was not among the elements of the adjustable-peg system of foreign exchange rates?
(a) each nation defined its monetary unit in terms of gold or dollars
(b) nations bought and sold their own currencies to stabilize exchange rates
(c) nations were allowed to devalue their currencies when faced with persistent payments deficits
(d) the deposit by all nations of their international reserves with the IMF

21. With the demise of the Bretton Wood systems, the United States "floated" the dollar. This meant that:
(a) the value of the dollar was to be determined by the demand for and the supply of the dollar
(b) the dollar price of gold was to be increased
(c) the price of the dollar was to be set by international agreement
(d) the gold content of the dollar was to be reduced

22. A system of managed floating exchange rates:
(a) allows nations to stabilize exchange rates in the short term
(b) requires nations to stabilize exchange rates in the long term
(c) entails stable exchange rates in both the short and long term
(d) none of the above

23. Floating exchange rates:

(a) tend to correct payments imbalances

(b) reduce the uncertainties and risks associated with international trade

(c) increase the world's need for official international reserves

(d) tend to expand the volume of world trade

24. Exchange controls are subject to all of the following problems, except which one?

(a) distortions of trade patters

(b) favouritism towards some importers over others

(c) black markets where foreign exchange is sold at illegal exchange rates

(d) loss of control of the nation's money supply

25. Which of the following is an *incorrect* statement about currency speculators?

(a) speculators' activity sometimes cause excess currency volatility

(b) speculators' activity generally lessens exchange rate fluctuations

(c) speculators in currency futures markets absorb some of the risk that others do not want to bear

(d) on balance, speculators' activity is detrimental to international trade

DISCUSSION QUESTIONS

1. What are foreign exchange and the foreign exchange rate? Who are the demanders and suppliers of a particular foreign exchange, say, the French franc? Why is a buyer (demander) in the foreign exchange markets always a seller (supplier) also?

2. What does a nation's balance of payments summarize? What are the principal sections of a nation's balance of payments?

3. How does a nation finance a balance of payments deficit and what does it do with a balance of payments surplus?

4. Is it good or bad for a nation to have a balance of payments deficit or surplus?

5. What types of events cause the exchange rate for a foreign currency to appreciate or depreciate? How will each of these events affect the exchange rate for a nation's currency?

6. How can floating exchange rates eliminate balance of payments deficits and surpluses? What are the problems associated with this method of correcting payments imbalances?

7. How may a nation employ its foreign exchange reserves to fix or "peg" foreign-exchange rates? Be precise. How does a nation obtain or acquire these official international reserves?

8. How can foreign exchange controls be used to overcome a payments deficit? Why do such exchange controls necessarily involve the rationing of foreign exchange?

9. If exchange rates are fixed, what kind of domestic macroeconomic adjustments are required to eliminate a payments deficit? To eliminate a payments surplus?

10. How did the gold standard operate? How did the gold standard correct payments imbalances? What were the disadvantages of this method of eliminating payments deficits and surpluses?

11. What is the "critical difference" between the adjustment necessary to correct payments deficits and surpluses under the gold standard and those necessary when exchange rates are flexible? How did this difference lead to the demise of the gold standard during the 1930s?

12. Explain: (a) why the IMF was established, and what the objectives of the adjustable-peg (or Bretton Woods) system were; (b) how the system worked, and how it stabilized exchange rates in the short run; and (c) why and how the system was to allow for long-run exchange rate adjustments.

13. What was the role of the US dollar under the Bretton Woods system? Why was the dollar used by nations as an international money, and how could they acquire additional dollars?

14. Explain what is meant by a managed floating system of exchange rates. When are exchange rates managed, and when are they allowed to float?

15. Explain the arguments of the proponents and the critics of the managed floating system.

16. How does speculation affect the currency markets, and therefore international trade?

ANSWERS

FILL-IN QUESTIONS

1. dollars, franc

2. 0.747

3. (a) supply of, demand for; (b) demand for, supply of

4. tourism, freight, shipping, interest, dividends

5. (a) credit, +; (b) debit, -

6. (a) goods, less, goods; (b) investment, transfers, negative

7. (a) in that nation, real, financial, other nations, abroad, that nation, real, financial; (b) greater

8. (a) selling, borrowing; (b) buy, lend

9. (a) foreign monies, central; (b) sold; (c) deficit, surplus

10. is not; (a) depreciate; (b) decrease, increase, decrease

11. depreciate

12. less expensive

13. greater, purchasing power parity

14. diminish, worsened, recession, inflation

15. (a) buy; (b) sell

16. (a) taxing, subsidizing; (b) import, export, government (Bank of Canada)

17. (1) gold; (2) money, stock; (3) exported, imported

18. (a) stable; (b) out of, decreased, rose, fell, recession

19. adjustable-peg; (a) gold, US dollars; (b) selling, selling, borrowing from; (c) devalue; (d) stable, flexible

20. managed floating

PROBLEMS AND PROJECTS

1. (a) (1) 3, (2) 3, dollars, 150, pesos; (b) (1) 3, (2) 3, 3; (c) (1) demand for, supply of, (2) increased, decreased

2. (a) surplus, 4; (b) -4; (c) gained

3. (a) (1) 4.00, (2) 0.25, (3) 300, (4) 1200; (b) buy, 300, 1500 (5.00 x 300)

4. (a) D, (b) D, (c) A, (d) A, (e) A, (f) D, (g) A, (h) N, (i) D, (j) D

TRUE-FALSE

1. T   so we can buy foreign currency to pay for imports
2. T
3. T
4. F   + sign (credit) because foreign exchange is earned by Canada
5. T
6. T   the German buyer transfers money to Canadian seller
7. T   the three accounts must add to zero
8. T
9. F   it is a reciprocal relationship: 1/1.35 =0.74
10. T
11. T   to minimize currency fluctuations
12. T   this is an application of the law of demand
13. F   no, because it must also be selling C$
14. F   the supply of $ will increase, not the demand
15. T
16. T   they will then be buying some C$ off the market
17. T   because 3 francs and 1 pound are worth an equal amount of gold
18. T
19. T
20. F   a persistent surplus calls for an appreciation
21. T   the painful adjustments would be a consequence of rigidly fixed rates

MULTIPLE-CHOICE

1. (c)   100,000/25,000
2. (d)   in all cases Canadians need to make payments abroad
3. (c)
4. (d)   in all cases foreigners make payments to Canadians
5. (d)   all would produce additional credits on the capital account
6. (b)   of exactly the same magnitude as the capital account surplus
7. (b)   this will stimulate export demand (more credits) and cut import demand (less debits)
8. (c)
9. (a)   capital flows into Canada, causing a demand for C$, as people try to take advantage of favourable return on Canadian financial assets
10. (c)   a capital inflow creates more demand for C$
11. (b)   the appreciation changes the relative prices of domestic and foreign goods

12. (c) our import demand grows faster than Sweden's, so our net exports fall

13. (d) because this country's goods become relatively more expensive

14. (d) this is the key advantage of such a system

15. (d) all of the measures suggested would work in the right way to resolve a deficit, not a surplus

16. (a) in fact under the modern gold standard most countries made no use of gold as money

17. (b) and its money supply, employment, and price level would all tend to rise

18. (c) with the money supply shrinking the interest rate would rise

19. (d) monetary policy could not be used for domestic stabilization

20. (a) this describes a fixed-exchange rate system

21. (a) breaking the link to gold

22. (a) intervention in the short term can smooth out some fluctuations

23. (a) automatically

24. (d)

25. (d) on balance, speculation is helpful

Answers to Key Questions

■ CHAPTER 6

6-3 They are excluded because the dollar value of final goods includes the dollar value of intermediate goods. If intermediate goods were counted, then multiple counting would occur. The value of steel (intermediate good) used in autos is included in the price of the auto (the final product).

This value is not included in GDP because such sales and purchases simply transfer the ownership of existing assets; such sales and purchases are not themselves (economic) investment and thus should not be counted as production of final goods and services.

Used furniture was produced in some previous year; it was counted as GDP then. Its resale does not measure new production.

6-8 (a) GDP = $215
(b) NDI = $174

6-11 Price index for 1984 = 62.5; 60 percent; real GDP for 1984 = $112,000 and real GDP for 1992 = $352,000.

6-12 Values for real GDP, top to bottom of the column $68.1 (inflating); $49.0 (inflating); $226.6 (inflating); $468.0 (inflating); $598.6 (inflating); $738.7 (deflating); $921.7 (deflating).

■ CHAPTER 7

7-2 Growth rate of real GDP = 4 percent (= $31,200 - $30,000)/$30,000). GDP per capita in year 1 = $300 (= $30,000/100). GDP per capita in year 2 = $305.88 (= $31,200/102). Growth rate of GDP per capita is 1.96 percent = ($305.88 - $300)/300).

7-4 The four phases of a typical business cycle, starting at the bottom, are trough, recovery, peak, and recession. As seen in Figure 8-1, the length of a complete cycle varies from about 2 to 3 years to as long as 15 years.

Normally there is a pre-Christmas spurt in production and sales and a January slackening. This normal seasonal variation does not signal boom or recession. From decade to decade, the long-term trend (the secular trend) of the Canadian economy has been upward. A period of no GDP growth thus does not mean that all is normal but that the economy is operating below its trend growth of output.

Because durable goods last, consumers can postpone buying replacements. This happens when people are worried about a recession and whether there will be a paycheque next month. And firms will soon stop producing what people are not buying. Durable goods industries therefore suffer large output declines during recessions. In contrast, consumers cannot long postpone the buying of nondurables such as food; therefore recessions only slightly reduce nondurable output.

7-6 Labour force = 230 [= 500 – (120 + 150)]; official unemployment rate = 10% [= (23/230) x 100].

7-8 GDP gap = 8% [= (9 – 5) x 2]; forgone output = $40 billion (=8% of $500 billion).

7-10 This year's rate of inflation is 10% or [(121 – 110)/110] x 100.

Dividing 70 by the annual percentage rate of increase of any variable (for instance, the rate of inflation or population growth) will give the approximate number of years for doubling of the variable.

(a) 35 years (= 70/2); (b) 14 years (=70/5); (c) 7 years (=70/10).

■ CHAPTER 8

8-5 Data for completing the table (top to bottom). Consumption: $244; $260; $276; $292; $308; $324; $340; $356; $32. APC: 1.02; 1.00; .99; .97; .96; .95; .94; .94; .93. APS: –.02; .00; .01; .03; .04; .05; .06; .06; .07. MPC: .80 throughout. MPS: .20 throughout.

(a) See the graphs below.

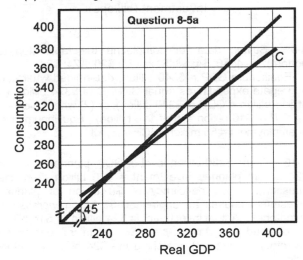

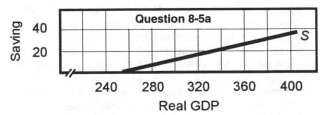

(b) Break-even income = $260. Households dissave borrowing or using past savings.

(c) Technically, the APC diminishes and the APS increases because the consumption and saving schedules have positive and negative vertical intercepts respectively. (Appendix to Chapter 1). MPC and MPS measure *changes* in consumption and saving as income changes; they are the *slopes* of the consumption and saving schedules. For straight-line consumption and saving schedules, these slopes do not change as the level of income changes; the slopes and thus the MPC and MPS remain constant.

8-7 See the graph. Aggregate investment: (a) $20 billion; (b) $30 billion; (c) $40 billion. This is the investment-demand curve because we have applied the rule of undertaking all investment up to the point where the expected rate of return, r, equals the interest rate, i.

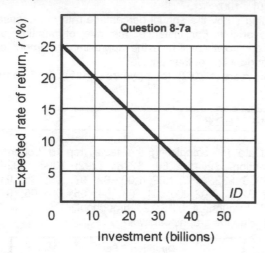

8-9 Saving data for completing the table (top to bottom): $–4; $0; $4; $8; $12; $16; $20; $24; $28.

Equilibrium GDP = $340 billion, determined where (1) aggregate expenditures equal GDP (C of $324 billion + I of $16 billion = GDP of $340 billion); or (2) where planned I = S (I of $16 billion = S of $16 billion). Equilibrium level of employment = 65 million; MCP = .8; MPS = .2.

8-10 At the $380 billion level of GDP, planned saving = $24 billion; planned investment = $16 billion (from the question). This deficiency of $8 billion of planned investment causes an unplanned $8 billion *increase* in inventories. Actual investment is $24 billion (= $16 billion of planned investment *plus* $8 billion of unplanned inventory investment), matching the $24 billion of actual saving.

At the $300 billion level of GDP, saving = $8 billion; planned investment = $16 billion (from the question). This excess of $8 billion of planned investment causes an unplanned $8 billion *decline* in inventories. Actual investment is $8 billion (= $16 billion of planned investment *minus* $8 billion of unplanned inventory disinvestment) matching the actual saving of $8 billion.

When unplanned investments in inventories occur, as at the $380 billion level of GDP, businesses revise their production plans downward and GDP falls. When unintended disinvestments in inventories occur, as at the $300 billion level of GDP; businesses revise their production plans upward and GDP rises. Equilibrium GDP — in this case, $340 billion — occurs where planned investment equals saving.

8-17 The multiplier effect is the magnified increase in equilibrium GDP that occurs when any component of

aggregate expenditures changes. The greater the MPC (the smaller the MPS), the greater the multiplier.

MPS = 0, multiplier = infinity; MPS = .4, multiplier = 2.5; MPS = .6, multiplier = 1.67; MPS = 1, multiplier = 1.

MPC = 1; multiplier = infinity; MPC = .9, multiplier = 10; MPC = .67; multiplier = 3; MPC = .5, multiplier = 2; MPC = 0, multiplier = 1.

MPC = .8: Change in GDP = $40 billion (= $8 billion × multiplier of 5); MPC = .67: Change in GDP = $24 billion ($8 billion × multiplier of 3). The simple multiplier takes account of only the leakage of saving. The complex multiplier also takes account of leakages of taxes and imports, making the complex multiplier less than the simple multiplier.

8-20 (a) $400
(b) Net exports: $2, –$2, –$6, –$10, –$14, –$18, –$22, –$26. Aggregate expenditures, open economy: $242, $278, $314, $350, $386, $422, $458, $494. Equilibrium GDP: $350. Equilibrium GDP is lower because of imports.
(c) $300; $400; level of imports and equilibrium GDP are inversely related.
(d) Open economy multiplier = 1/(MPS + MPM) = 1/(0.2 + 0.08) = 3.57.

8-23 The addition of government through equal increases of G and T of $100 billion increases equilibrium GDP from $340 billion to $440 billion. This is the balanced-budget multiplier at work. It comes about because the effect of an increase in taxes on AE is not direct, as is an increase in G. Increased taxes work through their effect on C. When MPC is 0.8, increased T of $100 billion results in a decreased C of $80 billion [= 0.8($100 billion)] (with the balance of the tax increase being paid through a $20 million decrease in saving [= 0.2 ($100 billion)]).

With a multiplier of 5 = 1/(1 – 0.8), an $80 billion decrease in C causes a $400 billion decline in equilibrium GDP. But the $100 billion increase in G causes a $500 billion increase in equilibrium GDP, which therefore, with the two effects at work, increases by $100 billion (= $500 – $400 billion).

8-25 (a) Recessionary gap. Equilibrium GDP is $600 billion, while full employment GDP is $700 billion. Employment will be 2 million less than at full employment. Aggregate expenditures will have to increase by $20 million at each level of GDP to eliminate the recessionary gap.
(b) Inflationary gap. Aggregate expenditures are excessive, causing demand-pull inflation. Aggregate expenditures will have to fall by $20 billion at each level of GDP to eliminate the inflationary gap.

■ **CHAPTER 9**

9-3 (a) See the graph. Equilibrium price level = 200. Equilibrium real output = $300 billion. No, the full-capacity level of GDP is $400 billion, where the AS curve becomes vertical.

(b)　At a price level of 150, real GDP supplied is a maximum of $200 billion, less than the real GDP demanded of $400 billion. The shortage of real output will drive the price level up. At a price level of 250, real GDP supplied is $400 billion, which is more than the real GDP demanded of $200 billion. The surplus of real output will drive down the price level. Equilibrium occurs at the price level at which AS and AD intersect.

(c)　See the graph. Increases in consumer, investment, government, or net export spending might shift the AD curve rightward. New equilibrium price level = 250. New equilibrium GDP = $400 billion. The intermediate range.

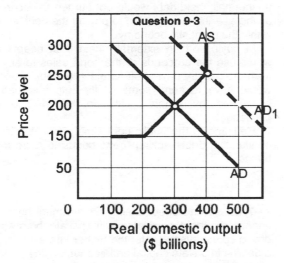

Question 9-3

9-4　(a) Productivity = 2.67(= 300/112.5). (b) Per-unit cost of production = $.75 (= $2 × 112.5/300). (c) New per-unit production cost = $1.13. The AS curve would shift leftward. The price level would rise and real output would decrease. (d) New per-unit cost of production = $0.375 ($2 × 112.5/600). AS curve shifts to the right; price level declines and real output increases.

9-6　(a)　AD curve left; (b) AD curve right; (c) AS curve left; (d) AD curve right; (e) AD curve left; (f) AD curve right; (g) AS curve right; (h) AD curve right; (i) AS curve right; (j) AS curve left; (k) AD curve right; AS curve left; (l) AD curve left; (m) AS curve right.

9-7　(a)　Price level rises and no change in real output; (b) price level drops and real output increases; (c) price level does not change, but real output rises; (d) price level does not change, but real output declines; (e) price level increases, but the change in real output is indeterminate; (f) price level drops, and real output declines.

9-11　(a)　$280; $220. When the price level rises from 100 to 125 [in aggregate supply schedule AS(P_{100})], producers experience higher prices for their products. Because nominal wages are constant, profits rise and producers increase output to Q = $280. When the price level

decreases from 100 to 75, profits decline and producers adjust their output to Q = $75. These are short-run responses to changes in the price level.

(b)　$250; $250. In the long run, a rise in the price level to 125 leads to nominal wage increases. The AS(P_{100}) schedule changes to AS(P_{125}) and Q returns to $250, now at a price level of 125. In the long run, a decrease in price level to 75 leads to lower nominal wages, yielding aggregate supply schedule AS(P_{75}). Equilibrium Q returns to $250, now at a price level of 75.

(c)　Graphically, the explanation is identical to Figure 11-10. Short-run AS : P_1 = 100; P_2 = 125; P_3 = 75; and Q_1 = $250; Q_2 = $280; and Q_3 = $220. Long-run aggregate supply = Q_1 = $250 at each of the three price levels.

■ CHAPTER 10

10-1　Reduce government spending, increase taxes, or some combination of both. In the real world, the goal is to reduce *inflation* — to keep prices from rising so rapidly — not to reduce the *price level*. A "conservative" economist might favour cuts in government spending, since this would reduce the size of government. A "liberal" economist might favour a tax hike; it would preserve government spending programs.

10-5 The cyclically adjusted budget employment budget (also called full employment budget) measures what the federal deficit or surplus would be if the economy reached full-employment level of GDP with existing tax and spending policies. If the full-employment budget is balanced, then the government is not engaging in either expansionary not contractionary policy, even if, for example, a deficit automatically results when GDP declines. The "actual" budget is the deficit or surplus that results when revenues and expenditures occur over a year if the economy is not operating at full-employment.

Looking at Figure 10-3, if full-employment GDP level was GDP₃, then the full-employment budget is contractionary since a surplus would exist. Even though the "actual" budget has no deficit at GDP₂, fiscal policy is contractionary. To move the economy to full-employment, government should cut taxes or increase spending. You would raise G line or lower T line or combination of each until they intersect at GDP₃.

10-7　It takes time to ascertain the direction in which the economy is moving (recognition lag), to get a fiscal policy enacted into law (administrative lag), and for the policy to have its full effect on the economy (operational lag). Meanwhile, other factors may change, rendering inappropriate a particular fiscal policy. Nevertheless, discretionary fiscal policy is a valuable tool in preventing severe recession or severe demand-pull inflation.

A political business cycle is the concept that politicians are more interested in re-election than in stabilizing the economy. Before the election, they enact tax cuts and spending increases even though this may fuel inflation. After the election, they apply the brakes to restrain inflation. The economy will slow and unemployment will rise. In this view the political process creates economic instability.

The crowding-out effect is the reduction in investment spending caused by the increase in interest rates arising from an increase in government spending, financed by borrowing. The increase in G was designed to increase AD but the resulting increase in interest rates may decrease I. Thus the impact of the expansionary fiscal policy may be reduced.

The next export effect also arises from the higher interest rates accompanying expansionary fiscal policy. The higher interest rates make Canadian bonds more attractive to foreign buyers. The inflow of foreign currency to buy dollars to purchase the bonds drives up the international value of the dollar, making imports less expensive for Canadians and Canadian exports more expensive for people abroad. Net exports in Canada decline, and like the crowding-out effect, diminish the expansionary fiscal policy.

■ CHAPTER 11

11-1 a) There is practically no potential for using fiscal policy as a stabilization tool under an annually balanced budget. In an economic downturn, tax revenues fall. To keep the budget in balance, fiscal policy would require the government to reduce its spending or increase its tax rates, adding to the deficiency in spending and accelerating the downturn. If the economy were booming and tax revenues were mounting, to keep the budget balanced fiscal policy would have to increase government spending or reduce taxes, thus adding to the already excessive demand and accelerating the inflationary pressures. An annually balanced budget would intensify cyclical ups and downs.

(b) A cyclically balanced budget would be countercyclical, as it should be, since it would bolster demand by lowering taxes and increasing government spending during a recession and restrain demand by raising taxes and reducing government spending during an inflationary boom. However, because boom and bust are not always of equal intensity and duration, budget surpluses during the upswing need not automatically match budget deficits during the downswing. Requiring the budget to be balanced over the cycle may necessitate inappropriate changes in tax rates or levels of government expenditures.

(c) Functional finance pays no attention to the balance of deficits and surpluses annually or over the cycle. What counts is the maintenance of a noninflationary full-employment level of

spending. Balancing the economy is what counts, not the budget.

11-3 Two ways of measuring the public debt: (1) measure its absolute size; (2) measure its size as a percentage of GDP.

An internally held debt is one in which the bondholders live in the nation having the debt; an externally held debt is one in which the bondholders are citizens of other nations. Paying off an internally held debt would involve boosting taxes or reducing other government spending and using the proceeds to buy the government bonds. This would present a problem of income distribution because holders of the government bonds generally have higher incomes than the average taxpayer. But paying off an internally held debt would not burden the economy as a whole — the money used to pay off the debt would stay within the domestic economy.

In paying off an externally held debt people abroad would use the proceeds of the bond sales to buy goods from the country paying off its external debt. That nation would have to send some of its output abroad to be consumed by others (with no imported goods in exchange).

Refinancing the public debt simply means rolling over outstanding debt—selling "new" bonds to retire maturing bonds.

11-7 Cause and effect chain: Government borrowing to finance the debt competes with private borrowing and drives up the interest rate; the higher interest rate causes a decline in private capital and economic growth slows.

However, if public investment complements private investment, private borrowers may be willing to pay higher rates for positive growth opportunities. Productivity and economic growth could rise.

■ CHAPTER 12

12-3 M1 = currency (in circulation) + chequable deposits. The largest component of M1 is chequable deposits. If the face value of a coin were not greater than its intrinsic (metallic) value, people would remove coins from circulation and sell them for their metallic content. M2 = M1 + personal savings deposits and nonpersonal (business) notice deposits. M2+ = M2+ deposits at trust and mortgage loan companies, and deposits at *caisses populaires* and credit unions, plus money market mutual funds, and deposits at other institutions.

Near-monies represent wealth; the more wealth people have, the more they are likely to spend out of current income. Also, the fact that near-monies are liquid adds to potential economic instability. People may cash in their near-monies and spend the proceeds while the monetary authorities are trying to stem inflation by reducing the money supply. Finally, near-monies can complicate monetary policy because $M1$, $M2$, and $M2+$ do not always change in the same direction.

12-5 In the first case, the value of the dollar (in year 2, relative to year 1) is $.80 (= 1/1.25); in the second case the value is $2 (= 1/.50). Generalization: The price level and the value of the dollar are inversely related.

■ CHAPTER 13

13-2 Reserves are assets to chartered banks in that they are cash that belongs to these banks: either cash with which the bank started operations, or profits, or money deposited in the bank by its customers and for which the bank has created in exchange a deposit liability. Excess reserves are cash owned by a chartered bank over and above what it desires to hold as its cash reserves to meet its customers' demand. Excess reserves may safely be lent by the chartered bank; when they are, the money supply increases by the amount of the loan.

13-4 Banks create or add to chequing, or demand, account balances when they make loans; these demand deposits are part of the money supply. People pay off loans by writing cheques. Demand deposits fall, meaning the money supply drops. Money is "destroyed."

13-8(a) $2,000. Column 1 of Assets (top to bottom): $22,000; $38,000; $42,000. Column 1 of Liabilities: $102,000.

(b) $2,000. The bank has lent out its excess reserves, creating $2,000 of new demand-deposit money.

(c) Column 2 of Assets (top to bottom): $20,000; $38,000; $42,000. Column 2 of Liabilities; $100,000.

(d) $7,000.

13-13(a) Desired reserves = $50 billion (= 25% of $200 billion); so excess reserves = $2 billion (= $52 billion - $50 billion). Maximum amount banking system can lend = $8 billion (= 1/.25 • $2 billion). Column (1) of Assets data (top to bottom): $52 billion; $48 billion; $108 billion. Column (1) of Liabilities data: $208 billion. Monetary multiplier = 4 (= 1/.25).

(b) Desired reserves = $40 billion (= 20% of $200 billion); so excess reserves = $12 billion (= $52 billion - $40 billion). Maximum amount banking system can lend = $60 billion (= 1/.20 • $12 billion). Column (1) data for assets after loans (top to bottom); $52 billion; $48 billion; $160 billion. Column (1) data for liabilities after loans: $260 billion. Monetary multiplier = 5 (= 1/.20). The decrease in the desired reserve ratio increases the banking system's excess reserves from $2 billion to $12 billion and increases the size of the monetary multiplier from 4 to 5. Lending capacity becomes 5 • $12 = $609 billion.

■ CHAPTER 14

14-3 (a) and (b)
Consolidated Balance Sheet
All Chartered Banks (billions of dollars)

		(1)	(2)
Assets:			
Reserves	$4.8	$4.7	$5.0
Securites	20.0	20	19.8
Loans	71.2	71.2	71.2
Liabilities:			
Deposits	$96.0	$95.9	$96.0
Advances from Bank of Canada	0.0	0.0	0.0

Balance Sheet
Bank of Canada (billions of dollars)

		(1)	(2)
Assets			
Securites	$15.8	$15.7	$16.0
Advances to Chartered Banks	0.0	0.0	0.0
Liabilities			
Reserves of Chartered Banks	$4.8	$4.7	$5.0
Government of Canada Deposits	0.1	0.1	0.1
Notes in circulation	10.9	10.9	10.9

(c)(1) Money supply (deposits) *directly* changes only in (a); in this case, it decreases by $0.1 billion.
(2) See balance sheets.
(3) Money-creating potential of the banking system decreases by $2 billion in (a), and increases by $4 billion in (b).

14-4 (a) The level of nominal GDP. The higher this level, the greater the amount of money demanded for transactions. (b) The interest rate. The higher the interest rate, the smaller the amount of money demanded as an asset.

On a graph measuring the interest rate vertically and the amount of money demanded horizontally, the two demand-for-money curves can be summed horizontally to get the total demand for money. This total demand shows the total amount of money demanded at each interest rate. The equilibrium interest rate is determined at the intersection of the total demand for money curve and the supply of money curve.

(a) Expanded use of credit cards: transaction demand for money declines; total demand for money declines; interest rate falls. (b) Shortening of worker pay periods: transaction demand for money declines; total demand for money declines; interest rate falls. (c) Increase in nominal GDP: transaction demand for money increases; total demand for money increases; interest rate rises.

14-8 (a) Sell government securities in the open market. This would immediately decrease the money supply by the amount of the securities sales. If the banks had been fully loaned up, they would now have to decrease their loans by a multiple (because of the money multiplier) of their bond sales. This would force up interest rates (this, added to the immediate effect of the bond sales, would tend to drive down their prices, that is, drive interest rates up), and decrease aggregate expenditures.

(b)   Switching government deposits from the chartered banks will reduce excess reserves, thus banks could loan out fewer funds, thereby decreasing the money supply.

14-9   The basic objective of monetary policy is to assist the economy in achieving a full employment, noninflationary level of total output. Changes in the money supply affect interest rates, which affect investment spending and therefore aggregate demand.

(a) A steep demand curve for money makes monetary policy more effective since the steepness of the curve means that only a relatively small change in the money supply is needed to produce large changes in interest rates. A relatively flat investment demand curve aids monetary policy since it means that only a small change in the interest rate is sufficient to change investment sharply. (b) A high MPC (low MPS) yields a large income multiplier, meaning that a relatively small initial change in spending will multiply into a larger change in GDP.

An easy money policy increases the money supply. The increase in GDP resulting from an easy money policy will also increase the transactions demand for money, partially offsetting the reduction in the interest rate associated with the initial increase in the money supply. Overall, investment spending, aggregate demand, and GDP will not rise by as much. The reverse is true for a tight money policy.

14-10 The intent of a contractionary monetary policy would be shown as a leftward shift of the aggregate demand curve and a decline in the price level (or, in the real world, a reduction in the rate of inflation). In an open economy, the interest rate hike resulting from the tight money policy would entice people abroad to buy Canadian securities. Because they would need Canadian dollars to buy these securities, the international demand for dollars would rise, causing the dollar to appreciate. Net exports would fall, pushing the aggregate demand curve farther leftward than in the closed economy.

■ CHAPTER 15

15-1   (a)   See Figure 15-2 in the chapter. Short run: The aggregate supply curve shifts to the left, the price level rises, and real output declines. Long run: The aggregate supply curve shifts back rightward (due to declining nominal wages), the price level falls, and real output increases.

(b)   See Figure 15-1. Short run: The aggregate demand curve shifts to the right, and both the price level and real output increase.

Long run: The aggregate supply curve shifts to the left (due to higher nominal wages), the price level rises, and real output declines.

(c)   See Figure 15-3. Short run: The aggregate demand curve shifts to the left, both the price level and real output decline. Long run: The aggregate supply curve shifts to the right, the price level falls further, and real output increases.

15-3 In the short-run there is probably a tradeoff between unemployment and inflation. The government's expansionary policy should reduce unemployment as aggregate demand increases. However, the government has misjudged the natural rate and will continue its expansionary policy beyond the point of the natural level of unemployment. As aggregate demand continues to rise, prices begin to rise. In the long-run, workers demand higher wages to compensate for these higher prices. Aggregate supply will decrease (shift leftward) toward the natural rate of unemployment.

In other words, any reduction of unemployment below the natural rate is only temporary and involves a short-run rise in inflation. This, in turn, causes long-run costs to rise and a decrease in aggregate supply. The end result should be an equilibrium at the natural rate of unemployment and a higher price level than the beginning level. The long-run Phillips curve is thus a vertical line connecting the price levels possible at the natural rate of unemployment found on the horizontal axis. (See Figure 15-7)

15-5   Economist Arthur Laffer observed that tax revenues would obviously be zero when the tax rate was either at 0% or 100%. In between these two extremes would have to be an optimal rate where aggregate output and income produced the maximum tax revenues. This idea is presented as the Laffer Curve shown in Figure 15-8.

The difficult decision involves the analysis to determine what is the optimum tax rate for producing maximum tax revenue and the related maximum economic output level. Laffer argued that low tax rates would actually increase revenues because low rates improved productivity, saving and investment incentives. The expansion in output and employment and thus, revenue, would more than compensate for the lower rates.

■ CHAPTER 16

16-1 The four supply factors are the quantity and quality of natural resources; the quantity and quality of human resources; the stock of capital goods; and the level of technology. The demand factor is the level of purchases needed to maintain full employment. The efficiency factor refers to both productive and allocative efficiency. Figure 16-1 illustrates these growth factors by showing movement from curve AB to curve CD.

16-5 In the graph shown, both AD and AS expanded over the 1990-1999 period. Because aggregate supply increased as well as aggregate demand, the new equilibrium output rose at a faster pace than did the price level. P2 is 20% above P1 and GDP2 is 33% greater than GDP1. Note that it is also possible that in early 1990s when unemployment was above natural rate that some of the expansion of AD took place in the horizontal portion of AS curve, but that is not the situation depicted here.

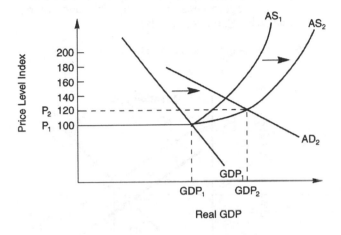

16-6 Refer to Table 16-2. Between 1961 and 1999 35.9% of Canada's growth came from increased quantities of capital, 30.7% from increased quantities of labour, and the remaining 33.4% attributed to aggregate total factor productivity. Among the key factors contributing to economic growth are technological advance, improved education and training of the work force, greater exploitation of economies of scale, and better allocation of resources.

16-9 Each of the above is a characteristic of the New Economy. The rate of productivity growth has grown substantially due to innovations using microchips, computers, new telecommunications devices and the Internet. All of these innovations describe features of what we call information technology, which connects information in all parts of the world with information seekers. New information products are often digital in nature and can be easily replicated once they have been developed. The start-up cost of new firms and new technology is high, but expanding production has a very low marginal cost which leads to economies of scale – firms' output grows faster than their inputs. Network effects refer to a type of economy of scale whereby certain information products become more valuable to each user as the number of buyers grows. For example, a fax machine is more useful to you when lots of other people and firms have one; the same is true for compatible word-processing programs. Global competition is a feature of the New Economy because both transportation and communication can be accomplished at much lower cost and faster speed than

previously which expands market possibilities for both consumers and producers who are not very limited by national boundaries today.

■ CHAPTER 17

17-4 (a)   New Zealand's cost ratio is 1 plum = 4 apples (or 1 apple = 1/4 plum). Spain's cost ratio is 1 plum = 1 apple (or 1 apple = 1 plum). See the graphs.
(b)   New Zealand should specialize in apples, Spain in plums.
(c) See the graphs.

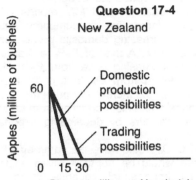

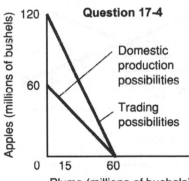

(d)   Total production before specialization and trade: 40 apples (20 + 20) and 50 plums (10 + 40). After specialization and trade: 60 apples and 60 plums. Gain = 20 apples and 10 plums.

17-6
At $1: import 15,000. At $2: import 7,000. At $3: no imports or exports. At $4: export 6,000. At $5: export 10,000.
Canada will export corn, France will import it.

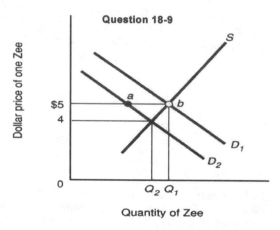

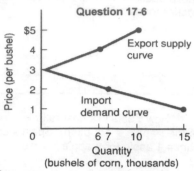

Question 17-6

Export supply curve

Import demand curve

Quantity
(bushels of corn, thousands)

17-7

See the graph. Canada does not have a comparative advantage in this product because the world price P_w is below the Canadian domestic price of P_d. Imports will reduce the price of P_w, increasing consumption from nontrade Q_c to Q_e and decreasing domestic production from Q_c to Q_a. See the graph. A tariff of P_wP_t (a) harms domestic consumers by increasing price from P_w to P_t and decreasing consumption from Q_e to Q_d; (b) aids domestic producers through the increase in price from P_w to P_t and the expansion of domestic production from Q_a to Q_b; (c) harms foreign exporters by decreasing exports from Q_aQ_e to Q_bQ_d.

An import quota of Q_bQ_d would have the same effects as the tariff, but there would be no tariff revenues to government from these imports; this revenue would in effect be transferred to foreign producers.

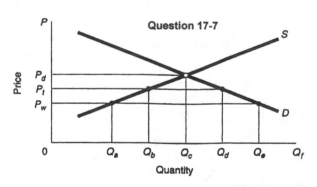

Question 17-7

■ **CHAPTER 18**

18-2   A demand for francs is created in (a), (c), and (f). A supply of francs is created in (b), (d), (e), and (g).

18-3   Balance of trade = $10 billion surplus (= exports of goods of $40 billion minus imports of goods of $30 billion). Balance on goods and services = $15 billion surplus (= $55 billion of exports of goods and services minus $40 billion of imports of goods and services). Balance on current account = $20 billion surplus (= credits of $65 billion minus debits of $45 billion). Balance on capital account = $30 billion deficit (= Foreign purchases of assets in Canada of $10 billion minus Canadian purchases of assets abroad of $40 billion). Balance of payments = $10 billion deficit.

18-6   The Canadian demand for pesos is downsloping: When the peso depreciates in value (relative to the dollar) Canadians find that Mexican goods and services are less expensive in dollar terms and purchase more of them, demanding a greater quantity of pesos in the process. The supply of pesos to Canada is upsloping: As the peso appreciates in value (relative to the dollar), Canadian goods and services become cheaper to Mexicans in peso terms. Mexicans buy more dollars to obtain more Canadian goods, supplying a larger quantity of pesos.

The peso appreciates in (a), (f), (g), and (h) and depreciates in (b), (c), (d), and (e).

18-9   See the graph illustrating the market for Zees.

Question 18-9

(a)   The decrease in demand for Zees from D_1 to D_2 will create a surplus (ab) of Zees at the $5 price. To maintain the $5 to Z1 exchange rate, Canada must undertake policies to shift the demand-for-Zee curve rightward or shift the supply-of-Zee curve leftward. To increase the demand for Zees, Canada could use dollars or gold to buy Zees in the foreign exchange market; employ trade policies to increase imports from Zeeonia; or enact expansionary fiscal and monetary policies to increase Canadian domestic output and income, thus increasing imports from Zeeonia. Expansionary monetary policy would also reduce the supply of Zees: Zeeons would respond to the resulting lower Canadian interest rates by reducing their financial investing in Canada. Therefore, they would not supply as many Zees to the foreign exchange market.

(b)   Under a system of flexible exchange rates, the ab surplus of Zees (the Canadian balance of payments surplus) will cause the Zee to depreciate and the dollar to appreciate until the surplus is eliminated (at the $4 = Z1 exchange rate shown in the figure).